STRATEGIES IN BROADCAST AND CABLE PROMOTION

WADSWORTH SERIES IN MASS COMMUNICATION

Rebecca Hayden, Senior Editor

STRATEGIES IN BROADCAST AND CABLE PROMOTION

Commercial Television · Radio · Cable
Pay-Television · Public Television

Edited by

Susan Tyler Eastman
Indiana University

Robert A. Klein
Klein &

Wadsworth Publishing Company
Belmont, California
A Division of Wadsworth, Inc.

Rebecca Hayden, Senior Editor
Production Service: Mary Forkner, Publication Alternatives
Text Designer: Don Fujimoto
Cover Designer: John Edeen
Manuscript Editor: Don Yoder
Technical Illustrator: Milton Hamburger
Signing Representative: Winston Beauchamp

Printed in the United States of America

1 2 3 4 5 6 7 8 9 10—86 85 84 83 82

Library of Congress Cataloging in Publication Data
Main entry under title:

Strategies in broadcast and cable promotion.

    Bibliography: p.
    Includes index.
    1. Television broadcasting—Marketing. 2. Radio broadcasting—Marketing. 3. Community antenna television—Marketing. I. Eastman, Susan Tyler. II. Klein, Robert A., 1928–
HE8689.6.S85   384.55'4'0688   82–2724
ISBN 0-534-01156-X   AACR2

Contents

Preface

This book is intended for both the student of broadcasting and the professional. Promotion is an expanding arena for entry-level jobs for college graduates interested in station promotion, programming, sales, production, and design as well as management. Students will find the subjects of public broadcasting and commercial radio especially useful since much entry-level employment is in those areas. Additionally, the evolving strategies for pay-television and cable promotion will be of special interest since expansion in those fields is creating a sizable number of entry-level positions. Many general managers, programming executives, and promotion department staff members currently employed in the industry need to become more familiar with broadcast audience marketing strategies in order to respond to the changing economics of broadcasting. And information on effective public service campaigns will be especially valuable to small-market stations.

The proliferation of new technology and new media is bringing about the greatest change in broadcasting since the advent of radio. Different services mean more competition, more importance for marketing strategy, and more jobs of greater stature. This textbook appears at a crucial juncture in the history of the communications industry.

In the chapters that follow, all of which are original contributions, the authors examine the promotional strategies and techniques used by a variety of decision makers. The chapters in Part I establish a framework and vocabulary for the remainder of the book. The balance of the chapters divide into parts on audience promotion, sales promotion, and public relations—all of them introduced by the editors.

Since technical language of promotion is still evolving, a glossary of current usage is appended. All terms appearing in boldface in the text are defined in the glossary. A bibliography of books, periodicals, and teaching materials follows the text, but key items are listed at the end of the major parts of the book. Sources mentioned in footnotes are not included in the bibliography unless they refer to materials of a substantive nature. A guide to suppliers and consultants for music, graphics, and animation provides a handy reference tool for newcomers to the art of promotion. All stations, networks, syndicators, and suppliers mentioned in the text are included in a comprehensive general index.

The editors especially want to thank the following people for their generosity with assistance and ideas: Lucy Bodanza, David Bradbury, Harry Chancey, Jr., Gene Davis, Sydney W. Head, Lewis Klein, David LeRoy, Judith LeRoy, Gail Love, Teddy Reynolds, Christopher H. Sterling, Herbert A. Terry, and Lou Zaccheo. Our reviewers, El Dean Bennett of Arizona State University, Stuart L. Brower of ABC-TV and the University of Southern California, Mike Flynn of John Brown University, Richard J. Goggin (retired) of New York University, Lawrence D. Thompson of the University of Denver, G. Norman Van Tubergen of the University of Kentucky, John C. Weiser of Kent State University, Brian J. Williams of Dutchess Community College, and others, provided invaluable criticism and numerous practical recommendations. Rebecca Hayden, senior editor for Wadsworth Publishing Company, was a warm source of encouragement and facilitation. The Department of Radio-Television-Film at Temple University and the Department of Telecommunications at Indiana University were most generous with their support.

SUSAN TYLER EASTMAN
Indiana University

ROBERT A. KLEIN
Klein &

The Role of Promotion

Part I provides the framework for the balance of the book by exploring elements that are common to all broadcast and cable marketing situations irrespective of size, location, or budget. To understand the rest of the book, one must become familiar with the concepts and vocabulary of Part I. Chapter 1 defines the different forms of promotion in television, cable, and radio and gives examples. It covers the historical changes that have infused the field of promotion with new urgency and suggests a set of fundamental marketing models from which promotion strategies can be derived. The chapter also looks at the purchase of services from nonbroadcast production companies and discusses the relation of legal issues and ethics to promotion.

Chapter 2 covers the objectives of promotional strategies. It specifies the unique problems facing broadcast promotion and the general methods for implementing marketing goals in on-air and other media. It deals with promotional decision making by station management for broadcast and nonbroadcast services and also details the importance of research in the whole process of developing goals for specific situations.

Chapter 3 analyzes the role of the promotion manager from the perspective of commercial and noncommercial television and radio station management. It covers the differences implied by the range of titles for the promotion manager's job (from creative services director to public information officer) and the position's concomitant range of responsibilities. The chapter reports the findings from the 1968, 1976, and 1980 Broadcasters Promotion Association surveys on salaries, status, and background of commercial promotion managers and speculates on the likely upgrading of key positions during the 1980s and 1990s.

Chapter 4 details budgetary strategy for television and radio stations. It prescribes a plan that can be adapted for most promotion departments to acquire sufficient budget from station management without undue limitation on the way the money can be spent. This chapter concentrates on estimating and accounting procedures that provide the flexibility demanded by innovative and responsive promotion.

Chapter 5 reviews the techniques of on-air television promotion. It spells out the benefits and limitations of in-house production and the special effects, music, animation, and other services available from out-of-house production companies. It looks at the use of wraparounds and news graphics along with the issues in writing and producing original music, buying original music, and buying syndicated packages.

The five chapters in Part I establish the definitions, goals, limits, responsibilities, and procedures of promotion. They focus on the evolving concepts and vocabularies of the field and the marketing strategies common to all television, cable, and radio promotion.

The Scope of Promotion

by
Susan Tyler Eastman

Susan Tyler Eastman joined the faculty of Indiana University in 1981 in the Depart ment of Telecommunications. She had been on the faculty of the Department of Radio-Television-Film at Temple University in Philadelphia since 1977. She has a B.A. degree from the University of California, an M.A. from San Francisco State University, and a Ph.D. from Bowling Green State University. Her teaching experi ence includes broadcasting and film production, programming, promotion, and research. In addition to producing, directing, and scholarly publication credits, she was senior editor of Broadcast Programming: Strategies for Winning Television and Radio Audiences *(Belmont, Calif.: Wadsworth, 1981) with coeditors Sydney W. Head and Lewis Klein. In 1980 she received one of the two charter faculty internships from the National Association of Television Program Executives and interned at WCAU-TV in Philadelphia. She served as coordinator for the 1980 Broadcast Educa tion Association Faculty/Industry Seminar on programming and directed Temple University's telecommunications policy seminar in the summer of 1981 in Washing ton, D.C.*

Promotion has become a vital component of broadcast and cable strat egy since the mid-1970s. The immediate cause of its emergence was a startling rise in programming costs for television and attendant risks. No longer is promotion a secondary tactical device; it is now a primary marketing function enabling competitive **positioning** of stations, net works, or services in their markets. Because the public regards televi sion programs and radio formats as much alike, management executives must find ways of luring viewers or listeners to their stations or chan nels. Promotion is an indispensable tool for creating and exploiting dif ferences—that is, for convincing the public that one network, one station, one service, or one program differs substantially from its competitors.

Promotion encompasses such diverse elements as the on-air spot, print advertising, publicity, merchandising, and public relations within both the trade and the local community. It facilitates the sale of pro grams by **syndicators** and the sale of advertising time by stations and-networks. Promotion has become crucial to the success of both television and radio, independent stations and network affiliates, commercial networks and public broadcasting, pay-television, and the burgeoning cable industry. Each of these situations calls for a particular set of strategies, and command of the strategies of promotion is one of the major attributes demanded of outstanding professionals in the fields of broadcasting and cable. Moreover, promotion has become a new path into executive management for college graduates.

The most important division among types of promotion lies between audience promotion and sales promotion. (See Figure 1-1.) *Audience promotion* is directed toward viewers and listeners. *Sales promotion* is directed to clients—that is, advertisers (or potential advertisers) and their agencies. *Public relations* is directed toward media representatives, such as journalists and editors, and toward opinion leaders in the industry and competing stations and networks, advertising agencies, syndicators, and program producers, for the purpose of building visibility and a positive image. The terms publicity and merchandising are loosely applied in all three spheres, but they can be understood as forms of audience promotion on most occasions. Public service, as explained in Chapter 16, can be used to tie together many aspects of promotion and advertising.

Figure 1-1 Types of Promotion

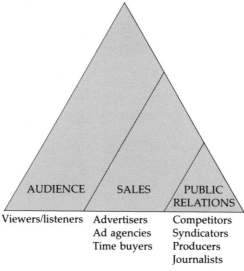

Viewers/listeners   Advertisers   Competitors
                     Ad agencies   Syndicators
                     Time buyers   Producers
                                    Journalists

THE INFLUENCE OF THE 1970s

The importance of the study of promotion lies in five significant changes in broadcasting economics: lessening of the dominance of the commercial networks; increases in program costs; education of management about promotion; pressure from cable and pay-television; and the removal of some federal impediments to open competition. These five influences have combined since the mid-1970s to bolster the status of the job of promoting programs and images.

Network Ratings Effects

Until the mid-1970s, affiliated stations depended on their networks to establish their rating positions in local markets. But it now appears that no single network may dominate the ratings for any great length of time in the future; consequently, a network's position no longer automatically determines a local affiliate's market ranking. A station's image no longer depends solely on the success of its network's programming, and local promotion directly influences station positioning.

Costs

One sudden change in broadcast economics has been the escalating cost of programming that began in the early 1970s. Once Paramount broke the pricing pattern for syndicated materials with *Happy Days* and *Laverne and Shirley*, the whole pricing structure for television programs altered drastically. An episode that cost $600 in 1965 cost on the order of $6,000 by 1980.[1] Thus managers are more eager than ever to get their money's worth out of every program.

Moreover, by the late 1970s independent television stations began to pay high prices for off-network hits, transforming independents from low-ante/high-profit operations into equal contenders for the mass audience and shares of market dollars. In the top twenty or thirty markets, this programming factor has driven affiliates and independents into head-to-head competition (outside of primetime), escalating the need for effective promotion by both affiliates and independents. Competition for the purchase of movies by the major pay-television services has driven up the costs for films and further reduced the available supply of programming.

---

[1]Costs for single episodes of especially popular situation comedies exceeded $65,000 by 1979 in the top markets. See Edward G. Aiken, "Independent Station Programming," in *Broadcast Programming: Strategies for Winning Television and Radio Audiences*, ed. S. Eastman, S. Head, and L. Klein (Belmont, Calif.: Wadsworth, 1981), p. 77. Aiken discusses the changes in pricing structure initiated by Paramount and the movement by stations to purchase "futures" in programs.

Management's Attitude

Another, more gradual, change has occurred in the attitude of station managers. Persuaded by program consultants and scientific research into broadcasting, management has become educated to the subtleties of program decision making and the role of promotion. The knowledge of images and programs provided by influential "news doctors"—such as Frank N. Magid Associates, McHugh-Hoffman, and a burgeoning number of other media consultant firms—has increased greatly since 1975.

The same trend is evident in the attitudes of local advertisers. They have come to realize the crucial importance of local news in local advertising and are willing to pay high prices for time on a local news program. In turn, they demand the biggest possible audience. This demand then escalates the importance of news and station promotion.

New Competing Media

A fourth change influencing broadcast economics was the advent of competing media such as cable, pay-cable, subscription television, videocassettes, and videodiscs. Some of these newer forms are drawing substantial audiences and are cutting into the ratings base of local stations (and the networks). As the ratings base (total viewers) decreases, so potentially will advertising dollars for broadcasting. During the mid-1980s, it is anticipated that the new media will gain more than 30 percent penetration (perhaps as high as 50 percent penetration for cable alone by 1990) while commercial over-the-air broadcasting will decrease up to 40 percent.[2] Total viewership, however, is projected to hold steady or increase.

Advertising agencies are beginning to be attracted by the new media and their specialized audiences. As the mass audience fragments, the importance of promotion in attracting and holding viewers becomes ever greater.

Deregulation

Another change is the long-term trend toward deregulation. In 1980, the Federal Communications Commission (FCC) voted to lift two major restrictions on cable television affecting **distant signal importation** and **exclusivity rights** for syndicated programs.[3] These decisions, if upheld

---

[2]Nancy P. Clott, "Cable Etc.," *Marketing and Media Decisions,* September 1980, p. 86.

[3]Lawrence Van Gelder, "Freeing of Cable TV by F.C.C. Faces New Challenge," *New York Times,* 24 July 1980, C18–C19.

in the courts, will free cable operators to expand the range and quality of programs carried; clearly they will stimulate the need for station and program promotion. Image promotion will be required to give visibility to individual stations; program promotion will be accelerated by the demand for large audiences for high-cost programming.

In 1981, the FCC acted to remove restrictions on radio. In addition to eliminating requirements for maintaining program **logs** and determining community views on programming needs (the process called **ascertainment**), the commission dropped its processing guidelines covering the quantities of nonentertainment material aired (such as news and public affairs) and hourly limitations on the number of commercial minutes.[4] These two changes will have long-range effects on promotional strategy in commercial radio. It is possible, moreover, that television broadcasting could be similarly deregulated, in which case the amount of air time devoted to advertising would have no centrally imposed restrictions. Certainly this step would lead to increased flexibility in on-air promotion and give greater salience to television promotional campaigns.

All of these changes add up to a new focus on the role of promotion in the 1980s. People trained in the strategies and techniques of promotion will be in great demand in the decades ahead, and a growing number of college courses and industry seminars are already addressing the need for informed practitioners of broadcast and cable promotion.

THE FORMS OF PROMOTION

Promotion is the overall term for the types of marketing used in the broadcasting and cable industries. It encompasses *audience promotion* (in the specialized forms of on-air spots, advertising, publicity, and merchandising), *sales promotion*, and *public relations*. All are company-initiated means of gaining audiences or advertisers and building positive images in communities and markets.

Promotion departments at stations are usually responsible for getting people to watch programs and for preparing materials used by sales departments to persuade advertisers to buy commercial time. In addition, some public relations duties fall under the purview of promotion departments. At many stations, the promotion department functions as a catch-all for image-building (or image-saving) activities that other departments are too busy to handle. The major activities of promotion, whether for broadcast stations, cable, or pay-television, can be classi-

---

[4]"The FCC Ends Curbs on Radio Stations," *New York Times*, 15 January 1981, A1 ff. See also *Deregulation of Radio*, 84 FCC 2d 968 (1981).

fied according to whether they have to do with audiences, with advertisers, or with other media specialists (journalists, editors). The major functions of audience promotion, sales promotion, and public relations are depicted in Figure 1-2—although functions often overlap and terminology may differ from department to department.

Figure 1-2 Forms of Promotion in Broadcasting

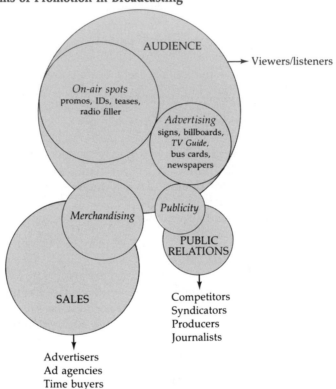

PROMOTION TO AUDIENCES

On-air refers to television **promos** (spots), radio **filler**, **IDs** (identifications), and **teases** appearing on a broadcaster's own air time intended to draw audiences (or hold them) for specific programs or groups of programs. On-air collectively creates an identity for a station, network, or service while dispensing information on program time and place.

Promos

Commercial and noncommercial television stations make heavy use of on-air promos; usually they produce their on-air spots in their own studios. Most on-air spots for television are produced in standard 30- and 60-second lengths, although 10-, 15-, and 20-second spots are also useful in scheduling to fill other lengths of air time (unsold **availabilities**).

To create movie promos, stations usually add introductory and closing material to exciting segments taken from movies. For local newscasts, producers frequently videotape a news anchor announcing an upcoming news story or use lively segments of news footage. Most distributors of syndicated series supply edited segments of each episode; the local station then adds its own channel number and the episode's air time.

The networks devote substantial budget resources to production of on-air spots. They create developmental campaigns to introduce new programs and encourage viewing of primetime and daytime network series, talk and variety programs, and national news. On-air promotion of network entertainment series is especially active during the fall season introductions and in the November, February, and May ratings periods.

There are two basic types of promotion content: generic (also called general) and specific (also called topical). Most network promotion and locally produced promotion is program-specific—that is, it consists of visuals tied to the daily content of individual episodes and newscasts. However, stations often produce generic promotion to support their newscasts and substantial changes in station image or format. Distributors of syndicated off-network reruns typically supply generic promotional materials for their programs because of the production time required to create specific promos for each episode. A single program-specific promo is called a **topical** at CBS; ABC and NBC use the term **episodic**.

Radio Filler

On-air for radio consists of a broad spectrum of live and prerecorded talk directed to listeners by disc jockeys. For music format stations, filler typically includes contest activities such as prize announcements, statements on rules, and telephone calls taken over-the-air. It includes announcements of guest interviews and features, repetition of the station's slogan, and informative bits on time, weather and traffic. On radio, however, content and game announcements tend to be live filler between recordings and commercial spots rather than the tightly prerecorded promos that characterize on-air television. Promotion for specific programs plays a lesser role in radio because most stations adhere to continuous formats rather than discrete programs. In markets that have several radio stations with virtually identical formats (such as album-oriented rock or top-forty music), on-air promotion is the major means of distinguishing between stations.

IDs

In addition to on-air promos, both stations and networks air brief IDs (identifications) at the half-hour and on the hour as required by the FCC. An ID must give the station's call letters and place of signal origination (city or area of dominant influence); it often includes the channel number (for television stations) or dial frequency (for radio stations). Although identifications are seldom more than 3 to 5 seconds in length, they have become useful devices for reiterating a promotional theme or advertising an upcoming program. Figure 1-3 depicts the NBC logo in its storyboard form (the registered trademark of the stylized letter N and a peacock) combined with its 1979–1980–1981 season promotional theme of "proud as a peacock." A radio ID briefly announces the station's call letters and the city in which it is licensed. Dial frequency and a station slogan are commonly given, often to the accompaniment of background music. Announcers for the all-news AM radio station in

Figure 1-3 NBC Logo (*Courtesy of National Broadcasting Company, Inc.*)

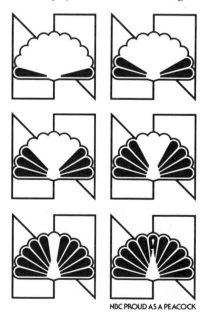

NBC PROUD AS A PEACOCK

Philadelphia say, "This is KYW News Radio in Philadelphia," for example, and may add "1030 on your radio dial."

Teases—Bumpers

Another type of on-air spot, used most commonly in television, is the tease or bumper. This is a brief visual announcement, as short as 3 seconds, asking viewers to stay tuned through a series of commercial announcements in order to watch an upcoming news story or series episode. Teases are commonly used at the end of a program to encourage viewing of local newscasts and upcoming programs.

Cable On-Air

On-air promotion for cable and pay-television refers to brief spots similar to those used by broadcast stations and networks. However, cable services can also dedicate an entire channel to program listings, and many services use on-air **print crawls** (created by video **character generators**) to keep viewers informed of the offerings on various channels, especially any locally produced cable programming.[5]

Advertising

Advertising is the term applied to on-air or print promotion for which a station, network, service, or occasionally a syndicator, pays or trades. The ads may appear as radio spots purchased by a television station (or, conversely, television spots paid or traded for by a radio station). Print advertising about guests or new programs commonly appears in newspapers as illustrations adjacent to schedule listings. Similar ads are placed in *TV Guide* and other program-listing supplements. Bus display cards and billboards are often used for promotion by stations, networks, and cable services. Radio stations in major markets make frequent use of billboard advertising along main roads (as in Figure 1-4) while television stations emphasize print advertising. One study of promotion for a small-market public television station compared several types of print advertising (in various local media) with on-air promotion and radio promotion on a sister station.[6] Illustrated advertising in the local newspaper appeared to be more effective in enlarging the audience for a program than the station's own on-air promos. This finding

[5]"Locally produced" in this case means produced by cable operators in local studios for distribution only over a dedicated cable channel.
[6]Wilma Pokorny, "An Experimental Study of Program Promotion by WBGU-TV," masters thesis, Bowling Green State University, 1970.

Figure 1-4 Billboard Advertising Radio (*KFWB, Westinghouse Broadcasting, 1980. Used with permission.*)

is only suggestive, but it does indicate the value of paid print advertising to television.

Publicity

Publicity focuses on unpaid space such as free mentions in newspaper columns. It includes nonmedia giveaways such as T-shirts with the station's call letters distributed at concerts. Publicity also involves releasing details—production dates, stars appearing in special episodes, and air dates—to television and feature editors to create awareness of new programs and special programming. One publicity stunt has become legendary in the annals of television: that was the time radio station WKRP dropped live turkeys on Cincinnati to promote its new image![7]

Merchandising

Merchandising is another name for the aspect of publicity concerned with selling a station or network's image with premiums. Figure 1-5

---

[7]This episode of the situation comedy called *WKRP in Cincinnati* first aired in 1979.

Figure 1-5 HBO Premiums (*HBO, 1980. Used with permission.*)

shows the types of premiums offered by Home Box Office. Merchandising includes special promotions such as introducing the new fall schedule, holding contests, giving records away, and using mascots to get the public's attention. These techniques are considered aspects of audience promotion when they are directed largely toward viewers or listeners; when they are directed toward advertisers, they become sales promotion.

SALES PROMOTION IN BROADCASTING AND CABLE

Sales promotion in broadcasting refers to anything that helps sales executives sell commercial time on the station or network to advertisers.

It also includes aids that help syndicators sell their programs to individual stations, the three commercial networks, and the major pay-television services, all of whom are clients for syndicated wares.

Sales promotion especially refers to the printed materials and premiums prepared by promotion departments to help sales executives sell time. Printed sales promotions range from **leave-behinds** to customized brochures that analyze ratings data. Sometimes mass mailers are sent to existing and potential clients; these mailers are often handled by companies specializing in direct-mail campaigns to clients. Leave-behinds and mailers are selling materials based on the station or network's strong points—particularly specialized analyses of the age and sex of program audiences. Gifts bearing station call letters (sometimes called **merchandising**) are another part of sales promotion strategy.

Figure 1-6 shows a one-page leave-behind intended to persuade an ad agency buyer or local retail advertiser to purchase commercial time on WCAU-TV in Philadelphia.

Sales promotion also covers the use of **tradeouts** (from travel agencies and other firms) to build good relations with clients. These items, provided in exchange for on-air spot advertising time, include cruises, fishing trips, and bottles of scotch at Christmas. On music radio stations, most tradeouts are used for contest prizes. Trading is less pervasive in television, but most stations acquire some tradeouts to use as gifts for local retail advertisers. Also, television and radio stations in the same market often trade air time for promotional spots.

PUBLIC RELATIONS AS PROMOTION

Public relations refers to management's interactions with the press, government, pressure groups, and the public on a broad scale. In

---

Figure 1-6 WCAU Leave-Behind (*WCAU-TV, 1981. Used with permission.*)

Tuesday, March 17, 1981   Philadelphia Daily News

'Live at 5' Is Knockin' 'Em Dead

The local Nielsen TV ratings for the month of February are in, and at Channel 10, they're celebrating the news.

Simply, according to Channel 10 spokesman John Tarquinio, the station's introduction of the "Live at 5" newscast in January has given it a head start on the formidable competition at Channel 6. And that jump has meant that 10 has been able to peck away at its competitor's lead.

CHANNEL 6 ANNOUNCED on Friday that it, too, would start its evening news at 5 o'clock beginning Monday, April 27. It conceded that Channel 10's demonstration that there was an audience for news at that hour had had something to do with its decision.

The numbers also help explain that decision. According to Tarquinio, at 5 p.m., when the Channel 10 news is competing with the last half-hour of

Merv Griffin on 6 and "Prisoner: Cell Block H" on 3,.Channel 10 gets a 12 rating and a 28 share versus 9 and 21 at Channel 6, and 6 and 14 at Channel 3. (The rating figure represents the percentage of all TV sets in the area tuned in to a station; the share is the percentage of sets actually in use that are tuned in and measures head-to-head competition.)

broadcasting, two specialized forms of public relations have developed that are crucial to the industry: trade press relations and public service promotion.

Trade

Trade press relations involve unpaid publicity and paid advertising in the trade magazines and newspapers intended to influence executives in advertising agencies, media buyers, advertisers, and, to a lesser extent, government officials. These activities are handled primarily by promotion departments at smaller and mid-sized stations. For the larger stations, trade press relations are often contracted to outside firms. The networks devote whole departments to public relations quite separate from their on-air promotional activities. Publicists doing trade press relations make use of printed mailers, press releases, and gifts of merchandise.

Community

Public service promotion is a form of community public relations that makes use of on-air and print promotion in organized campaigns. Public service promotion is intended to build a positive image for a station (or conceivably a network) in its market. Apart from its audience, other targets include civic leaders and national as well as local pressure groups and public service organizations. Public service promotion has two aspects: participation in community events and on-air public service campaigns supporting efforts, for example, to reduce smoking or encourage bicycling. These campaigns make use of publicity and may use merchandising and public relations releases, but they generally have very small budgets intended only for unavoidable costs. Public relations have special importance in a government-licensed and regulated industry that has been enjoined by Congress to be responsive to the public interest.[8]

MARKETING MODELS FOR BROADCASTING AND CABLE

In the field of marketing, experts frequently distinguish between advertising (a means of informing a public) and promotion (a means of persuasion). In broadcasting, this distinction is not clearly maintained. Promotion staffs at local stations handle both print advertising and on-air promotion and aim to inform and persuade in all their efforts. The pay-television services maintain staffs at their headquarters that purchase print advertising and distribute promotional materials to cable

---

[8]The Communications Act of 1934 contains the fundamental principles governing regulation of the broadcast industry by the Federal Communications Commission.

operators. Most on-air for pay-television is distributed with the programming as in national network television. The particular persuasive strategies behind promotional messages depend on the type of station, or service network, that originates them.

Marketing Functions

Otto Kleppner's three-part model of marketing functions visually depicts the three overall strategies of broadcast and cable promotion: acquisitive, competitive, and retentive.[9] His model is adapted in Figure 1-7 to show the relative importance of the three functions for different broadcast and cable situations. Generally, a single dominant strategy characterizes a promotional campaign (or on-air spot or advertisement).

Strategies for promoting new programs have an *acquisitive* function, as do strategies for promoting new services (such as pay-television and

Figure 1-7 Models of Promotional Strategies

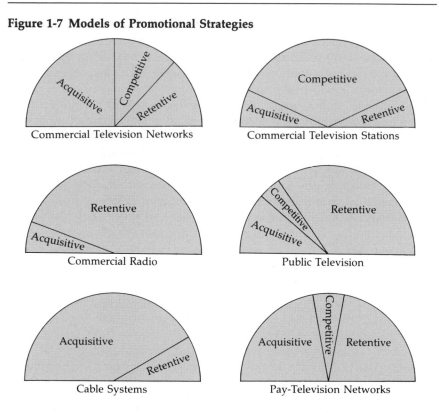

[9]Otto Kleppner, *Advertising Procedure*, 6th ed. (Englewood Cliffs, N.J.: Prentice-Hall, 1973), pp. 77–91.

cable). They are intended to get potential viewers or listeners to sample the program or service or format. Acquisitive strategies derive from studies of human needs and the process of diffusion of innovations throughout societies.[10] Thorough promotion of the new fall season of entertainment programs and midyear replacement series and specials occupies the bulk of network promotional efforts and budgets.

Since cable and pay-television are relatively new services, they spend a far greater proportion of their budgets on acquisition of new subscribers than do commercial broadcast stations. Cable's first task is to persuade viewers to pay to have cable service connected. Broadcasters need only persuade viewers (or listeners) to sample their pro grams. When a radio station uses billboards on busy highways to encourage sampling of its new format, it is using an acquisitive strategy. Public television places great emphasis on acquiring viewers for specific programs through promotion. (Public radio varies widely and more closely resembles commercial radio.) National public television (PBS), on the other hand, is moving away from wholly acquisitive strategies into competitive ones as the struggle for corporate funding stimulates a need for larger and more varied audiences.

The greatest promotional effort at most commercial TV stations goes into *competitive* promotion. Competitive strategies such as counterprogramming derive from advertising models of programs as "products" to be sold to consumers by means of advertising messages. Each station tries to draw the largest possible (or most finely targeted) audience from the pool of available viewers in the market.[11] Competitive promotion uses on-air spots and persuasive print advertising in mass publications such as viewer program guides and newspapers. Competitive messages may focus on station image and use emotional appeals rather than factual content, but most of them are program-related and informational.

Since viewers pay directly for pay-television and cable services, they can cancel a service in the same way one cancels any monthly service. This fact gives special prominence to *retentive* strategies on the part of pay-television services and cable operators. However, all stations, networks, and services struggle to retain their audiences if they are suitable for their advertisers or funders. It is all a question of **demographics**—the audience's vital statistics of age and sex. If viewers tend to be older, for example, than the audience desired by advertisers, a station may drop a program or entire format and try to capture a more desirable audience.

[10]Abraham Maslow's classification of needs as applied to marketing is briefly described in Richard E. Stanley, *Promotion: Advertising, Publicity, Personal Selling, Sales Promotion* (Englewood Cliffs, N.J.: Prentice-Hall, 1977), pp. 41–42.

[11]The "pool" refers to all households with television sets in the market, but an independent television station may, for example, target a group not being served by affiliate newscasts at 6 pm.

Public stations have traditionally adopted retentive rather than competitive strategies, but some evidence of new trends is visible. Retentive programming strategies such as **block programming** are designed to preserve the same audience from one program to the next. The three commercial networks place heavy emphasis on retaining their viewers in primetime and in daytime. Spots for following programs are inserted to motivate the audience to stay with the station (and not tune elsewhere); these strategies derive particularly from studies of audience habits and lifestyles. Retention is increasingly the concern of pay-television services that attempt to persuade viewers that a pay programming service matches their lifestyle and is worth the monthly cost.

In all broadcast and cable situations, the three basic strategies—acquisitive, competitive, and retentive—govern target audience selection (demographics), media selection (print or on-air), and media placement (scheduling). The strategy determines the goals that can be achieved and must be compatible with techniques. Only one strategy should dominate in a single campaign, but all three should be given weight in long-term promotional planning.

Elements of Marketing Technique

Promotion is the mass marketing of programs and images through the mass media.[12] It is mass selling over a mass medium. Promotion involves the four basic elements of any marketing technique: information, design, distribution, and presentation.

Information in broadcast promotion refers to the practical who/what/when/where incorporated in a promotional spot (or leave-behind or mailer). The basic concern of promotion is to ensure that adequate information reaches the audience in memorable form.

Design in broadcast promotion is the set of appeals used in ads or spots. The classic appeals for mass media are conflict/competition, comedy, information, personality/sex, and human interest. These combine with other appeals such as sympathy for the underdog, nostalgia, and greed for prizes to create the design thrust of a spot or ad. The choice of appeals is based on ratings and other audience feedback (combined with data on the desired markets for advertisers' products). An appeal may be highly emotional or very factual; it may be appropriate for children or adults, for males or females, for the traditional family or single adults.

Distribution refers to the technical means for communicating the message. A message can be distributed by print or through on-air television

---

[12]William C. Nichols, *Marketing in Communications and Promotion* (Columbus, Ohio: Grid, 1976), p. 9.

or radio, for example. Either video or film can be used for on-air television spots.

Presentation refers to the esthetic production and graphic art techniques and the form of audio copy. Editing pace and directing style affect the way that information and appeals are communicated and must be appropriate for the medium of distribution. Presentation may reinforce the other elements of marketing technique, rendering the strategy behind a campaign effective; or it may instead neutralize the other elements, rendering the campaign impotent.

All four of these broad elements of marketing technique combine in varying degrees. For example, a television station's early **fringe programming** (a cartoon, say, at 4 o'clock) may primarily draw children between the ages of 7 and 12. In this case the sales strategy might be to interest retailers of computerized games to buy commercials in that time period; the promotional strategy might try to attract new viewers of the same ages. Moreover, the station might decide to place persuasive messages for the 4 o'clock program via on-air promos inside Saturday morning programs and primetime situation comedies. Each spot must communicate where and when the cartoon can be seen. The content and vocabulary level must be appropriate and appeal to children between 7 and 12 years old. The distribution medium can be video on the station itself or combined with audio spots in radio programs with the desired demographics. The directing and editing of the promos should involve the same rapid cutting that (doubtless) characterizes the cartoon.

The six models of promotional strategies shown in Figure 1-7 are useful for analyzing broadcast and cable promotion materials in combination with the four elements of technique. Only one of the three possible strategies (acquisitive, competitive, or retentive) should dominate in a single campaign or a single promotional spot or ad. Station management, promotion managers, and design and production staff need to agree on the dominant strategy behind an effort and determine how the elements of information, design, distribution, and presentation can be combined to realize this strategy. Confusion regarding the overall strategy or the proper proportions of these four elements is a major source of ineffective broadcast promotion.

THE ROLE OF OUTSIDE RESOURCES

Broadcasters have outside resources available—advertising agencies, public relations firms, art services, printers, music producers, animators, film and tape production services, and research consultants. But by comparison with the advertisers who buy their air time, few broadcasters make use of outside resources. Elaborately produced promotional campaigns are rare outside of those commissioned by commercial networks, pay-television services, and stations in the top ten markets—due to their high cost. Since the mid-1970s, however, competition in the marketplace has stimulated an increase in the volume of outside work.[13] Higher standards for the quality of on-air promos and advertising materials have spotlighted the need for specialized skills. While the bulk of day-to-day promotional work is generally handled by in-house resources, the most sophisticated visual effects, music, and graphics are usually produced on the outside by specialized companies.

Custom Production Services

Apart from advertising agencies, some companies specialize in creative production services for broadcasters: animation houses, music producers, news promotion producers, and syndicators who have prepackaged campaigns for television and radio stations. Most outside resources are listed periodically in industry trade publications, and the seminars and conventions of the Broadcasters Promotion Association (BPA), National Association of Broadcasters (NAB), National Association of Television Program Executives (NATPE), and National Cable Television Association (NCTA) contain exhibits of the best work. To find high-quality outside resources, one can always ask colleagues for recommendations and examine outstanding materials prepared for other stations. It is important to talk to producers without assuming that something is "too good" or "too expensive"; promotion prices are usually negotiable. The guide to suppliers in this book is another place to begin. New companies come into the field every day, however, and most cannot afford to seek out all potential clients.

In general, station promotion staffs should not try to prepare all promotion materials themselves. In highly competitive markets, high-quality visual materials and music are the norm; in mid-sized markets, expenditures for outside assistance in promotion may be the element that alters ratings. Moreover, professional relationships with outside resources may encourage learning and creative growth among station staff members.

Advertising Agencies as Resources

Because most broadcast promotion material is for on-air and relatively little is commissionable media,[14] few advertising agencies are able to

---

[13]For example, the ABC-owned stations spent $350,000 out-of-house in 1981 for movie and prime-time access promotional materials instead of doing all the work in-house.

[14]"Commissionable media" is time or space purchased on behalf of an advertiser and subject to the traditional 15 percent agency commission.

handle broadcast accounts profitably. Few agencies understand the special needs of on-air promotion and its overriding importance to broadcast marketing plans.[15] At the same time, advertising agencies are capable of providing expertise in marketing and creative concepts and can help to develop outdoor, print, and radio spot campaigns.

Promotion managers should generally be able to negotiate a fee or reduced commission (less than a full 15 percent) in return for media consultation and placement services or anything short of full agency service. The obstacle to full service is the lack of commissionable media. The commissions have to be supplemented by fees that, in most situations, make the full agency relationship too expensive.

In selecting an agency, it is best to explore these problems fully in advance. Agencies doing excellent work in the market will readily make presentations for comparative purposes. However, it is unethical to ask for speculative creative presentations without paying for them.

To develop promotional materials, broadcasters often seek outside creative collaboration. As the station's chief marketing representative, the promotion manager is responsible for locating resources, assembling a creative team, and proposing a budget. Professional outside services are only as effective as the guidance and budgets they receive from their broadcast clients. Thus the promotion manager can maximize their usefulness by providing clear directives, adequate support, and strong encouragement. At the end of this book is a representative list of advertising agencies, creative services, production companies, graphic effects, animation, and music services that are active in the broadcast promotion field.

LEGAL CONSTRAINTS ON PROMOTION

Promotion is governed by the legal restrictions on advertising when it is paid but falls into a special classification when it is unpaid (and not traded). The government agencies that regulate broadcasting, as well as the major industry trade organizations, have taken special note of promotion.

The Federal Trade Commission (FTC) is the government agency traditionally responsible for eliminating deceptive advertising practices. Since promotional spots on a station's own air involve no payment to a sponsor, they are not considered advertisements. The same promotional announcements placed on another station's air or in print, however, may be paid advertising.[16] Although promotion is obviously a

---

[15]A comprehensive description of the services provided by advertising agencies is contained in Stanley, *Promotion*, pp. 174–178.

[16]Sydney W. Head, *Broadcasting in America*, 3rd ed. (Boston: Houghton-Mifflin, 1976), p. 260.

form of self-advertising, it has never come under the scrutiny of the FTC because no one has seriously attempted to prove that economic injury resulted from on-air promotion or that consumers were being defrauded or otherwise misled in an injurious way. No legal damage uniquely pertaining to broadcast promotion has been demonstrated in the courts.

The FCC licenses broadcast stations (periodically renewable) and requires written logs of all broadcast matter (for designated days) from television stations.[17] The FCC's official forms classify on-air promotion separately from advertising (commercial matter), and the FCC has not adopted guidelines on appropriate quantities of on-air promotion.

The television code of the National Association of Broadcasters (NAB) does specify standards for the quantity and placement of non-program material, however. Although NAB codes are in no sense laws, frequent or excessive violation of these standards is likely to invite FCC scrutiny—a hazard generally to be avoided due to potential delays in license renewal and the high cost of legal assistance in public hearings. Adherence to the codes is wholly voluntary; no means of enforcement exists. Individual station policies vary from strict to loose compliance with the code guidelines. Station practices also tend to vary with seasonal and election year pressures. Under the NAB codes, the requirements differ for affiliates and independent television stations and for radio.

For network-affiliated stations, the NAB Television Code recommends no more than 9 minutes and 30 seconds of commercials, billboards, and promotional announcements during any hour of primetime, but it does permit averaging of allowable minutes within programs of 90 minutes or longer.[18] Moreover, the code specifies that, at the discretion of the broadcaster, an additional 30 seconds of promotional announcements may be inserted per hour. Excluded from the code restrictions on total nonprogram material for affiliates are public service announcements and announcements concerning the scheduling of unusual newscasts or delayed programs (affected by sports and other special-event programming of indeterminate length).

In time periods other than primetime for network-affiliated stations, the NAB Television Code restricts nonprogram material to 16 minutes in any 60-minute time period. It imposes stricter limits on children's programming on weekdays (12 minutes of nonprogram material) and weekends (9 minutes and 30 seconds). The code in no way specifies

---

[17]Broadcast licenses have been renewable for a maximum of three years since the 1940s. In 1981, however, Congress lengthened license periods to five years for television stations and seven years for radio stations.

[18]National Association of Broadcasters, *The Television Code*, 21st ed., January 1980, pp. 18–23.

how much of nonprogram material may consist of promotional announcements. It does, however, limit code subscribers to no more than five consecutive announcements of nonprogram material in any daypart (of which a maximum of four can be commercial interruptions) and no more than three such announcements during a station break. Public service announcements are not included in the code's consecutive announcement count for affiliates.

Independent television stations have different limits under the NAB Television Code. Nonprogram material is defined to include public service announcements as well as promotional spots (and, of course, commercials). The code restrictions are 14 minutes per hour of primetime of nonprogram material and 16 minutes per hour of nonprimetime. No more than four announcements of nonprogram material may be scheduled in a row, including public service announcements, and the limits on announcements in children's programs applying to affiliates apply also to independent television stations.[19]

The NAB Radio Code makes no direct mention of promotion. The distinction between program and nonprogram material applying to television has no counterpart in radio; all material has been logged separately (as public service announcements, promotional spots, or commercial matter).[20] The code does not specify limits on the frequency of interruptions or the kinds of material that may be included in a single interruption. It does, however, repeat the warning included in the Television Code that contests may not be lotteries.

Lotteries

Few legal issues affect promotion practices directly; most are shared by all producers (copyright) or other businesses (sales practices). The one area of unique legal concern to broadcasters is that of lotteries, since many states have declared lotteries otherwise legal. Indeed, special laws had to be passed by Congress to permit the reporting of state lottery results on television and radio in the states where they are permitted.[21] However, Congress has expressly forbidden radio or television broadcasters to air games or contests that are lotteries.

The manager of a contemporary music format radio station needs to be an expert in what constitutes a lottery. The FCC has spelled out the

---

[19]It should be noted that the NAB Television Code makes exceptions on the number of consecutive announcements within long programs having fewer than the maximum number of interruptions.

[20]National Association of Broadcasters, *The Radio Code*, 22nd ed., January 1980, p. 17. The FCC acted to eliminate program log requirements for radio stations in 1981, but logging continues as a commercial record.

[21]Public Law 93-583 (18 U.S.C. 1307).

combination of characteristics that are illegal.[22] The three main criteria are prize, consideration, and chance. Any game or contest that involves luck and reward and simultaneously requires a specific action of viewers (such as making a purchase or paying an admission price) is a lottery. In addition, many retail sales promotions have certain characteristics of lotteries and cannot be advertised in broadcast commercials if they meet all three criteria. The NAB guidelines for radio stations spell out common pitfalls and possible solutions regarding games and contests involving chance, prize, and consideration.[23]

Broadcasting a lottery actively endangers a station's license; in fact, the FCC has responded emphatically to demonstrated violations in the past with fines or nonrenewal of licenses. The game of bingo is becoming increasingly common in cable programming but falls outside the definition of a lottery since no consideration is involved. (That is, one need not pay to play.) Furthermore, the issue of whether the FCC could in fact regulate the programming contents of a cable channel is open (since cable is not federally licensed but locally or state franchised).

Sales Promotion

Another area for concern is sales promotion. Any practice that is illegal or unethical in selling goods or services—such as discounting for certain buyers among competing companies—is illegal also in selling broadcast time.[24] Federal laws relating to sales practices can be enforced by the FTC and the FCC.

The NAB codes explicitly enjoin broadcasters and networks from unfair trading practices in the sale of time. The shift from prepublished station cards to flexible patterns of time pricing (since there are now several ratings books from which to choose audience estimates) has blurred station time sales transactions. However, many network discounting practices that traditionally favored major advertisers such as Proctor & Gamble (and tended to create monopolies) have been eliminated in recent years due to investigative efforts by the FCC and FTC.

Another sales practice that occasionally affects promotion staffs is that of cooperative advertising in which two or more retailers (or a manufacturer and a retailer) share advertising costs. In 1969 the FTC revised its guidelines on co-op advertising; it now prohibits a wide va-

---

[22]18 U.S.C. 1304.

[23]*Legal Guide to FCC Broadcasting Rules, Regulations and Policies* (Washington, D.C.: National Association of Broadcasters, May 1977).

[24]The details of the Robinson–Patman Act of 1936 applying to interstate commerce, portions of which have been adopted by many state governments, are covered in Stanley, *Promotion*, pp. 84–85.

riety of practices.[25] Although these regulations apply more directly to sales efforts rather than to promotion, an employee seeking cooperative contracts for public service efforts, for example, should consult the station's legal advisor to see if the arrangement falls within the FTC's guidelines.

Copyright

Two other areas of legality relating to promotion are trademark protection and copyright. Network and station logos and slogans can be registered as trademarks to receive protection within the United States. Moreover, many attention-getting symbols, characteristic sounds, original program titles, and distinct personalities may be protected. Advice on what a station can protect is available from the National Association of Broadcasters.

Copyright looms as an important concern to all producers of local materials. Music, scripts, photographs, slides, maps, motion-picture sound tracks, designs—all are protected under the Copyright Act of 1978. Typeface designs are not covered under present legislation.[26] Contracts for materials produced by production resource companies spell out the limitations on a station's use of the materials supplied. Generally, the station may make unrestricted use of videotaped and filmed logos, leaders, front and end segments (**sandwiches**), music and sound effects, and associated print designs and photographs for a designated period of time (such as one year). After that time, the station loses the right to air the materials except under a renewed contract. Of course, the station never possesses the right to sell or give away material produced *for* it (not even to public stations or organizations).

All music registered with the American Society of Composers, Authors, and Publishers (ASCAP), Broadcast Music Incorporated (BMI), and the Society of European Stage Authors and Composers (SESAC) is protected from use without payment of fees. Similarly, photographs and drawings not created by station employees must be purchased (or leased) from the copyright holders before they can be incorporated in promotional productions. However, the fair use provision of the Copyright Act allows a station to use a creator's work as illustration in a promotion that advertises that person's presence on a program, without seeking explicit permission.

Under the Copyright Act of 1978, cable operators must pay a proportion of their revenues into a fund administered by the Copyright

[25]James F. Engel, Hugh G. Wales, and Martin R. Warshaw, *Promotional Strategy* (Homewood, Ill.: Richard D. Irwin, 1975), p. 157.
[26]Tad Crawford, *The Visual Artist's Guide to the New Copyright Law* (New York: Graphic Artists Guild, 1978), p. 6.

Tribunal. These funds are intended to be distributed annually to the composers and publishers whose material was used by cable systems (by importing distant signals into markets in which they were previously not available). Inequity between the amount broadcasters pay for original rights and the amount cable systems pay for redistribution is a source of friction among broadcasters and cable system operators.

Release Forms

Release forms permitting the use of someone's face or voice are required before the likeness may be broadcast. This stipulation applies to both hired actors and members of the public; it does not apply to news footage or celebrities or public officials. Shots of people participating in large-scale public activities, such as rallies, parades, or fairs, are exempted from the need for releases. Recognizability is the criterion determining when a signed release must be obtained from a casually recorded member of the public (who did not seek recording and was not participating in a mass activity). If the person (passing on the street, for example, in the background of promotional footage) is recognizable, a signed release is required by law.

Billboard Advertising

Another matter of occasional concern to station promotion managers is local law relating to billboards and other outdoor signs. Although such laws are largely the responsibility of the company that leases the space, local stations should be familiar with restrictions that limit certain design concepts (such as projecting elements or flashing lights). There is no point in planning elaborately for what may be an illegal sign.

ETHICS IN PROMOTION

Since on-air promotion (in a station's own schedule) is not legally defined as advertising by government regulations, those responsible for producing and scheduling program promotion need not concern themselves with the legal requirements for commercial matter. Promotion departments do, however, share ethical responsibility with other employees of broadcast stations for the social effects of both the broadcast programs and the commercial advertising messages. Quantities and types of violence and sexual contents in programs, commercials, or promotions are issues of broad social concern that reach far beyond quibbles about good taste or puffery. Another fundamental social concern is the long-term effect of mass consumerism in broadcast programming in a world where many do not possess even the necessities of life.

It must be pointed out that most broadcast networks and stations have enforced strict limitations (continuity acceptance standards) on the content of commercials; over the long term, the industry has raised the level of advertising as a whole.[27] Stations exercise control for several reasons. Perhaps the main reason is that their licenses may not be renewed if they broadcast illegal material. But apart from this danger is the station's need to develop a positive image in the minds of audience members—an image that encourages viewing and listening. Stations also wish to avoid angering advertisers. And, of course, in some cases controls are imposed by the personal ethical standards of station owners and managers.

The widespread subscription to the voluntary codes of the NAB indicates the direction of the broadcast industry, although proportionately more television stations subscribe than radio stations.[28] Stations with only marginal financial success are under economic pressure to adopt "flexible" ethical policies.

There are five practices relating to audience promotion that should be considered unethical despite their frequent occurrence: (1) the use of excessive hypoing to boost audience ratings artificially; (2) the creation of erroneous impressions of program content or the conditions for winning prizes; (3) the use of warnings about content unsuitable for children actually intended as come ons; (4) the airing of phony testimonials by celebrities, actors, or members of the general public; and (5) the toleration of payola or plugola.

Hypoing

During rating periods, stations and networks alter their schedules and increase their promotion and advertising to boost their ratings. On television, blockbuster movies, specials, and prime episodes of series are scheduled and receive more on-air and print promotion than other movies and episodes; special news series on exploitable subjects such as rape and drugs are common; and interview programs tend to be loaded with big-name guests. On radio, on-air contests get extra attention. These practices are widespread in the industry and are apparently acceptable to the FTC, the Broadcast Ratings Council, and the rating services, although they violate the spirit of their public pronouncements and guidelines (see Figure 1-8).

[27]Stanley, *Promotion*, p. 94.
[28]Head, *Broadcasting in America*, p. 434.

Figure 1-8 Warnings to Avoid Hypoing (*Arbitron Ratings Books, 1977 to date. Used with permission.*)

The FTC Guidelines Regarding Deceptive Claims of Broadcast Audience Coverage contain language which points out that TELEVISION STATIONS ...

" should not engage in activities calculated to DISTORT or INFLATE such data — for example, by conducting a SPECIAL CONTEST, or otherwise varying ... usual programming, or instituting UNUSUAL ADVERTISING or other promotional efforts, DESIGNED TO INCREASE AUDIENCES ONLY DURING THE SURVEY PERIOD. Such variation from normal practices is known as 'HYPOING'."

It is the opinion of Arbitron that while many television stations that engage in promotional activities during a survey period are not attempting to hypo audiences, some stations may conduct their promotional activity for the specific purpose of increasing audiences artificially during the rating period. This activity could affect the behavior of the viewing audience, thereby making the audience estimates higher than they would have been if no promotional activity had been conducted during the survey period.

The purpose of this notice is to call attention to the text of the FTC Guidelines and to call attention to report users where there is a possibility that some kind of hypoing might have been conducted during the survey period by one or more stations reported in the market.

Relating to On-Air Survey Announcements ... the NAB is "CONCERNED WITH THE EFFECTS of the practices, engaged by some stations of exhorting the public to cooperate with television ratings surveys in process."

... The BRC opposes "any attempt by stations to exhort the public to cooperate with television audience measurement services whether over the air or by any other means, and recommends to syndicated audience measurement services that the practice be DISCOURAGED because of its POSSIBLE BIASING EFFECTS." The BRC has ammended its minimum standards to define On-Air Survey Announcements as hypoing ...

The AAAA "opposes any attempt by any medium to exhort the public to cooperate with the audience measurement surveys by CALLING ATTENTION to such research by ANY MEANS."

... The Television Advisory Council has also stated their opposition to On-Air Survey Announcements.

Certain practices are actively discouraged by the rating services, however. These practices, classified as **hypoing**, constitute flagrant artificial inflation of viewing or listening in order to maintain audience allegiance and drive up the measures on which advertising rates are based. Prohibited are on-air mentions of diaries or ratings (particularly in connection with the station's call letters) and the conduct of field surveys (about programming or news or viewing preferences) during a rating period or the preceding four weeks. Scheduling documentaries or news interviews about ratings during this period is especially discouraged by the rating services.

Unfortunately, prohibitions against hypoing are largely unenforceable. The rating services obtain their information haphazardly from competing stations, and it frequently arrives too late for publication. A notice does appear on the front cover of Arbitron ratings books (and under "Station Research Activity") whenever a station reported in that book has apparently attempted to influence diary measurements. (The most common violation is when radio announcers direct those filling out diaries to note down that they are listening to, say, Station WXXX.) When a station attempts to hypo the ratings, Arbitron cautions against hypoing as in Figure 1-8.[29] The rating services' most extreme sanction is total removal from ratings books—a sanction that is rarely practiced and one that has little disadvantage for many radio stations (especially those who do not purchase the books anyway).

False Impressions

Creating an erroneous impression in on-air promotion is unethical. Promotional spots sometimes make misleading suggestions regarding the importance of roles played by celebrities or use titillation as a come-on to series episodes. These practices may not harm the public, but they can minimize the effectiveness of other promotional efforts. Moreover, continued discrepancy between on-air promos and actual programs (especially local news) may cause audiences to tune out.

A more serious concern, for radio stations especially, is misleading information about on-air contests. This failing is most commonly the by-product of spontaneous announcing by inexperienced disc jockeys. The FCC requires broadcasters to disclose periodically all the terms of a contest on the air. Continued misleading impressions can lead to investigations by the FCC and are emphatically prohibited in the NAB Radio Code.[30] Games or contests that result in disruption of the community are also prohibited by the FCC.

Warnings

Warnings about the level of sexual explicitness and types and quantities of acts of violence in programs were initially introduced to placate critics of television. On the surface, advisories are intended to inform parents so they can restrict their children's viewing. It appears, however,

[29]Nielsen euphemistically mentions offending stations (when reported) under "Special Notes" in its station ratings books but does not include guidelines or warnings in individual station ratings books.

[30]NAB, *The Radio Code*, p. 17.

that many so-called warnings are in fact designed to draw adult audiences and have little effect on the numbers of children tuning the programs.[31] The NAB Television Code specifically cautions broadcasters on the placement and content of warnings.[32]

Testimonials

Using an actor to pose as a celebrity or public figure is obviously misleading; so is false testimony solicited by producers of spots; both practices violate code guidelines and FTC regulations. Other practices may not be so obvious, however. Public display of microphones and television cameras influences people's responses in subtle ways in "man-on-the-street" interviews, a common means of gaining content for local promotional spots. Most people tend to give positive responses if they anticipate some reward such as a giveaway. Also, such interviews are prone to biases arising from the subject's assumption that any negative responses will be edited out of the broadcast material.

Payola and Plugola

The dividing line between promotion and advertising becomes blurred when stations join with advertisers (in, for example, a promotion for a rock concert) in any fashion that promotes the interests of both the advertiser and the station. Television licensees have to be careful about precise logging of such promotions, and both radio and television management must be watchful for instances of staff payola and plugola.

Payola refers to illegal payment for promoting a recording or song on the air. **Plugola** is the variant in which material is included in a program for the purpose of covertly promoting or advertising a product without disclosing that payment of some kind was made. The penalties for violating payola or plugola regulations include fines up to $10,000 or a year in jail or both for each offense. These penalties have been imposed by the FCC in many cases. However, numerous instances of payola or plugola go undetected by the FCC but remain ethical problems for local station management.

The subject of ethics for promotion involves questions of personal values rather than purely legal issues. Ethics are also a matter of concern throughout the industry. Many articles in the BPA's newsletter

[31]Alan Wurtzel and Stuart Surlin, "Viewer Attitudes Toward Television Advisory Warnings," *Journal of Broadcasting* 22 (Winter 1978):19–29.
[32]NAB, *The Television Code*, p. 3.

have addressed borderline promotional practices and exhorted promotion managers to adopt high standards.[33]

SUMMARY

Promotion is an evolving field with an imprecise vocabulary. This chapter defined the major forms of promotion in words and illustrations as they apply to audience promotion, sales promotion, and public relations. Since industry events in the 1970s gave increased visibility to promotional practices, advocates of modern marketing have been drawn into the field and added their concepts to the pool of broadcasting and cable terminology. In the 1980s, television on-air promotional spots combine the elements of visual design, sound, and live action or episode sequences to create persuasive and informative messages aimed at broadcast and cable audiences. Radio promotion focuses on contest and personality chatter. Characteristic of the 1980s is the increased use of outside production resources for promotion by small and mid-sized market stations as well as major market stations. Although most FCC regulations and NAB code restrictions have only an indirect bearing on promotion, hypoing by both television and radio stations persists as a substantial legal and ethical issue.

Analysis by means of the six general models and the set of techniques discussed in this chapter ties together specific strategies for the different situations of radio, television, and cable and applies in both public and commercial broadcasting. The remaining chapters in Part I delineate strategies and techniques by examining goals, responsibilities, and methods. The chapters in Parts II, III, and IV subdivide strategies and techniques according to specific promotional situations. The overall marketing models described here provide a framework that the reader can apply to the views expressed in subsequent chapters.

---

[33]A typical example is Don B. Curran's "Curran Challenges Promoters to Excel on Station Team," *BPA Newsletter*, August 1976, reprinted September 1980, pp. 14–15.

Goals and Concepts of Promotion

by
Robert A. Klein

Robert A. Klein is founder and president of Klein &, a Los Angeles firm that creates and produces communications concepts. Klein & employs a full-time staff of twenty-five to operate creative, design, audio and visual production, copy, and music departments. The company has received awards for its work from the International Radio and Television Society, CLIO, and American Advertising Federation, among others. The firm's clients include the Post-Newsweek stations and the ABC-owned stations; it has done work for the Group W (Westinghouse Broadcasting Co.) stations and productions; CBS-TV Network and its owned stations WCAU-TV in Philadelphia and WBBM-TV in Chicago; NBC-owned WKYC-TV in Cleveland; General Electric-owned KOA-TV in Denver; Columbia Pictures, MGM, United Artists, and Twentieth Century-Fox Television; and more than a dozen top corporations in the Fortune 500. Klein & has recently branched out into the cable/pay-television field, helping companies like Warner, Oceanic, Rainbow, and Times-Mirror develop promotional strategies and materials. Klein & worked with the University of California in pioneering a center to develop the educational potential of all the media; the work culminated in 1980 in a daily, live current events service on PBS stations produced by Klein, Walter Cronkite, and the Public Broadcasting Service. Robert Klein has lectured at the University of California at Los Angeles and San Diego, the University of Southern California, the University of Illinois, and for the American Management Association. He served on the national board of the Pacifica Foundation for five years.

In any market, examples of the basic marketing problems of radio and television stations abound, problems that need to be dealt with in broadcast promotion:

- The top-rated station may be trying to maintain its leadership despite aging on-air personalities and audience demographics.
- A challenger may be engaged in building and communicating stability, aggressiveness, and identity in the market.
- A station that has radically altered its programming, format, or network affiliation may be trying to reestablish itself.
- A long-time loser may be trying to turn itself around.

- A station with a new manager who wants to change everything may be fluctuating without defined objectives.
- A public television or radio station may be endeavoring to raise enough money to keep out of the red for another season.
- A newcomer in cable or subscription television may be trying to establish itself in the crowded marketplace.

Broadcast marketing problems ultimately divide into the need to: (1) attract audience, (2) maintain audience, (3) increase audience, (4) alter the demographics of an audience, or (5) improve image.

The problems for network television affiliates in the 1980s tend to be concentrated in newscasts, news personalities, and news lead-in and **lead-out** programming. For independents, the challenge is to counter the programming and the promotion of network affiliates. In radio, the problems relate to format and consistency (as in music mix), to on-air personalities, or to overall service. The problems in cable are to get subscribers, keep them, and persuade them to purchase additional services. The problem of public television appears to be survival. At the same time, the television networks are engaged in a three-horse race to maintain mass audience numbers with the new specialized media coming up on the outside.

In all these situations, overall marketing strategies for the 1980s have five major aspects to their design:

1. Building program popularity
2. Generating loyalty that results in extended viewing and listening
3. Appealing to the entire coverage area
4. Identifying the specific television or radio station or cable system with the needs and interests of its community
5. Developing a competitive position in relation to the growing number of media alternatives in the market

These are the fundamental objectives of promotional strategies.

Comprehensive marketing plans covering all five objectives are called "total identity concepts" and involve collaboration between management, programmers, and promotion personnel in backing a coordinated approach and a single theme over a considerable period of time. A station or network's unified approach is then reiterated in all on-air, display, print promotion, and public relations materials; ideally this effort has a cumulative effect on the audience. This is the most basic strategy behind a comprehensive marketing plan.

SPECIFIC AND GENERIC STRATEGIES

Programs (or in radio, personalities) are the basic product for promotion. Day by day, week to week, promotion must continually reinforce the audience's impulse to tune in. Routine program information is the equivalent, in broadcasting, of retail marketing strategy and can be called *specific* strategy.

Traditionally, broadcasters have referred to the marketing of their stations and programs as promotion or creative services, designating advertising and public relations as activities supporting the total effort. However, the overall strategies are in fact a specialized form of marketing. Promotion, advertising, and public relations are the broadcaster's tactics. The cable and subscription television industries have already adopted marketing terminology and concepts, and it is likely that the broadcast industry will gradually fall in line.[1]

In addition to programs, the other principal consideration in broadcast marketing strategy is the development of image or identity in the marketplace—an equivalent of institutional advertising. The words *image* and *identity* can be used interchangeably to refer to the character of a network, station, or service as it would like to be perceived by the audience. This emphasis on image is *generic* strategy.

The objective of generic strategy is to develop long-term audience loyalty to a particular broadcaster. Elements of identity occur in identifications (IDs) by means of thematic concepts, music, and graphics. The **ID** is one of the most demanding elements of promotion. It provides the possibility of summing up all the station's attributes in a single symbol, a theme, a line of copy, a sound, an attitude—and in a manner that can be communicated to viewers or listeners in the space of 3 to 5 seconds.

Yet all too often, broadcasters settle for slogans rather than marketing themes. A useful test for differentiating the two is to ask if any other broadcaster can make the same statement; in other words, is the message unique? Marketing themes are exemplified in "We're 4" (WBZ-TV, NBC affiliate, Boston); "(11) Alive" (syndicated theme); and "NBC Proud as a Peacock" (NBC Television Network). Familiar examples of slogans are "Tune In, Turn On," "We've Got It All," and "Looking Good." A station or network may be in such a dominant position (or so lacking in dominance) that other considerations are more crucial than the unique quality of a marketing theme. Nevertheless, it is al-

---

[1]When a commercial broadcast station goes on the air, its programs are automatically available to the audience free. In cable and subscription television, the public must be persuaded to pay for the service. The aggressive marketing approach of companies like HBO will probably influence commercial broadcasters as the systems become more and more competitive.

ways preferable to promote with something that is special, individual, and comprehensive.

Rosser Reeves of the Ted Bates Agency coined an excellent phrase that sums up what marketing people try to create in order to achieve these objectives.[2] He calls it USP—the unique selling proposition—the concept that sets one product or service apart from its competitors and communicates most effectively with consumers. Promotion managers would always do well to ask themselves if a message, whether it is topical or cosmic, specific or generic, presents a unique selling proposition.

The television networks have considered overall identity a basic part of their marketing strategy since their days as radio networks—remember "CBS, The Stars' Address."[3] Each year they launch their fall seasons with new themes, music, graphics, and hoopla. Generally, they offer affiliates adaptations of the fall campaigns for local use. Sometimes the material is given free; sometimes it is offered for sale at nominal prices.[4] Most network campaigns are designed largely to attract program sampling, however, particularly in the fall season. The three television networks rely on their affiliated stations to develop their own community identities or images. A fundamental strategic consideration for a network affiliate is deciding the extent to which the station should identify with the network campaigns. For many years, it was advantageous for affiliates of CBS and NBC to ride their network's promotional coattails. However, three factors have made station reliance on network image a less and less satisfactory strategy: (1) the rise of ABC in the mid-1970s, (2) the unpredictability of competitive standings among the three networks, and (3) the continuing proliferation of new media choices.[5] Since these circumstances are likely to continue through the 1980s, the best strategy is to seek a strong local identity designed to exist independent of, but complementary to, network image in a total marketing plan.

A similar debate about marketing strategy already exists in pay-television. Local systems are wondering how much emphasis to place on nationally promoted services and how much on local identity. There is no pat answer, but balance is desirable.

---

[2]Rosser Reeves was president of Ted Bates in the 1950s and 1960s and was one of the prime advocates of "hard sell" advertising.

[3]This was the theme adopted by CBS Radio in 1948 after it had hired a number of the top NBC stars for its roster.

[4]All three networks usually give basic campaign graphics, music, and cooperative advertising allowances to their affiliates. They also offer customized versions of their material to the stations at prices based on market size.

[5]Even some network-owned stations now choose to emphasize their own local identity themes rather than using network campaign adaptations.

BALANCING SPECIFIC AND GENERIC PRIORITIES

The two main goals of a broadcaster's marketing efforts are to support programs or personalities and build an overall image. At television stations, the prevalent view for many years was that any dollar not devoted to specific program promotion was a dollar down the drain.[6] Since the early 1970s, however, research has demonstrated the strong impact of a station's overall service and personality in developing and sustaining audience loyalty.[7] Another factor that increased the salience of promotion was the attention focused on television's community role during the urban unrest of the late 1960s and early 1970s. Stations began to accept an active responsibility for ascertaining community needs and reflecting them in programming.[8]

Recognition of the importance of these factors gradually led to an understanding of total identity and the value of the umbrella concept of promotion. The term *umbrella* refers to the unifying promotional concept that ties together all of a station or network's identity strategies under a theme, style, and attitude. A unifying concept should be related to community involvement, leadership, or uniqueness of service. This concept needs to be communicated to the audience in a way that encourages a loyalty that goes beyond loyalty to a specific program. The umbrella, then, is the theme that unifies a total identity concept.

GOALS FOR ON-AIR PROMOTION

In television, the most important vehicle for marketing networks' and affiliates' programs and images is their own air. At one time or another during the week, most viewers tune in to each of the network affiliates. A different priority exists for radio, independent television stations, cable, pay-television, and competitively weak affiliated stations. In these cases, emphasis upon on-air must be shared with advertising in other media in order to attract substantial sampling by potential audiences. The broadcaster's objectives are always to hold onto audience members when they do tune in and to get them to come back more often and for longer periods. Hence on-air is ultimately the best place for most stations to extend viewership or listenership and build loyalty.

[6]During the period when the networks provided the overall promotion, local programming was also subservient. Vietnam, Watergate, and the civil rights movement led to an emphasis on local news. The Prime Time Access Rule, in effect after 1971, increased the importance of the postnews timeblock in local ratings and revenues.

[7]Probably the first television station identity concept was "The Land of the 3," introduced by Post-Newsweek Stations when it purchased Channel 3 in Hartford in 1974.

[8]The ascertainment procedure for television stations was instituted by the FCC in 1971 and continues in force.

Networks and radio stations typically understand the value of on-air promotion and use it extensively. Such has not always been the case with television stations. From 1950 until the mid-1970s, on-air promotion primarily filled unsold air time. Often that meant that successful stations had no spot time for their own promotion except by sharing the 2- or 3-second station IDs with quick bursts of program information. Management could not really be blamed for its attitude; VHF stations were sold out much of the time, making healthy profits, and did not require more promotion than they were getting. The programs sold themselves. And for affiliated stations, the networks did the rest by providing an umbrella and the daily excitement of specials and special events. Affiliated stations got a free ride.

Over the years it has been difficult to persuade sales managers to take spots out of inventory and dedicate them to station promotion. Nevertheless, there are two persuasive arguments: In a highly competitive market, if a station does not promote, it cannot dominate; and the more successful promotion is, the more likely rates can be increased, at least offsetting the losses of inventory. When competition heated up in the mid-1970s, however, television stations began contracting with their sales departments for set schedules of spots that could reach the audiences the stations needed if they were to achieve their promotional goals.

As of 1981, most comprehensive marketing plans give major emphasis to their on-air component. Although broadcasters may invest advertising dollars in other media to attract sampling, the payoff is in what the stations say to the huge flow of viewing audience on their own air. Therefore, on-air promotion must present a message in harmony with the advertising that attracted the viewer in the first place. It must deliver on the promises made in the other media. It must be consistent. All the promotional weapons—the IDs (legal and shared), the promos of varying lengths (generic and specific), the public service spots and promotions, the programming itself—must synergize to achieve the one basic goal of all commercial broadcasters: attracting a larger share of salable audience more of the time and satisfying the taste and needs of that audience so that they reward the stations with their continuing loyalty.

GOALS AND CONCEPTS IN PUBLIC TELEVISION

To understand how *public* television operates promotionally, it is necessary to picture its complex of components.[9] The Public Broadcasting

---

[9]Chapter 11 deals specifically with promotion in community-supported stations.

Service (PBS) is not a network with affiliated stations; it is a service that offers programs to public television stations.[10] There are actually four different types of public stations: community stations, educational stations, municipal stations, and state networks. Each has a different relationship with PBS and with one another. Some are instructional; others are combinations of instructional, cultural, and informational programming. Most carry some PBS programs. But only recently have PBS public stations across the country agreed to carry some network programs on the same nights at the same times. Only with common carriage can the public network develop positive strategies for promotion with some hope of substantially increasing the national audience.[11]

Community by community, public stations face an enormous number of limitations in developing identity and achieving promotional impact. Lack of sufficient funds is a problem common for all. Reluctance to use public funds or private contributions to finance ambitious on-air promotion plans is another. A third problem is one of constituencies. Where commercial broadcasters concentrate on reaching the largest salable audiences, public broadcasters offering general cultural programming have to deal with a number of active constituencies in their community—the educational establishment, the cultural establishment, and ethnic and social minorities. All are pressing to be served.

In these situations promotion managers face the nearly insurmountable task of setting priorities that will satisfy their constituencies and still reach their critical goals: broadening the composition of the audience, increasing the number of subscribers and viewers, raising money, and creating an identity for their station in the community. In light of these complex burdens, the top priority seems to fall on fundraising and program funding.

Lacking funds for advertising or staffs for on-air promotion, public stations have devised innovative techniques such as marathons and auctions that build emotion and financial support while spotlighting programming of specific interest. These are areas of promotion unique to public broadcasting and seem to receive the most attention, staffing, budget, and creativity.

There is considerable movement in the instructional area of public broadcasting. America's schools are well on the way to being fully equipped for television.[12] Instructional programming is offered daily by most stations, regional networks, and the national network. Programs

---

[10]Public television stations are not required to carry PBS programs.

[11]"Common carriage" refers to the agreement by all stations to carry a set of PBS programs in the same time slot in each time zone. Initial agreement between the member stations and PBS occurred in 1979 and was reiterated in 1980.

[12]As of 1980, more than 90 percent of public schools had access to television or video playback equipment.

are promoted ahead of time on the air and via a variety of educational publications, direct mail, personal contact and meetings, and closed-circuit teleconferencing. Instructional television appears to have established a reason for being—to supplement classroom education with information in the form of programming that no single station or school system could afford to finance individually.

No definitive reason for being has yet emerged for PBS or the community stations in the cultural arena. With the new video media moving heavily into the cultural sphere and with cultural programming available on videocassettes and videodiscs, public broadcasting promotion must have as its overriding priority the development of deep and abiding community loyalties that can ensure its survival.

THE SPECIAL CASE OF CABLE

In its initial period of growth, cable (then called CATV) was marketed as a utility—a service to enhance the quality of in-home television reception.[13] The goal of marketing was to make known to the communities, neighborhoods, and residences that the service was available; the system's goal was to wire as many of the dwelling units as possible. Promotionally, this strategy will continue in many areas until virtually the entire nation has been wired. In the meantime, this priority has been superseded in importance by the marketing of various free and pay services made possible by the expansion of the business, by government deregulation, and by advances in multichannel technology.[14]

THE SPECIAL CASE OF PAY-TELEVISION

For the operators and suppliers of pay-cable and over-the-air pay (STV) stations, the overriding goal is getting subscribers. Acquisition of subscribers requires a traditional product/service marketing approach using conventional media campaigns concluding with a direct phone number to call in order to subscribe. The various media are measured in terms of their cost per inquiry and their cost per subscriber. The most productive ones receive most of the budget. Commercial television probably gets more than its share of pay-television and subscription television

[13]After initial introduction of CATV in the 1950s and early 1960s to provide importation of signals to communities too far away or cut off by mountains from regular broadcast transmissions, cable operators began the more lucrative process of wiring dense population areas with mid-to-high income in the 1960s, but they were held back by FCC regulations that protected over-the-air broadcasters until the late 1970s.

[14]Cable and pay-television marketing are discussed in detail in Chapter 12.

(STV) media dollars because its reach surpasses that of all the other media. Commercial broadcast television spots carry messages that create awareness (image) and inform the mass audience of pay-television's availability. The majority of media investment relating to cable comes from the major pay and STV services (Home Box Office, Showtime, Warner-Amex, CBS Cable, and ON TV) as they expand their services nationally.

The second main objective—keeping subscribers—involves strategies that are still in the process of evolution. This objective becomes the most important priority by far once sufficient subscribers have been signed up. One device common to all services is the program guide, usually a monthly publication displaying the complete program schedule, promotional materials on the programming, and teaser promotions on upcoming programming.

While keeping subscribers is a main objective, only a handful of program suppliers are using on-air promotion in a sophisticated manner to influence the flow of audience and develop audience loyalty. Consequently, a serious marketing problem has surfaced: the problem of **disconnects** or, as some wag has put it, the "DCs." Disconnects are people who are disappointed with the service they have paid for—either the basic cable service or the pay services. Their expectations are not being met by the product or its promotion.

One way to solve this problem is by improving the product (more movies, more often; better movies, more often). Another way is by adding tiers of services on additional channels. But a substantial responsibility for lowering the rate of **churn** falls to on-air promotion.[15] In commercial television and radio, promotion staffs are accustomed to devising concepts that make the audience feel satisfied with what it is receiving. In cable television that process is only beginning.

BROADCAST PROMOTION IN OTHER MEDIA

All broadcast marketing plans must contain a strategy for using other media. Although media planning for specific broadcast and cable needs is addressed in subsequent chapters, a number of basic views are commonly held among promotion people and appropriate to most situations.

Newspapers are playing a decreasing role in broadcast promotion while radio is surfacing as an effective targeting device for both commercial and public television stations. Television advertising is the ma-

---

[15]Churn is the marketing term for turnover among subscribers. It is the percentage of subscribers who disconnect or cancel in a given month versus the number of remaining subscribers. (One might say, for example, that 10 percent churn occurred in January/February.)

jor medium for achieving increased sampling. Many radio stations consider it too expensive, although syndicated campaigns are reducing costs. Outdoor billboard advertising is effective in those markets with extensive billboard coverage. Pay-television is discovering the advantages of on-air television spots in promoting its programs. And *TV Guide* remains the giant among magazine guides to programming and is crucial to topical network promotion and image promotion of stations. It is increasingly becoming a tool for pay-television as well.

Newspapers

Newspaper readers tend to be older than the typical mass television audience and the dominant radio audience.[16] They also tend to be upper class economically.[17] These two facts limit the use of newspapers as a major advertising medium for broadcasters. On the other hand, newspapers reach an influential, opinion-making public and a news-interested audience.[18] Consequently, they can be effective as an institutional medium for communicating overall image. They can also be used successfully to project news image (or format) and to advertise special series and promote personalities.[19]

Because of the influential individuals they reach, newspapers have traditionally been used to launch major campaigns and new seasons, programs, services, and formats. In recent years, however, they have come to be considered supplementary to on air promotion and, in many cases, to radio.

Promoting Television on Radio

Radio is an ideal medium to supplement television's own air. It is especially effective for topical advertising.[20] If a station's objective is to increase the quantity of specific day-to-day program promotion, radio is probably the most flexible medium. Stations can be selected which pinpoint the very audiences that television is most interested in reaching at the times of day when listening is at its peak. Public television stations are making increasing use of commercial and public radio sta-

---

[16]Newspapers claim 79 percent readership (ages 45–55) versus 40–45 percent of the television viewing audience in the same age group.

[17]About 84 percent of newspaper readership is in the $30,000 to $50,000 range versus 46 percent for viewers in the same economic range.

[18]Newspaper readers (especially subscribers) tend to be more serious about the content and quality of their news, and they also tend to voice their opinions strongly on reported issues.

[19]Major market television stations tend to use newspapers during major rating periods and to gear news specials for exploitation via the major dailies.

[20]Some television stations actually use live radio spots, generally during the late afternoon traffic periods, to promote their early evening news.

tions that have the right target audiences to promote their television programs.

Moreover, radio allows for the **piggybacking** of two different messages within one 60-second spot. This practice is especially desirable for promoting the lead-in or lead-out for local evening news (early fringe to news to access programming). This is also the highest revenue-producing time period for most television stations.[21]

Promoting Radio on Television

Television is generally regarded as the highest-impact medium for radio advertising.[22] Most radio formats can be sold very effectively on television in 30 seconds, and the medium is unexcelled at creating awareness and generating **sampling** of new programs by large numbers of viewers.

Television time is expensive, however, as is television production; a radio station's message competes for attention with national and regional spot commercials combining high creativity, sophisticated production values, and big budgets. To meet this problem, spot campaigns have been developed for syndication that market specific radio formats. It is likely that the more radio broadcasters make use of these syndicated campaigns, the greater the choice.

Pay-Television on Broadcast Television

Several pay services have begun extensive on-air spot advertising on commercial television stations. In Chicago, for example, ON TV, a subscription television service, advertises on WGN, the second largest superstation. Many network-affiliated stations, viewing the pay services as direct competitors, have refused to accept pay-television advertising. On-air television can serve the dual purpose of informing current subscribers about upcoming movies while urging other viewers to subscribe in order not to miss out. Superstations such as WGN and WTBS are especially effective because they reach widely dispersed geographical areas.

Magazines

TV Guide is the one publication essential to commercial television networks and stations and PBS. It is the publication most viewers read,

---

[21]The 4 to 8 pm period, running from early fringe through access, accounts for approximately 92 percent of a network affiliate's revenue.

[22]Many radio stations have begun to emphasize television spots using animation, graphics and laser art to stress the "look" and the "feel" of their sound. Others promote their personalities in "Face Behind the Voice" campaigns.

and its readership is made up wholly of viewers. There is no waste circulation. In some markets, the newspapers' weekly television supplements reach greater numbers of people than *TV Guide*, in which case they too become "must buys."

Magazines other than the guides printed by pay and subscription television services are generally peripheral to the basic goals of broadcasters. They should be used carefully when specific programming objectives and magazine demographics coincide, and then preferably as **tradeouts**.[23] Pay-television services will continue to create separate programming guides until multiple-listing guides covering pay-television usurp the function of individual magazines.

Outdoor Advertising

Outdoor advertising is expensive and one of the least flexible of all advertising media. However, it is extremely effective in establishing programs, personalities, and themes in markets that are heavily posted and heavily trafficked.[24] Unfortunately, most broadcasters use outdoor advertising so seldom that they lack expertise in making the space work for them to maximum advantage. It is advisable to consult outdoor companies and take advantage of their recommendations in preparing copy and art.

An old truism claims that an outdoor message cannot have more than five words in it and still be effective. By and large, that is probably true, but it does not deal with the fundamental challenge of how to design an outdoor message that makes a memorable impact on the passing viewer. Most outdoor advertising is used passively. Advertisers are content to show the product with a copy line tied into a current umbrella (campaign) theme. When these same advertisers use radio, however, and especially television, they are much more inventive in the ways they involve the audience in the message.

These are the conceptual problems that furnish marketing people with their most creative challenges. There are a number of publications that can prove helpful and challenging in the use of outdoor advertising and all the graphic arts.[25] Ultimately, however, promotion managers

---

[23]Tradeouts are reciprocal agreements by the promotion department (usually in conjunction with the sales department) in which station or network spot time is exchanged for space. Sometimes these reciprocal arrangements are made on a dollar-for-dollar basis, but often the broadcast media are able to trade their air time for more space because of its extra reach or the other media's special needs. Sometimes the trades are part cash. Some companies prohibit tradeouts entirely.

[24]Billboards (and other outdoor advertising) take weeks to produce and are difficult to change once posted, but they can create a continuing impression for the faces, personalities, and titles of new shows.

[25]See *Art Direction, Graphis, Communication Arts, Printers Ink*, and the awards annuals of the major art directors' clubs. BPA, CLIO and IRTS provide samples of award-winning work. The Broadcasters Promotion Association maintains a library of promotion work at San Diego State University.

must become students of all outside media—to become knowledgeable about each of the media and its dynamics when combined in a media mix, to tailor the most relevant messages for each.

SETTING GOALS

When setting promotional goals, commercial broadcast promotion managers deal with an uncertain commitment on the part of their managements. Promotion is the most discretionary budget a broadcaster has to manage. Moreover, broadcast station managers typically lack training or experience in marketing.[26] Thus a large part of the promotion manager's efforts must be devoted to educating management and working toward practices that place a high priority on marketing strategy. As the media marketplace continues to fractionalize, management will inevitably be forced to give promotion increased importance. In radio, the advent of year-round ratings is already leading to a significant increase in the priority of marketing strategy.

At most television and radio stations, the promotion manager reports to the station manager.[27] At stations where promotion receives a high priority, it is usually because the promotion manager serves as a catalyzing force among the other department heads involved in the process of setting station goals.

The aggressive promotion manager takes the lead in tying together the views of management, programming, news, sales, public affairs, and public relations by organizing them into a coherent marketing plan. Having involved the department executives in the process, the promotion manager should try to enlist their support before presenting a marketing plan and budget to the station manager. A thorough and businesslike approach is the best way to counter the high degree of subjectivity that typifies reactions to creative concepts. And a broadcast marketing plan is, to a considerable degree, a piece of creative work. In the ideal situation, it is the promotion manager who, each year, guides the department heads and station management toward agreement on a set of goals for the coming year.

Broadcasters have barely begun to face the need for three-year and five-year marketing plans, although stations have adopted long-range budget and capital equipment projections. Long-term promotional

---

[26]Most station managers have moved up from sales. A minority move up from programming. The smallest minority move up from promotion. See Chapter 3.

[27]In some stations, promotion managers report to the program manager—which creates one more barrier in the decision-making process unless the program managers themselves are experienced in promotion.

plans create measurable criteria. They provide standards for comparison from year to year. They also give a sense of direction to everyone involved, a direction that tends to build confidence, morale, and momentum. If promotional plans are failing to meet stated goals, that failure often puts the problems in clear perspective and leads to effective action.

The first goal in broadcast marketing is to define the audience a station, network, or service wants to attract. Commercial broadcasters are strongly influenced by the requirements of their advertisers and tend to define their audiences as those that are most salable. Public broadcasters tend to divide their audiences into two: the loyal core group and the potential but thus far uninvolved growth group. Cable operators and pay-television services deal with three groups: the total audience to be wired; the total audience to be sold on pay services; and the many special-interest audiences to be attracted to programming designed to appeal to them.[28]

There are two approaches to defining a salable audience; one is quantitative, the other qualitative. Since no single message can reach everybody, commercial broadcasters attempt the next best thing—to reach the largest number of viewers or listeners consonant with advertisers' needs. Commercial broadcasting seeks a mass audience measured in gross numbers and demographics. Gross numbers represent total numbers of viewers or listeners; demographics represent the major age groups and sexes.

As of 1981, the most popular mass audience, quantitatively, is young consumers, particularly women, between the ages of 18 and 49. As the American population grows gradually older and more productive at older ages, however, the popular demographic range is moving toward 25 to 54, now the fastest-growing age group in advertising agency avail requests.[29] For the 1980s, though, most mass appeal television programming will still be aimed at the 18 to 49 mass consuming audience.

In radio, stations pursue more specialized mass audiences via special-interest formats such as all-news, popular music of various types, and conversation. These larger categories break down into a dozen or more variations—thus popular music becomes adult contemporary, album-oriented rock, beautiful music, and so on. Each of these formats appeals to a specific portion of the mass audience spectrum. Rock music, of course, has particular appeal to the younger end of the age spectrum, while news and talk formats appeal generally to a mass

[28]The term **narrowcasting** has been coined to differentiate the mass audience approach of the commercial broadcasters from the growing number of special interests appealed to by cable, pay-television, and STV.

[29]An avail or availability is an unsold spot. Avails refer to a station or network's unsold inventory of spots.

of older listeners.[30] Radio stations offer programming to these large fractions of the mass audience because it is profitable. Cable and pay-television are beginning to offer specifically formatted services because they attract paying subscribers and, in some cases, advertisers too.

The major objectives of marketing are common to all the profit-making entities involved in broadcasting—service, stability, and profitability. Without service, no broadcaster, no cable, pay, or STV operator, and no program supplier can retain the audiences they attract. Service is the "better mousetrap" that audiences and advertisers want. Stability comes from managing and marketing the service in such a way that it is consistently and competitively appealing to its audiences and, usually, growing. Standing still is not really a stable situation. Profitability remains the primary concern of management in a free enterprise society. That concern must be understood and shared in the marketing effort, which takes the three objectives of service, stability, and profitability and tries to communicate the first two in a way that ensures the third. Hence the acquisitive-competitive-retentive model applies.

THE ROLE OF RESEARCH

Quantitative and qualitative research together provide the raw material to establish the goals for a marketing strategy. They offer the road map for promotional efforts. Broadcast research generally falls into two categories—behavioral measurement and attitudinal measurement. Behavioral measurement focuses on quantifying audiences (size, channel selection, and demographic variables); attitudinal measurement attempts to determine the "why" behind viewing and listening preferences. Broadcasters acquire research by subscribing to syndicated rating services (Arbitron, Nielsen) and by initiating special market research projects using outside consulting and research firms.

Ratings Research

From the point of view of marketing, the Arbitron and Nielsen ratings are analogous to the initial steps of a medical checkup. Basic ratings can pinpoint a broadcaster's program-by-program strengths and weaknesses and isolate demographic problems (male/female characteristics, age-related symptoms). Ratings can also show how well the station's

---

[30]Some further examples: for upper-income and older listeners—classical, news, talk radio, beautiful music, big bands; for students 18 to 24—album-oriented rock and golden oldies; for blue collar—country and country-western; for blacks—ethnic; for foreign—Spanish, German.

or network's blood (the audience) is flowing. The additional research studies used by broadcast and cable service management are like the detailed parts of a checkup such as blood tests and EKGs.

Apart from standard ratings, Arbitron and Nielsen also sell useful information computed from the giant data bases gained by their regular measurement of audiences throughout the country. This information includes audience flow studies, duplication of audience studies, reach and frequency studies, and county-by-county studies:

- Audience flow studies show what audiences do and where new tune-in goes at a given time or between adjacent programs.
- Duplication studies measure shared viewing among programs that are not adjacent to one another.
- Reach and frequency studies (marketed as AID by Arbitron and NSI-PLUS by Nielsen) show when and how audiences are duplicated between numerous programs throughout the day or thoroughout the week.
- County-by-county studies determine the geographic composition of audience strengths and weaknesses in each part of the coverage area.

Behavioral information is an integral part of identifying audiences— and, therefore, understanding viewers and listeners. In particular, it is useful to support promotional strategies intended to influence the flow of audience, determine when a station's own on-air promotion will reach segments of competitors' audiences, and target geographical areas where the station's audiences are weakest.

Attitudinal Research

Most attitudinal research is developed through surveys that use quantitative measurements.[31] These surveys can be supplemented by quali-

---

[31]Surveys are interviews among a random sample of a population. If properly designed, they produce information that is representative of that population. Interviews are conducted in person (usually in the home) or by telephone; both techniques have their advantages and disadvantages.

With face-to-face contact, questionnaires can be complex and detailed and utilize visual aids such as photographs, lists, or scales. In-home interviewing has its drawbacks, however. It is costly. It usually takes substantial time to complete. It is not as representative as telephone surveys because of the difficulty or even impossibility of interviewing certain segments of the population—especially in metropolitan areas where people are less willing to open the door for strangers or where security precludes access to high-rise apartments. Finally, quality control can be a problem because of the inability to supervise the interviewing.

Telephone surveys do provide a means for reaching virtually everyone in a population. Moreover, experience has shown that people are more willing to cooperate with an interviewer over the phone. These surveys are also quick and less costly. Interviewing can be carefully controlled because it can be done from a central facility. But telephone interviews are generally somewhat short and less open-ended; furthermore, the interviewer cannot show visuals to elicit a respondent's reactions.

tative research, usually by means of focus groups. Attitudinal research goes beyond the ratings to explore the nature of the audience itself, to determine the audience's perceptions of programs, personalities, formats, and the station's overall image, and to define trends in the tastes, habits, and interests of the audience. The objectives of attitudinal studies are virtually endless, and their designs are varied. The results are used by programmers to define the different components of a program or format; they are used by promotion managers to identify opportunities to be exploited and weaknesses to be overcome through promotion.[32] There are three major types of attitudinal research: psychographic research, personality research, and focus groups.

The major television stations are increasingly turning toward **psychographic** (or lifestyle) **research** to gain detailed pictures of their audiences for specific programs. Lifestyle analysis typically examines daily habits of viewers and elicits their attitudes, interests, and opinions on a wide variety of topics. This information aids stations in developing daypart strategies for promoting key programs and suggests motivational appeals for ad copy.

Most broadcasters want **personality research**—that is, evaluation of their on-air personalities. The networks as well as some major market stations have used "Q" ratings **(TvQs)** to measure the familiarity and popularity of news and program talent. Episodes of entertainment series that show signs of slippage in the ratings may receive this sort of analysis as the producers and network program executives try to determine which character to replace, which to reemphasize, which plot line to focus on. On a very different level, but with the same goal in mind, the owner/manager of the smallest 250-watt radio station asks lunch partners what they think of the new morning man or woman. Everybody wants to know how their talent is perceived in comparison to the competition.

General audience surveys can elicit viewers' perceptions of on-air personalities in minute detail. Stations generally hire consulting firms to perform this research or, if the expertise is available, may handle it with in-house staff using telephone surveying techniques and hire and train callers themselves. Promotion staffs use personality research to

---

[32]In this regard, promotion managers should not lose sight of the fact that promotional claims not supported by reality can backfire. Broadcast history abounds with cases of solid promotional campaigns that introduced a "new and different" news program or personality; but when audiences sampled the fare (and sample they did in droves because the promotion was effective), what *they* saw was something new and even less acceptable than what it replaced. It is extremely risky to commit major promotion to news programming prematurely—before research gives some idea of audience acceptance. The net effect is not only rejection of the present program or personality but a reluctance to believe the next claim made by the station.

develop strategies for selling the personalities. Research provides the keys—to the pluses to be exploited and the minuses to be neutralized.

A **focus group** is a small panel (usually ten to twelve people) brought together for a free-flowing discussion of a topic. A skilled moderator guides the discussion and probes deeply into their attitudes and opinions. Focus groups enable station management to hear programs described from the audience's viewpoint and in their own words—and the results are often startlingly different from management's perceptions of its programs. The disadvantage of focus groups is that they are comprised of only a few people and thus represent too small a sample base to permit generalization. The insights gained, however, are so valuable that focus groups should be included whenever possible in attitudinal research programs.

Focus groups are typically used in two ways. The first is at the start of a research program; in this case they serve as a means of developing hypotheses to be tested in follow-up surveys. The second is after a survey; in this case specific types of people can be brought together to gain further insight into the reasons behind certain attitudes and opinions measured in a survey.

Audience studies can define the aspects of a newscast that are most appealing: the personalities, the coverage, the equipment (helicopters, mini cams), and the types of features. As of the 1980s, market research at affiliated television stations concentrates primarily on newcasts because news is the most profitable of all programming. It is generally assumed that no station can maintain long-term audience dominance in a market without achieving local news leadership. A television network affiliate typically conducts a series of focus groups and then an in-depth audience survey to learn what news viewers think about the various components of the local newscasts in the market. These studies can also measure how other factors—such as the station's overall image in the community, audience habits, the effects of past promotion, lead-in/lead-out viewing—affect the choice of which newscast to watch.

Management might learn that most people who regularly watch the station's local newscast particularly like the blend of personalities and like the way one of the anchor teams goes out to report the news rather than remaining desk-bound. These hypothetical findings point out promotional directions—the need to get people to sample the program and to see the unique aspect of the station's major personalities vis-à-vis the competition. Promotion can use personality research data to develop strategies that maximize newcasters' active images and encourage more outside assignments for anchors and then cover those activities extensively in promos and teasers.

Independent television stations use research to define the audiences least compatible with affiliate programming and to clarify local tastes and attitudes. An independent station's goal is to lure audiences away from affiliates. Hence, in the early evening, comedy is offered as an alternative to news; during the latter part of primetime, 10 o'clock news is scheduled as an alternative to staying up later (for affiliate newscasts) or to entertainment; children's programs are offered as an alternative to adult programs; and, on weekend afternoons, movies are promoted as an alternative to sports. By identifying the profile of viewers of this counterprogramming, promotional staffs can develop media plans that efficiently reach these select audiences.

Because radio is so highly formatted, the demographics of audiences are fixed (unless a station is contemplating a format change). Of greatest interest in most radio research is the target audience—the particular segment that the format is attempting to attract. Typically, news and talk stations examine in detail the reactions of the 25- to 54-year-old group. Popular music stations want to know how the "adult contemporaries" are reacting. Each format wants to use promotion to achieve strict, selective targeting.

Hypothetically, a radio station that plays contemporary music might conduct a survey among young adults in the area and learn that people think of it as a "station for teenagers" because of the "loudness of its DJs" and its lack of helpful information such as news updates and traffic reports. The station might then make changes by toning down its on-air personalities and adding more news and information segments. The promotion manager gains a new product to promote and, more important, finds that the station's advertising must depict *adults* enjoying the station (to show that the station is not just for teenagers).

At the television networks, program research is largely devoted to testing new programs (usually pilots) in controlled situations. Audiences are invited into theaters, shown pilots, and asked to register their reaction—manually via knobs or electronically via galvanic skin responses. The results help to determine whether the program should be added to the next season's schedule. Promotion departments at the networks also use these data in preparing the fall season campaigns. They are likely to put some effort behind a show that looks like a potential blockbuster and to highlight the characters that elicited a strong audience reaction.

Sales Research

In commercial broadcasting, every marketing effort is an attempt to position the product—programming—in a favorable light to advertisers and their agencies. To an increasing extent, this is also true in marketing basic cable services that accept advertising. Promoting to advertisers is largely the task of the sales staff; they interpret ratings (demographics, share of audience, audience flow, audience trends) to make the strongest possible case for the commercial availabilities within local programs and adjacent to network programming (or, in some instances, for local program sponsorship). In addition to specific program successes, advertising success stories circulated to sales **reps**[33] and advertising agencies can provide convincing evidence of the broadcaster's ability to move advertisers' products and services.[34]

Sales promotion research goes hand in hand with program and audience promotion research. Findings that are useful in audience promotion can generally be turned into sales marketing tools as well. This is especially the case with trend information. If a station (or network) is weak but gathering strength, it can be sold "on the come."

Strength in one demographic grouping can help overcome weakness in others. Many broadcasters rank second or third in share of audience but lead in the key group of women aged 18 to 49 (shifting in the 1980s to women aged 25 to 54). This information, turned into trade advertising and promotion, may result in attracting more business than the competitor who is rated number one. In radio there are, literally, a dozen ways to be number one: for example, in weekly **cumulative audience,** quarter-hour listening, drivetime, women from 25 to 54. All are salable. Promotion helps sales make the most of every advantage.

Ascertainment

Marketing and public relations benefits can come from an expanded form of the ongoing community ascertainment process required by the FCC for television station license renewal. Commercial and noncommercial television station executives must interview a broad cross section of community leaders to ascertain the local issues that require media attention.[35] For broadcasters who wish to maintain a high community profile, these ascertainment interviews are educational and useful. If audience loyalty is based on a station's image as an involved

[33]Reps are national sales representative organizations. Their primary responsibility is to represent large numbers of commercial television and radio stations in the solicitation of national spots. But they also supply a great deal of information on network and syndicated program strengths and weaknesses—helping promotion people to understand the product they promote.

[34]The success letter is the basic promotional vehicle for demonstrating to potential advertisers and their agencies the power of the station to sell. The station's sales staff solicits these letters from satisfied advertisers. The promotion department then reproduces them on station promotion sheets, often pointing up salient phrases by setting them off in headline form with boldface type.

[35]In addition to community interviews, commercial television stations are required to perform an audience survey during the license renewal period to determine the important issues and needs in the minds of their general viewing audience. As of 1981, radio stations are no longer required to perform formal ascertainments by the FCC—though the deregulation ruling is being appealed in the courts.

community institution, ascertainment can be a productive way to keep a broadcaster's finger on the pulse of the market. Ascertainment interviews indicate the issues to be dealt with in programming and locate opportunities for effective public service promotion. (This topic is covered in detail in Chapter 16.)

Research Uses in Promotion

In the interpretation of research, promotion people must be concerned about credibility. In some markets, viewers are unlikely to accept the promotional image of an aggressive journalist/anchor unless that journalist/anchor is regularly seen in the field covering stories often enough to support the claim. First comes the reality, then the promotion.

A major problem facing marketing staffs is to achieve balanced research. The promotion manager still has to fight long and hard to have promotional efforts measured. Since all survey research or audience testing begins with the research questionnaire, the promotion manager needs to take the initiative at the inception of a new study by preparing the precise questions promotion wants answered and ensuring that they are included. Otherwise, station research usually ends up being filtered through the news department's perspective. The total station perspective can easily get lost.

Research findings should not be accepted slavishly, however. Error creeps into all broadcast research from cost/effectiveness compromises as well as from statistical estimation. Broadcast research is not an exact science. Constructing a valid questionnaire requires skilled researchers to make sure that respondents answer truthfully and not as they think they *should* respond and to eliminate such human biases as the tendency of respondents to pretend to be aware of something for fear of appearing stupid. Moreover, every survey has statistical variance and is subject to a certain amount of sampling error. The recommendations of news consultants are, at best, educated opinions. In consequence, promotion managers should use research as guidelines rather than gospel.[36] Nevertheless, research is essential to marketing. The seat of the pants is the weakest location from which to make a decision.

Broadcast research will undergo tremendous changes during the 1980s—principally because of the growth of specialized programming and the new competing technologies. Cable television is likely to have

---

[36]Suppose, for example, that major changes have occurred in a news team. A news consultant may conclude that the new anchor team has not established a strong impression but the long-time weatherman and the new helicopter are major strengths and should be emphasized. A sensible response might well place part of the emphasis on these known strengths while going to work on the image of the new anchor team. If they are going to make it, the new news team needs promotional help.

the most immediate impact. Tests are under way to determine how cable audiences should be measured and to monitor accurately the effect of cable viewing on the audience size of broadcast stations.

BEYOND THE MEDIA

Beyond the use of paid advertising media, marketing links up with the great traditions of theatrical showmanship. Publicity demands exploitation—involvement in everything from rock concerts to 10-kilometer runs, from circuses to squiring stars. No textbook can teach exploitation. The best way to learn it from books is to read about P. T. Barnum and the circus or Ziegfeld and vaudeville; read the exploits of the flamboyant flacks of Broadway and Hollywood who turned their shows into front-page events and created stars on assignment. Today's promotions are the direct descendants of the circus parades, carnival come-ons, and personality buildups that have been the stock-in-trade of theatrical showmanship for generations.

Exploitation in broadcasting usually falls within the purviews of both the promotion and the public relations departments. The subject is examined in several chapters of this book; Chapter 15 gives an overview of current practice in the broadcast industry. The *Broadcasters Promotion Association Newsletter* and the annual radio workshops of the National Association of Broadcasters give a sense of what broadcasters are doing. Trade publications such as *Variety, View,* and *Billboard* often report on special promotions in entertainment and communications. Reading about the exploits of the great showpeople can supply a background and respect for the craft, but imagination and a little craziness are required if one is to create new and effective exploitations.

SUMMARY

Broadcasting is a field that grows more competitive by the year. Selling a station or network or service to the public requires a marketing approach in order to achieve goals efficiently. Ratings and research are essential in order to counterbalance the natural spontaneity and subjectivity common in the field. The promotion manager leads the planning with other department heads in developing and updating a total marketing strategy and budget. The two basic goals of station strategy are to support programming and personalities and to build identity (image). On-air promotion is the most important marketing vehicle for broadcast promotion, but other advertising media may be essential in attracting new viewers, subscribers, or listeners and in supplementing on-air promotion. In pay-television and cable, the goal of attracting subscribers is surpassed in importance only by the objective of keeping them and selling them additional services. In public broadcasting, the challenge is to be competitive in supporting a quality product paid for with public funds. The strategies discussed in this chapter apply broadly to all television, radio, cable, and pay services and provide the professional concepts and practical framework for doing an effective job.

The Role of the Promotion Manager

by
Charles E. Sherman

Charles E. Sherman became president and general manager of WRTF Television and Radio in 1979. (The station is owned by Forward Communications Corporation.) He came to Wheeling, West Virginia, from the position of professor and chairman of the Department of Telecommunications at Indiana University, Bloomington, and earlier was professor and associate chairman of Communication Arts at the University of Wisconsin. He holds a B.S. with honors and an M.A. from Temple University and a Ph.D. in mass communications from Wayne State University. He has published in the Journal of Broadcasting, Journalism Quarterly, and Feedback and has written a monograph entitled Issues in International Broadcasting. *He gained producing experience with WHAT-Radio and WFIL Television in Philadelphia and has served as chairman of the international seminar and the international interest group for the Broadcast Education Association. He chaired the Task Force of Citizen's Rights and Access for the Wisconsin Commission on Cable Television.*

The organizational structures in broadcasting are not consistent. Responsibilities in stations and networks depend on such factors as corporate policy, tradition, market and station size, income, mission, and management style. The role of promotion manager is rapidly evolving into a position with prominence. No longer a temporary assignment on the way up or a place to put the burnt-out members of the staff, the job has become professionalized and now demands special knowledge and advanced skills. Increasingly, promotion managers are being designated as creative services, advertising, or marketing managers to indicate their new status and involvement in management decisions.

This name change is not cosmetic. It reflects greater emphasis in broadcasting on management theory, goal setting, research, and acquiring professionally educated personnel. Shifts toward a marketing perspective are symptomatic of stations and networks that saw their gross annual revenues and profits increase at the rate of at least 10 percent per annum during the 1970s and wanted to retain their profit margins. The new stress on promotion was also a result of higher costs

55

for programs. As expenses rose, management increased its efforts to achieve greater audience shares, and larger promotion budgets were a key element. Government regulations also had their impact. As the FCC paid greater attention to lotteries, payola, hypoing, and community relations through its ascertainment process, promotion personnel had to become sophisticated in legal matters to avoid jeopardizing their station's license. Finally, the role of the Broadcasters Promotion Association (BPA) should not be overlooked. As this organization grew, it showed management the contributions that promotion could make.

ORGANIZATIONAL HIERARCHIES

Even under changing circumstances, it is still possible to generalize about the positioning of promotion personnel in management hierarchies. Promotion has recently achieved prominence in the organizational structures of networks, stations, and broadcast groups.

Network Configurations

The networks have complex structures ranging from dominance by the overall parent corporation to separate and independent divisions for television, radio, news, and owned-and-operated stations. As conceived by ABC, the most recent addition to network structures is the entertainment division, mainly responsible for developing programs. This restructuring began in 1975 when Fred Silverman joined the network. By 1980, CBS and NBC had adopted this pattern. Since this innovation, no single person on a daily basis remains totally responsible for all phases of network operations, sales, and programming. Promotion was affected by these shifts.

At the highest company level, a vice-president is responsible for corporate public relations. This person is not involved with program promotion or advertising, however. These assignments are under the aegis of various entities, depending on the network. CBS places these responsibilities, including news promotion, in the entertainment division; ABC splits them between the entertainment and network divisions; the NBC unit reports directly to the top NBC corporate level, bypassing both the entertainment and network divisions.[1]

Whatever structure is utilized, the activities at each network are generally grouped into three broad categories: on-air promotion, print advertising and promotion, and affiliate advertising and promotion.

---

[1]Although these organizational arrangements were in effect when this chapter was written in January 1981, the networks are constantly shifting their promotion units.

These categories (except for affiliate advertising and promotion) may then be subdivided to deal with such specific program content as daytime, comedy, variety, specials, children's, news, and sports. Within the network hierarchies, there is usually a press information unit that is involved with program kits, press releases, interviews, and star tours. Several hundred people, situated on the East and West Coasts, are assigned to these activities.

Station Staff Size

At the station level, of course, these tasks fall to fewer people. Staffs range in size from only one to ten. In the small radio station (49 employees and under) and small television station (99 and under), promotion is usually handled by one or two people as Table 3-1 indicates.[2] This table also reveals that the size of the promotion staff in such stations has not expanded. This situation is not caused by a lack of faith in promotion or the absence of competition. It is a matter of smaller budgets and fewer economic resources than those enjoyed by larger operations. It is not unusual in small operations for promotion assignments to be shared with other duties.

On the other hand, Table 3-2 indicates that the larger stations, generally located in the larger markets, are increasing their promotional

Table 3-1
Promotion Staff Size for Small Stations: 1968–1976

Staff Size	Radio[a]		TV[b]		Radio/TV Combined[b]	
	1968	1976	1968	1976	1968	1976
1–2	64.3%	62.7%	46.5%	47.5%	31.8%	35.1%
3–5	11.9	11.2	13.3	12.4	11.6	10.4
Over 5	1.0	1.8	0.6	1.0	0.0	1.3

Note. The data for this table came from the 1976 BPA survey. The original BPA table encompassed all stations. For this analysis, the BPA data were divided into small and large stations based on the number of employees. However, the original percentages are retained in this table and derived from 100 percent of the respective radio, television, and radio/television combination samples for 1968 and 1976. To verify the percentages, add the respective columns for 1968 and 1976 in this table and Table 3-2.

[a] Stations with 49 employees or less.

[b] Stations with 99 employees or less.

[2] Data are from "Broadcast Promotion Survey—United States and Canada," prepared by the Broadcast Promotion Association and Bradley University Department of Journalism in 1976 (hereinafter referred to as the 1976 BPA Survey). Questions on staff size and budgets were not included in the 1980 BPA Survey conducted by *Television/Radio Age*.

Table 3-2
Promotion Staff Size for Large Stations: 1968–1976

| | Radioᵃ | | TVᵇ | | Radio/TV Combinedᵇ | |
Staff Size	1968	1976	1968	1976	1968	1976
1–2	9.9%	11.3%	12.2%	10.9%	15.9%	16.9%
3–5	16.8	11.3	24.3	17.3	37.7	23.4
6–10	1.0	5.2	2.2	10.4	1.4	13.0
Over 10	1.0	0.9	0.6	0.5	1.4	0.0

Note: The data for this table came from the 1976 BPA survey. The original BPA table encompassed all stations. For this analysis, the BPA data were divided into small and large stations based on the number of employees. However, the original percentages are retained in this table and derived from 100 percent of the respective radio, television, and radio/television combination samples for 1968 and 1976. To verify the percentages, add the respective columns for 1968 and 1976 in this table and Table 3-1.

ᵃ Stations with 50 employees or more.

ᵇ Stations with 100 employees or more.

staff sizes from the 3–5 range to 6–10. Nevertheless, most still employ three to five people for promotional jobs. These larger staffs result from several conditions. First, there are more media outlets in the larger markets, increasing the promotional challenge. Greater available total advertising dollars and financial rewards to be gained enhance the competition. Lastly, larger stations produce more discretionary income, which gives management, if it desires, a greater opportunity to emphasize promotion.

TELEVISION STATION STATUS

An important indicator of promotion's influence is its relative position in the station's personnel hierarchy. In television's early years, the promotion manager frequently reported to (or was) the program director. This person had little access to top management, especially at the larger stations. As staffs grew larger and assignments more complex in the late 1960s and the 1970s, however, a direct reporting line was instituted from the promotion manager to the station manager and, even more frequently, to the general manager. This arrangement allows the promotion manager to work on an equal basis with all department heads and to have a voice in important policy matters. Furthermore, by the mid-1970s, most managers (over 60 percent) no longer had split functions but were responsible only for promoting the station.[3]

[3]1976 BPA Survey, p. 8.

Radio Promotion

While the largest radio stations have evolved hierarchies similar to those in television, most are still relatively simple organizations. Market size, economics, power, automation, and commitment of top management determine the role of promotion. In most radio stations, the promotion functions are borne by the station or program manager and occasionally by sales. As the 1976 BPA survey indicates, 35 percent of the radio sample held titles associated only with promotion.[4] Nearly 65 percent had dual roles in station, program, or sales management. Nevertheless, with increasing competition, it is expected that radio stations will establish more exclusive promotion departments or positions.

Group Ownership

Of increasing importance is group ownership. As groups expanded between 1960 and 1980, they tended to standardize their promotional efforts in their commonly owned stations. This development enhanced corporate identity, allowed for greater use of research expertise, and spread promotional costs. At the major groups, a unit or person at the corporate level coordinates promotional efforts, consults on local promotion problems, and conducts joint meetings among station department heads, frequently in tandem with top management.[5]

SALARIES

Another concrete example of promotion's value to a station is the money spent on salaries and budgets. There are two ways to evaluate the position of promotion managers: in comparison to other employees' salaries and in comparison to past salary levels for the same job. When compared to the average salary figures reported for general managers, general sales managers, and program directors, promotion managers do not fare very well. Figure 3-1 shows that general managers typically make three times as much as promotion managers and that program directors do half again as well as promotion managers.[6]

[4]1976 BPA Survey, p. 8.

[5]From discussion with personnel from Corinthian Broadcasting, Group W, Ziff-Davis, and Klein &.

[6]Averages for general managers, sales managers, and program directors reported in "Station Executive Salaries Up Over '78; Impact of New Technologies Assayed," *Television/Radio Age,* 28 January 1980, p. 78. These figures are based on 500 responses to *Television/Radio Age's* annual survey of station executives in January 1980. The average for promotion managers is reported in "Radio, TV Promotion Execs Happy with Work, Average over $22,000, Survey Indicates," *Television/Radio Age,* 2 June 1980, p. 41. The graph is based on an April 1980 survey of the membership of the Broadcasters Promotion Association conducted by *Television/Radio Age.*

Figure 3-1 Average Television Executive Salaries in 1980

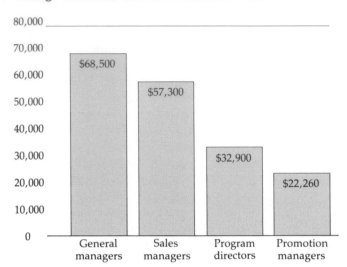

When we examine salaries over the twelve years from 1968 to 1980, a different picture emerges. But before proceeding, several factors should be kept in mind. These data are drawn from BPA surveys of its membership in 1968, 1976, and 1980. Thus inflation plays a role in these increases. There are also some inconsistencies in the salary figures between radio and television. As *Television/Radio Age* states:

> *BPA membership among television stations is more broadly representative of small-, medium-, and large-sized markets than among radio stations. BPA radio station promotion people tend to come from the major markets, where larger stations have both the pressures and the economic wherewithal. . . .[7]*

Despite these limitations, these salary data clearly demonstrate promotion's growing importance.

In the 1968 BPA survey, 33 percent of the television and 34 percent of the radio respondents earned less than $10,000 annually. Forty percent working in television made between $10,000 and $14,999 while 35 percent did so in radio. Twenty-one percent in television and 23 percent in radio made over $15,000. The remainder did not answer this question.[8] By 1976, only 5.3 percent of the radio respondents and 9.0 percent in television earned less than $10,000 while 26.3 percent and

[7]"Radio, TV Promotion Execs Happy with Work, Average over $22,000, Survey Indicates," *Television/Radio Age*, 2 June 1980, pp. 41–42.
[8]1969 BPA Survey.

54.6 percent, respectively, made between $10,000 and $14,999. Salaries of $15,000 and over were received by 68.5 percent working in radio and 36.4 percent in television.[9]

Salary levels increased dramatically when the 1980 study was taken. None in radio earned less than $10,000, while only 3.6 percent did in television. Executives in the median salary range of $10,000 to $14,999 had declined to 20.9 percent in radio and 14.5 percent in television. The vast majority in both media now made more than $15,000 a year. More-over, 53.4 percent of the television respondents and 47.3 percent in radio made $20,000 or more. The average television promotion executive's salary was $22,300; in radio it was $22,600.[10]

There is, however, a wide disparity in salaries paid to men and women. In 1968, some 75 percent of the women versus 30 percent of the men were earning less than $10,000, while 25 percent of the men were paid $15,000 and over compared to only 8 percent of the women. The situation had not changed significantly by 1976: Seventy-five per-cent of the women in promotion earned less than $15,000 whereas 59 percent of the men made more than $15,000.[11] With stricter FCC en-forcement of equal employment opportunity as well as the general im-pact of the women's movement, women were faring a little better at the time of the 1980 BPA survey. In television, 35.8 percent of the male respondents earned less than $20,000 versus 62.3 percent of the women. In radio, the respective percentages were 26.3 and 71.7. On the other hand, women were still not evident in significant numbers at the upper salary levels. While 11.5 percent of the males in television and 26.4 percent in radio were paid more than $35,000 annually, only 1 percent of the women in television were. None in radio reached this level.[12]

This wide discrepancy in salary was produced by several factors, the most obvious being discriminatory hiring practices. Tenure is another cause. The longer one is with a company, generally the more money one makes. Longevity also gives executives a greater chance to build successful records that often invite other companies to bid for their services. Furthermore, male promotion executives report that they are responsible for a broader number of functions than women are.[13] What-ever the reason, female promotion managers have made some eco-nomic strides in the past fifteen years, but parity is still a long way off.

[9]1976 BPA Survey, p. 10.
[10]"Radio, TV Promotion Execs . . .," p. 41.
[11]1976 BPA Survey, p. 12.
[12]"Radio, TV Promotion Execs . . .," p. 42.
[13]"Radio, TV Promotion Execs . . .," p. 42.

BUDGETS

Tables 3-3 and 3-4 provide further evidence of promotion's growing influence. These data are from 1968 and 1976; unfortunately, comparable figures are not available for 1980.

As Table 3-3 indicates, most respondents at small radio stations (49 employees or less) in 1968 and 1976 had promotion budgets of $5,000 or less. Nevertheless, between these years there was an important shift. While 61 percent had less than $5,000 in 1968, the majority were working with more than that amount by 1976 and almost a quarter of them had at least $25,000. A similar shift took place at the small television stations (99 employees or less). In 1968, 64 percent had budgets under $25,000. Seven years later, most respondents (54 percent) had $25,000 or more at their disposal, and 26 percent were budgeted between $50,000 and $250,000.

The larger stations witnessed even more dramatic growth. In 1968, most radio stations (64 percent) with 50 employees or more spent less than $50,000 on promotion. By 1975, 72 percent exceeded $50,000; slightly over a third were budgeting more than $100,000. The large tele-

Table 3-3
Promotion Budget Levels for Small Stations: 1968–1976

Budget Level[a]	Radio[b]		TV[c]		Radio/TV Combined[c]	
	1968	1976	1968	1976	1968	1976
Less than $5,000	46.1%	33.3%	13.2%	10.7%	17.7%	11.8%
$5,001 to $10,000	12.5	14.2	6.8	4.6	3.2	5.3
$10,001 to $25,000	7.7	8.4	18.8	12.7	16.1	9.2
$25,001 to $50,000	4.8	5.8	10.1	16.7	1.6	13.1
$50,001 to $100,000	1.9	7.5	8.8	11.2	6.5	6.6
$100,001 to $250,000	2.9	4.2	2.5	4.1	0.0	1.3
Over $250,000	0.0	0.0	0.6	0.5	0.0	0.0

Note: The data for this table came from the 1976 BPA survey. The original BPA table encompassed all stations. For this analysis, the BPA data were divided into small and large stations based on the number of employees. However, the original percentages are retained in this table and derived from 100 percent of the respective radio, television, and radio/television combination samples for 1968 and 1976. To verify the percentages, add the respective columns for 1968 and 1976 in this table and Table 3-4.

[a] Excluding salaries and reciprocal trade.

[b] Stations with 49 employees or less.

[c] Stations with 99 employees or less.

vision stations (100 employees or more) were well within the $100,000 range in 1968; 61 percent had promotion budgets of $100,000 or less. During 1975, promotion expenditures of more than $100,000 were reached by 66 percent of the respondents, and almost a third spent over $250,000. This figure represents doubled spending at similar levels from seven years earlier.

THE PROMOTION MANAGER'S RESPONSIBILITIES

Whether a person is situated at a network, group, or station, the diverse responsibilities associated with promotion require broad knowledge. In small operations most of this expertise will be used daily, whereas specialization will be needed in larger organizations. In any case, promotion personnel are generally charged with four distinct functions to enhance the station's or network's economic position, programs, and image: audience promotion, sales promotion, community relations, and research.

Table 3-4
Promotion Budget Levels for Large Stations: 1968–1976

Budget Level[a]	Radio[b]		TV[c]		Radio/TV Combined[c]	
	1968	1976	1968	1976	1968	1976
Less than $5,000	1.9%	0.8%	0.6%	0.0%	0.0%	0.0%
$5,001 to $10,000	2.9	0.8	2.5	0.5	6.5	3.9
$10,001 to $25,000	3.9	0.8	3.8	1.0	4.8	1.3
$25,001 to $50,000	6.7	5.0	7.5	3.6	9.7	5.3
$50,001 to $100,000	4.8	9.2	9.4	8.1	14.5	11.8
$100,001 to $250,000	1.0	6.7	9.4	13.7	11.3	18.4
Over $250,000	2.9	3.3	5.6	12.2	6.5	11.8

Note: The data for this table came from the 1976 BPA survey. The original BPA table encompassed all stations. For this analysis, the BPA data were divided into small and large stations based on the number of employees. However, the original percentages are retained in this table and derived from 100 percent of the respective radio, television, and radio/television combination samples for 1968 and 1976. To verify the percentages, add the respective columns for 1968 and 1976 in this table and Table 3-3.

[a] Excluding salaries and reciprocal trade.

[b] Stations with 50 employees or more.

[c] Stations with 100 employees or more.

The following list shows many of the specific duties a promotion manager may have.[14] In addition to the four functions just noted, these duties may involve station image, press relations, news, and general administrative responsibilities.

The Job of the Promotion Manager (*Used with permission.*)

1. Audience promotion
    *   On-air television
        1. Scripting
        2. Previewing tapes, films, music tracks
        3. Selection of talent if needed (actors, actresses, announcers)
        4. Scheduling
        5. Maintaining inventory
        6. Ensuring the consistency and creativity of each spot as well as each entire campaign
        7. Directing creative process
        8. Evaluating effectiveness of spots
    *   On-air radio
        1. Writing
        2. Editing music and sound, selecting voices
        3. Evaluating media
        4. Arranging for spots at various times to reach appropriate audiences
        5. Recommending and coordinating trade arrangements with radio stations
    *   *TV Guide*, newspaper advertising
        1. Preparing schedule based on priorities and available information
        2. Securing artwork and graphic materials for the production of ads
        3. Copywriting
        4. Supervising artwork and design including selection of type and overall appearance of ad
        5. Determining size and frequency of ad
        6. Coordinating trade arrangements
        7. Securing approval and delivery of finished artwork to the publication before deadline

---

[14]This list was prepared by Morton A. Slakoff and originally appeared in *Facts, Figures, & Film*, June 1980.

- Magazine advertising
  1. Preparation as above
  2. Contact and recommendations for trade arrangements
- Outdoor and transit advertising
  1. Exploring trade arrangements
  2. Researching costs and effectiveness of these campaigns
  3. Selecting locations
  4. Supervising creative concepts
  5. Supervising production within budgets
  6. Postcampaign evaluating
- Other forms of audience promotion: many ingenious and unusual promotional ideas can bring attention to individual programs and the station. This category is limited only by one's imagination. The promotion director must organize, arrange, compensate—cash or trade—and follow through to make these forms of promotion work. Here are a few examples: laundry stuffers, ticket envelopes, supermarket bags, tie-ins with department stores, retail outlets, book and record stores, painting the sides of buildings, skywriting, parades, fireworks, mailings, posters, personal appearances.

2. Sales promotion
   - Promotion directors must have a thorough understanding of research and sales and marketing techniques in order to write and supervise the layout and production of:
     1. Customized sales presentations
     2. Sales brochures
     3. Single sheets
     4. Major client presentations
     5. General sales presentations (written and audiovisual)
   - Coordinating graphics for commercial operations (camera cards, commercials)
   - Supervising agency and client receptions (development of theme, selection of appropriate facility, budgets, catering, entertainment, invitations, decorations)
   - Supervising gifts, premiums, client giveaways (must be familiar with suppliers, sources, new and inventive gifts)
   - Preparing client reports after the promotion

3. Research
   - Working with the research department to ensure that all research bulletins and published research materials are presented in the most professional and creative manner
   - Taking research statistics and translating them into clear concepts with impressive headlines

4. Community relations
   - Working closely with community relations director (if there is one) since many community projects end up in the promotion department:
     1. Public service campaigns
     2. Community tie-in promotions
     3. Keeping track of public service activities for FCC filing
     4. Station tours
   - Participating in ascertainment
   - Assisting with community receptions
   - Helping to answer letters and calls from viewers
5. Station image
   - Coordinating overall graphic look of the station (on-air station IDs, use of channel number, corporate identification, stationery, order forms, billing forms, everything seen by client and audience)
   - Supervising use of station logo wherever it appears
   - Preparing and submitting presentations for awards for various programs and projects
6. Press relations
   - Obtaining approval for all press relations
   - Developing and maintaining close press contacts (lunches and personal meetings)
   - Ensuring accurate newspaper and *TV Guide* listings
   - Developing feature stories on:
     1. Station personnel
     2. Visiting celebrities
     3. New programs
     4. Specials
     5. Unusual events
   - Keeping accurate clipping file to measure effectiveness of press activities (how much space does your station get compared to the competition)
   - Organizing press receptions and screenings including invitations, catering, press kits
7. News
   - Working with news director on:
     1. Set problems
     2. All on-air news graphics
     3. News logo
     4. All aspects of news advertising and promotion
8. General administration
   - Building an effective promotion department

- Supervising art department
- Preparing and monitoring a budget
- Keeping close touch with the division (if part of large corporation)
- Working closely with other stations in the group
- Coordinating projects with other corporate divisions
- Preparing a monthly report
- Attending station staff meetings
- Keeping in touch with program suppliers for promotion materials
- Cultivating reliable and reasonable suppliers for printing, photos, and so on
- Keeping updated bios and photo file on station personnel and programs
- Keeping track of salaries, raises, vacations, sick time for department employees
- Helping department members with company procedures
- Supervising training of new personnel and interns
- Keeping track of competition's promotional activities (budgets, staffs, campaigns)
- Assisting general managers with intrastation communications
- Keeping abreast of all new technologies, equipment, trends in graphics and current fads and popular themes in order to shape the station's overall look
- Staying aware of advertising legal restrictions and station and company policy (including use of trademarks and copyright information)

Audience Promotion

Many avenues are used in audience promotion—including on-air, consumer publications such as newspapers and magazines, and outdoor advertising. To a lesser degree, direct mail, tie-ins with local merchants, cross-promotions with books and records, and personal appearances are used. The list of possibilities is limited only by the ingenuity and budget of the promotion managers.

The first avenue is on-air promotion. Certainly the station's own air is the most effective means for promotion. To use it creatively, the promotion staff must be skilled in writing, selecting appropriate visuals and music, choosing talent, applying production techniques, scheduling, and maintaining and rotating inventory. Tight fiscal management by the manager is also required, as well as the ability to establish a creative environment that encourages talented people to function effectively.

Promotion managers must also be knowledgeable about using the "other" broadcast medium. In television's early years, many stations were owned by local radio outlets. Tentatively at first, and then with greater frequency, these radio stations were used to promote the new medium. This situation continued unabated even when local co-ownerships were separated, and by 1980 radio had become a prime outlet for local and network television promotion.

Many arrangements are trade deals in which time is swapped on a quid pro quo basis and little cash is involved. Radio, however, was slow to take full advantage of advertising on television and only began using it effectively and with greater frequency in the 1970s.

Numerous syndicators have developed radio promotions especially for television that are available on a market-exclusive basis throughout the United States. Using the same basic production techniques, these promotions can be adapted to each station. One that has appeared in many markets opens on the face of a beautiful woman. The camera zooms in to her lips, and she lip-syncs the sounds, including announcers and music, of the station. For a tag, the camera zooms back, and she says, in her own voice, "We have a beautiful radio station."

In the BPA surveys noted above, promotion managers consistently agreed that the role of on-air has substantially increased in importance over the decade. In 1968, some 90 percent of the television promotion managers surveyed specified on-air as their major function as compared with 58 percent in radio and 85 percent at combined radio/television operations. These percentages increased respectively to 98 percent for television, 87 percent for radio, and 89 percent for combined operations by 1980.[15]

Another avenue for audience promotion is consumer publications. According to the BPA surveys, preparing materials for other consumer media, particularly print publications, is generally listed slightly behind on-air as the promotion manager's most important job. This task requires skills in writing, art design, layout, type selection, color formats, page placement and size, and determination of the most effective number of runs for each ad. Moreover, knowing which publications the local audience uses most often will determine the division of budget, although the decision to advertise might be based also on reciprocal trades of print space for air time. At all television stations, the local

15"Radio, TV Promotion Execs . . . ," p. 43.

circulation of *TV Guide* is given special consideration, and most stations have trade arrangements with this publication.

To negotiate effectively, promotion managers must establish and maintain credible relations with many sectors of the press. Print media contacts must be confident that program schedules will be as accurate as possible and delivered on time. More feature stories and press releases will be used by print contacts if close relations persist and mutual trust exists. Frequent press luncheons and parties help in this regard.

The third major avenue for audience promotion is outdoor advertising. Using outdoor advertising and related forms such as posters and transit ads requires the ability to encapsulate a campaign in a few words to attain quick impressions. Layout, color, graphics, location—these are the vital communication elements. The goal is to choose the sites that the station's audience is most likely to pass regularly. Trade arrangements may be used, but they are not so common as in other consumer media. Television and radio respondents in 1968 and 1976 did not give a high ranking to billboard use. Radio promotion executives tend to use them more frequently.[16]

Sales Promotion

Promotion managers generally agree that sales-related functions rank among the highest in their order of responsibilities. In 1969, some 68 percent of those surveyed listed sales promotion as a prime duty; 73 percent did so in 1980.[17] Trade publications account for most of this work. But other forms are involved—ranging from quick one-page handouts, usually treating rating data or new program introductions, to highly customized sales brochures that convey major station/network themes and enhance corporate image.

Client presentations are sometimes within promotion's purview, although to a lesser degree (30 percent according to the 1969 survey) than other sales assignments. This activity includes the preparation of audiovisual aids and program preview tapes. In conjunction with the sales department, promotion plans and supervises client receptions as well as the selection of gifts to clients.

Community Relations

In the past eleven years, an increasing emphasis on community relations has been demonstrated by the BPA surveys. In 1969, community

[16]1969 BPA Survey, pp. 9–10; 1976 BPA Survey, p. 6.
[17]1969 BPA Survey, p. 8; "Radio, TV Promotion Execs . . . ," p. 43.

relations were listed by radio and television promotion personnel as their top *secondary* responsibility, but only one-third of those surveyed rated it as a primary duty. In the 1980 survey, 76 percent in radio, 60 percent in television, and 69 at radio/television combinations named community relations as a key duty.[18] Fewer promotion managers are involved at television stations because many have community relations directors, while radio is more likely to combine the functions of community relations and promotion.

This increasing emphasis on community relations can be traced to several sources. But first it should be noted that many stations have been involved for years in community activities. They needed no provocation other than the belief that community involvement was simply good business practice as well as a social commitment. Nevertheless, others needed prodding that came initially from increased media competition.

Since broadcasting's early years, promotion managers (or some designated persons) have been involved in community tie-in and public service campaigns, station tours, and answering letters and telephone calls (see Chapter 16). These activities took on increasing importance, however, as competition grew. They served as a constant demonstration of the station's community concern. It is difficult to measure the effectiveness of such activities. But one might hypothesize (with a fair degree of certainty) that the station with the best community image is probably the audience leader as well.

Another factor has been the increasing militancy of minority groups and others who seriously began to challenge station licenses in the late 1960s and the 1970s. At license renewal time, stations, especially in the larger markets, had petitions to deny filed at the FCC by groups who felt that their needs and interests were not being served. Most stations retained their licenses but were chastened in the process—and issued directives to spend more time and money on community affairs, especially in previously neglected areas.[19]

The FCC took a more formal approach toward community relations in the 1970s. It promulgated regulations requiring broadcasters to meet formally with community leaders and ascertain their views of the area's problems and needs. In turn, some of these problems and needs were to be addressed in the station's programs. Stations complied with these requirements but worked vigorously for their repeal. As of 1981, radio station requirements are being relieved by the FCC, but formal television compliance continues.

---

[18]1969 BPA Survey, p. 43.
[19]Erwin G. Krasnow, Lawrence D. Longley, and Herbert A. Terry, *The Politics of Broadcast Regulation*, 3rd ed. (New York: St. Martin's Press, 1982).

Research

Most promotion managers give research a low ranking in the order of their job priorities. In 1969, some 32 percent of the television respondents (and 33 percent in radio) indicated that research was a prime duty; 45 percent at combined operations had this responsibility. By 1980, no change was evident at separate stations, while 58 percent of those surveyed at joint operations reported the conduct of research as within their purview.[20]

This lack of involvement in data collection is not surprising. Conflict frequently exists between those who rely on their instincts to make programming decisions and those who believe that human behavior can be predicted through scientific investigation. Quantities of new numbers cannot replace the human insight that creates a new concept.

On the other hand, accurate data collection and detailed analysis can be important tools in the overall decision-making process. Quantitative studies, for example, can indicate which programs or newspapers a target audience prefers. Census and zip code data can reveal where these people live to aid in making use of billboards.

But exposure is one thing, effect another. Once a message is received, surveys may determine whether the campaign has been effective. While such studies have their limitations, they should not be discounted. Promotion managers need expertise in interpreting data and conducting, or at least contracting for, audience research to aid their missions.

A CASE STUDY

To see how these responsibilities might mesh, consider the following case. This example, using the CBS Television Network program *The Pride of Jesse Hallam*, which starred Johnny Cash, demonstrates how a network and its affiliates can work together to maximize the local audience. It focuses on distribution and does not take into account all of the prerelease work, including production, that takes place at the network.

Network distribution encompasses the following:

1. Stations are sent camera-ready art for newspaper ads that include space for local programs, taped radio spots, photographs, slides, press releases, and story lines. To stimulate the campaign, co-op dollars are provided for the network and station to share in the

[20]1969 BPA Survey, p. 8; "Radio, TV Promotion Execs . . . ," p. 43.

cost of local newspaper ads. Because this program deals with the struggle of a middle-aged man to overcome illiteracy, it is included in the CBS Television Reading Program in which full scripts and teachers' guides are made available to local schools. A closed-circuit feed of the program is available for showing to educators and local newspaper critics. There is also a late news tie-in if a local story can be obtained on illiteracy.

2. Consumer publications are sent schedules, press releases, photographs, and story lines. *TV Guide* receives the same materials and, in addition, a full-page ad is bought giving the channel numbers of the local affiliates served by that edition. Note that the network, and not the station, is responsible for the times of network programs that appear in *TV Guide*.

3. On-air promotional spots are scheduled in network programs. Radio network time is bought. Interviews are arranged on such programs as *Morning*.

At the local affiliate level, the promotion manager takes these steps:

1. Inside the station, the promotion manager works with other managers:

    - The general manager or station manager confirms the overall strategy and budget. After the program, the promotion manager reviews the campaign to determine its strengths and weaknesses.

    - Sales personnel are asked if there are special sales opportunities and what materials would be most valuable.

    - The program manager or operations manager schedules the production needed for customizing television and radio spots. The promotion department prepares a local program schedule that includes the network offerings and distributes them to print media.

    - The traffic manager schedules extra local spots.

    - The art director prepares visuals for television spots and also customizes camera-ready newspaper art with call letters and an ad promoting the late news.

    - The public affairs or community affairs director contacts local school systems to invite their participation in the School Reading Program. At the station's expense, or if an underwriter can be found, scripts and teachers' guides are sent free of charge to the participants.

    - The comptroller pays the bills after verification by the promotion manager and attempts to keep the budget within set limits.

2. Outside the station:

- Newspaper ads are placed, and reporters are encouraged to use press releases and photographs.
- Radio spots are placed, and talk show hosts are contacted to consider illiteracy as a topic.
- A community luncheon is arranged so that educators and news reporters can preview the program.

This list is by no means complete. It only provides an illustration of the myriad details that must be accomplished to bring one program to the public's attention.

EDUCATION

Job responsibilities, ranging from the highly creative to the social scientific, require executives with a broad educational background. In fact, promotion managers ranked this diverse challenge, along with creativity, as the most favorable aspect of their job.[21] To prepare for this challenge, almost 90 percent of those surveyed by BPA in 1968 and 1976 had at least some college.

Furthermore, the increasing complexity of promotion apparently had an impact on the educational achievement of the respondents between the two surveys. In 1968, some 66 percent employed in radio, 75 percent in television, and 65 percent at the radio-television combinations had attended college or attained an undergraduate degree, while 18, 15, and 23 percent respectively had done graduate work.[22] A greater emphasis on advanced education was evident by 1976 as 22.2 percent in radio, 32.5 percent in television, and 31.2 percent at the combinations worked toward or achieved a graduate degree.[23] These advanced degrees are also indicative of a growing professionalism in the ranks of promotion.

Aside from formal education, most people who do not start in promotion positions generally receive their initial broadcast training in production and performance. Other entry-level points include ad agencies, sales, and news.[24]

[21] 1969 BPA Survey, p. 10; 1976 BPA Survey, p. 15.
[22] 1969 BPA Survey, p. 5.
[23] 1976 BPA Survey, p. 10.
[24] 1969 BPA Survey, p. 12; 1976 BPA Survey, p. 15.

PERSONAL COMMENTS

From personal observation, confirmed by the 1980 survey, it is obvious that promotion people love their jobs. They are among the most dedicated and hardworking people at stations and networks. The promotion manager's slot is also one of the most difficult positions to fill. Where does management find individuals who have a broad range of knowledge and appropriate talents combined with a competitive spirit and the even temperament to cope with the exigencies of an intense ratings race? The descriptive data in this chapter only begin to provide an answer.

As a television/radio general manager (and a former university professor), I think that definitive answers must come from several sources. First, management must clearly articulate the role and position of promotion at various levels of the industry. In preparing this chapter, little data were available to define precisely the differences in the promotion manager's specific functions at small, medium, and large radio or television stations. The network situation is even worse. It is possible to glean bits of information here and there, but an intensive study is needed to provide an accurate assessment. This book is an important step in that direction.

Once such data are available, they should be brought to the attention of the academic community that is training personnel for the industry. Certainly BPA could be a vital conduit, as it has already established a working relationship with such institutions as San Diego State, the University of Nebraska, and Michigan State University.[25] In addition, internships for both students and faculty can bring the classroom and the field into sharper focus. Just as important, universities should consider advanced training seminars for promotion personnel. An appropriate model would be the Harvard University course in management and sales that has been offered each summer for more than two decades. The dynamics of promotion require continuous training.

But from a management perspective, training is only one aspect of personnel development. Of even greater priority is the question of how to attract the best and the brightest. Again, management must set the example. Too often the commitment to promotion is tentative. It is frequently among the first items to disappear in a budget pinch, and one of the last to be restored, especially at the smaller stations. Management must demonstrate that opportunities for advancement to the top levels are in fact available. As the 1968 and 1976 BPA surveys demon-

---

[25]San Diego State University provides a home for the BPA library of videocassettes, audiocassettes, and award-winning materials; the University of Nebraska and Michigan State have hosted the BPA awards competition.

strate, most promotion personnel aspire to top station management and ownership positions and not to programming as is often thought.[26] These personnel should be given more insight into station operations to prepare them for the future. It is also common sense to follow this practice regularly, as it is the promotion manager who is frequently charged with representing the station or network to the community.

Finally, there are several role models in broadcasting who provide vivid proof that a bright and talented promotion manager can achieve considerable managerial success. Such examples include Fred Silverman, former president and chief executive officer of NBC; Brandon Tartikoff, president of NBC Entertainment; Thomas E. Bolger, former joint board chairman of the National Association of Broadcasters; and Lawrence Grossman, president of PBS. These people might be the forerunners of an industry trend in which the growth of competitive media makes it increasingly essential for the leadership to be well versed in promotion.

SUMMARY

This chapter reports findings on the sizes of promotion department staffs at commercial television-stations in large and small markets and discusses the position and importance of promotion at the commercial networks, radio stations, and television stations. Organizational shifts at networks and stations in the 1970s and 1980s reflect a new prominence for promotion, as do the dramatic increases in salary for promotion managers at stations. The growth of promotion department budgets during the 1970s also demonstrates promotion's increased value—especially at large-market stations. As for the relative importance of the elements of their jobs, promotion managers rank on-air and print promotion as their two most important responsibilities. A hypothetical case study illustrates the interrelationships of the various duties of promotion managers. The chapter concludes with a call for improved academic training and greater management commitment to promotion.

[26]1968 and 1976 BPA Surveys, p. 11, p. 14, respectively.

Promotion Budget Strategy

by
Diane K. Bagwell

Diane K. Bagwell is assistant program director/promotion manager at WIS-TV in Columbia, South Carolina. She buys and schedules syndicated programming, designs and administers budgets, and is responsible for local program production and statewide program feeds. Before coming to WIS, she was promotion manager/public service director at WCIV-TV in Charleston, South Carolina, after serving as associate producer of community affairs. She is a graduate with honors from the University of South Carolina and is a member of the board of directors of the Broadcasters Promotion Association.

The myths that surround the budgeting process can be dispelled by analyzing exactly what a budget is. In simple terms, a budget is a management tool—a plan for what a station wants to do expressed in numbers. Promotion managers must formulate and execute on-air and print advertising campaigns that will increase audiences, solidify the station's image, and promote that image in the local market. To meet this challenge, a plan of action is needed. Promotion budgets are the monetary guidelines within which promotion departments accomplish their goals.

BUDGETING OBJECTIVES

Advertising and promotion departments are usually regarded as "support" arms for stations. Therefore, promotion managers need to know the goals of all the station's departments before devising their plan of action. Communication and coordination with sales, programming, news, and public affairs, as well as other departments, provide starting points for outlines of objectives. The following questions provide essential information:

- How many sales promotion/client parties are forecast for the coming year?

- Will there be a major revision in the station's programming lineup—and if so, when?
- How will the station advertise the new fall season?
- Is the news department planning a change in format or style?
- Is it intending to add new features or new anchors?
- What kind of community activities are planned for the coming year?
- What major changes are expected in the competition's programming?

The promotion manager should spend time with each department head searching for information about projects that may need promotional support.

After gathering facts and figures from departments in the station, the promotion manager combines the station's overall goals with the promotion department's plan for routine advertising and promotion expenses. Key questions relating to promotion strategy are:

- When are the rating periods?
- When and where will the department make multimedia buys?
- Will they be ongoing or focus on rating periods?

To answer these questions, the promotion manager must understand the station's position in the market, know the potential weaknesses in programming that will need substantial promotional support, and anticipate promotional and programming moves by the station's competition. Detailed discussion with other department managers should provide the critical information for effective promotion budgeting.

A formal system for promotional planning requires four categories of information on the station's plant, the on-air and print promotional product, the department's personnel, and its measurements of effectiveness. These four divisions should guide strategic planning sessions and systematize budgetary considerations in the promotion department.

The broad guidelines discussed in the following paragraphs need interpretation to fit the needs of specific stations or departments. The key, however, is to make promotional goals *measurable*. Assign a date for completion of each goal and indicate who is responsible for each task. A detailed written plan is an effective motivational tool for staff members and should be presented to the station manager for approval. When the plan is approved, the promotion manager can move on to the next step.

Plant

Plant refers to the promotion department's work area. Will it need additional equipment, studio space, or editing space? Will it require minor changes to facilitate on-air or graphics efforts in the coming year? These items need to be estimated for the budget after discussion with the station's engineering staff. Many companies budget for major renovations in their capital budgets, however, not the operational budget each department prepares annually.

Product

The second division of department budgeting—product—includes plans for in-house production of on-air advertising. It also entails purchasing jingles, audio identification packages, animation, and spot production done out-of-house at production companies. Product also involves the development of sales support materials, routine advertising strategies for the coming year, and any new projects (such as community service) requiring materials that the promotion department must design for the station. In addition to new projects, stock materials for the production of graphics and on-air video need to be estimated from previous consumption.

Personnel

Plans for hiring, training, and development of the promotion department's personnel (seminars, workshops) should be included in this category. Schedule evaluations, salary increases, and specific goals for each member of the promotion department should be outlined here.

Productivity

To be effective, the promotion department must gather adequate information and make efficient use of its internal facilities. This goal involves (1) evaluating the station's position in the market by means of research materials on a quarterly basis, (2) analyzing the competition's advertising strategies monthly, and (3) developing plans for increased use of studio production time for on-air promotion. These needs give rise to budgetary inclusions.

APPLYING DOLLAR FIGURES TO GOALS

Once the promotion manager has a firm grip on the station's overall goals, other departments' plans for operation, and promotion's own plan of action, in written form and approved, the basic framework for budgeting exists. The next step is to apply dollar figures to each goal. And herein lies the greatest challenge in the entire budgeting process: to budget in the most *economic* and *effective* manner to garner maximum results.

The first step in the mechanics of budgeting is direct contact with the station's business office. It will supply the proper forms, a chart of account numbers, and the administrative information needed to complete sections of the promotion department's budget. The forms for budgeting generally are broken down into about nine categories. Each category has a separate account number, but all are part of the promotion budget. The following paragraphs describe a basic budget; certain line items are specified to pinpoint what belongs in each category.

Personnel Administration

The section of the budgeting form known as personnel administration includes costs for (1) base salaries for the personnel in the department, (2) the projected overtime, (3) insurance, (4) FICA taxes, (5) profit sharing plans, and (6) training and development programs. The station's business manager can provide tips on how to arrive at monthly and grand total figures for such items, and all such costs will be charged to a specific account number (see Figure 4-1).

Office Administration

Items in the category known as office administration include (1) dues and subscriptions, (2) office supplies, (3) postage, (4) copying expenses, (5) telephone, (6) shipping, and (7) other supplies. Past budget records will suggest how much to allocate for such expenditures. If records from previous years are inadequate, estimates must be based on the department's goals. The business manager can advise on the cost of supplies and services and can also project inflationary increases in the cost of various items.

Travel and Entertainment

Many of the station's community commitments require (1) luncheons, (2) special video presentation, (3) travel, (4) entertaining, and (5) trips to conferences, seminars, and meetings in distant cities. Be sure to allocate enough money for food, transportation, hotels, taxis, and tips in this account. The station's calendar of events will indicate holiday functions, community events, and special projects that require promotion department planning and expense.

Figure 4-1 Proposed Departmental Budget

PROPOSED DEPARTMENTAL BUDGET

STATION _____   YEAR _____

Page 1 of 2

ACCT. NO.	DETAILED OPERATING EXPENSES	19____ ACTUAL	19____ BUDGET	19____ ACTUAL ESTIMATED	19____ PROPOSED BUDGET	LONG RANGE (000s OMITTED) 19____	19____
0010	Base Salaries						
0020	Overtime						
0021	Overtime & Prem. - Prod.						
0030	Sales Commissions						
0040	Staff Talent						
0050	Non-Staff Talent						
0060	Temporary Services						
0070	Salary Reimbursements						
0080	Salary Contingency						
0090	Salary Allocation						
0100	Workmen's Compensation						
0110	Group Insurance						
0120	Profit Sharing						
0121	Supplemental Retirement						
0122	Profit Sharing - IBEW						
0130	FICA Taxes						
0140	Unemployment Taxes						
0150	Employee Welfare						
0160	Recruiting Expense						
0170	Training & Development						
0200	Travel & Entertainment						
0201	T & E - Corporate Conf.						
0210	Parking						
0220	Company Car Expense						
0230	Dues and Subscriptions						
0240	Other Supplies						
0250	Postage						
0260	Freight & Express						
0270	Copying Expense						
0280	Other Expenses						
0290	Small Equipment						
0300	Telephone Expense						
0310	Line & Switching Charges						
0320	Electricity, Fuel & Water						
0330	Building & Grounds Maint.						
0400	Film Processing						
0490	Film Prod. Allocation						
0500	Program Rights						
0510	Program Rental						
0520	Program Shipping						
0530	Network Coop						
0540	Music License Fees						
0550	Purchase of Station Time						
0600	Art Supplies						
0601	Art Supplies - Corp. Conf.						
0610	Studio Props						
0620	Music Recordings						
0630	Tapes & Reels						
0700	Tube Expense						
0710	Studio Lighting						
0720	VTR Heads						
0730	Other Equipment Maint.						
0740	ENG Maintenance						
0750	ENG Tube Expense						
0800	Print Media Adv.						
0801	Print Media Adv./TV Guide						
0810	Trade Paper Adv.						
0820	Broadcast Adv.						
0830	Outdoor Display Adv.						

PROPOSED DEPARTMENTAL BUDGET

STATION _____   YEAR _____

ACCT. NO.	DETAILED OPERATING EXPENSES	19____ ACTUAL	19____ BUDGET	19____ ACTUAL ESTIMATED	19____ PROPOSED BUDGET	LONG RANGE (000s OMITTED)	
						19____	19____
0840	Other Adv. & Promotion						
0841	Sales Promotion						
0850	Research						
0860	Printing						
0900	VTR News Service						
0910	Wire Services						
0920	Slide Services						
0930	Stringer Services						
1000	Real Estate Rent						
1010	Technical Equipment Rent						
1011	Tech. Equip. - Corp. Cont.						
1020	Data Processing Rent						
1030	Other Equipment Rent						
1040	Chartered Aircraft - News						
1050	Auto & Truck Rental						
1060	Outside EDP						
1101	License Renewal Expense						
1110	General Insurance Expense						
1120	Property Taxes						
1130	Other Taxes						
1200	Bad Debt Expense						
1210	Credit & Collections						
1300	Charitable Contributions						
1310	Professional Fees						
1311	Professional Fees - SRC						
1320	Misc. Operating Expense						
1600	Headquarters Allocation						
1601	HQ. Exp. - Profit Sharing						
1610	Chgs. To/Fm Other Depts.						
1620	Trans. to Direct Expense						
1630	Capital Charges						
	TOTAL CASH EXPENSES						
	TRADE AND BARTER						
3050	Non-Staff Talent						
3150	Employee Welfare						
3500	Program Rights						
3510	Program Rental						
3610	Studio Props						
3800	Print Media Adv.						
3810	Trade Paper Adv.						
3820	Broadcast Adv.						
3830	Outdoor Display Adv.						
3840	Other Adv. & Promotion						
3900	VTR News Service Trade						
4030	Charitable Contribution						
4310	Professional Fees						
	TOTAL TRADE EXPENSES						
	TOTAL EXPENSES						

Technical Supplies

To execute the promotional job during the coming twelve-month period, the department will need (1) art supplies, (2) audiotape, (3) videotape, (4) film, and (5) film processing. Be sure to forecast such expenditures in the promotion budget if they are not accounted for in another department's budget.

Advertising Expenses

The items grouped under advertising expenses sound familiar to promotion staffs. This category is commonly broken down into such line items as (1) print media (newspaper), (2) print media (*TV Guide*), (3) electronic media, and (4) outdoor advertising. This category is the most time-consuming section of budgeting. Before putting dollar figures to the promotion department's goals, the promotion manager must be familiar with the rate cards, coverage area, circulation, and breakdown of audience demographics for every local and regional advertising outlet. After conducting research into other media's costs, the promotion manager can determine which advertising outlets will be most effective for the station. The station's statement of goals should specify how and when to allocate advertising dollars throughout the year.

Printing

Many stations have their own print shop to handle printing for the entire company. When this is the case, supplies such as (1) ink, (2) masters, (3) typesetting, and (4) other print-related costs may be included in the print shop budget or may have to be accounted for in the promotion budget.

If printing is done outside the station, it is necessary to determine print costs for various types of jobs and apply the costs to the number of print pieces the department anticipates for the coming year. These jobs typically include (1) special invitations for parties, (2) rate cards for the production department and sales department, (3) brochures that advertise news reporters, anchors, and programming, and (4) special printing for community projects that the station plans to undertake in the coming year.

Sales Promotion

The category known as sales promotion is used for the production of sales materials. The station's goals should indicate how many sales aids are to be designed monthly, quarterly, and for the total year and indicate also their general format: one-pagers printed in-house or complex and costly four-color booklets. Other sales items such as availability sheets, coverage maps, or special one-time-only programming sales sheets belong in the sales promotion category. The wisest approach is to budget for what is known and then add contingency amounts for the special presentations that are bound to occur.

Research

Although dollars for research are generally handled in news, programming, or sales department budgets, tailoring other departments' projects to promotional needs may be a cost-efficient means to improve the promotion department's effectiveness. Station management, the station's rep firm, and fellow promotion managers can advise on add-on research costs. Too many novice promotion managers skip over this category because they do not know how to evaluate their effectiveness and how to assign a dollar value.

Other Advertising and Promotion

Every station should have an account number for "other advertising." This category includes such things as (1) out of house production of music jingles and video and film animation and (2) community activities that the station sponsors. If the station's goals for the year include special "other" items, it is the promotion manager's responsibility to find out the projected cost of such undertakings.

ACCOUNTING FOR TRADES

This chapter has so far dealt with cash expenses. However, there are many ways to pursue advertising, promotion, and publicity by using trade (barter) agreements. Each station has its own philosophy regarding trade agreements. Some do it, and some do not.

Trade maneuvering is limited only by the promotion manager's imagination and the station's attitude. It is crucial to understand that the station's air-time inventory is being traded away—typically for (1) air time on a radio station, (2) newspaper space, (3) outdoor billboard space, or (4) concert or sporting event tickets.

The general manager and sales manager should be consulted before the promotion manager enters into any trade agreement. Contracts must be drawn up, signed, and kept on file; oral agreements are absolutely inadequate. Although cash does not change hands, the sales and accounting departments must specify the dollar value of traded air time and whatever was received in return. If a station trades for five hundred circus tickets to distribute via an over-the-air contest, the sales department must know the total worth of the tickets so that equivalent value in spots for the circus show are broadcast by the station.

PREPARING THE PRESENTATION

After reviewing the various line-item expenses, the promotion manager should write a detailed explanation of proposed expenditures. Making notes during the formulation of costs aids in writing the explanation. Under the heading of travel and entertainment, for example, only total figures such as $15,000 appear, but the promotion manager must attach a description of how that $15,000 will be spent over the course of the year. A narrative description is necessary for each line item and will be particularly helpful when the promotion manager has to make the formal budget presentation. Figure 4-2 shows a typical line-item budget.

MONTHLY SPREADS

After the promotion manager has applied dollar figures to goals, arrived at totals for each line item, and written a short descriptive narrative for each expenditure, the budget takes on a completed look. The promotion manager is only halfway home, however. After thousands of feet of calculator tape, there is more to come. The grand total for the year is the bottom line for the department budgeting process. Before a budget can mean anything on a day-to-day, month-by-month basis, the total figures have to be spread across the total year to produce the "monthly spreads."

It is crucial to know not only how much the promotion department wants to spend for the whole year but also *when* it wants to spend it. Estimating expenses month by month will indicate key periods of heavy expenditure and give an accurate picture of activities to be accomplished on a monthly basis. Referring to goals that have been assigned dates helps to determine monthly expenses. At some stations the promotion manager is asked to total department expenses quarterly. (This happens typically when stations are group-owned and corporate budgeting requires quarterly expenditure reports.)

The final touch in preparing the budget is the cover page that divides the contents into major sections. While every company's budget forms vary, basic accounting principles require (1) information for the current budget, (2) estimates of how close to budget a department anticipates

Figure 4-2 Example of a Line-Item Budget

```
                              1981  PROPOSED  BUDGET



ACCOUNT  NUMBER


    0010        BASE  SALARIES                                  $54,616

                Salaries for Promotion Manager and
                Assistant Promotion Manager, and
                part-time secretary


    0020        OVERTIME                                           900

                Client Reception        300
                Premiere Party          300
                Community Project        300


    0130        FICA                                             3,632

                6.65% on wages up to $29,700 per
                employee


    0140        UNEMPLOYMENT TAXES                                 423

                2.35% of first $6,000 in earnings
                per employee


    0200        TRAVEL AND ENTERTAINMENT                        15,000

                Client reception (January)      1,000
                Network regional meeting          500
                BPA Seminar (New York)          1,000
                Premiere Party                  7,000
                Local Travel                      500
                Community Project               5,000
```

being at the end of the current budget year, and (3) the figures the promotion manager is preparing for the next budget year.

After compiling all these figures, the promotion manager may be asked to come up with long-range projections for the next two, three, or five years. While these figures will be estimated totals only, the long-range budget requires considerable anticipation of the goals that could be set over the next few years, simultaneously projecting for expenses as accurately as possible. It is necessary to keep in mind the rate of inflation, potential growth in the department, future costs of office administration, changes in media expenditures, and possible tactical changes in the station's promotional plans in the future.

When line items have been tallied and cross-checked and the narrative descriptions of each line-item expense have been drawn up, the first draft of the budget is complete. Research, computation, and creativity should come together in a neat package that describes the promotion manager's plans for the next twelve months. The next step in the budgeting process, however, is probably the most interesting of all.

FORMAL PRESENTATION

The presentation of the budget is more accurately the *selling* of ideas on the best way to promote the station in the coming year. In this case the audience consists of the station's top executives. Many first-time presenters lose a lot of sleep over this formal encounter with the chiefs. There is a certain pride of authorship involved in presenting a budget for approval. Working day and night for weeks, to come up with the facts, figures, and proposed techniques, leaves many promotion managers ill-prepared for adjustments from higher management. Each department's budget is only a part of the whole, however, and the station's management has greater knowledge of the station's total operation than do individual department heads. Information on revenue projections, where and when economic declines may come, how greater profit might be gained (due to experience or knowledge of the marketplace)—all these factors affect management's decisions.

Department heads should approach the budget presentation session in a positive and flexible frame of mind. The presentation allows three things: (1) a chance for the promotion manager to identify opportunities, define problems, help coordinate efforts, formulate new programs, and propose new actions; (2) an illustration to top management of how creative and practical the promotion manager's plans are; and (3) an opportunity to push for acceptance of promotion's proposed budget and to defend its programs.

After the presentation, the promotion manager may have to make structural or dollar changes before receiving final approval. Usually the station's business office issues the final copy of the budget to each department. This action starts the next phase of the budgeting process: execution.

BUDGET EXECUTION

Execution of a formal budget requires a certain amount of accounting knowledge. Periodically it is wise to review accounting procedures with the business manager or chief accountant. Limits on purchases vary. Some promotion managers may order and sign for a $100 or $200 item; others need countersignatures. Some items require a purchase order *before* ordering. Procedures for check requests and expense vouchers and monthly accounting deadlines differ from station to station. Once department heads have approved budgets to work with, they have sole responsibility for day-to-day administration, but they are advised to determine the accounting department's preferences.

Forecasting

Forecasting is of considerable value in administering budgets effectively. Set aside one day a month (say the fifteenth or twentieth) to analyze the activities and expenditures planned for the upcoming month. This practice invites advance planning from calendar notations on start dates for certain projects—first to make sure that they are completed on time but also to account for expenses in the correct month. Execution of a budget necessitates both forecasting and accountability— the measurement of how well the budget held up in the last month.

Accountability

A successfully executed budget requires a built-in system of accountability. This system should provide information that permits monitoring and directing the activities of the promotion department. Usually such a system is called a monthly variance report. Some companies do it by quarter, some weekly. A variance report allows the department head and the station's management to keep tabs on expenses.

To fill out a variance form (Figure 4 3), the promotion manager needs to know the budgeted amounts (projected) for the month versus what was actually expended during the thirty-day period. The station's business office provides this information after they have closed the books for the month. It is the promotion manager's responsibility to explain any variances between budget forecasts and actual expenses that is, whether the amount is higher or lower than it was projected to be. This information lets department heads know exactly where they stand at any given time during the year. Frequently companies ask for a quarterly report on departmental budgets as well as a report at midyear. Reports of this type should be regarded as "promise versus performance" reports. Those who are behind will be the first to know and will be able to revise their plans accordingly.

SUMMARY

A budget that is carefully researched and planned becomes the road map for departmental activities during the following year. Preparing a

Figure 4-3 Variance Report

STATION: WXXX-TV

DEPARTMENT: Promotion

MONTH/YEAR: January 1982

BUDGET VARIANCE EXPLANATION

ACCOUNT	(OVER) UNDER BUDGET				EXPLANATION OF VARIANCE
	MONTH		YEAR TO DATE		
	AMOUNT	%	AMOUNT	%	
0800 Print Advertising	+500	10%	+500	10%	Additional lineage purchased to advertise special prime time movie in January.
0820 Broadcast Adv.	+480	20%	+480	20%	Additional radio buys made to advertise same movie
OTHER					
TOTAL					

budget for the first time is a demanding learning experience, and *executing* the budget is an ongoing opportunity to strengthen one's budgeting skills. Monthly variances supply invaluable information in drawing up the next budget. An ongoing file of ideas, projects, rate changes, and substantial variances can be referred to when the time comes to prepare the next year's budget. There are no shortcuts in the budgeting process. It requires familiarity with accounting principles, the station's philosophy, and knowledge of the marketplace; it demands well-thought-out objectives and a great amount of research, creativity, and patience. While budgeting may not be exciting, it is essential for accomplishing promotional goals.

The Tactics of On-Air Promotion

by
Richard J. Weisberg

Richard J. Weisberg has been promotion manager for Post-Newsweek's WDIV-TV in Detroit since 1979 after serving as executive producer/creative services. He is presently director of marketing services for the station. His efforts have contributed directly to major ratings and demographic successes and to the repositioning of the station in the market. Before coming to WDIV, he was art director for WJZ-TV in Baltimore from 1976 to 1979 and associate art director for WSBK-TV in Boston after moving up from graphic designer (1973 to 1976). He has a B.F.A. degree from the Massachusetts College of Art in Boston (1973) and taught principles of advertising and visual fundamentals at Chamberluin School of Retailing in Boston from 1973 to 1975. He received a Boston Art Directors Club Annual Design Show award in 1976, three Desi awards for graphic design in 1978, four individual Emmy awards in 1980 from the Detroit chapter of the National Academy of Television Arts and Sciences for on-air promotion, and two BPA awards for on-air promotion in 1981.

Just as warring legions select from a variety of tactical options such as direct assault, encirclement, or infiltration, the on-air promotion tactician chooses from approaches such as hard sell, soft sell, emotional appeal, and factual appeal. The approach can be very specific with limited objectives or it can be a total effort designed to build a superior identity. There is no right or wrong to these approaches, only a right or wrong time to use them and a right or wrong way to apply them. If an army were to rely solely on massed frontal attacks, it would become predictable and defeatable. Similarly, surprise, variety, spontaneity, and shrewdness are all valuable characteristics of competitive tactical planning for on-air promotion.

THE APPROACHES

The two basic approaches to achieving promotional objectives are the direct and the indirect (along with their variations and permutations).

Here is an example of the direct approach that is hard sell and emotional:

SEVERED HEAD ON THE RAILROAD TRACK. DETAILS AT 11.

This direct approach is factual:

POLICE INVESTIGATE A DECAPITATED BODY ON THE RAILROAD
TRACKS. CLUES AT 11.

The indirect approach can be factual:

MURDER CLAIMS ANOTHER VICTIM. THE I-TEAM INVESTIGATES
TONIGHT AT 11.

The indirect approach can also be soft sell, generic, and emotional:

JOIN CHANNEL 2'S "HANDS UP" CAMPAIGN AND HELP FIGHT CRIME.

The demarcations among the various tactics are not very rigid. Admittedly, promoting coverage of a murder story is far different from spearheading a crime prevention program. But while these are extreme examples, they are also widely used promotional approaches, as are all the variations in between. A message can be soft sell or hard sell *and* factual, or soft sell or hard sell *and* emotional. Each approach has advantages and traps. All of them work. Each of them can fail.

Hard Sell

A direct, hard-sell approach is the most efficient approach when time or space is limited. This is particularly true of short promos of 10 seconds or less and with small-space advertising. The number of words that can be used are so few that the selling message must be stated directly. Copy for a 5-second ID promoting a familiar off-network situation comedy might read as follows:

WATCH *ALL IN THE FAMILY* TODAY AT 4:30 ONLY ON CHANNEL 4.

There is no time to be more elaborate. The message is concise and efficient and written as a command. This form is direct and more difficult to ignore than other less specific requests.

If time permits, commands should be backed up by promises of benefits. After all, demanding that an action take place, without showing proper rewards, can have only limited effectiveness. Sooner or later viewers ask, "What's in it for me?"

A hard sell backed with a direct factual approach can answer this question, but it requires more copy. Facts take time or space. For example, the following **voice-over copy** is appropriate for a 10-second promo during which clips from a program have been selected for the video portion:

Announcer: ARCHIE'S A HERO, HE'S SAVED A HUMAN LIFE. BUT THE LADY HE'S SAVED TURNS OUT TO BE NO LADY. (Surprised laughter up, then under.) DON'T MISS *ALL IN THE FAMILY* TO-DAY AT 4:30 ONLY ON CHANNEL 4.
Video: Archie tight shot.
Cut to transvestite pulling off wig.
Cut to Archie's reaction.
Graphic tag.

This 10-second spot uses a topical approach to promote a familiar program. It offers a specific reason (the plot) why the viewer might want to watch. It offers proof of a promise of benefit (the laughter; the look of shock on Archie's face) and indicates that the time spent watching will be rewarding.

Soft Sell

Longer promos of 30 or 60 seconds serving a more generic purpose often call for a softer approach. The **shelf life** of a soft-sell spot is longer than that of a hard-sell spot. Soft-sell spots may not necessarily prompt tune-in on a specific day, but they will reinforce good feelings from viewers and can educate or entice nonviewers. Here is an example of a 30-second generic promo using a soft-sell approach:

Audio: Archie and Edith singing the opening theme up and under.
Announcer: REMEMBER THE GOOD OLD DAYS ON *ALL IN THE FAMILY?*
Followed by sound bites of great moments from outstanding episodes.
Announcer: WATCH *ALL IN THE FAMILY* WEEKDAYS AT 4:30 ONLY ON CHANNEL 4.

This soft-sell approach has been tagged with a hard-sell request. A harder sell would be:

WATCH *ALL IN THE FAMILY* TODAY AT 4:30.

Combining this approach with a topical tag combines a soft-sell approach with a hard sell:

ARCHIE BECOMES A GRANDPA ON *ALL IN THE FAMILY* AT 4:30 TODAY ON CHANNEL 4.

In one of the most effective uses of soft sell, WJZ-TV in Baltimore (a station that dominated the ratings in its market at the time—the late 1970s) sought to remind viewers of its various successes. WJZ created a campaign that interspersed popular network stars with local news personalities. This tactic tied two successes together: WJZ's local news was number one, and ABC, WJZ's affiliated network, was number one. Their on-air promos created mutual identification of network and affiliate by viewers. They used generic spots: No specific tune-in information was given; only the channel number was repeated. Viewers were reminded of all the things they favor about this station—the things that had made WJZ number one in the market during this period.

Another example of the soft-sell approach is "The One & Only"—a theme that has been used successfully by WTOP-TV (WDVM) in Washington, D.C., WPLG in Miami, and WJXT in Jacksonville. "The One & Only" sums up the unique reasons for making a particular station a steady habit. The objective of all these approaches is sustained viewer loyalty. The following example shows "The One & Only" at work in music and lyrics (with appropriate pictures) as WJXT used it to celebrate its thirtieth anniversary, summing up reasons for loyalty—past, present, and future:

> You make us THE ONE
> Thirty years we've run
> We've been bringing the world to Jacksonville
> And we're going at it still
> Tomorrow there's more
> THE ONE & ONLY TV 4
> In the '50s we'd just begun
> And TV was a wondrous toy
> You'd love Lucy
> Murrow was newsy
> And Sullivan brought Sunday joy
> You gave us the eye
> Made us fly so high
> All those wonderful years with CBS
> You're the stars of our success
> The best is in store
> THE ONE & ONLY TV 4.

Soft sell is, in most cases, selling by association. It requires the presentation of some quality that evokes a positive response from viewers in the hope that this response will transfer to the program or station associated with the emotion. The obvious liability to this approach is that only limited connections are stated. Ideally, an image (soft sell) promo leads viewers to an emotional response that is useful in evoking goodwill toward a station, program, format, or personality. If this is not the result, the promotional effort was counterproductive.

Unlike the soft-sell approach, when hard sell reaches the point of viewer saturation, the message can become abrasive. Although station research may show a positive audience reaction to a selling message, the promotion manager should sense the danger of oversaturation. Here is an example of how a liability can be turned into an asset by turning a hard sell into a soft-sell approach. WDIV-TV in Detroit was using "Go 4 It" as a hard sell tune in message constantly in 1977. WDIV is Channel 4 in Detroit, so the play-on-number as well as the play-on-words became a natural combination. The slogan was turned into a hard-sell jingle accompanying topical program promotion. After more than a year of constant use, however, the message began to annoy many viewers.

Rather than abandoning the approach, the slogan was expanded and given more meaning through a soft-sell approach. "Go 4 It" was explained as a positive ideal, even a goal in life. Slice-of-life commercials were produced to illustrate common states of mind: an athlete trying to jump higher than before, dancers limbering muscles and calling them into perfect interaction, a teenage boy's victory over a used car ready for the junkheap.

The vignettes were set to original music expressing common aspirations. A major recording artist was selected to perform the vocal, ensuring a high level of quality in the performance and leaving viewers with something beyond a commercial jingle: the performance of an artist. A signature was created from the word *Go*, the station's logo number, 4, and the word *It.* This signature was added in an animated style at a climactic point at the end of each promotional spot, associating the visual and the music with the station (Figure 5-1). The result was an effective booster for civic pride with substantial credit and goodwill going to the station.

Hard sell is the most common approach to advertising and promotion. It is easier to create and produce than soft sell and is therefore considered safer. Soft sell and emotional approaches require more highly developed skills, subtlety, a finely tuned writing style, and production finesse. That does not necessarily make them better tactics, only harder to do.

Each time broadcasters go into battle promotionally, they carry the station's message. In developing that message, a choice must be made as to which approach is most appropriate and whether the resources are available to deliver the message effectively.

Figure 5-1 Signature for WDIV-TV in Detroit (*Used with permission.*)

W D I V / D E T R O I T

SPECIFIC VS. GENERIC SPOTS

Hard sell and specific promotion direct immediate action. Generic promotion and soft sell entice. A specific approach is aimed directly at the audience's decision making; it gives a command. Generic promotion provides broad information and tries to communicate overall feeling. Specific promotion asks viewers to make up their minds; generic promotion attempts to leave behind a memory of positive relationships. In other words, generic promotion creates *images*. It is more often applied to stations and groups of programs (comedy, adventure, news) and personalities than to individual programs.

Regardless of the approach chosen, promotion's goal is always to communicate a convincing message to audiences. Beyond marketing strategies, broadcast promotion is a *creative* service; hence there is always a premium placed on originality that challenges designers and producers to develop talent and craft, to reach further.

DECIDING ON A TECHNIQUE

Techniques facilitate the production of promotional messages; they do not create the messages. Techniques, however, demonstrate styles of communication that affect the viewer's perception of messages. Style has a direct impact on the feel of a promo and should reflect a station's cumulative feel. Promotional style contributes to the cumulative effect of television experiences provided by an individual channel and makes a direct contribution to shaping tastes for that brand of television.

When examining viewer loyalty and dominance of a market by a single television station over a long period of time, one inevitably discovers a consistency in feel in the bulk of that station's programming and promotion. Therefore, when deciding on a production technique, consideration should be given to the effect it will have as a link in the continuing chain of viewing experiences. Will the technique under consideration enhance the concept or confuse it? Will it distract the viewer from the selling message or bring the message home? Is it affordable? Will quality be sacrificed for expediency or vice versa? Does it complement the station's style? What is the technique's impact on budget, available studio time, and facilities?

Promotional approaches for rerun episodes of a network series should differ in style and tone from the same episodes in their first run. Rather than "Radar is on his way out of the 4077th tonight" (first run), the local (syndicated) version might go "Tonight, a classic M*A*S*H—when Radar finally goes home." It is essential to match the copy approach to the way the audience perceives the show.

One choice the promotion manager must face is whether to produce on-air materials at the station or commission them from a specialist. Going outside assumes that a concept cannot be realized effectively by working in-house. Going outside requires spending production dollars, in turn demanding accountability for the impact of this expenditure on budgets. This requirement can cause confrontations with station management if sufficient need has not been established to justify going outside.

The end product of the outside expenditure should solve the promotional problem in a way that creates visible benefit and prestige for the station. It should provide something extra—something special in concept, in production, in music—with the added impact usually available only from specialists. This something extra not only gives the station management something to boast about but reduces resentment from staff technicians and engineers.

These personnel, part of the daily work force at every station, often feel that promotion producers return with high-cost results that could have been produced with station equipment and personnel. If the need is legitimate and the result is successful, however, a feeling of pride surfaces as the staff admires the quality and professionalism of the outside work. They acquire pride through association because the technical look of the station is positively reflected back onto them.

BASIC TECHNIQUES

A wide variety of specialized terms are used by promotion department staffs to describe their techniques. In the following list of common

Figure 5-2 Station Logo (*Used with permission.*)

WSBK-TV Boston

terms, several may mean approximately the same thing (donut/wrap-around/sandwich, for example, or logo/signature):

- **Logo:** A logo is a concise, visually identifiable signature repre-senting a network, station, or programming service. Its success depends on (1) distinctiveness in the marketplace, (2) consistent, repetitive usage, (3) effective associations between the logo and various selling messages on behalf of the station, and (4) clarity of communication within 2 or 3 seconds. Figures 5-2 and 5-3 show typical station and network logos.
- **ID:** ID is short for identification. In the case of television stations, IDs in their simplest form state the channel number, call letters, and city of origin (or in some cases, the area of dominant influence). At their most complex, IDs are animated, musical state-ments of a broadcaster's identity. They run 2 or 3 seconds in

Figure 5-3 Network Logo (*CBS, Inc. Used with permission.*)

length. In some cases an ID may legally be shared. Shared IDs combine station and program identification—title, day, and time—as in Figure 5-4. They run 2, 3, or 10 seconds long. Usually part of the information is presented visually while the rest is delivered aurally.

- **Donut:** A donut (or wraparound or shell or sandwich) is a promotional form consisting of a fixed opening (or intro) and a fixed ending (or tag). The middle of a donut is open and can be filled with various topical promotional materials. The donut is a very efficient format since a set structure has been established for a particular show or a specific night of the week; all that is needed is to replace one episodic module with another.
- **Voice-over:** A voice-over is the narrative portion of a commercial, usually recorded by an announcer and containing the vital information for the spot.
- **Voice-over copy:** This is announcer's copy to be read as narrative over video.
- **Topical (or daily) promo:** A topical promo is a promotional spot showcasing a specific episode or program via edited highlights of that show.

Figure 5-4 Shared ID (*Used with permission.*)

- **Generic promo:** A generic promo is a promotional spot highlighting intrinsic qualities and appeals of a program, format, or service, rather than describing specific episode plots.

- **Tease:** A tease is a promotional announcement that provokes interest or curiosity about a program or event. Usually it is a short message that is incomplete in some way, intriguing viewers and, ideally, creating a desire to find out more.

- **Personality spot:** A personality spot is a promotional announcement aimed at creating a heightened awareness of particular on-air talent or talents by helping the viewer to know them better either as people or as professionals.

- **Sound bite:** A sound bite is a short clip consisting of video and audio information from a program or news story, used as it was recorded, to give viewers a quick taste of the actual program or story.

- **Film clips:** Film clips are selected scenes, generally from feature movies.

- **Music bed:** A music bed is a piece of music that is played under an announcer's voice or the sound track of a promotional spot.

- **Shelf life:** The shelf life of a spot is the length of time a spot can run before it wears out through overexposure.

- **Inventory:** Inventory refers to the amount of on-air promotional material on hand.

- **Tag lines:** A tag line visually and audibly sums up a promotional spot. Traditionally, a graphic tag for a 30-second promo for a local television program consists of three elements: program title, scheduled air time, and channel number. (The sequence of these elements can be varied.) The program title is the final product identification; the scheduled air time tells the viewer when the event will take place; the channel number tells the viewer where the program can be found. It is not necessary to have these elements simultaneously on the screen. Television graphics should not be designed as if they were print graphics; video information is communicated sequentially during a passage of time, and on-air promos should follow this principle, not the rules for print.

THE VISUAL RECORDING MEDIA

Videotape and film are two alternative techniques for communicating promotional messages to television audiences. Each has advantages and limitations, and both are widely used for on-air promotion by broadcasters.

Videotape

There are four forms, or configurations, of magnetic videotape of broadcast quality (named by their width): 2-inch, 1-inch, ¾-inch, and ¼-inch sizes. The first three are currently the broadcast standard configurations. All of them record, store, and play back audio as well as video signals with a single unit.

Two-inch tape has the highest quality due to finer resolution of its image. Because of its large surface area, 2-inch tape can store more detailed signals on its surface than the other configurations. This allows for greater clarity in the differentiation of frequency occurring in a video playback system. One-inch and ¾-inch tapes have respectively less resolution capability because of their smaller surface areas.

Videotape technology developed in synchronization with computerized editing systems and digital technology. Video has leaped ahead in editing sophistication leaving its elder relations, film splicing and audiotape editing, behind. Video editing can be a virtually instantaneous process with advanced, expensive equipment. State-of-the-art editing has the advantage of speed but the liability of lending itself to more careless employment than film. Film spots tend to be worked on by an editor for several days, whereas video editing is usually accomplished in single show sessions. Video thus tends to be less deliberately worked over, which prompts the misleading assumption that its esthetic range is less than that of film. **Off-line preediting**, in which the rough footage is coded and transferred to cassette for previewing, planning, and sometimes rough assembly, gives producers an opportunity to invest more care and subtlety in tape productions—an investment that can put them on a competitive level with film.

Film

Film does many things that video does and, conversely, many things that video does not. It too contains picture and sound on the same reel. It too comes in different sizes: 70 mm, 35 mm, 16 mm, 8mm. The larger the format, the finer the resolution. The most common production formats for on-air television promotion are 35 mm and 16 mm.

Thirty-five millimeter, used professionally, is the technique of the feature film and most primetime television. Combined with professional direction and lighting, it offers the most dramatic possibilities, is most flattering to performers and personalities, and has the range and subtlety to bear a great deal more repetition than the other film and tape alternatives. It tends to be the choice in producing long-range image promotion campaigns.

Sixteen-millimeter has always been associated with documentaries. It has the qualities of grittiness and graininess that suggest "reality."

Nevertheless, 16 mm is fast being replaced by tape and the reality of on-the-spot coverage.

Live Action Promos

Other than movie and syndicated series promos using program segments (clips) placed within donuts of front matter and end matter, the most common source for video and film images for promotional messages is live action. On-air promos vary from documenting the superior coverage of news events to showcasing the skills of a station's news team. Live action promos can be documentary, dramatic, or humorous. They can feature station personalities, people on the street, or professional actors and actresses.

The typical promotional spot for a local commercial television station airs in breaks surrounded by other commercial spots. Adjacent spot images are, consciously or subconsciously, compared by viewers. Weak production techniques become obvious to the detriment of the promotional message. Live action spots do not happen by accident. They are the result of skilled technicians and creative people paying attention to details. Elements like makeup, wardrobe, lighting, and props should be regarded not as luxuries but as necessities. As often as possible, newly finished spots should be viewed as part of a commercial cluster to determine their comparative strengths and weaknesses.

A live action promo flows from two sources—the material and the concept. It originates from a promotional need. Sooner or later in broadcast promotion, the need will arise to turn a dashing Don Juan sportscaster into an avid athlete or a close confidant of the local sports stars; to transform a bland meteorologist into a colorful character; and to take disparate (and sometimes not particularly friendly) groups of news "personalities" and try to mold them into "teams" through promotion. These are the challenges that are won and lost in a day's work.

One warning: The sum total of marketing goals, strategic concepts, techniques, production, and the message itself had better be believable. If the sum is not credible, the whole exercise will have no value and will probably have a negative impact. It is often tempting to think that silk purses can be created out of sows' ears, but this gift is rarely bestowed on mortals.

Topical Promos*

From a purely quantitative point of view, most of the promotion produced for television is in the form of daily topical spots. On-air pro-

*These guidelines were contributed by Stuart L. Browar, vice-president, On-Air, ABC Entertainment.

motion production is the training ground for promotion management. A few guidelines can aid in approaching the process of creating and editing promotional spots (**promo cutting**):

- A spot should open with something gripping—either video or audio or both. A scream, a pratfall, a provocative line of dialogue—all of these moments grab an audience's attention and direct them to what is coming next. If the spot builds properly from there, by the time the audience knows what is happening, the hook is in, and the message has been communicated.

- Pacing is important. Each spot needs its own rhythm and tempo. A promo montage for *Wide World of Sports* or a local sports event is paced and cut differently from a big dramatic scene from *General Hospital*, even though there is more game playing in a soap opera than on the polo field. Either way, the images must make sense visually (no jump cuts) and convey the message. The spot must look and feel funny, or romantic, or action-oriented—whatever the show demands.

- The audio and video need not be run in synch in a promo. Audio can be "slipped" to run over a scene differently than it appears in the program itself. This can be done to save precious seconds or to make special promotional statements. For example, letting a speech from Archie Bunker about Edith's "dingbat" qualities play over shots of Edith's funny takes might be very effective. The point is that the audio and video elements of a promo spot must be considered as separate components to be used as the producer of the promo sees fit, not as the producer of the show deemed best for the episode.

- A common mistake made by novice producers is to overuse narration, telling the entire story in the voice-over. "Wall-to-wall" narration generally is not as effective as allowing the characters to tell the story through their dialogue and actions. It is better to let James Earl Jones (as Alex Haley) exclaim "I have found you, Kunta Kinte, I found you!" than to have an announcer proclaim that "Alex Haley finally reaches his roots."

GRAPHICS

Promotion producers in television rely heavily on graphic designers to help convey promotional messages. Although graphic designers originally worked mainly in the print media, they are increasingly part of the video team. Well-constructed, well-designed graphics ensure communication of promotional messages and add other visual dimensions to what viewers see. There are two major categories of graphics: stills and motion. Both are used regularly in on-air promos for television, although complex animation is generally produced by specialist companies.

The most basic graphic is the still, which includes various camera cards, slides, mounted photographs, and drawings. Video and film animation are the moving media that come under the control of graphic designers. Stills and motion and sounds are mixed with live (or prerecorded) video images to create the final promo for on-air use. Promo producers in all but the smallest markets use multiple studio cameras, multitrack audio consoles, **video switcher** effects, and **telecine film chains** to achieve final mixes in the same way that program producers use these elements. The control room time designated for this purpose is called a **mix session.**

Stills

Camera cards for promotion graphics generally consist of a channel number or logo design for the station dry-mounted on 11 × 14 inch cards. Promotion staffs make heavy use of 35-mm slides to assemble stills of program content and to store logos and other commonly repeated graphics. The slides themselves can be projected from a telecine film chain or magnetic discs into a composite piece of art. Increasingly, graphics are being stored on magnetic floppy discs, eliminating the need for slides and slide chains.

Photographs are mounted by graphic designers but are typically shot and developed elsewhere at a station. Drawings are solely the province of graphic designers and range from simple line sketches in a single color to complex renderings of faces or scenes.

Some promotional spots consist largely or entirely of still graphics. In fact, there have been award-winning examples in recent years. In some cases, spots composed entirely of graphic materials have proved more cost-efficient and easier to control than video or film animation. When stills are animated or edited into a tempo or pattern, the technique is called **kinesthesis** (moving stills).

Contemporary Animation Techniques

Animation includes images recorded on traditional animation stands as well as any type of frame-by-frame recording of calculated stop/start sequences. The following paragraphs examine the major animation techniques: video animation, film animation, cartoon images, and kinesthesis.

Video animation achieves single-frame shooting of numerically ordered sequences through computer-assisted digital technology. More simply, video animation is the generation and regeneration of video signals fed repeatedly through digital circuitry. The content is developed from a single black and white point or series of points (called intersections) within a video matrix screen. The projected path of the video sequences has been preprogrammed into a computer and translates into images on cathode tubes. Video animation is customarily supplied by outside companies in major markets. These companies create design concepts based on station-generated art, or they will supply the basic creative concept if requested. Video animation is quick and less expensive than film animation, but it tends to be less than a top-quality technique and is commonly associated with retail advertisers. Simplified video animation equipment is beginning to be acquired by stations, primarily for use in generating news graphics; its use in day-to-day promotion will no doubt follow.

For decades, *film animation* was labor-intensive because each sequence of **cels** was individually painted and arranged numerically. Now digital technology for film produces sequential generation of images and numbering systems with a limitless world of possibilities. It represents the evolution of the art from *Mickey Mouse* to *Star Wars*.

Film animation is the actual recording, frame by frame, of individual images through a lens onto light-sensitive film. Whether these images are back-lit or front-lit, hand-rendered or photographic, the recording process remains fundamentally the same. However, film animation can be digitally computer-assisted so that commands for camera movements, such as a zoom, pan, tilt, or rack focus, are controlled by a computer or overridden by hand. The more sophisticated the animation and the animator, the more computer-assisted technology is involved in the finished product. The use of computers also contributes to higher final costs, of course.

The cost of this technology is so high that neither networks nor stations are likely to possess state-of-the-art film equipment; it appears that only outside resource companies that specialize in film animation can do this sophisticated work profitably. While the cost of advanced film animation can be the most expensive per second on the air, a highly produced 3-second ID using a campaign theme with an open-close adaptation for promos will probably end up costing less per actual use than anything else on the air if it is used extensively.

Recording hand-drawn images in single-frame sequences is *cartoon animation*. This type of animation varies from elaborate Walt Disney productions to a simple linear underscore drawing across the screen to emphasize a word in a tag line at the end of a spot. Cartoon animation is a comparatively costly investment, but it can add great entertainment value and memorability to the station's overall promotional identity. Sports, weather, advances in station technology (mini-cams, helicopters)—all are messages that offer the creative range to employ cartoon animation effectively. Everybody in the television audience was a child at least once—and most of us continue to find cartoon work irresistible.

Kinesthesis, in its most advanced form, is the moving of cutout images along specific plotted paths as they are recorded on film. This technique looks like stop-motion filming. Kinesthesis traditionally requires an animation stand for production. With the advent of the frame storer, however, stations can approximate some of the excitement of quick-cutting news or entertainment images. Certainly kinesthesis can get attention. Digitally assisted, the sequences of movement can become quite sophisticated. The kinesthesis sequences for *Monty Python* are examples of this technique at its most entertaining.*

In a day of viewing television, anyone can see the whole wide range of graphic techniques in use—in commercials, programs, titles, and promos—some of it dazzling, some dreadful, but most of it mediocre and uninspired. Broadcast promotion requires the inspired—even though stations are often reluctant to pay for it.

AUDIO TECHNIQUES

Audio production for promotion consists of audio accompanying video (for television) and audio communicating on its own (for radio). In video production, audio constitutes 50 percent of the end product, but historically it has not received equal creative emphasis. Television promotion cannot succeed by images alone. Just silence the audio portion and see how often the video portion of a promo lacks clarity and realism. When the audio portions of video promos are compared to promos produced for radio, the differences are clear. Typically, audio quality and imagination show to a greater degree in radio, communicating an entire selling message without the "advantage" of accompanying video images. Sound alone can create startling, realistic, poignant, unforgettable audio commercials that deliver a very effective selling message.

Excitement, suspense, comedy, danger—these are just some of the emotions that can be conveyed through the effective use of music and sound effects played against video action (with little or no voice-over or dialogue). If a picture is really worth a thousand words, imagine how many words a striking montage of pictures *with* sound can convey! A killer stalking a victim, lovers in a clinch, a great touchdown run, all matched with appropriate music and sound effects, are ready-made promo situations that can be selected from program footage to intrigue and attract viewers.

Thematic music should not be overlooked as a major promotional tool. The thematic music associated with individual series and movies

*A more sophisticated form of kinesthesis is multi-plane animation that creates the effect of dimensional montage. The main title of *Entertainment Tonight* is a recent example.

is available as well as the music composed for network and station campaigns. The themes from *All in the Family; Happy Days; M*A*S*H; Welcome Back, Kotter;* and *The Rockford Files* are instantly recognizable and are a tremendous help in promoting those shows. When the films *Jaws* and *Rocky* aired on television, the promotion producers would have been foolhardy to ignore the built-in audience identification with their main themes.

Television is the *demonstration* medium. It can document precisely. Radio can only describe an event or record what it sounds like; the listener must fill in the detail. Imagination and perception come into play as part of the audio communication process, and illusions are created quite readily and inexpensively. A stadium crowded one minute is suddenly empty—simply by throwing a switch. No payroll for thousands of extras is needed for audio, just good writing, sound effects, music, reality, and good voice actors. These are what make the "Theater of the Mind" come alive. Multichannel audio production consoles have been commonplace since the 1960s in most audio production studios. They began to appear in most television production studios in the late 1970s, making possible more ambitious in-house audio production.

Music in On-Air Promotion

Apart from its use in promos, music at television stations typically underscores entertainment programs, news titles, sports, and public affairs programming. Music adds color and memorability to a station's image.

Music helps create identity. As with formatted radio stations, the repetitive use of a selected musical sound or style will contribute directly to the viewer's perception of a television station. Music can make a station sound young, traditional, contemporary, or ethnic. The way a station sounds has a direct effect on its demographic appeal. As a result, the promotion staff should be intimately involved in the selection of music as one of the station's production tools. This selection process should support the central programming and promotional strategies of the station. It should also enhance the total selling message. Music can become the heartbeat by which production values keep time, and the end result will be gratifying both to producers and viewers.

Television viewing audiences change from daypart to daypart. On the whole, they are a transient group. Accordingly, television programming changes in order to serve the audience. As changes in the broadcast day occur, they present opportunities to change the mood of the station in keeping with each daypart, its programming, and its audience. Late-night programming feels different from daytime programming; it can sound different as well. Music is a *mood* medium.

Producers should consciously match up the right mood with the right product and daypart. Music is a tool for packaging the television station from sign-on to sign-off.

Finding a Musical Theme

There are only two ways to obtain music: Either it already exists or it will have to be created. The best place to find existing music is in record libraries. These are collections of prerecorded arrangements and compositions that can be rented or bought for broadcast purposes. The rights to broadcast any of the selections are usually held by the owner of the library (a production company, syndicator, or any other source of license). Music from a library is either rented by the piece (called a **needle drop**) or in music packages. A **rights use contract** usually gives the renter exclusivity within a certain market or geographic area for a specific time period with optional renewal terms.

The second way to obtain music is to create it or have it created. Since few television producers can create their own production music, they usually turn to outside composers, arrangers, or music producers. Here the producer's job is to define the music production needs to the collaborator as completely as possible. The musical product will be a negotiated refinement of this wish list.

When an agreement is made to finance the creation of production music, a four-part arrangement is common. First, a fee is paid to the composer and lyricist for development of a demonstration (**demo**) of the basic creative approach. Second, an additional fee is paid to the composer and music producer for the creative energy expended on the project. This fee usually covers the planning, writing, arranging, and booking of the studio and musicians. Third, another set of fees is paid for the actual production sessions. These costs cover studio time, musicians' session fees, instrument rentals (if any), and tape costs. Fourth, financial consideration should be given to licensing rights, residuals, royalties, and reuse fees as required by the American Federation of Musicians and AFTRA. Any residual creative fees should be negotiated in advance.

When purchasing an overall sound or music package for a station, look for music that concentrates on a single theme and encourages multiple variations. If the station's promotional identity is summed up in a phrase, it is best to have the musical theme fit that phrase, vocally and instrumentally. The easiest thing to vary is length. Make a list of the most common times required—for example, 2 seconds, 10 seconds, 20 seconds, 30 seconds, and 60 seconds. These times represent the most common lengths of promos and IDs. If a station is buying needle drops from a library, listen for potential edit points that might allow these variations to be created through editing. An **edit point** is a place in the music that will allow an existing arrangement to be extended or abbreviated. For best results, consult an audio engineer for guidance.

If music is being custom-made for a station, consider alternate mixes of existing tracks, or supplemental tracks, that vary texture or mood. Some examples are: a solo instrument replacing a lead vocalist; male voices replacing female voices; no lead vocal or instrument (useful under strong announcer voice-overs); strings, brass, or some novelty percussion (sleighbells for a seasonal version). Each musical texture adds up to a mood change if properly selected.

Another way of creating harmony within a station's music package and an overall musical thematic feeling is by selecting or producing elements of the musical package in the same or complementary keys. This strategy creates a harmony of sympathetic chords and encourages a smooth flow in and out of each music bed. Using a complementary key signature connects the ends of programs with promos and other station announcements in a continuous fashion. Many stations include programming as well as promotional needs when commissioning music packages for promotion.

Original sound effects can be effective selling tools. Any sound that is distinctive can be used repetitively in association with a specific product. To help sell "Go-Getters," a news promotion concept in the Detroit television market in 1980, WDIV-TV had a custom effect created that sounded like rushing air. Inside this sound, television viewers also heard the words "Go-Getters" being whispered. This concept was very effective as a sound track accompanying "Go-Getters" animation. It reinforced the feeling of momentum. After the sound effect had been successfully associated with the concept visually on television, it became a valuable production tool when the station produced radio spots promoting its newscasts. These promotional spots reinforced the visual impressions of radio listeners who had seen the television promos.

Radio Spots

In producing radio spots promoting television programs, just as in video on-air promotion, the station's musical theme packages are the most effective accompaniments to the announcer's voice-over. They add consistency, mood, and pace—the identity associated with the television station. These are key factors for effective television promotion via radio. In a sound-only medium, television as an advertiser can substitute music and sound for pictures to help demonstrate its selling points.

Care must be given to timing and copy length. When there is too much information or too many elements in too short a time, the message is likely to sound rushed and confused. Wall-to-wall copy is no more desirable in radio advertising than it is on television. Success is achieved not by getting all the copy points in but by making one or two points uncommonly well. This is a basic rule of advertising, and it applies equally to promotion.

It is also important to choose the kind of voice that is best for the spot and the subject matter. Avoid mechanical voices that do not communicate. Voices that are distinctive and those that project dramatic emotions are most valuable. Use announcers who have proved that they can relate to the subject matter and to the desired audience. Announcers should be selected the same way music is selected—by listening, feeling, and associating feelings with the copy.

GOING OUTSIDE

A few guidelines can help promotion producers establish productive relationships with outside resources. They focus on goals, costs, and personal involvement.

- Outside resources are only as good as the direction they receive. If the station understands its problem and communicates clearly and thoroughly, good outside resources—companies carefully chosen—will do good work. If not, they are likely to drift off into flights of creative fancy. The result may be solutions that do not fit problems.

- Understand what outside resources are likely to cost. The woods are full of stories of suppliers who overcharge clients. They are also full of stories of clients who underpay suppliers. This is particularly true in broadcast promotion, where the lack of priority often obliges producers to try to persuade suppliers to work for less than they would charge for the average advertising assignment. This is why some top-quality resources refuse to work for television and radio stations.

- Establish budget parameters, familiarly referred to as "ballparks." Know approximately what can be spent on a project, and share that information with the supplier. The resource who works with clear budget guidelines in mind will usually create and produce realistic solutions. The resource who is flying blind tends to create an ideal solution that has to be pared down to fit the budget. The realistic concept usually turns out to be more effective than one that gets compromised. The most unproductive guideline imaginable is: "See what you can come up with, and I'll see what I can shake loose."

- Stay with a project all the way through. Do not farm it out. Attend the shoot. Go to the edit. These activities are part of the producer's job. They are also a valuable learning experience every time.
- Foster outside creative and production specialists. They often provide valuable guidance to talent inside the business.

SUMMARY

When a viewing experience prompts an idea, a connection is made and information is produced. Everyone who sends promotional messages is trying to bring about this connection. The information is carefully chosen by promotion producers so that, ideally, the encounter between viewer and selling message flows perfectly. All elements of the finished product contribute to this flow while stimulating the desired connection. The major technical tools of television promotion production are logos, promos, musical signatures, and donuts. The visual elements can be produced on videotape or film and can come from in-house or out-of-house services. Music can come from libraries or out-of-house production companies. The content of promotional spots can be classified by the selling approach (hard sell or soft sell) and the type of promotion (generic or specific). All these elements contribute to the station's overall promotional strategy, but they must be used at the right time and in the right place.

Part I ■ Suggested Readings

"The Broadcast Promoter: No Longer the Last to Know, the First to Go." *Broadcasting* (5 June 1978):8.
A special report on promoters and marketing in the broadcasting industry; covers the future of promotion and the importance of modern marketing techniques.

Fitch, Dennis. BPA Big Ideas: Creatively Servicing the Budget. Lancaster, Pennsylvania: Broadcasters Promotion Association, 1981.
A booklet based on a 1981 BPA seminar workshop on promotion budgets; contains a budgeting system and sample forms.

Hadley, William T. "Business Magazines." *Media Decisions* (April 1976):74.
An assessment of the role of the Broadcasters Promotion Association; gives information on what they do, where they do it, and the value of promotion to the broadcasting industry.

Legal Guide to FCC Rules, Regulations and Policies. Washington, D.C.: National Association of Broadcasters, 1977.
Explanation and interpretation of the Federal Communications Commission's regulations and rulings as they apply to broadcasters.

"On Air Graphics." *Print* 34(March/April 1980):33–79.
Special issue devoted to the use of graphics on television.

On-Air Promotion Handbook. Lancaster, Pennsylvania: Broadcasters Promotion Association, 1980.
Handbook of broadcast promotional ideas; discusses use of the station's own on-air, viewer motivation, tools and styles of promotion, and scheduling.

Pocket Pal: A Graphic Arts Production Handbook. 11th ed. New York: International Paper Company, 1976.
First published in 1934 and now in the eleventh edition, this handbook presents material in accessible format for beginners. It is a guide to printing processes, type and typesetting, copy preparation, photography, stripping and imposition, platemaking, printing, binding paper, and inks. The handbook includes a glossary, a section on copyfitting, and many tables and charts.

Potts, Joseph. "Accounting for Trade-Outs: Solving an Industry Headache." *Broadcast Financial Journal* 3(November 1973):8–10 and 4(January 1974):6–7.
Budgetary procedures for evaluating traded promotional air time.

"Radio, TV Promotion Execs Happy with Work, Average Over $22,000, Survey Indicates." *Television/Radio Age* (2 June 1980):41.
Findings of a 1980 survey of Broadcasters Promotion Association members covering salaries, professional experience, and job satisfaction; includes members' evaluation of promotional materials made available by major suppliers.

"Roving Reporter." *P.D. Cue* (February 1979):44.
   Collection of opinions from broadcasting executives on the role of promotion managers and their positions in the industry.

Vella, JoAnn. "Production Houses: A Survey of Rates." *Video Systems* (October 1979):24–26.
   Results of a cross-country survey of video production houses reviewing rates and cost averages for remote productions, studio productions, and post-production editing.

Part
II

Audience Promotion

Part II examines the unique features of promotion at networks, stations, and cable outlets. Most of the chapters focus on station-level strategies, and television news is given special attention because of its basic function in local station economics. All these chapters examine *audience-directed* strategies.

Chapter 6 on network promotional strategies stresses the promotion of entertainment programs. Part II begins with this chapter because the commercial networks dominate decision making in the broadcasting industry. The language and concepts of promotion were first developed for network programs and images, and their patterns still set trends at the station level.

Chapter 7 covers promotion at network-affiliated television stations. It analyzes the positive and negative sides of network affiliation, the ways of dealing with conflicting attitudes and goals, and the kinds of cooperative advertising that can be undertaken by an affiliate and its network.

Chapter 8 analyzes the problems of independent television stations that lack network resources. It focuses on the strategies and procedures for promoting alternatives to network and affiliate fare, especially movies, rerun series, and sports.

Chapter 9 looks at early and late evening television news on local stations. This chapter explains the importance of promoting news for stations and its integral role in the station's whole marketing plan. It covers the different pressures resulting from the station's ranking in the market and the criteria for allocating budgets, staffs, and facilities for news promotion.

Chapter 10 is devoted to commercial radio promotion. It details the pivotal role of contest promotions and merchandising for contemporary music format stations.

Chapter 11 examines promotion from the vantage of the noncommercial broadcaster, delineating the function of auctions and station subscriptions in supporting public radio and television.

Chapter 12, the last chapter in Part II, spells out the problems behind the promotional strategies of local cable franchise operators and the commanding influence of national pay-television on overall cable promotion. It covers the strategies of the pay-cable services, subscription television, and multipoint distribution systems. Understanding the functions of promotion in competing media (network versus pay-television) and symbiotic media (affiliates and networks) leads to informed decision making in a changing economic environment.

In all these chapters, the authors deal primarily with the medium's need to market itself and its programs to the public. This part of the book contains chapters on the circumstances that govern audience marketing activities. These limitations are characteristic of hundreds of stations (or cable systems and networks and pay-television suppliers) and are not likely to change until a new generation of executives persuades higher management of the benefits of sophisticated, long-term promotional strategies combined with the short-term strategies now commonly practiced.

Network Television Promotion

by
Symon B. Cowles

Symon B. Cowles has been with ABC Television for eighteen years. Since 1974, he has served as vice-president of creative services. Prior to that he was vice-president in charge of sales development and presentations. Initially, he was director of advertising and public relations for the ABC-Owned Television Stations Division. He received a B.A. and an M.A. from the City College of New York and began his career at Warner Brothers Pictures as an advertising copywriter. He was promotion director at WCKT, Miami, and directed advertising and promotion for two Metromedia stations, WTTG in Washington and WNEW-TV in New York, after which he became director of advertising and promotion for Metromedia Television Stations Division.

At the ABC Television Network, the promotion department is called Creative Services, a catchall covering five departmental activities linked by their creative aspects. The most visible function is on-air promotion—that is, the body of commercial announcements that networks and stations put on their own air to get people to watch their own programming. The second most important function is advertising, which covers magazines, newspapers, radio, outdoor, skywriting, and any other imaginable form of paid communication. The other functions of the department are sales promotion and presentations, art, and conference planning.

Departmental structures vary from network to network. Moreover, the internal organizational structures are ever-changing. What does not change, however, is the basic goal of network advertising and promotion departments: to get audience sampling. The means for achieving this objective are on-air promotion and advertising incorporated in an annual cycle of network promotional events. A set of assumptions about audience behavior underlies this promotional calendar.

THE MARKETING APPROACH

The total promotion of a network requires a total marketing approach. Getting an audience starts with the first announcement that a show

115

will be going on the air. That very first announcement is the beginning of a campaign which reaches a climax with the premiere of the show and then continues in an ongoing denouement for as long as the show remains on the air. The first phase—the publicity buildup—includes (1) the photo sessions for the picture service that publicity departments provide to newspapers, (2) talk show exposures, and (3) plugs on radio—all the free things that serve to announce new programs.

The next chronological phase is the on-air campaign that starts two, three, or four weeks in advance of the air date, depending on the project. Most start about ten days in advance of the premiere. On-air campaigns begin by introducing the concept of a program to establish the identity of the personalities and indicate the time and place of the shows.

Television is not a medium that has to be sold in the same way that a new product is marketed. Television does not face the problem of creating a desire for programs. People *want* to watch television.

The uniqueness of television is that the three commercial networks compete with each other with virtually identical products. Therefore, the goal of each network is to make its programs more interesting to viewers than its competitors' programs. Each network's objective is to be sure that the audience learns what programs are offered and to endow them with unique appeals. If the appeals coincide with what the audience wants, they will watch. If the appeal of the program does not relate to viewers' interests or needs, they will try other stations . . . or other activities.

The function of advertising and promotion in television is to let audiences know what is on the air in an interesting and memorable way. On-air campaigns should define the nature of individual programs, identify the casts of the programs, and make clear when the programs are on the air. Those are the three basic questions that need to be answered for viewers. Most people make an almost instantaneous judgment when exposed to a new program idea. Subconsciously viewers react emotionally and almost immediately to questions like "Does that appeal to me? Do I have an interest in it?" In that moment most program decisions are made.

People also want to know *who* is in the program. People are attracted to certain actors or actresses. In television, however, the real persona must relate to the fictional character to be successful. Many "stars" have failed in television when the role they played did not match their personal appeal. Conversely, television has the ability to make stars of performers who absorb the identity of a fictional character. Simply having performers appearing on a successful program will not automatically draw an audience. Exposure on network television is not equivalent to audience appeal. The appeals have to be quite clearly defined in viewers' minds before they tune to a program specifically to see a personality.

But networks deal with such broad audience needs—they cater to so many different aspects of society and need to reach so many different people in so many different parts of the country—that they must use all of the possible appeals in their promotional strategies. Some people only want to know what a show is about; others care very much who appears in the show; others are repelled by certain stars or certain stories. Promotion's goal is to get as much appealing information as possible to as many people as possible. Television networks are the most successful mass medium ever; they deal with everybody all the time.

Overnight Ratings and Marketing

Life in the network promotion business used to be simple—before the advent of overnight ratings. When the overnight ratings started in Los Angeles in 1972 (they began as early as 1960 in New York), promotion suddenly became very busy, and budgets went through the roof. Every day the networks got a report on their "sales," that is, how many people were watching or "buying" the product—network primetime programs.

Overnight ratings measure the effects of promotion. When a show debuts on a Monday, the networks have a strong indication of its popularity by Tuesday morning. During the second week of a new program, there is an opportunity to increase the on-air, print, and radio promotion for a promising show. Program promotion is akin to watching the shelves empty in a retail store. Merchants need to know which way to invest promotional dollars and how to rearrange the shelves to display products that are not moving.

Research and Marketing

Everybody in a network promotion department is aware of research in varying degrees of sophistication. Promotion is discussed constantly with the research department, and research staffs sit in on a good deal of promotional planning. Because promotional research can be directed to specific audiences, it can provide the data necessary to produce and schedule different spots for different time periods.

Programs also can be promoted by region. If a network's research department finds that a certain show is not doing well in a certain part of the country, radio campaigns can be directed immediately to that region. If, on the other hand, a show is not doing well with a specific audience segment on a national basis (if, for example, all of a sudden, fewer women watch because of something the competition is doing), promotion can be redirected toward that audience segment. Research is the measuring device used to direct network advertising and promotion in terms of gross numbers of homes, demographics, and regional appeals.

Research is also used in developing advertising approaches. For example, research has been helpful in developing print-advertising formats. Experimental work often uses twenty or thirty different design ideas and copy approaches. Five or six are eventually field-tested with focus groups in five, six, or seven different markets around the country.

With demand approaching four thousand spots a year, there is no time for testing on-air promotion. Certain basics come from experience, however. Finding something in a show that is promotable is relatively simple after talking with the people who make the show. Network promotion departments today maintain day-to-day, hour-to-hour, minute-to-minute liaison with network entertainment divisions, news divisions, sports divisions, and the producers who make the programs. Nowhere in other successful businesses do manufacturers make products, deliver them to advertising departments, and then go on vacation for six months, leaving the advertising people to figure out what to do with them. Liaison between producers and promoters is absolutely essential to the marketing of any product, and certainly the marketing of television programs.

How promotion departments tell the public about programs is where promotional creativity comes in. Do they show audiences a clip? Do they edit fast cuts of some kind? Do they use animation? Do they do man-on-the-street interviews? Do they screen a show and elicit people's reactions to it? Do they have the stars talk about it? All kinds of approaches are possible. Networks are no longer locked into showing clips. In the 1970s, however, when CBS and NBC were adopting ABC's techniques, everybody cut clips and stacked them, and most network promotion looked pretty much alike.

NETWORK ON-AIR PROMOTION

Until the early 1970s, the only type of television promotion that viewers saw on the air was a 30-second piece of film (a clip) with an announcer saying nice things about the show (with voice-över). A few were more sophisticated, and sometimes the dialogue in the clip came through so that viewers might hear a joke or a scream or the screeching of tires.

Promo Evolution

Gradually, the networks began editing clips in the manner of movie trailers, snipping a piece from here and a piece from there and putting them together in such a way that they communicated the essence of the show in an entertaining or exciting way. That was a very effective promotional technique for its day (the mid-1970s). Because of facilities and technical problems, however, production was limited to three or four hundred spots per year. That was about what could be done with film.

In 1974, ABC began to use *tape* to edit promos. The advent of tape and digital sophistication in editing changed the entire strategy of the networks starting around 1975. Obviously, there was inherent flexibility in on-air promotion. But before the mid-1970s, on-air promotion was a static medium using slides, **telops,** or, God forbid, just a voice-over (which sounded like radio coming out of a box with a picture on it). Television caught up and surpassed anything that print could offer in terms of flexibility, speed—and, most obviously, sight/sound-created emotion.

In the first year of tape editing, ABC went from 300 promos to 1,600. Editing with tape became much more sophisticated than had been possible with film. It was a lot faster; a lot more pizzazz was involved. By 1980 ABC was producing up to 3,500 promos per year and moving toward 4,000. CBS and NBC soon followed suit.

Certainly tape editing of promos must be considered a technical and conceptual revolution. When Fred Silverman arrived at ABC in 1975, he had strong feelings about the use of promotion. He was a firm believer in the philosophy that "if good people in promotion cannot cut a good promo for a show, then we must have a bad show." And he would go back to the show and attempt to fix it. Today, with the aid of research and the flexibility of tape editing, networks have learned to make spots fit specific needs.

Promo Scheduling

Television in the 1980s deals with different demographics during the day and at night. The Saturday morning audience is mostly children, the Monday to Friday daytime audience is mostly women; primetime audiences are whole families. But certain shows have different appeals for different people.

In editing and producing different spots for different time periods, both the content (appeal) and the scheduling of the spots become critical functions. A network cannot simply make a spot and run it eighteen times. Rather, it must make eighteen spots and run them one at a time in specific places to appeal to specific audiences.

For a show that is dramatic and has a lot of action, emphasis can be placed on the action; the spot can then be scheduled on sports programs or on another action show. A spot emphasizing love interest in the same show could be produced and run in the daytime. By 1980, the networks suddenly found themselves producing a great number of spots for single programs, rather than running a single spot all over the schedule. That indeed was a revolution in promotion.

Cross-Plugs

According to research findings, the highest number of sets-in-use is at 9 pm. The strategy of **cross-plugs** is to begin building that audience at the start of primetime. The credit for this contribution must go to Michael Eisner. It was Eisner who, in the programming department at ABC in the early 1970s (later becoming president of Paramount Pictures Corporation), came up with the concept of producing a specific spot for a show and using it in the preceding program. It was cross-pollination—for example, at the end of *Happy Days*, a spot specifically promoted *Laverne & Shirley* which followed; at the end of *Laverne & Shirley*, a spot appeared specifically for the show that followed. The goal of these cross-plug spots was to guarantee maximum audience flow from 8 to 8:30 to 9 pm and on through primetime.

Multiple Spots

The **multiple spot** is an answer to a specific need. Promotional time is limited; networks do not have unlimited availabilities. They are governed by the NAB Television Code and follow its nonprogram material requirements judiciously. The more competitive the network television business became, the more important on-air promotion became; every program acquired its own priority ranking. The flexibility of tape made it possible to fractionalize on-air spots—that is, instead of one 30-second spot advertising one show, groups of shows can be promoted in one spot.

This practice has been extended until, finally, an entire night's lineup has been promoted in a single spot. This can be bad promotion, however, since audiences can absorb only so much information in 30 seconds. A multiple spot works when dealing with easily identifiable programming in a stable schedule, but it can create overload on a night in which two or three shows out of five or six are new or specials. The mind cannot absorb sufficient information in 23 seconds (the usable amount in most 30-second promos). But there are no reliable research findings on just how much information people can absorb about six television shows in 30 seconds, so the subject of how many programs to include in a multiple spot remains controversial.

Multiple spots have become a necessity, though. Saying "Don't do that because it's bad promotion" elicits responses such as "Well, which show can we remove? We don't want to lose any time periods; we want the audience to stay with us throughout the night." Decisions about what to eliminate are never easy. But without hard thinking, promotional strategy is ultimately self-defeating. Starting in 1979, ABC cut back considerably on stacking within its on-air spots. No longer does the network promote six shows in one 30-second spot.

GENERIC CAMPAIGNS

Thematic promotions with slogans are a device to help introduce a sense of excitement about the new season. Their goal is to create anticipation for new programs, the programs returning in new time periods, the movies, and the regular lineup. Nobody tunes in to hear a slogan in television, though. An audience never tunes into a network or a show because it has a catchy theme or slogan: People tune in for programs. Even more fundamentally, audiences members do not sit down in front of a television set and say "Let's see what ABC has on." There is a network habit, but no network loyalty.[1]

Each network has meetings to discuss problems other than the selling of individual shows. How does a network get audiences excited in anticipation of new material? Networks use the summertime for their fall generic campaigns. In January the networks start thinking about what they are going to do in the summer to get people to anticipate the new fall season.[2] In the summertime the networks whet appetites with thematic material. CBS did it with the "Looking good, looking good together" campaign two years in a row; NBC did it with "Proud as a peacock" and ABC with "We're still the one" and "It's you and me and

[1]Others will disagree, arguing that networks must be marketed and that there are messages that go beyond slogans and lift a network's prestige and popularity. This was Lou Dorfsman's philosophy at CBS. But two different audiences are involved. Dorfsman's philosophy probably applies only in sales promotion.

A network's image plays a part in an advertiser's decision to use that network. Certainly image influences an advertiser who looks at magazines for their editorial environment, choosing carefully where to place advertising. To some extent advertisers and agencies also look at the environment of a television network. A network sells environment created by the image the network projects in its programming *and* in its promotion. The CBS promotion that Dorfsman and Bill Golden before him created was successful in terms of its sales and its audience appeal. But its audience appeal, in my view, has little to do with its image. The advertisers bought CBS programming in the 1960s and early 1970s because it delivered the audiences, because it delivered the demographics, and because it provided them with a good-looking editorial environment. There is no such thing as a national image for ABC, CBS, or NBC from the audience's point of view. Audiences see what the local station shows them, and local stations show them a blend of what the network feeds, local programming, plus local station involvement in the community. That is the total image. It is really a function of station promotion, not network promotion.

[2]This strategy is not unlike that of the automotive industry, which tries to generate excitement over the new models by showing teaser pictures of the cars covered with canvas, draped in flags, and hidden by a bevy of girls.

ABC." Generic campaigns for fall try to characterize a network in terms of what the audience can anticipate.

With "Let us be the one" in 1976, ABC was on the verge of a breakthrough—almost, but not quite, number one. The network then began to develop the idea that people were actually rooting for ABC—not just as viewers, but as onlookers at a contest. Television is a part of American life, and the public is well aware of the competition among the three networks. This fact has almost nothing to do, however, with the shows they watch on a particular night. Promotional spots cannot get people to give up a favorite show simply because it is not on the number one network. Nevertheless, there is a "rooting" appeal for the underdog. ABC played on that appeal and developed a "get on the bandwagon" approach. This is a basic concept in promotion that dates back to the oldest circuses. If you are number one, people want to be with you. Thus "number oneness" is one strategy of promotion. It has a good deal of influence on sales, affiliate relations, station clearances, momentum, enthusiasm, morale. It worked for CBS for twenty years and for ABC subsequently.

ABC started by saying "Let us be the one," then "We're the one," then "We're still the one." Most professionals fail to recall, however, that every one of those slogans said "Let us be the one *you turn to*" . . . "We're still the one *for Laverne & Shirley and Happy Days.*" Every one of the promotional spots said "This is the place for the *programming* you want." It was not "We are number one." The actual tune-in device was "If you want to see *Happy Days,* watch us."

ABC was able to combine two different sales objectives: selling programs and selling leadership and oneness. ABC became "the hot network" in sales, and hotness rubs off both in sales and at affiliates. ABC went from 184 stations to 207 stations during the late 1970s—and not only because ABC was doing better in ratings; it was also a question of image. Thus the job of network promotion is not just tune-in advertising: It covers many different aspects of broadcast operation including affiliate needs, sales needs, and, of course, audience needs.

FALL CAMPAIGNS

Fall campaigns are intended to achieve one primary goal—to get the greatest number of people to sample as many of a network's primetime shows as possible. If six shows are new in the season, they have the highest priority. Returning shows in new time periods have second priority. Movies have third priority at the networks because they represent 4 hours or more of primetime programming per week. Shows that return in their previous time periods have fourth priority.

Fall campaigns involve certain tangibles for stations. Starting in the summer, the networks send their affiliates on-air promotional materials via closed circuit for local use. All the fall promos, graphics, animation, and music go to the stations. All they have to do is record them, edit them, and fit them into local needs. However, the biggest thing the networks do is send money for cooperative advertising.

The networks also supply tapes of the music and lead sheets for all their music. Stations get all this at no charge. In addition, affiliates receive generic print ads for adaptation into local stacked ads or individual tune-in ads. Networks also supply slides and artwork for use in shared IDs. Stations put their own call letters on slides that promote network programs which identify stations at the local level.

Networks also produce radio spots, prerecorded and supplemented with scripts for local live tag copy. They supply posters featuring new shows and photographs of personalities starring in network shows. The networks arrange for affiliates to tape or film local promos by sending stars to the stations. Promotion experts are available to help individual stations.

Moreover, a 30-minute film that deals with the network's primetime programming is distributed free to affiliates at the end of June or the beginning of July. Affiliates use it for local sales promotion. None of the three networks clear their promotional films for airing because of contractual complications. The opening and closing of those films serve as the basis for close ties between station spots and the network's generic/thematic approach to the fall campaign.

YEAR-ROUND PROMOTION

Reliance on the fall campaign—traditionally the only major network campaign—is weakening. In 1966, ABC introduced the second season. Since then, both programming and promotion have moved away from concentration on the fall and adopted a year-round strategy. By 1980, promotion had become a fifty-two-week operation. Ratings are year-round; budgets are year-round. No longer are there slow periods in network promotion. There is a peak in the third and fourth quarters, and there is another peak in the first quarter with new programming. But with so many preemptions for specials and movies, and with new programs being introduced all the time, there is no such thing as a slack time. Every period is measured by research companies and looked at by the industry. Since networks must work to maintain audience levels throughout the year, they need advertising and promotional support throughout the year.

STATION ADAPTATION OF NETWORK CAMPAIGNS

In recent years, networks have assigned the rights to the concepts, music, and graphics that make up their fall campaigns to outside companies that subsequently customize the material and sell it to affiliates. The affiliates use this material in combination with their own localized copy and artwork. For a modest amount, stations can buy expensive music and graphics.

Networks do not engage in this customization themselves because it is inefficient and costly. Network promotion departments are not in the retail business, and when they try to supply materials fitting the needs of individual stations, they frequently run into problems because, surprisingly, they lack sufficient staffing. Work for stations is best handled by free-lance companies specializing in graphics; they can also supply customized lyrics for the network music that tie in with a local community.

Over the decade of the 1970s, affiliates have gotten more sophisticated in their use of network material. They want their call letters included in all materials, and they want their own stars mixed in with the network stars. As long as the networks and their affiliates were dependent on film, it was difficult for stations to customize because they lacked the technology. As local stations become proficient with tape technology, they will be able to edit most of what the networks give them (or purchase the customized versions).

The local promotion manager's job has changed drastically in its relationship to the network. Promotion managers used to be hired because they were good at print-oriented advertising; often they came from radio promotion. Today it is virtually impossible to get a job at a television station without knowledge of on-air production.

Network promotion departments have staffs who see that the affiliated stations get what they need to promote the network. They provide promotional kits on all network shows containing slides, ad mats, print publicity, photographs, and other materials. Moreover, all three networks have an advisory committee for affiliate promotion—a group of promotion managers elected as representatives to the networks by the promotion managers of the affiliated stations. Since they are selected from small, medium, and large markets and six regions of the country, they represent a cross section of station needs. Meetings are held several times a year.

All three networks use closed-circuit video to keep their affiliates up to date, promotionally, when opportunities occur. Network closed-circuit video communicates with both promotion managers and general managers. When the networks have established a relationship with affiliated general managers, they can readily implement their promotional program at the local level through promotion managers.

PRINT ADVERTISING

Print advertising, from the television network's point of view, represents the final effort to get viewers to tune into television programs. Print is not the last word in promotion strategy. (The last word is the stay-tuned announcement just before a show goes on the air.) But an ad appearing in newspapers on the day that a show goes on is akin to a point-of-purchase display that says, "You know that item you've been thinking about, the one we've been telling you about in other media for so long; well, here it is now right on the counter in front of you." Tune-in advertising is supposed to do precisely that.

The basic function of **stack ads,** which only appear in newspapers (before 1980, they used to appear in *TV Guide* also), is to be carry-alls for an evening's programming. They are akin to the department store's full page ad that lists all the merchandise on special sale that day. The stack ad (Figure 6-1) is a unit listing all related programs (or those that are most attractive to the audience). Listing programs chronologically is efficient.

Before the advent of sophisticated tape editing, the networks put as much emphasis on stack ads as they did on on-air promotion because there was more flexibility to print advertising. A print ad could be put together, placed, and run in about 24 hours. By the late 1970s, however, the roles of print and on-air had reversed. Normally, the networks place print advertising only in the five markets in which they own and operate television stations and in *TV Guide*, which provides a national subscriber base. The networks do not usually place entertainment print advertising outside their five markets. They expect affiliated stations to place their own advertising in their own markets.

CO-OP ADVERTISING

All three commercial networks have co-op advertising programs for special campaigns. They want affiliated stations to advertise network programming in any measured local media. Stations decide what media serve their needs best in their markets. In the past, network co-op

Figure 6-1 Network Stack Ad (*ABC, 1980. Used with permission.*)

STAY TUNED FOR THE ABC NEWS MAGAZINE 20/20

funds came with strings attached, but by the late 1970s the ground rules had been relaxed.

Co-op print campaigns generally last three weeks, usually the first three weeks of the fall season. In 1980, ABC announced the first year-round co-op arrangement, giving affiliates the lead in planning uses of co-op funds.

Co-op advertising is a fifty-fifty arrangement; the networks return 50 cents per dollar spent to affiliated stations. A fixed amount is allotted per market. Each station is in charge of that budget, and ABC affiliates can spend it any time of the year and for any program within prime-time. (Priority recommendations are supplied by the networks.) Thus far, CBS and NBC still limit co-op advertising to the fall campaign.

Network co-ops are strictly for primetime network programming. For instance, stations promoting the 10:00 and 10:30 pm network programs along with their 11:00 local news would not be eligible (under the co-op) for funds for the local news. However, it is good strategy for stations to promote the network 10:00 shows and add a local ad to that space, so the networks pay 50 percent of the network portion. The attention-getting qualities of such ads are heightened by further network advertising.

Commonly print ads tie early evening local **access** shows at 7:30 to the network programs that follow. Although stations pay extra to put their access shows ahead of the primetime schedule in the ads, the connection with network shows (for syndicated shows especially) is very important to stations. And the networks of course, want the strongest possible lead-ins to primetime. Co-op strategy is becoming even more important as the television marketplace becomes more competitive. Network strategy is to maximize support even in the smaller markets.

PUBLICITY

Publicity is not an official part of creative services at any network, although publicity work is done daily. If the goal of promotion is total marketing, then publicity should be included because free space obtained in newspapers or magazines, on talk shows, or on radio has effects on the public's desire to see programs. Nevertheless, publicity remains largely a station concern.

NETWORK NEWS PROMOTION

News viewers change their attitudes and therefore their viewing habits very slowly and sometimes reluctantly. News ratings on a national level change through the course of years rather than in weeks as with entertainment programs. The messages—both verbal and graphic—in news promotion make lasting impressions that strongly influence viewers' choice of newscasts. Every ad or television spot should be designed to assure the public that a news organization and its personalities are reliable, competent, and knowledgeable. How that impression is transmitted is limited only by creative imagination.

All the means of promoting entertainment shows are available for news promotion: on-air, newspaper and magazine advertising, radio, billboard. But specialized magazines, news-oriented radio stations, and sections of the newspaper other than the television listing page are the most useful for reaching news viewers.

Although ABC normally buys newspaper advertising for entertainment programs only in the five markets in which it owns television stations, its news advertising is often placed in as many as fifty markets beyond the top five. This practice aids topical news advertising. The advanced closing dates for national magazines (*TV Guide* needs its ad materials three weeks in advance) force the networks to use newspapers to achieve national exposure for their news program content.

In on-air promotion of news, it is important to tie the national and local newscasts into a unified service. In addition to the spots they produce for their own news programs, the networks make special promos that tie in local news personalities or network news personalities.[3] In print advertising, cooperative ventures that join the local and national news programs have become the norm. In some cases the network provides special advertising materials free to stations for local integration; more commonly, the network pays half the media costs for ads that feature a combination of local and network news.

When Walter Cronkite retired from CBS News, ABC seized the opportunity to promote its own *World News Tonight* in a concerted co-op campaign using on-air, newspaper, magazine, and radio. The campaign was launched with a full-page ad that offered a salute to Walter Cronkite from ABC News. It featured a picture of Cronkite and a headline which read, "Thank you, Walter." This ad became the subject of numerous comments by the press across the country and was doubtless the best-read ad in that edition of the *Wall Street Journal*.[4]

PROMOTIONAL TECHNIQUES

All kinds of promotional techniques are available: comedy, documentary, cartoon and graphic animation, demonstration, star and public endorsements, and others. Advertisers use them all on the air every night in commercials. The question is whether the techniques of television advertising are applicable to program promotion. Few people, even in the television industry, think of promos in the same terms they apply to television commercials. The industry tends to denigrate television promos in comparison with television commercials. Commercials seem to have an environment and prestige of their own.

Network television promotional operations are probably as sophisticated as commercial production, however. Network practice requires

---

[3]Peter Jennings in London once taped a hundred or so spots in one day, using the concept that "This is Peter Jennings in London. Be sure to watch Joe Smith in Wichita on *Eyewitness News* and then stay tuned for *ABC World News Tonight* at 7:00." He did that for at least fifty markets, two spots per market. For many years Walter Cronkite also did regular promotional taping sessions for CBS's affiliated stations. Stations could send in almost any copy. It was reviewed by CBS's network news promotion staff, and Cronkite then taped the copy for local newscasts or combinations of local and network news. In 1980, CBS did its first overall news promotion campaign—"Cronkite and Company," an all-out, all-media campaign. They offered to buy space for print ads in which half was for the network ad and half was for local ads. When ABC launched *World News Tonight*, it also used a co-op campaign in which local news programs and the network news program appeared together, and ABC shared the cost. The news department at ABC now has its own unit for producing on-air promotion for news. NBC began working to develop its news operation in 1981.

[4]The Starch Readership score (an industry measure of ad visibility) may have been the highest ever recorded by any ad in that publication.

dealing 24 hours a day with pictures that move and with sound. It is necessary to make images interesting because of the amount of exposure television promotion receives; boredom easily sets in. Constant change is required. Yet there have been classic exceptions to the transience of promotional work. Certain film graphic pieces have emerged from promotion's changing patterns and become permanent: the CBS eye; the ABC circle seven logo; the *ABC Sunday Night Movie* opening.

Techniques that compress energy, excitement, and color into two or three memorable seconds are valuable tools indeed. Time is precious. Promotional impact has to be instantaneous, and memorability is the key to all promotion because most promotion leads to an ephemeral moment in time. Once the program goes by, there is no second shot. Even when *Roots* is rerun, it is sold in a different way and does not get the type of audience that watched the original showing.

Film graphics offer the most powerful means of harnessing energy and excitement in short bursts. Film graphics are warm because they reflect human thought and creative work by a pair of hands. They are an arresting medium. An artist works on each frame, one at a time; therefore, each frame has a built-in variable. On the other hand, computer graphics are pseudo-three-dimensional. They are limited by what artists can put in, and their limits show clearly.

A network's image is the sum of all its parts—the promotion as well as the programming. And the technical and esthetic qualities of on-air promotion are central to the creation of image.

SUMMARY

Network promotion strategies have yet to feel the impact of the new technologies such as cable, pay-television, and STV. Gradually there will be a lowering of sets-in-use, but more viewers per set are likely so the audience that advertisers buy will not decrease for a number of years. Meanwhile, advertisers will enjoy the same exposure in a slightly different package. The technologies arriving in the 1980s will change not only the programs, but promotional practices as well. Different kinds of creativity will be required by network promotion. Year-round promotion will become the standard at all three networks for primetime programming. Affiliated stations will become increasingly sophisticated in their use of network-supplied promotional materials, and the role of co-op advertising will increase at all three networks. On-air promotion will remain, however, the cornerstone of network promotional efforts.

Television Network Affiliate Promotion

by
David P. Tressel

David P. Tressel joined WTAR-TV in Norfolk, Virginia, in 1979, which became WTKR in 1981. He is in charge of all on-air promotion, outside advertising, and sales promotion. He was formerly programming/promotion manager of WIFR-TV in Rockford, Illinois. From 1977 to 1978, he was advertising/promotion director for WDHO-TV in Toledo, Ohio. He holds a B.A. degree from Ashland College and an M.A. from Bowling Green State University, both in Ohio, and is currently working on a doctorate at Bowling Green State University. He served two years as a member of the CBS Affiliate Promotion Managers' Caucus. For his news promotion campaign at WIFR in 1979 he received a Broadcasters Promotion Association Award and a Rockford Advertising Club Award.

Two-way relationships exist between television networks and affiliated stations for many departments—programming, news, press and public relations, promotion, public affairs, traffic, business affairs. Each department has exact counterparts working in both network and affiliate organizations. Since the late 1970s, network promotion and local station promotion departments have grown much closer. There was a time when networks and local stations worked independently, but this attitude was rapidly abandoned in the face of spiraling costs and increased competition. From the network perspective, Steve Sohmer, vice-president of CBS Advertising and Promotion,* has said, "You cannot be the number one network nationally, unless you are number one in each and every market across the country."

The turning point in network thinking came during the 1976 and 1977 television seasons. These two seasons marked the rise of ABC as the programming leader. ABC had been the leader in innovative promotion for years, but it had relatively weak programming. In 1976, however, *Roots* and the summer Olympics broke the programming barrier for ABC and became the symbols of its breakthrough. CBS and

---

*Steve Sohmer became vice-president of advertising and creative services for NBC in March, 1982.

NBC had the weaker network/affiliate promotional efforts, so ABC achieved the winning combination of good programming and good promotion. Since 1977, both CBS and NBC have worked extensively to improve their advertising and promotional strategy and their promotional relations with affiliates.

UNDERSTANDING NETWORK/AFFILIATE RELATIONS

A network is a group of stations interconnected through a single programming source so that all affiliated stations are able to broadcast the same program material simultaneously.[1] Expensive, high-quality programming requires wide distribution to offset its production or purchase costs. Consequently, the three commercial networks are the traditional chief program suppliers.[2]

The network/affiliate relationship is built on the principle that the network supplies programming and the affiliate is its outlet by contractual agreement.[3] One station is the primary distribution outlet for one network in a particular market.

THE ROLE OF THE PROGRAMMING MIX

How does local programming fit with network programming? Is audience flow being sought? Or do local programmers go after available audience blocks during particular dayparts without considering the lead-in effects on network programs? Are network programs used as lead-outs? How promotion managers treat the affiliate/network programming mix establishes their relationship with the network. Only after developing a strategy regarding the programming mix is it clear what is and what is not important from a promotional viewpoint.

One of the first things a newcomer to an affiliate's promotion department learns is that a station cannot promote everything. Affiliates must set priorities. There is not enough time to produce promotional

---

[1]This definition of the three commercial networks emphasizes the networks' role in the development of television. It is extremely expensive to produce or purchase original, first-run, high-quality television programming. Unlike other forms of distributing program material (bicycling tapes or films between stations), the ability to broadcast simultaneously ensures program originality and permits coast-to-coast coverage of national news—live or recorded.

[2]The recent development of low-cost satellite communication systems has opened the door to other ways of distributing first-run, high-quality programming—by means of cable and other programming services.

[3]For this service, the station receives compensation from the network. This revenue is paid to the station not for airing program material but for airing the network commercials within the programming. The network has sold its air time using audience projections based on the number of affiliates agreeing to air a program. If, for any reason, a network commercial is not aired by a local affiliate, the compensation payment is reduced. It is also up to each station to clear each network program. If a station preempts an episode or does not clear a series, compensation is based on the network's hourly rate in the station's contract.

material for all of a station's programming in on-air, print, radio, press releases, and other types of promotion. The affiliate's promotion manager studies the station's programming mix in relation to its established goals and then develops a plan for all advertising and promotion. Affecting this plan are the guidelines for the working relationship between promotion managers and their networks. The three commercial networks provide slightly different materials to their affiliates, but the basic services are similar.

THE FALL SEASON

For the networks' promotion departments, the year begins in late January or early February with planning sessions to determine the theme and direction of next fall's new campaign. At these meetings, networks and affiliates also plan for the April close of the current season. This planning is important since April promotion (even though it is not in a rating period in most markets) usually reflects the race between the networks for the number one spot for that season. Being number one for an entire season leads to higher rates and more revenue for that network's following season in September. It also means higher local rates for spots adjacent to network programming. Thus April usually contains a strong promotional push by the networks. Network requests for local promotion time for network shows are quite common.[4]

Plans for promoting the new season are completed by spring, and work begins on campaign development. All promotion must be ready by May for the network/affiliate meetings (usually held on three consecutive weeks in Los Angeles). Station owners and general managers attend these meetings, and there are sessions for promotion managers. At this time, the new season's program schedule is revealed, along with the network promotional campaigns.

The Timing Problem

In the past, promotion managers received their first glimpse of the fall campaign during meetings scheduled just before and after the annual Broadcasters Promotion Association Seminar (held in early June). Since general managers, station managers, and program directors all saw the

---

[4]The network promotes network shows within network programming. These promos cannot be deleted. It is only natural for the station to promote local shows in local programming. Any unsold local spot positions in network programming usually go to local show promotion. Since promotion time is scarce and very valuable to local show promotion, strong justification is needed for a local station to air a network promo. If the programming mix is such that network programs are important to local programming as lead-ins, the station may decide to air network promos.

new fall campaign weeks before the promotion manager, the promotion manager was at a disadvantage during station-level planning sessions.[5] In 1979, NBC held its first promotion managers' meeting immediately after the general managers' meeting in May; CBS adopted this practice in 1980. This adjustment encouraged a better understanding of the new season's goals among promotion managers and station managers during the early planning sessions.

The Samples

At the promotion managers' meetings, the new season's campaign is revealed—campaign themes, graphics, music, network package tie-ins, fall premiere co-op plans, and on-air, radio, and print samples. Each manager is given a kit containing this information; the kit becomes a bible for the new season and often the year. Promotion managers who do not attend their meetings receive the promotion kits by mail with detailed explanations.

Sample on-air promos, shown at these meetings, reinforce network themes and also reinforce the stations' positive participation in tie-in packages. If they look effective, affiliates want theirs to look that way too. (They do not always look effective, however.) Radio and print samples are discussed to encourage positive participation in cooperative plans. Print samples offer stations an opportunity to adapt their print formats to the network's look. This adaptation is required if affiliates participate in the co-op plan. The networks help affiliates to produce high-quality print ads, even for local shows, by providing massive amounts of support material (ad layouts, press type, and other print pieces).

Co-Ops

For a new season (or at other times during the year when a **co-op** is available), the networks will pay their affiliates half the cost of running ads for a network program in local media (other than on a station's own air). Co-ops are offered only during network-prescribed periods and within the network-budgeted co-op amounts for each station.[6] Some networks also require that the advertising be limited to designated network programs on designated days.

---

[5]Promotion managers were especially handicapped when general managers formulated opinions concerning a station's participation in network campaign packages and co-op arrangements before promotion managers had a chance to see the material and come to their own conclusions.

[6]Other co-op periods throughout the year generally include (1) the November rating period, (2) the January mid-session replacements, (3) the February rating period, (4) the television season's end in April, and (5) the May rating period.

The typical co-op ad is a **stack ad** containing an evening's lineup of programming. Space is provided at the top of the stack ad for the station's news or prime access programs. The network reimburses stations for only half the ad, the network programming portion. Affiliated stations must pay for the entire space used for advertising local programs.

Tie-In Packages

A strong network campaign becomes even stronger when it is made easy for affiliate stations to tie into it through custom animation and music packages (available to stations at modest prices). ABC was the first network to offer local customization of a network campaign; then CBS, and finally NBC, followed suit.

Use of these tie-in packages helps the network gain added theme exposure during off-network dayparts when stations produce promos for their local and syndicated programs using network-style animation and music. These promos are aired during local station times. The stations themselves benefit from tie-in packages because they gain theme exposure during high-viewing periods such as primetime when the networks run their promos for network shows. Tie-in packages are also attractive because they are less expensive than custom campaign packages developed for just one station. Both networks and stations are strengthened by a unified approach to promotion.

Tie-in packages are not always the answer to a station's search for a good campaign theme. A weak station in a market, affiliated with a weak network, should think twice about participating in a network tie-in package. Tie-in packages should also complement a station's established theme.

Tie-in packages vary from network to network and from year to year, but they usually include (1) ID animation customized with local channel number; (2) on-air promo head-and-tail animation in the campaign style; (3) various cuts of music (full vocal, **donuts,** and instrumentals of various lengths—all with local station designation sung); and (4) animation of various titles such as the days of the week, "Weeknights," and "Special." As an option, character-generator **type fonts** with the network's typeface can also be purchased. Figure 7-1 shows a typical tie-in title.

NETWORK SUPPORT MATERIALS

Summer is the time when stations prepare for the fall premiere of the new season. During the summer the networks send the stations com-

Figure 7-1 Animated Tie-In Title: 30-Second Promo Tag Sequence for the *Donahue* **Show** (*Used with permission.*)

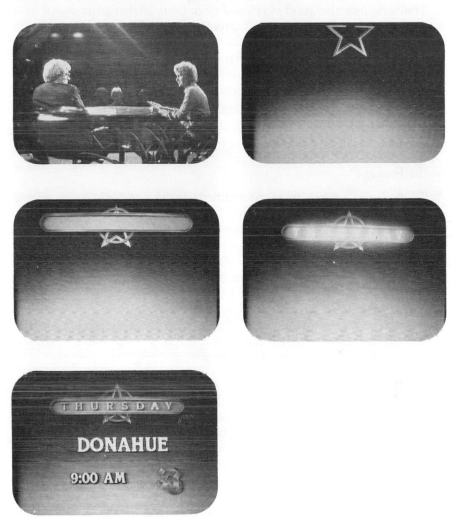

pleted episodes of new fall programs via closed circuit.[7] Promotion managers record them for promotional use and for the sales department to use as sales aids. Also sent via closed circuit are the network presentation tapes that were first shown at the affiliate meetings. These

[7]An affiliate is connected to its network by a series of microwave and land-line links. Only one signal can be sent to a station at a time. When the network is not sending programming for simultaneous airing, it uses this hookup for closed-circuit transmissions such as news feeds, advanced programming, and promotional announcements.

presentations inform station staffs and are included with local program information in sales presentations to prospective clients.

The networks also send via closed circuit completed promos for new and returning shows with new campaign animation and music. Some networks also produce combination promos with an open space at the beginning for insertion of material about local access shows. These combination promos stimulate audience flow—not only from local to network programs but also in reverse when a strong network show aids local prime access shows. Advanced tune-in is encouraged when the audience recognizes that the programs are a combination (especially if they are similar in appeal).

Wild Footage

Wild footage—scenes from programs cleared for local promotional use—is also sent via closed circuit. This clearance is given only when actors and actresses in a series have agreed, by contract, to allow their performances (apart from the actual broadcasting of episodes) to be used for promotional announcements. All main characters must agree to this promotional use, but minor one-time performers need not. Before the station selects footage from network series episodes for promotional use, it is advisable to determine which characters appear in that footage. When producing a local promo for a network program, and not using specifically cleared wild footage, it is advisable to contact the network concerning cast and clearance.

Promotion Kits

Promotion kits containing network program profiles, photographs (color and black and white), biographies, and slides for on-air use begin to arrive at stations in midsummer. From this material, stations construct their own kits containing new season information on both network and local programming. These kits are used by sales departments in materials sent to clients.

Stations typically host fall premiere parties in midsummer or late August. The main attraction at such parties is the elaborate presentation of new programming keyed to network campaign themes. Since the mid-1970s, the networks have locked in their fall program schedules by May, thus permitting stations extra time to prepare their fall campaigns.

New-Season Premieres

Premiere week for the network's new season occurs in September. Affiliates try to schedule the premieres of new local programming simultaneously with those of the networks. Since it is important that shows do well in premiere, network co-op money is available at this time.

An affiliate's participation in a co-op plan depends on the value the station places on outside media promotion of network programming. At one time, networks provided co-op funds for *TV Guide* ads shared with stations on a market by market basis. During fall premiere week, ad space for the numerous returning shows gets especially costly. But since the mid-1970s, the networks have realized that exposure in *TV Guide* is too valuable to let local affiliates control it by deciding whether they want to participate in a co-op plan. To ensure new-season exposure, the networks now pay for 100 percent of all network advertising space during fall premiere week, just as they normally do during the rest of the year. After the new-season premiere, network promotional support remains constant; a steady stream of day-to-day promotional aids is sent to affiliates.

Weekly and Daily Activities

The networks inform station promotion managers weekly about anticipated closed-circuit promotion presentations, batch mailings, and other promotional aids. Network promos, wild footage, and other video sent via closed circuit are scheduled at predetermined times throughout the week. Since materials may not be seen or taped the first time they are transmitted, repeats are common. Videotaping capacities are usually limited at the station level, making it difficult to schedule a taping of closed-circuit material during busy periods of the day.

Batch mailings include program listings with episode descriptions three or four weeks in advance. These are helpful in producing newspaper stack ads because of supplements' long deadlines. These batch or advance listings provide a good promotional picture for upcoming weeks.

Much of the advance promotion material is also sent directly to local newspapers by the networks. Included with press information are black and white pictures, outlines of specific episodes, and names of guest stars. All this material is sent to the newspapers with the hope that it will be used as feature or fill material.

Other network services are star weekends and star junkets. Star weekends take place at various times of the year, usually at least once before new-season premieres (summer) and again near the second-season premieres (January). Stations are invited to bring their own local talent and camera crews to a central location, usually a large hotel. There the network assembles a cross-section of stars who are at the station's disposal to do promos, interviews, and material for the fall preview parties (or anything else within reason).

Star junkets are promotional trips made by network stars (usually performers in daytime programs) throughout the country. Junkets are scattered throughout the year. The network arranges stops at a number of affiliated stations, which are asked in advance if they are interested in participating. The network pays the performers' airfare and expenses; the stations are usually responsible for hotel and limousine charges. While a star is in town, the affiliate can arrange television and radio interviews, press conferences, shopping center appearances, and, of course, promo tapings at the station.

Local news talent junkets are also arranged throughout the year. For these, affiliates typically send their anchor teams to New York for promo taping sessions with network anchor people and key reporters.

NETWORK NEWS SERVICES

News graphics and artwork are sent via closed-circuit transmission from the networks to their affiliates. Network news departments also offer affiliates various support materials for special projects. During national elections, for example, blueprints of a network's election set, along with sample materials, are sent to stations so that the affiliates can, if they choose, coordinate their set design with that of the network. Since set design relates to a station's news image, it is not unusual for the promotion department to be consulted in such cases. With heightened competition between the three network newscasts, co-op news campaigns are also becoming more common.

Community Affairs

Since the networks are concerned with the audience's perception of how programming decisions are made, they have produced videotape and slide presentations dealing with television's impact on society. These presentations are made available to the affiliates without charge, and their use is encouraged. From the station's promotional viewpoint, these presentations, along with other materials supplied by the network, are useful when the station's representatives are asked to speak to citizens' groups such as PTAs, Rotary Clubs, high school classes, or local community television activists.

Network Special Services

CBS supplies a unique service called the CBS Reading Program. The network sends its affiliates scripts of selected CBS specials that are television adaptations of classic novels. The affiliates then distribute these scripts to local school systems for classroom use in conjunction with the network's televised presentation of the novels. Teacher guides suggesting classroom activities and tests are also prepared by CBS. The CBS Reading Program helps local education and creates audiences for the long-awaited air dates of the novels the students study. The other networks also supply educational and public service aids periodically.

THE IMPORTANCE OF ON-AIR SCHEDULING

The scheduling of on air promotion is certainly as important as making it. A well-produced spot not only needs to be seen, but it needs to be seen by the right audience. Most television stations make ineffective use of their own air time. For years, promotion departments have gotten what was left—the unsold commercial positions. At some stations, the public service department selects positions for their spots among these availabilities (**avails**) before the promotion department to ensure that the station meets its public service announcement commitment.[8]

Scheduling promos in leftover availabilities runs against all good advertising principles. Morale is depressed when top-quality promos can only be run during undesirable periods of low ratings. (When a prime-time availability goes unsold, many sales account executives do their clients a favor by moving spots scheduled for less expensive time periods to better times.) This attitude toward promos can be blamed on the time when promos were merely announcements of upcoming program titles accompanied by the scheduled air time. But today, with increased competition, promotional announcements need to sell.[9] And the station needs to schedule promos in the same way It handles spots for its best client. The leftover avails are generally not good enough to sell a station effectively; and when the station and the economy are strong, there are seldom leftovers.

Stations that recognize the importance of selling themselves work out systems for clearing promotion spots during all time periods, regardless of the sales climate. Such a system is commonly called **fixed-position promotion** because the promotion department actually contracts with the sales department for fixed times throughout the day that cannot be sold. These may be specific times (30 seconds at the 3:00 break) or for specific dayparts (90 seconds between noon and 3:00 pm).

---

[8] A weekly minimum commitment of public service units is required for license renewal. The FCC, throughout the license period, requires proof of performance during yearly composite week programming reports.

[9] The new competition comes from stations imported on cable, movies, delayed program viewing through use of off-air home video recording, and prerecorded tapes and discs marketed for home use.

A billing system is usually established for these spots for internal accounting purposes.

There are ways to maximize leftover positions and create other on-air opportunities at stations with limited fixed positions or no fixed positions at all. Combo spots that mention more than one program maximize the effectiveness of the positions that are available. They also help create audience flow between programs.

It is important to know what avails exist before producing on-air promotional materials. Commercial breaks are usually divided into 30-second multiples: 30, 60, or 90 seconds. Therefore, if the sales department sells a heavy schedule of 10-second spots to a client, this creates 20-second avails, but few advertisers produce 20-second commercials. When promotion managers know this in advance, however, they can produce 20-second promos especially to fill these avails. Promotion managers should have access to sales availability reports so that promo production plans can be tailored to a possible overabundance of abnormal lengths such as 10-second or 20-second spots.

Another on-air promotional opportunity, often ignored, is the shared ID. In a shared ID, the legal information shares the position with a promotional announcement. Since the FCC only requires a legal ID to identify the station's call letters and city of license with either video or audio, there are many ways to construct a promo/shared ID. For example, topical video of a special guest can be pulled from a talk show and combined with a topical audio announcement. Video can either be action (moving) or a freeze frame. The legal portion of the ID can be video located under an animated station logo. Shared IDs combining a slide and prerecorded audio on a cartridge are also popular since they are easy to produce and do not require a 2-inch video tape recorder for production or playback. (See Figure 7-2.)

The networks too have adopted shared IDs. Not only do they add opportunities for promoting network programming during network service times, but they encourage network program promotion during local programming.[10] Networks now send topical shared ID material to their affiliates daily via closed circuit. Affiliates need only add local voice announcements and a visual logo.

Another effective method in a spot crunch is the audio-only promotional announcements that can be used over the credits of a program. The copy is usually mixed with the last 5 seconds of the program's theme music while the credits are rolling. This announcement is called a voice-over credit promo (VOC) or an audio promo (AP)

---

[10]Because of the abundance of station IDs throughout the broadcast day, affiliates are more willing to share IDs with their networks than give up 30-second avails in local programming for 30-second network promos.

Figure 7-2 Station/Program Shared ID Slide (*Used with permission.*)

or an over-the-crawl (ATC).[11] Locally produced VOCs can only be used over local or syndicated programs, not network program credits.

ON-AIR PROMO SCHEDULING

The process of scheduling on-air promotions varies from station to station, but two basic methods are used: hand or computer. Most television stations have computerized printing of their daily logs according to parameters delineated in each station's contract. Computer-generated logs are then checked by the various departments to ensure proper scheduling. Daily changes in programming (talk show guests, news topics) often necessitate rescheduling of promotional spots in order to target to specific audiences. Billing and other accounting functions are also computerized to produce invoices for promotional time used. The computer aids in recordkeeping and measuring promotional effectiveness.

Some stations still produce logs by hand. All programming, commercials, promos, and PSAs are entered on log sheets, and all billing is also done by hand. Under this system, promotional spots are not invoiced for time used because of the added paperwork.

[11]ABC, CBS, and NBC terminology, respectively.

To ensure the effectiveness of well-produced promos, six guidelines should be followed in scheduling on-air promos at network-affiliated stations:

1. *Establish promotional priorities.* Promotional priorities are the product of three-way communication between the programming (or news), sales, and promotion departments. Priorities are especially crucial during rating periods. Since everything cannot be promoted, find out what is important to sales. Know what a rating point is worth during particular time periods. Understand the rationale behind programming decisions—target demographics, audience flow. Once priorities are set, campaigns can be created and scheduling goals determined. Some promotion managers use a **gross ratings point** (GRP) system with weekly goals.[12]

Since the highest-rated syndicated programs are usually the most expensive to buy (or soon will be), promotional emphasis on these programs is needed in order to ensure their popularity and justify their cost. Programs that fall into this category include *M*A*S*H, Donahue, PM Magazine,* and *All in the Family.*

2. *Use topicals before generics.* Unless a show is a newcomer and needs thematic (generic) promotion, topical (specific) promotion is always best. Topical promos should also be run more times per day than generic. This added exposure is needed because the topical promo changes each day.

3. *Target on-air promotion.* Schedule promotion in programming that reaches the desired audience. A promo for *Captain Kangaroo* is wasted if it airs in the *CBS Evening News.* Another consideration is that certain material (particularly sex and violence) should be kept out of certain time periods (for example, Saturday morning cartoons).

One way to target promos is by using an **audience flow** analysis. A flow analysis, performed on the rating data collected during a sweeps period, gives a profile of audience viewing patterns. This profile reveals how viewers flow between programs and between stations; it also shows how many are new tune-ins and tune-offs. This information suggests ideal placements for on-air promos.

4. *Give news promotion priority.* Local newscasts dominate a station's image. A highly rated early newscast aids network news ratings that in turn lead into access time programs. Because of the importance of news, a base should be established for the early and late newscasts

---

[12]Gross ratings points are sums of all the rating points in a week's availabilities. In this case, the quarter-hour ratings for programs on either side of a break containing a promo are averaged to get a "break rating," and all the break ratings for the week are added up.

with good generic image promotion. The base should then be reinforced with daily topical promotion. Anchor personalities are vital promotable elements of local newscasts. Specific spots for top personalities
should be produced and scheduled in addition to those for the entire
newscast and topical news features.

5.   *Keep a good rotation.* Separate promos by at least half an hour. This
separation allows for sufficiently frequent exposure without excessive
repetition. An exception to this guideline occurs when there is a drastic
shift in audiences between programs. For example, a topical *PM Magazine* promo can be scheduled during the last break of the afternoon
movie. The same promo could air in the first break in the early news
following the movie because the audience changes between the two
programs.

6.   *Keep informed of network on-air promotion.* Keeping an eye on network
promo schedules helps in evaluating the network's promotional efforts
for individual programs. Spot-matching is essential when the affiliate
is supporting network programming. The station must avoid promo
duplication when switching between network and local feeds during
breaks. In addition, an important rule pertains to network promotional
announcements. When a network program is preempted, affiliated stations must cover the network promotional spot for a preempted program with a promotional spot for *another* network program.

SUMMARY

The role of the affiliate is vital to networks in supporting their efforts,
just as the functions of the networks are crucial to their affiliates. The
networks supply the bulk of the local stations' on-air and print designs
and can supply music and other special (and customized) graphics if
affiliates want to purchase them. The key question in promotional strategy is the extent to which affiliates should tie their images to that of
their networks. This decision is usually based on the national ranking
of the parent network in comparison to the other two networks. In
some markets, however, national rankings are not a reflection of a network's local prestige, so every decision must take local market conditions into account. The next most important promotional consideration
is the placement of on-air promos, since ineffective scheduling can
waste a spot or an entire campaign. The networks make a wide range
of professionally produced materials available to their affiliates that can
enhance the on-air look of even small-market stations.

Independent Television Station Promotion

by
Morton A. Slakoff and Lee A. Helper

Morton A. Slakoff has worked on the marketing and on-air promotion of series and films for television group-owners, film and series producers, and a network division. He moved from Triangle Stations (1957–1959) to National Telefilms Associates to Allied Artists Television to NBC Films, gaining a decade of experience in sales, advertising, and promotion. In 1968 he joined Wolper Production, which evolved into Metromedia Producers Corporation, later moving to Time/Life Films and then Viacom as director of creative services. From 1977 to 1981, he was vice-president for creative services at Metromedia Television. In 1981, he became vice-president for creative services for MCA TV. He holds a B.A. degree from Penn State University (1956) and an M.A. from the University of Iowa (1957) and teaches advertising and promotion at the New School for Social Research in New York City. He currently serves on the board of directors of the Broadcasters Promotion Association and is active in the Academy of Television Arts and Sciences and the International Radio and Television Society.

Lee A. Helper became director of the West Coast office of March Five Public Relations Inc. in 1979. He is responsible for the publicity and promotion of a large number of nationally syndicated television programs on behalf of clients such as Viacom International, Post-Newsweek Stations, Telepictures, Scholastic Productions, Metromedia Producers Corporation, Time-Life Television, and Operation Prime Time. After graduating from Emerson College in Boston in 1975, he worked briefly for WWWM-FM in Ohio as director of public relations, for Design Concepts International as partner and graphics consultant, and then formed Helper and Associates in 1976. In 1977, he joined Dudley-Anderson-Yutzy Public Relations as an account executive and worked for The Softness Group and Harshe, Rotman and Druck in New York. In 1978, he re-formed Helper and Associates and established affiliations with Harshe, Rotman and Druck and D.A.Y. before joining March Five on the West Coast. Lee A. Helper has been a speaker at John Carrol University, Ohio University, and Colby College. In 1978 he received an Outstanding Publicist's Award from the Publicity Club of New York.

The promotion manager at an independent television station functions with little outside support in advertising, promotion, press regulations, or on-air and general promotion. Unlike networks' affiliates and their owned-and-operated stations, independents have no preex-

144

isting network concepts, promotional spots, graphics, press releases, or built-ins. They are largely on their own.

THE VALUE OF SUPPORT

While the promotional needs of network-owned and affiliated stations and independently operated outlets are similar, their promotional priorities are different. Network-owned stations (O&Os) and affiliates receive promotional packages that accompany daytime and primetime programming provided by the network. Independent television stations purchase most of their programming from program distributors that generally make some promotional materials available but spend significantly less on promotion than the networks. Consequently, on-air promotion provided by program distributors often reflects low-cost production and hastily constructed announcements.

Press kits, too, are often shortchanged by program distributors who do not spend the money to hire publicists and photographers during the production of their properties. The artwork, photographs, and background materials supplied by syndicators for creating advertising and promotion may vary widely from the desired quantity and quality.

Large additional sums of money are certain to be spent by the networks in their own station markets to bolster their programming. Each network develops on-air promos for its programs, versions of which are made available to affiliates at no cost. Newspaper and television guide advertising, publicity in the national press and local newspapers, tours by celebrities, and other forms of promotion emanate from the networks and benefit their affiliates at no cost to them.

Independents face the perplexing problem of promoting 17 to 24 hours a day of programming without national promotional support. Although syndicators purchase large quantities of advertising space, it is almost exclusively in the trade press and directed toward selling their programs to stations; it is seldom in the consumer press and directed toward audiences. This pattern prevails because syndicated programs are picked up by scattered stations and aired at different times of day and on different dates (in contrast to the simultaneity of affiliate programming).

Audience promotion by syndicators would require enormous staffs. They would have to overcome the logistics of different episodes of a program playing on different stations at different times. The cost would be prohibitive. However, the advent of satellites for program distribution is bound to make national promotion easier for program distributors.

The promotional challenge at independents is to create what is not supplied: attractive newspaper ads, innovative merchandising, engaging on-air promos, and effective publicity. Promotional materials on in-dependent stations must have the same professional look and quality that viewers, press, advertisers, and agencies have come to expect on the networks—at a fraction of network budgets.

THE INDEPENDENT STATION'S IMAGE

The only identity that an independent station has is the one it creates for itself. The more successful an independent is in promoting its im-age, the more impact it creates for every program promoted. The iden-tity crisis that faces independents in the 1980s is a by-product of the growth period of the 1970s when competition and financial necessity prompted the programming of off-network reruns, local sports, old movies, and cartoons. Prices for commercial spots were markedly lower than on the network affiliates. And when the market was soft, inde-pendents were quick to take commercials rejected by affiliates (such as 2-minute sales pitches, paid religion, and **per-inquiry** commercials).[1]

At the same time, the network affiliates could afford to take first choice of off-network reruns for daytime and early fringe programming and also new game shows for early evening. The rejected programs were only then made available to independents. Agency advertising budgets, dictated by ratings, demographics, and clients' wishes, typi-cally went to affiliates first. Viewers were accustomed to thinking of independents as rerun stations, old movie stations, kids' stations, and junk advertising stations.

By depicting viewers of independent stations as predominantly blue-collar workers, children, and low-income groups to potential advertis-ers, the networks and their affiliates misrepresented the audience de-mographics of their independent competition. The independent's image did not change until management began to outbid network-affiliated stations for high-priced shows like *M*A*S*H*, *Happy Days,* and *All in the Family* and program them against the heart of affiliated schedules in early fringe, news, and **access** time.

A 1977 study conducted by the Arbitron Company compared the qualitative characteristics of independent and affiliated-station audi-ences.[2] They concluded that there were no differences in the quality of independent and affiliated-station audiences. This finding has been ex-tremely important in the overall marketing of independent stations. It has been used in sales promotion to change potential advertisers' per-ceptions of independent television station viewers.

---

[1]"Per inquiries" are commercials that are paid according to the number of viewer (customer) responses.

[2]This research was conducted in twenty-three markets covering 142 counties representing over a third of the nation's households. There were thirty-nine independent television stations and sixty-nine affiliated stations in the twenty-three markets studied.

Figure 8-1 An Independent Strategy (*Used with permission.*)

How to create an image.

An image is only what happens on the screen. And that's exactly how Metromedia Television has come to be identified with quality programming. Some of our recent image makers?

Well, there's Metromedia Producers Corporation's new Golden Circle project. Starting with the adaptation of Brian Garfield's novel, "Wild Times," this exciting, prime time drama venture includes four major four-hour productions this year...

The enthusiastically received *Against the Wind*, a powerful, 13-hour drama series underscoring man's inhumanity to man...

Scared Straight, the documentary that rocked the nation with its unorthodox prescription for scaring the crime out of defiant youngsters...

From London via satellite — the Royal Ballet's *Sleeping Beauty*, a fitting follow-up to earlier telecasts (also via satellite) of *The Royal Ballet Salutes the U.S.A.* and *Die Fledermaus*.

Our regular attractions are great for image-making, too. Like *The Merv Griffin Show*, *The Carol Burnett Show* and Metromedia's prime-time news in New York and Washington. Other quality offerings cover a wide gamut — from *Angel Death*, a chilling drug documentary narrated by Paul Newman and Joanne Woodward, to *All in the Family* and *M.A.S.H.*, two of television's most popular and most honored comedy series.

There's nothing mysterious about an image. It's on that screen — all season long.

Metromedia Television

New York, Ch. 5, WNEW-TV
Los Angeles, Ch. 11, KTTV
Washington, D.C., Ch. 5, WTTG
Houston, Ch. 26, KRIV-TV
Minneapolis/St. Paul, Ch. 11, WTCN-TV
Cincinnati, Ch. 19, WXIX-TV
Kansas City, Ch. 9, KMBC-TV

Represented by Metro TV Sales

Another study, conducted by Burke Research Services in 1980, confirmed that there is virtually no difference between the effectiveness of television commercials broadcast on independents or network affiliates.[3] This conclusion reinforces assumptions about the parity of independent-station audiences and affiliated-station audiences.

The combination of these research findings and a major commitment to competitive programming formed the basis for new and aggressive promotional positioning by independents. The most effective strategies have presented the independent station as an alternative to network-affiliate sameness. (See Figure 8-1.) As WNEW-TV puts it: "The choice

[3]Based on a survey of 200,000 viewers, released by Burke in January 1981.

is yours." KTVU in Oakland says: "There's only one 2." Creativity and individuality are at the heart of independent promotion.

PROMOTION FOR COUNTERPROGRAMMING

Independent stations have had great success in counterprogramming their affiliate competition. **Counterprogramming** is a basic strategy in which programs are scheduled to attract a target audience not being served by competitors' programs in a given daypart. Promotion for counterprogramming is *target* promotion. It consists of reaching the target audience at other times when it is tuned to the independent station or by advertising in media directed to that audience.

INDEPENDENT PROMOTIONAL PRIORITIES

Independents have many more programs per day to promote than affiliates. Affiliates program about 6½ hours on weekdays (between 7 am and midnight); independents program all 17 to 24 hours of their broadcast days. Thus independents must set promotional priorities favoring the entertainment programs that cost the most and have the greatest audience potential (such as *M*A*S*H* during access time).

Affiliates focus on newscasts; independents emphasize entertainment series and films. As of 1981, first-run programs dominate among entertainment shows and have the highest priority in promotion. Programs that fill large amounts of air time (movies), programs that are habit-forming (**stripped** talk-variety shows), and programs that change guests and features daily (topical magazine shows) occupy the next rungs of the promotional ladder.

Another high priority for independent promotion is original prestige programming.(Figure 8-2). Satellite transmissions of opera and ballet performances, first-run motion pictures, and long-form drama produced for television have premiered on independent stations. The mini-series funded and produced by Operation Prime Time are the outstanding examples of original prestige programming. Operation Prime Time and The Golden Circle are supported primarily by independent television stations. These are major undertakings, and they generally receive major promotional support from their producers and syndica-

Figure 8-2 Promotion for Original Prestige Programming (*Used with permission.*)

Your family is cordially invited to attend the Royal Ballet's performance of The Sleeping Beauty.

Metromedia Television is proud to present the Royal Ballet's performance of Tchaikovsky's "The Sleeping Beauty" via satellite from Covent Garden, London. With Merle Park in the principal role, this is widely considered to be the definitive version of choreographer Marius Petipa's classic.

The Los Angeles Times called the Royal Ballet's "The Sleeping Beauty" "a triumph of enlightened style."

The entire family will enjoy seeing this masterpiece come to life.

December 16, 1978 at 8 p.m. EST (7 p.m. CST)

To be repeated Christmas Day.

Metromedia Television
New York, Ch. 5, WNEW-TV
Los Angeles, Ch. 11, KTTV
Washington, D.C., Ch. 5, WTTG
Houston, Ch. 26, KRIV-TV
Minn./St. Paul, Ch. 11, WTCN-TV*
Cincinnati, Ch. 19, WXIX-TV
Kansas City, Ch. 9, KMBC-TV
In other cities, check local listings.
A Metromedia Television/
BBC-TV Coproduction.

*December 17, 1978 at 7p.m. CST.

tors. Consequently, the stations give them major emphasis in on-air and print promotion.

SCHEDULING ON-AIR PROMOTION

The scheduling of on-air promotional spots on an independent television station differs from the scheduling practices at affiliated stations. Generally, more time is available on independents for scheduling on-air spots, and stations have more programming that they must promote. Network affiliates have their daytime and primetime spots already provided by the networks. Affiliates mainly use station breaks for promotion and a limited number of spots within programs whereas independents are able to schedule promos heavily within programs. Thus independents are often able to avoid **clutter** at the breaks and gain prominence for their individual spots. They can also target specific program audiences.

PRESS RELATIONS

Independent station promotion strategies involve an entirely different approach to press relations than those of network-owned or affiliated stations. Because independents promote programming that is not seen in 100 percent of the country, they do not benefit from the national coverage that network programming often garners. Local newspaper editors tend to be less familiar with the titles of independent station programs and the names of their stars, so the newsworthiness of items is at first less salient.

Consequently, promotion managers, who generally supervise press relations at independent stations, need to create publicity materials and make strong personal contacts with local editors and writers and critics as part of the station's overall promotional strategy. When it comes down to the pragmatics of getting publicity in print or on the air, they are basically the same for all broadcasters. They hinge on three elements: interviews, features, and promotion kits. These need to be distributed by a persistent publicist (promotion manager) who recognizes the value of personal communication with the press.

Interviews

The distributor's release usually gives the name of the publicist or public relations contact for syndicated shows. This publicist will know whether stars are available for telephone interviews with local television editors. If the distributor fails to provide a press kit with feature stories, the station's promotion staff can conduct personal interviews over the telephone with stars or key production personnel.

Feature Stories

The following story was developed for the telefilm *Wild Times* at Metromedia Producers Corporation in May 1980. This program aired on a large number of independent television stations nationally, and local promotion managers adapted this story for local television and print features. (See Figure 8-3.) The purpose of such a story is to generate

Figure 8-3 Ben Johnson: You Won't Find a Nicer Feller (*Used with permission.*)

Ben Johnson: You Won't Find a Nicer Feller!

"Moviemakin' " and rodeos have always seemed to go hand in hand with one another for Ben Johnson. A world champion rodeo star and internationally recognized film actor, Johnson is perhaps best remembered by many for his role as "Sam the Lion" in Peter Bogdanovich's "The Last Picture Show" for which Ben won the 1971 Academy Award for best supporting actor.

Johnson's latest role is the portrayal of Doc Bagardus, the legendary and real-life world champion sharpshooter star of the 1860s in the upcoming television movie "Wild Times." "Wild Times" is an action-packed western based on Brian Garfield's best-selling novel. It is the authentic story of how dime novel heroes were born, how they began to believe their own created images, and how the wild west show originated.

Ben started out in the "moviemakin' " business in 1940 as a wrangler and a stuntman for Howard Hughes' production, "The Outlaw." Howard paid him $175 a week. That was enough money to help finance his principal interest, rodeo competition.

All his life he had wanted to be a world champion at something, "even if it was playing marbles." Seein' as how his father had been a world champion rodeo star, and after all Ben had lived and worked around cows and horses his entire life, why not go after the obvious, the world rodeo championship?

In 1947, Ben saw a glimmer of what the future might hold for him in rodeo competition. He had roped his first calf and set a new world's record. Six years later, in 1953, he won the world rodeo championship after perfecting his skills in the main events of team ropin', calf ropin', bull doggin', buckin' horse ridin', and bull ridin'. "I think the bull and buckin' horse ridin' were the most dangerous and difficult," Johnson recollects.

Having accomplished his life-long goal, he happily went home to tell his wife. Ben recalls her asking, "Do we have any money?" And he said, "No, but look at this big shiny billfold." She asked, "Can we eat it?" Fortunately for Ben he still had an acting contract with John Ford, who welcomed him back into the movies with open arms.

Does he have any regrets about leaving the rodeo circuit? "No. I'd accomplished what I set out to do. The movie business has been good to me and my family." Ben humbly adds, "Everybody in town (Hollywood) is a better actor than me, but none of them can play Ben Johnson as well as me." Talking to Ben Johnson will certainly convince you that this part Cherokee, Oklahoma-born gent is just doin' what comes naturally in real life and on the movie screen.

The last thing Ben Johnson ever expected to win was an academy award. "I always thought that a cowpuncher couldn't win one of those because he never had," comments the former $35 a week cowhand. "I really didn't expect to be nominated or win." At that time, Ben was working on a movie with John Wayne and Ann-Margaret. Ben recalls, "When I got word of the nomination, John lent me and Ann his brand new jet to fly up for the awards."

Ben was not only nominated, but he won as well. "I wasn't prepared to win, so I had to make up the speech between my seat and the stage. I began to thank everybody from the janitor on up. Then I sort of panicked and didn't really know how to end it and get myself off stage. And then it came to me, and I said, 'what I am about to say may stir up a lot of controversy around the world. It couldn't have happened to a nicer feller.' " He arrived at home to find stacks of telegrams from every state in the union. The caption on 95% of 'em read, "You're right, it couldn't have happened to a nicer feller!"

the print and electronic media's interest in the program by providing unusual and newsworthy information. While the story can be reprinted by a television editor in its entirety, it is more likely to serve as background for an interview or feature story.[4] Small-market newspapers with their small staffs are more inclined to pick up this kind of story in its entirety than large-market newspapers.

Promotion Kits

A promotion kit is used for dissemination of information and materials to the electronic and print news media. Promotion kits are sometimes supplied by program distributors, but they may be of uneven quality and lacking in essential ingredients. Should this be the case, the local station can develop the materials. The following elements should be included in the promotion kit for a telefilm or series:

- Announcement release (explaining what/why/where/announced by whom)
- Biographies of stars
- Show description or telefilm synopsis
- Cast list and production credits
- General information stories
- Photographs of stars and scenes
- Color slides

Promotion managers use these materials for features and photo stories.

The keys to successful press relations at an independent television station are (1) to develop tools that will enable promotion managers to communicate effectively on any program, movie, or special; (2) to establish strong personal relationships with members of the media; and (3) to work with members of the media and with the producers and other stations to generate as much national program coverage as possible.

Follow-Up and Coordination

Promotion managers should check with their national contacts to find out how much national coverage each program has obtained. Was a

---

[4]This release worked well for local stations and was successful in generating media coverage for the program. UPI used the story as background for an interview with Ben Johnson, and its feature ran throughout the United States during January, February, and March 1980.

telefilm promoted or reviewed in *Newsweek?* Was there a special appearance by one of the stars on the *Today Show?*

It is especially important to find out if a movie or special had a *TV Guide* "Close-Up." These inside features on specials or movies are prepared by *TV Guide* in its national office in Radnor, Pennsylvania, and sent to regional offices for the 110 individual weekly issues. Since each office decides independently on their use, a phone call from a local promotion manager may affect the decision. A similar process holds for other publishers of television schedules.

Promotion managers should also check with the television editors for every local newspaper regarding television inserts on movies and specials. These inserts are often assembled by a separate publisher who assumes editorial responsibility for compiling local listings and determining features. Although the inserts are kept current and look as if they were prepared locally, they are in fact similar to syndicated columns.

THE UHF INDEPENDENT

A UHF station is usually an independent station. In two-station and three-station markets, however, one sometimes finds a UHF network affiliate and, in the very top markets, VHF independents. When a new UHF station is added to markets having three or four VHF stations, the promotion manager of the UHF station must take on the task of convincing viewers that the new channel is easy to find on the dial. On the average television set, tuning a channel beyond 13 (such as 26 or 31) requires some adjusting (unlike click-stop tuning for channels between 2 and 13). The expansion of cable wiring and the advent of remote controls and continuous dialing have increased the public's accessibility to the higher-numbered UHF channels, but the public's attitude lags behind these innovations. It is up to promotion staffs to persuade viewers to sample the channel regularly.

TRENDS IN INDEPENDENT PROMOTION

Because television is unquestionably a changing business, it is crucial for promotion departments to keep up with developments in the field. Members of broadcast groups have a ready advantage in their ability to stay in touch with other promotion people in the same organization. Frequently group headquarters arrange seminars, workshops, and marketing meetings for the group's station promotion managers and staffs. Moreover, station reps can serve as effective promotional liaisons. The

Broadcasters Promotion Association's annual seminars provide similar opportunities.

The future will bring further fragmentation of television audiences, and independent stations will have to use every means at their disposal to get a share of the viewers. The licensing of low-powered stations, if pursued aggressively by the FCC, will be an added imperative for independents to program (and promote) for more select audiences.

Another innovation is the emergence of combined UHF and subscription television (STV) channels—the independent station programs and promotes the daytime hours while the STV management programs and promotes primetime. In these new media marriages, the participants have the additional challenge of developing strategies for promoting each service in the other's airtime.

Special programs like *Angel Death, Scared Straight,* and *Mom, I Want to Come Home* have aired on independents with success. Blockbuster movies like *The Deer Hunter* and *Sgt. Pepper's Lonely Hearts Club Band* had their television premieres on independents. So effective was the primetime scheduling of these specials in market after market that they cut significantly into the network ratings.

Independent television stations have a promising and profitable future. While primetime has traditionally belonged to the network affiliates, independents are increasing their ratings and consequently their advertising revenues. Since November 1976, there has been a 7 percent drop in network ratings and a 5 percent drop in network audience shares. The decline, which became evident in 1979, resulted from the increased popularity of independent broadcast television stations (as well as the proliferation of cable television services.[5] With the increased revenues comes the promise of increased promotional budgets and more competitive programming. The independent television station of the future will demand competent people to promote and program to a growing but more fragmented audience. This is a challenge to which new professionals can look forward.

SUMMARY

Promotional priorities differ between affiliates and independent television stations. Since the independent's programs lack national promotional support, its promotional efforts focus on enhancement of materials supplied by syndicators and film distributors. Independents are reversing this trend, however, by purchasing higher-quality programs, draw-

---

[5]David Crook, "Networks' Monopoly Being Challenged," *Los Angeles Times,* 17 February 1981, pt. IV, p. 1.

ing larger audiences, and actively involving themselves in community events. They are targeting their promotion to maximize the effectiveness of their counterprogramming. This strategy is particularly relevant in a period of media fragmentation. Independent television stations provide excellent opportunities for recent broadcasting graduates interested in entry-level promotional work. The job of the promotion manager at an independent is likely to be wider-ranging and more demanding of varied skills than that of a counterpart at an affiliated station, but the opportunity for creativity and challenge is equivalently greater.

Promoting the News

by
Gerald Minnucci

Gerald Minnucci is director of creative services for KABC-TV, Los Angeles. He has been with the American Broadcasting Company's Owned Division since 1971—originally at KGO-TV in San Francisco as director of creative services and in Los Angeles since 1973. He is responsible for the administration of local on-air radio and television promotion, print promotion, program information, and press and public relations. In addition, he is responsible for creative direction of outside advertising agencies and for supervision of the station's own in-house advertising and media placement agency. He graduated from Syracuse University in advertising and advertising design.

News is the arena in which most network affiliates (but few independents) choose to compete for ratings supremacy in a marketplace. At virtually all of the more than 600 affiliated television stations in the United States, promotion of news has the highest priority; at the approximately 175 independent stations, movies and sports often supersede news in importance. However, the station that is number one in news ratings is usually number one in overall ratings and in total dollar revenue.

Stations label programs "news" when they in fact range from local headline services to daily information capsules to in-depth magazine features. Newscasts, of course, generally have all three components.[1] Most news promotion consists of delivering some basic information about an early evening or late evening newscast to the largest possible

---

[1]As local newscasts grow in length, the need for features grows proportionately. At stations with unique news personalities, these magazine features usually present experts reporting in their professional spheres. Many stations have doctors turned news reporters, lawyers turned legal reporters, consumer advisers, and counselors on contracts and wills, for example, to give credibility to their newscasts. Added to these are other regularly scheduled magazine features such as grocery shopping, theater and movie reviews, child care, gardening and care of house plants, entertainment, and vacation tips. Others such as *The Butcher* and *Dr. Art Ulene* are available from distributors of syndicated materials. The list of possible "daily living" features is endless, but their use depends on the space in the newscast to accommodate them and the need for them in the marketplace. When feature reporters are especially skilled in their areas, demand grows for them on the air and as speakers in the community.

audience. Adding showmanship to the presentation enhances the effort, but the message is the key ingredient. News promotion messages fit into two broad categories: long-term campaigns (using **generic** spots) and short-term **topical** promos (using specific spots).

Long-term campaigns can advertise anchors and reporters or upcoming programs. They can also be used to mount competitive assaults on the ratings leader in the marketplace or to demonstrate bragging rights by the station leading in the ratings. The second type of news promotion is the daily topical that requires no more than one or two days of lead time. The subjects of these promotions are local story exclusives, special features for women, or timely reactions to public events (perhaps a court decision relating to a hot local topic—such as school busing). Whatever the category, every promotion should have a goal that is both achievable and measurable.

DEFINING NEWS GOALS

The three common objectives of news promotion are to gain ratings supremacy, personality acceptance, and newsgathering credibility. Typical strategies for achieving these goals are the hiring and firing of anchors, changing of newscast scheduling, or investing of big chunks of capital in sets or equipment. Everyday promotional tactics are as direct as simple announcements of news features or new program times or the acquisition of major newsgathering equipment such as mini-cams or news helicopters. More specific goals include altering the demographic mix of the audience by capturing the 18 to 49-year-old females currently viewing the competition or acquiring viewers from an ethnic group that makes up a significant portion of the demographics in a market.

THE IMPORTANCE OF RESEARCH

Survey research shows the times when a market's **HUT level** (homes using television) goes up. The typical causes are bad weather, a major news happening, or some other factor that causes more viewers to watch television news. Ratings analysis will spot which station gets most of the viewers during these increases. The station perceived as the most credible gathers the largest news audience during major news happenings. Stations with exploitative news reporting do better with coverage of weather disasters, family tragedies, and explosive accidents.

Successful promotion also causes the HUT level to rise. Analysis of a series of rating books will tell how much audience increase came from new "turn-ons" as opposed to "switches from competitors." When poor weather or some other outside factor causes the HUT level to increase for all stations in a market, the amount of increase at one station by comparison to competitors suggests the part promotion played.

In some instances, it is possible to plan for increased HUT levels. Southern California has a fire and mudslide season when weather becomes major news. Big winter storms in eastern cities and tornado warnings in the Midwest have a similar effect on HUT levels. Major sporting events such as the World Series and the Superbowl raise HUT levels especially in the cities of origin. News departments and promotion departments that plan in advance for these predictable HUT increases usually get the major share of audiences.

In highly competitive situations, stealing a rating point from competitors really amounts to a difference of two points: one the station gained and one the competitor lost. And two rating points, as any research director will say, is a substantial success story.

News Consultants

Virtually all news departments at network affiliates in the top hundred markets subscribe to outside research companies for periodic analysis of their newscast content, their news delivery, and the professional and personal appeal of their news personalities. This information is available to the promotion manager, who should participate in meetings between the station's news staff and research team.

One important agenda item with news consultants is discussion of how to use the station's news personalities for promotion. Research indicates that some anchor personalities are perceived by audiences as especially credible and consequently appear to deliver news promotion headlines better than others. Some anchor personalities appeal to younger audiences; others are more popular with women. Whatever the strength, such features should be exploited by the promotion department.

Other Media Research

Television supplements and daily newspapers have always been a staple in media advertising budgets. But other than circulation figures, little data are available on the readership of the various pages and whether television ads in newspapers are read at all.[2] It is assumed that the television section is the best place for a television ad, because

---

[2]Circulation figures are available from the Audit Bureau of Circulation (ABC).

of the attraction of the daily schedule listings, but other sections may have higher readership and better demographics for the individual news features a station wishes to promote.

Newspapers and television supplements conduct their own readership research, usually for internal use only. Like television programs, some pages rank higher than others on the readership charts, but the publications may be reluctant to give out this information. Nevertheless, some publications will share their findings with a local station when so requested.

In-House Interpretation

Equally as important as data gathered from outside research firms is information compiled internally from ratings books. Different programs on a schedule reach different audiences, but too often on-air promotion placement is taken for granted. Careful study of program audience demographics often suggests more efficient scheduling of on-air news promos.

More crucially, certain programs on a schedule reach more of the viewers of news competitors. If a station's goal is to steal a competitor's audience by programming special features, the placement of on-air promos before the proper demographic groups is an important strategic tool. Using detailed interpretation of Nielsen and Arbitron ratings to guide promo scheduling will, in the long run, stretch promotion budget dollars.

BUILDING THE MEANS

Whether a news promotion budget is large enough to do the job is a question almost impossible to answer since there is no effective method for drawing the line between "enough" and "overkill." Budgets are the key factor in anything a promotion staff accomplishes, and recruiting a budget is like recruiting a football team. If promotion managers do not get the players during the off-season, they are not likely to win many games come September.

In-House Production Budgets

The news promotion budget is directly affected by the amount of in-house production attempted at the station. Some large-market stations have extensive postproduction facilities available to the promotion department's producers. Some stations have both camera operators and film editors available to the promotion department. Graphic arts departments come in various sizes of personnel and equipment. Promotion managers should not accept the limitations given with a job, particularly the size of a news promotion budget. It is always possible to persuade management to enlarge a news promotion effort to cover more news content and give more visibility to news personalities. Promotion directors can show these additional costs to be more efficient in the long run because on-air then reaches larger audiences by making better use of existing inventory. Consequently, asking for a larger budget becomes a matter of documenting the cost of being in business to build bigger profits.

News Promotion Budget Strategy

Although news promotion budgets are submitted annually, the money is usually spent during three major periods of the year: September through November (which includes the fall kickoff); February; and May. These are the major rating periods when news campaigns and extra news features are packed into each newscast. Budgets should be planned according to rating periods or by quarter so that each promotion director has a periodic checkpoint for evaluating recent expenditures.

Calculating a budget requires estimates for five major elements: (1) the number of campaigns the promotion department intends to run during the year; (2) the number of mini-documentaries, special features, personality projects, and public service projects (associated with news) that the station intends; (3) the amount of media advertising needed; (4) the amount of in-house service required from other departments; and (5) the quantity of work desired from outside vendors. All these elements need contingency estimates to allow for unanticipated events and outright failures.

Extra budget allows a station to take advantage of competitors' mistakes and to deliver the extra push occasionally demanded by management. Extra budget also allows for the unplanned campaign or news promotion project brought on by the competition's change in anchor talent, newscast expansion, or an unexpected rise in the ratings.

Mini-Docs, Features, and Projects

Promotionally oriented news operations schedule news mini-documentaries, magazine features, and special news series to take advantage of their promotional potential. They are placed well in advance of air dates in major rating periods.

In some markets the major rating periods are so competitive that choosing and promoting these nonheadline news features has been polished into an art form. Since most of the headline news is common to all stations, rating battles are won and lost on these extra features.

Depending on the length of newscasts and the size of feature reporter staffs, news directors may schedule anywhere from one feature per rating period to two or three per week. If the news contains a sizable number of promotable features, the news promotion budget should take into consideration the cost and facilities needed to inform the viewers when and where the features will appear.

Media Advertising to Support News

A station's own air time is the most flexible kind of advertising since commercial availabilities can be used when unexpected news stories occur. Radio time is especially flexible because it is relatively inexpensive and requires little lead time for production. Most of the larger radio and television stations in a market have similar **ADIs**.[3] Talk radio and all-news radio have the ideal demographics for reaching evening television news audiences. Advertising on these stations has exceptional promotional value because of information radio's timeliness.

The largest type of out-of-home radio listening is generally conceded to be via car radio. In cities with little or no mass transit, the car radio is a distinct medium in its own right. The timing of drive-home traffic has significant carry-over effects for evening television news promotion. It is usually the television station's last chance to promote its latest headline story or remind the "arriving-home/turn-on-the-news" crowd of special features planned for that day's early newscast.

In many markets, the competing stations employ last-minute radio promotion by means of special telephone lines from their news facilities through the central telephone switching facilities directly to the radio stations. Produced and executed well, this last-minute news promotion via radio stations can achieve extra rating points, drive the competition down, and actually steal audiences from other media and outside activities.

The best way to plan for last-minute radio headline promotion is to purchase radio time during the major rating periods. Block out the portion of a radio schedule that best serves newscasts, both early and late news, and choose exact dates for each campaign or rating period. A good news tease promotes the coming exclusive stories on a station but does not give conclusions or become a miniature synopsis of a feature.

---

[3]ADIs (areas of dominant influence) refer to geographical market boundaries as defined by Arbitron. In this instance, the term includes Nielsen definitions—technically called DMAs (designated market areas).

Advertising on radio allows more content in promotions than either transit or billboard messages. For both campaigns and daily announcements, radio adds depth to the sales effort. And because spot radio advertising has some flexibility in length (30 or 60 seconds), several messages can be stacked on top of each other. Stacking is of special value for news because stations that have 60, 90, and 120-minute newscasts accommodate larger numbers of magazine and nonheadline news features than stations doing half-hour newscasts. Since news directors choose these features not just for their informational and credibility value, but to attract larger audiences, the station's on-air promotion producers can billboard several news topics within each 30-second spot.

If a newscast for a given day has magazine features on social security, the school busing situation, and Cher's latest Las Vegas act (soon to appear as a road show in this market), the station has news features appealing to (1) an audience of 60 years plus, (2) a parents' age group of 25 or 30 plus, and (3) a young entertainment/music-oriented group. If just one of those topics within that 30-second promotion attracts just one extra viewer, and if that viewer is counted by the A. C. Nielsen Company, the promotion manager will have accomplished the key promotional job.[4]

Print Space

Print space should be the most predictable portion of the news promotion budget. Because major news features and mini-documentaries are generally scheduled for major rating periods, the number and size of print ads to support them can usually be estimated accurately in the annual budget. At the beginning of each budget quarter or in advance of each rating period, projections can be corrected.

Most major newspapers have a Sunday television supplement, similar to *TV Guide*, that lists the entire week of television fare (sometimes included in the Saturday paper). These supplements generally have greater staying power near home television sets (and, in many cases, higher readership) than the newspaper's daily television section. Because of the supplement's longer ad deadline and the news department's planned features for known rating periods, annual amounts of news print promotion should be the easiest to plan for in budgets. If promotion managers are fairly accurate in print ad estimates, they can shore up last-minute news stories with radio and television on-air pro-

---

[4]A news promo on a social security magazine feature has little appeal to anyone under 50. It is a simple matter of efficient arithmetic to cover larger audiences with a shotgun approach and still use only one 30-second availability.

motion, thereby satisfying the news department's needs right up to newstime.

Out-of-House Resources

In addition to their creative contribution, promotion managers are responsible for coordinating outside suppliers into production units. Since outside suppliers are available in all price ranges, budgeting becomes a matter of the quantity of service the station needs and the quality of service the station can afford. Regardless of these variables, the number of advertisements and on-air promotional spots can be tabulated within reasonable allowances and allotments made within the budget for these outside services. A contingency amount in the budget for unknown projects and for improving quality is most desirable.

Building a news promotion budget from the ground up, with detail at every level, gives flexibility when it is needed and strength to the whole station's effort. A handy rule of thumb is that production costs run somewhere in the neighborhood of one-third of media costs. A quick check of past bills will provide a more accurate estimate of the station's promotion costs; thereafter spot checks should be sufficient. When submitting budgets, estimate a little high since unspent money at year-end can always be returned at year-end. Securing the means to carry out the news promotion is the single most important thing a promotion director can do.

At most stations, the production costs for preparing on-air promotion are included in the budget, but the value of on-air time is not.[5] The unsold availabilities used by promotion, as well as its planned inventory, frequently go untabulated. An effective way of securing enough producers and facilities is to total the costs of the air time used by promotion periodically. The sales manager can price the spots that come from sales inventory. Moreover, tabulating the spots used from nonsales/programming, voice-over credits, movie trailers, and shared IDs should generate a total big enough to stagger management.

A full-page $5,000 ad in a newspaper justifies production expenses in keeping with media costs. If a station uses $5 million worth of its own air time for promotion, the cost of postproduction facilities and talented on-air producers is readily justified for daily news promotion. Million-dollar budgets are now commonplace in major-market television promotion. If an amount is calculated for a medium-sized station's own on-air promotion inventory, the combination of cash, in-house services, and on-air time can exceed $10 million per year. Certainly the

---

[5]Air-time value is nominally the rate established on the station's rate card. Many television stations negotiate (within limits) for all air time, however, so exact rates are difficult to determine.

promotion manager's job has grown substantially since the early 1970s when promotion budgets typically consisted of unsold air time and reciprocal trade exchanges.

Considering the dollar value of promotional air time, management should be responsive to requests for funds, staffing, and facilities that do not shortchange the promotion department's ability to deliver effective promotion. The promotion manager's goal is to build the dominant staff and delivery system in a marketplace. The ability to promote news effectively depends above all else on proper budget.

NEWS GRAPHICS AND ANIMATION

Television news graphics often lack high priority in promotion department budgets because it appears possible to achieve rating superiority without them. Nevertheless, good art costs little more than bad art, and artwork may be the extra element that gives conceptual and esthetic coherence to a news program.

The typography in news promo signatures (whether animated or not) and the titles for news features should be coordinated with the station's overall look. These are significant elements in establishing station identity and are an important strategic tool.

When close identification with a network is intended, local on-air promo tags should use the same typography the network uses, unifying the local and network on-air promotion. Animated introductions or tags for on-air news promotion can grab attention. The problem comes when the showiness of animation overshadows the informational content of the promos.

News art should be selected with long-term use in mind. Corporate and news program logos are often retained for years (and then modernized rather than discarded). An effective station concept, embodied in news art as well as the other elements of station identity, should have longevity. Capturing the desired image in quality logo art and good animation are worth the extra cost and can be justified by amortization over the life span of their use.

PRODUCTION SUPPORT

The promotion department shares the television studios and editing facilities of the station with the producers of local programs and jockeys for adequate time to produce high-quality topical promos supporting the daily newscast. Almost every promotion manager could use another on-air producer. Creative and fast producers are the nucleus of news promotion staffs because promotion deadlines are so short.

Staffs

Writer-producers gather the news film, write on-air radio and television promotion, block out usage of postproduction facilities, secure announcers, and direct the videotape and postproduction technicians—all within minutes of the newscast itself. Any delay in production means that immediate on-air availabilities will be filled with promotion other than that day or night's news promotion. The loss of this immediacy means the loss of a promotional edge over the station's competition.

Facilities

Once a promotion manager has an adequate budget and trained staff, production facilities are the next priority. On-air promotion is considerably more costly than print promotion and also requires studio and editing time that other departments (generally news) are reluctant to surrender. Promotion departments usually produce on-air promos in the fringe time periods of very early morning, late night, and weekends—a situation that inhibits the timeliness of news promotion. Failure to take advantage of daily and late-breaking news features forfeits the opportunity to steal the competition's news audience as well as the possibility of attracting viewers interested solely in a single story.

Postproduction facilities for editing are a luxury most promotion departments do not enjoy. Every station needs some arrangement for last-minute production, however, even if only for talking-head headlines. Planning for adequate facilities makes the difference between timely, polished news promotion and delayed, technically weak, or even nonexistent promotion.

MEDIA ADVERTISING OPTIONS

In large, spread-out cities with little or no mass transit, radio (particularly car radio) and billboards have greater value for news promotion than in cities where train, bus, and subway advertising reaches millions of people daily. Because of the lead time for printing messages and the limited number of words that will be effective, billboard and transit advertising are usually restricted to announcements or daily reminders to watch a newscast. Sometimes they introduce new personalities or features or changes in program times. If a news promotion budget can afford general reminders to "Watch the news when you get home," train, bus, and subway posters are a good buy. Occasionally these media can be bartered, partially or entirely. Paper and production costs for outdoor advertising vary substantially from market to market, however.

Whatever the medium, the length of the advertising message must be measured against the cost per thousand people reached and against the speed of delivery. The history of both transit and billboard sales suggests that these forms of advertising can be traded for television air time. Other elements in media advertising strategy are the timing and size of buys. At certain times in the year, it is wise to overbuy in anticipation of major news events. In particular, planning for a last-minute need to advertise unknown news features during the rating sweeps is sophisticated strategy and money well spent.

The February rating period makes the point. Weather disasters then frequently drive the HUT levels up because the bad weather keeps people home and keeps them tuned in to hear what's happening and what is expected. A major share of that increased HUT level can be captured by planning for on-air television and radio promotion to be produced under short deadlines. Should there be no newsworthy event, the news director can be alerted to have promotion-worthy features on standby. Should the anticipated rain and snow storms wreak the usual damage, the promotion manager has the additional time blocked out to take full advantage of the high HUTs by outadvertising and outperforming the competition with the same story. Whatever the weather, the line between an adequate amount of advertising and overkill is less likely to be challenged during major rating periods when every news director welcomes all the advertising obtainable.

NEWS PROMOTION CAMPAIGNS

Good news campaigns sell something. They sell news personalities to the viewing public; they sell special features and special ideas; and they sell positioning in a marketplace. Like every commercial product ad, every promotional advertisement should "ask for the sale"—that is, ask the viewing public to buy this newscast.

However creative a campaign, this message comes first, and it should be embodied in a simple statement. A campaign concept that uses wordy messages can be broken into stages and taken one step at a time. The most successful advertising campaigns in television news have evolved from a simple statement/concept and continued to build in scope and reach. News teams seldom attain leadership position overnight; they take months or years to build momentum. Figure 9-1 shows

Figure 9-1 Print News Promotion (*KOLN-TV, 1978. Used with permission.*)

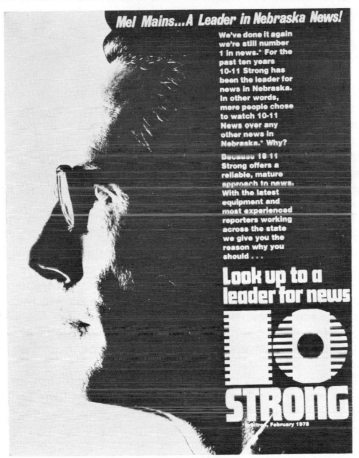

a print ad for an established news anchor combining visual simplicity and motivating content.

Television newscasts have different audiences. A half-hour television newscast may start with blue-collar appeal (all headline stories, exploitation of sensational news, accidents, tragedies). As newscasts expand to 60 minutes or longer, they typically include magazine features, investigative reports, quality-of-life segments. These features add credibility and reach for other income levels. Promotion for the news has to broaden from the 30-minute image of the news. It is no longer sufficient to promote the news personalities by themselves. Personalities should become associated with different news audiences and different news topics in promotion that reaches out for splinter audiences without losing the original audience.

DAILY NEWS PROMOTION

Everyday news promotion, whether on-air or in print, is more direct than campaign promotion. In most cases, the goal is to gain a viewer within 24 to 48 hours. The information a promo sells may be that day's headlines, a special feature, or a one-time-only live appearance of a nationally known personality. Most stations promote their mini-documentaries, one item to a promo. And if the mini-doc has segments lasting through an entire week of newscasts, it warrants an ad all its own.

As local newscasts expand from a half-hour to an hour, however, and then to 2 and 3 hours, news items tend to be stacked in promos and ads much as networks **piggyback** their primetime shows. News promos using multiple features are potentially more effective than network multiple promos because they consist entirely of features within the same newscast. It is unlikely that single viewers will watch 2 or 3 hours in a row unless the magazine or nonheadline news features change from newscast to newscast. But it is in the station's best interest to retain lead-in viewers, even if they migrate from newscast to newscast.

Billboard copy has six to eight words to cover the topic; print ads are much the same because fewer than 50 percent of all the people who see ads read beyond the headlines. Three and sometimes four features can be stacked in one 30-second on-air promo. It is important to sell everything salable about news features while keeping the words to a minimum. Daily promotion is quick selling, and a promotion manager has only a limited number of print, television, and radio availabilities to do the job.

News Teases

News headlines and **teases** are of even shorter length than shared on-air promos. Some stations take advantage of their 3-second station identifications to promote their news with a headline. The value of these station-break promos is so high that a price tag on one would equal all the rest of the newscast's on-air promotion.

Writing the headline itself goes one step beyond writing billboard copy. There is a big difference between saying "Duran beats Leonard for the welterweight title" and "See the Duran/Leonard welterweight decision at eleven." News headlines on television and radio should not be miniature newscasts but should whet the viewer's appetite for watching the news.

As often as possible, billboard-type headlines should refer to an exclusive feature in the next newscast. In this way, the station does not advertise the competition's news as well as its own. As interesting as the Duran–Leonard fight may sound to a station's sports viewers, for example, it is a feature likely to be on the competitor's news also.

Daily news promotion is a short-term sale. What is advertised that day is likely to be only on the air that evening. The next day's news promotion will probably deal with entirely different content. The ability to promote last-minute features quickly and creatively under the shortest possible deadlines will thrust a promotion department into center focus in management's overall strategy.

The Cost of Misrepresentation

News stories are not always well produced. Lack of expertise, lack of time to produce the story, equipment malfunction, or other shortcomings cause some news features to deliver much less than their potential. Misrepresenting news stories by inaccuracies in promotion will not only damage the station's credibility but lose viewers in the long run. News ratings depend on repeat viewers. If the audience feels cheated by not seeing what they were promised, it is harder to get them back than it was to attract them in the first place. Misrepresenting a single entertainment program may cost a station nothing more than bad reviews. Misrepresenting the news wastes advertising budget and damages the reputation of the person responsible for promotion.

ALMOST-FREE PROMOS

Cross-plugging news features is almost like getting a free promo. Cross-plugs are not charged to commercial time and do not show on the programming log. Their only costs come from the time for a newswriter or program producer to insert the plug somewhere in the program. Within the news itself, many newscasts tease the features coming up right after each commercial break with copy that reads, "Stay tuned for . . . right after these messages." This type of tease is also called a **bumper.**

Stations that have two early newscasts—at 5 pm and 6 pm, for example—can take advantage of the earlier newscast by having the 6 pm anchor appear about 45 to 50 minutes into the first hour with a tease for the 6 pm feature stories. The networks' morning shows all have local minutes blocked out in which stations can insert a mini-newscast.

Such miniature headlines may also contain a plug for exclusive news features in the early or late evening newscasts.

Weather breaks should always contain the name of the program, the channel number or call letters, or the name of the weather personality—as in, for example, "Channel Seven's Herb Brooks says we can expect rain later today." When people talk about the weather, they have a tendency to repeat the entire statement they heard and create their own word-of-mouth promos for a station's name or weather personality.

Network Cross-Plugs

Network news shows frequently make their personalities available to affiliates to cross-plug local and network newscasts. Prerecorded tapes, whether full length or tag lines, can ensure smooth transitions between network and affiliate news, thereby linking the two newscasts together. Should network news personalities be visiting locally, it is ideal to prepare on-air promotion showing both the local and network anchor people seated on the local news set. Taping several promos will allow frequent airing without wearing out the same promo in night-after-night display. It is the local news anchors, however, who carry the news burden in a market; seeing that they come off well in a tandem production with network news is the promotion manager's first priority.

Public Service Cross-Plugs

Since every station runs a large number of public service spots (generally thirty or more a day), it often becomes possible to have news personalities prepare charity or community-oriented announcements. Every free mention on the air is a personal promo for the station as well as for the news personality, generating goodwill and a sense of community involvement. Some of a station's personalities may only have time for one big project a year (such as requesting toys for a local children's hospital at Christmas), but they can also be asked to do on-air public service spots for the station. Outside press organizations frequently rally behind public service efforts, thus creating more news with rewards that go beyond personality promotion.

PRESS RELATIONS FOR THE NEWS

Facts about a station's news personalities and daily news features should not be overlooked in everyday press bundles. Most newspaper columnists shy away from reviewing mini-documentaries and news features, but at times special features can be telephoned to the newspapers. Uncommon timeliness or an outrageous fact uncovered may stimulate interest. When columnists have a slow day, they may be eager for that extra information.

A promotion staff member should make daily runs through the newsroom to inquire if the news anchors intend to make appearances on their own (not arranged by the promotion department). If so, the promotion department should furnish biographical materials, a photographer, or other useful assistance. In the larger markets, new personalities are celebrities of such magnitude that they frequently have agents or business managers to handle their public appearances. When this is the case, coordination is required to bring about the maximum amount of goodwill.

Promotion departments occasionally set up a speakers' bureau to assist station personalities (and often management and production staff as well) in public appearances.[6] Before initiating such a project, the station's news personalities should be polled to assure their interest in participating.

A speakers' bureau requires brochures to mail to community service and industrial organizations that regularly use speakers, parade personalities, contest judges, and grand marshals. Brochures should include the station's contact for each personality (the personality, an agent, or the station's promotion manager). If fees are a consideration, the copy should make clear that this person appears only for a fee, that a fee is sometimes requested, or that there is no fee at all. Brochures should also mention the type of appearance the personality will accept and list some of the topics he or she is willing to talk about (if willing to speak publicly at all). Mention should also be made of the willingness of certain news personalities to deliver guest lectures for university broadcasting and journalism classes.

The brochures need periodic updating and at least two mailings a year. Obviously some of a station's news personalities will welcome a speakers' bureau more than others, but the more a station's talent meets the public in functions, the easier it is for the promotion department to expand its viewing audience and create station goodwill. The ramifications extend all the way to the general manager's office and have residual effects at license renewal time when special-interest groups complain of a lack of attention and station support.

Press relations, as much as any other form of promotion, carry the station's image. Information on station personalities and special features needs print media distribution, and public appearances by station talent can contribute to the overall news promotion effort.

---

[6]Linda Nis of WDCN-TV in Nashville outlines five steps for setting up a speakers' bureau in "A Speakers Bureau Can Help Your Station," *BPA Newsletter*, December 1980, pp. 12–13.

NEWS PROMOTION IN THE 1980s

News promotion positions are being upgraded everywhere. Stations are recognizing that programs—news in particular—depend on good promotion not just during the rating sweeps but all year long. It is not coincidence that the status of promotion is growing at the same time most local newscasts are expanding. Promotion has become legitimate since competition increased in the mid-1970s, and it is gathering strength every year.

SUMMARY

Suppose a new promotion manager inherited a news program with a 40 percent share of the market, a creative and competent promotion staff, and a sizable budget. This imaginary promotion manager would need only maintain the momentum, since the job is already defined. Short of this dream, however, it becomes the personal and professional responsibility of a new promotion manager to devise a budget, build a promotion staff, and secure the facilities needed to do the job. Research and detailed budget accounting can guide the new promotion manager in planning, but the best strategy is to promote the promotion department as a revenue raiser. Promotion managers find that revenue raisers get greater compensation than money spenders. This orientation provides rewards in job satisfaction (greater budgets) and more frequent promotions; successful promotion managers tend to be judged more for their administrative ability to get jobs done than for specialized knowledge. More than any other position at a station, promotion is a full-circle job. It interacts with every other job and plays a major role in the station's overall success.

Commercial Radio Promotion

by
Harvey Mednick

*A long-time RKO Radio employee, Harvey Mednick joined the company as director of
advertising and promotion for WRKO-FM in 1967. In 1969, he became western
regional promotion manager for four RKO Radio stations in San Francisco and Los
Angeles, and he joined the corporate staff as vice-president of RKO Radio in 1973. He
presently advises RKO stations in advertising, marketing, and promotion. He is
also a principal of Klein/Mednick Special Projects, a promotional and programming
development group based in Los Angeles. He has written articles for the National
Association of Broadcasters'* RadioActive Magazine *and has lectured at several col-
leges. He is a member of the Executive Board of the Center for Public Resources
and the Board of Directors of the Association of Independent Radio Producers and the
Academy of Radio Arts.*

In the 1950s radio shifted from a network-dominated medium to specifically formatted stations. Although each station developed promotional practices to fit its format and locality, radio promotion does
contain several elements in common. The major stations use total promotional identity by combining image and format in short, thematic
slogans. All-news as a format becomes "All News All the Time" promotionally. Conversation radio becomes "Talk Radio" promotionally.
Country music becomes "LA Country."

Moreover, most radio promotion concentrates on the use of television as a primary advertising medium instead of print. As the largest
of the mass media, television is considered the major source of potential radio listeners. Outdoor advertising (billboards) continues to be
widely used for radio in heavily posted markets.[1] In markets with
heavy transit commuting, display cards become an effective advertising
medium for radio.

Where radio stations differ greatly is in the use of their own on-air.
Talk stations put major emphasis on showcasing their personalities.

---

[1]Markets with considerable automobile commuting that do not legally limit billboard placement are
suitable for outdoor advertising.

News stations promote their services (weather, traffic, sports, community involvement) or their immediacy and speed of reporting ("All News All the Time"). **Beautiful music** stations are unique in avoiding use of their own on-air in order not to interrupt its flow. Consequently, these stations tend to make heavy use of outdoor advertising and television. Classical radio stations traditionally adopted an elitist approach that denigrated self-promotion. With the acquisition of classical stations by major broadcasting groups, however, promotion has become more active. Some classical stations concentrate on program guides; others organize listeners' clubs with special benefits to members (such as bargain-rate tickets to local events).

The traditional powerhouse stations (often the old-time giant 50,000-watt clear channels), if they still attempt mass service to all audiences, tend to promote themselves much like television stations. They place heavy emphasis on their community identity ("KDKA, Pittsburgh, Someplace Special"; "WGN Is Chicago"). Figure 10-1 shows how WRKO in Boston declares its identity. Individual programs are singled out for regular topical promotion.

Popular music stations place overwhelming emphasis on contests. While rock stations make use of television, outdoor, and transit advertising, by far their major stress is on their own on-air. Contest promotion is especially significant in the highly competitive and lively rock radio market. More money is spent, and more energy expended, on contests than on any other kind of radio promotion. In addition, popular music promotion is the starting place for many newcomers to the field of radio.

THE THEORY OF CONTEST PROMOTION

Radio games and contests provide variation from predictable sound formats. The need for variation is especially important among young listeners who make up the audience for top forty radio. Contemporary music stations, especially those with top forty and similar formats, operate from **hot clocks** that outline the points in each broadcast hour at which each event takes place. Filler copy, news and weather, and on-air promotion might be scheduled as follows:

> :07 *One-liner promoting station*
> :19 *Weather report*
> :22 *Newscast*
> :33 *Promo invitation*

Figure 10-1 Promotion with an Emphasis on Community Identity (*Used with permission.*)

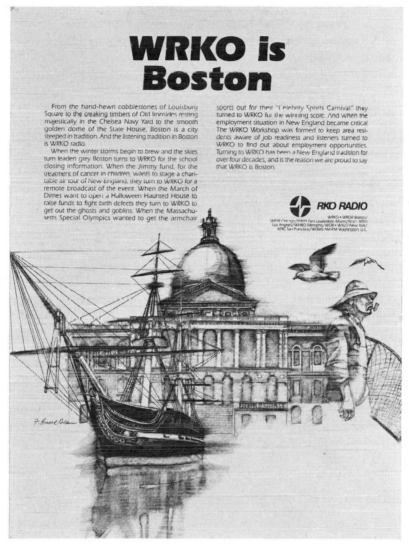

Listeners rapidly figure out such rotations and need something unexpected to catch their attention. On-air promotion fills this need.[2]

On-air games and contests also cater to the American dream of something for nothing. Listening to radio is free; participation in con-

---

[2]Alterations in programming are another way of gaining the audience's attention. Classical and talk stations use programming variations more commonly than do contemporary music stations.

tests costs listeners nothing. And in case of random selection contests, everyone has an equal chance of participating.

In crowded radio markets containing two or more stations with the same format, on-air promotion is a major way of creating identity. Games and contests can create distinct images for otherwise similar stations; to enhance this identification, many games and contests contain station call letters or frequency.

Radio promotion using games and contests also escalates audience ratings. Until the mid-1960s, radio ratings were made in two or four sweeps a year, each lasting four weeks. Stations offering enormous on-air prizes during the key sweep periods could inflate their audiences and, therefore, their ratings. This practice bolstered time sales to agencies that bought time on specific stations to reach particular demographic groups. Once this practice became widespread, Arbitron moved, in the major markets, to a 48-week rating collection period in an effort to halt it. Arbitron also attempted to develop more effective and unbiased survey techniques. In swift response to these new rating practices, organizations sprang up offering programs of promotional mailings to take maximum advantage of the dates of diary placement.

On-air promotion remains a major strategic tool of radio station decision makers. It is used most effectively by single-format music radio stations because most formatted stations have no identifiable programs to promote. On-air contests and games have become the major elements of audience appeal and station identity.

ON-AIR PROMOTION OF TOP FORTY

Top forty radio is the greatest practitioner of the art of on-air promotion. It uses a series of classic contests in cycles to provide variety without altering song lists. Though playlists vary from station to station, top forty developed on the supposition that familiarity breeds success.

Evolution of Top Forty Promotion

Todd Storz, one of the early giants of radio programming, is said to have stopped in a café during a car trip. He was having a cup of coffee when he was struck by what turned out to be a revolutionary perception. From time to time a customer would stroll over to the jukebox in the corner of the café, insert a coin, and play a record. What Storz noticed was that most of the patrons played the same four or five records over and over. And no one objected! Before 1950 it was supposed that radio stations were successful if they varied their music to avoid repetition, but here, right before Storz's coffee and cruller, the theory of a broad playlist with little repetition was being debunked. So Storz rushed, as the story goes, back to his station and instituted the practice of playing the "top forty" records on the charts.[3] The "forty" evolved because the jukebox of the 1950s had a capacity of forty records. With the institutionalization of top forty playlists, station programming became very restricted. Programmers added few records and maintained constant rotation of the few records they played.

Top forty radio evolved further when Bill Drake burst on the scene about 1960. Drake was a programmer from the Southwest who had great success at Gene Chenault's Fresno station and had moved forward to program the RKO chain of stations, which included such AM powerhouses as KHJ, Los Angeles, KFRC, San Francisco, and WRKO, Boston. Drake altered top forty by shutting up the jocks.[4] His assumption was that music hypnotized the audience and repetition of current hits aided the hypnotic effect. Anything that diminished the frequency or intensity of music acted as a negative element, and negative elements were likely to turn into irritants causing an audience to seek a competitive station.

The ensuing lack of talk between records, combined with frequent rotation of the hits, had another effect. It made top forty stations extremely predictable and bred a generation of disc jockeys trained only to speak time and temperature statistics. The stations needed something to relieve the predictability of top forty and at the same time give the DJs something to talk about. On-air promotion was the solution.

Originally, on-air promotion focused on events being sponsored by top forty stations. The first promotions urged attendance at concert appearances of such artists as The Beach Boys. This type of promotion forges a greater bond between the station and the music it plays. Before the advent of sophisticated research in the mid to late 1960s, programmers in the RKO/Drake axis concluded that top forty audiences did not care about the personal life and tribulations of individual disc jockeys.[5] In consequence, programmers focused on the base product of the station: the music played on the air.

A typical between-the-records rap in the frantic days of 1965 sounded something like this: "It's-4:31-the-Beach-Boys-are-comin'-time-on-KHJ-with-the-Real-Don-Steele"—all delivered in 4 seconds or less. This patter contains all the elements necessary to identify the time, the promotion, the disc jockey's name, and the call letters of the station.

---

[3]Other versions of this story attribute the innovation to another pioneer, Gordon McLendon. See Edd Routt, James B. McGrath, and Fredric A. Weiss, *The Radio Format Conundrum* (New York: Hastings House, 1978), pp. 3–8.

[4]According to Routt, McGrath, and Weiss, *The Radio Format Conundrum*, p. 4, this occurred at KYNO, Fresno, just prior to Drake's consulting work for KHJ in 1965.

[5]Routt, McGrath, and Weiss, *The Radio Format Conundrum*, p. 22.

Secret Promotions

This practice became tiresome, however. Acts in town worth associating with are not always available; concert tickets are valuable call-in rewards, but not always usable; and a sizable segment of the top forty audience does not attend concerts (teens because of inadequate transportation; older people because of noise and inconvenience; and some people simply because they do not like concerts). So the evolution of top forty continued.

Trivia questions asked on the air by DJs as fillers led to the discovery that many listeners were not much interested in the prizes or even in winning something; they simply enjoyed playing games in their cars or heads while listening. This perception gave rise to a whole spate of "secret" promotions—on-air contests in which audiences are challenged to identify a secret or mystery person or place. "The Secret Sound" is a classic contest. It requires the program director to record a sound somewhere in the community. For example, the immortal wooden naval ship of the Revolutionary War, *Old Ironsides*, is berthed at the Chelsea Navy Yard near Boston. Below decks, in an exhibit of the commonplace artifacts of revolutionary war naval service, is a display of shackles and restraints. In 1967, WRKO in Boston recorded the rattle of leg irons aboard the vessel and played this sound with great success.

To aid the audience in solving the mystery, clues are announced hourly; telephone callers are the ideal contestants. By cleverly timing the release of the clues, the station can manipulate the time of the end of the contest (although not the specific contestant). By strategically narrowing the content of the clues, the station can direct listeners toward the correct answer. Thus stations can use their control of the clues to drag out or cut short a contest according to its success with audiences and advertisers.

The secret sound has many offspring. In the "Black Box" contest, a mysterious black box appears in a public place and listeners are challenged to identify its contents in order to win them. In this contest, it is a *place* that needs to be pinpointed rather than a sound. These on-air games become powerful station promotion when they are used to advertise the station's call letters or names of the disc jockeys.

Personality and Call Letter Promotion

Two additional classics take advantage of contests to promote station recognition: "Jock-in-the-Box" and the "Stolen Call Letter." Most members of a radio audience can name one or at most two on-air personalities. The names most readily remembered are those of the station's morning DJ, since he or she is most heavily promoted by the station. To aid other personalities, and to give the DJs a reason to cross-plug their fellow performers, Jock-in-the-Box was born. On-air, the names of all the personalities are placed in an imaginary jack-in-the-box container. The DJ on the the air turns the handle of the box, and a caller has to name which personality will pop up. This game has at least four purposes: identification of the DJs by name; encouragement of cross-plugging among DJs; prizes for contestants; and fun even for listeners not interested in winning. Jock-in-the-Box meets these requirements successfully and was enormously popular in the 1960s and 1970s. It led to a host of variations such as car, motorcycle, and swimming races in which the caller had to guess which personality would finish first. The natural hook was the station's tie-in with local events (say stock cars at the fairgrounds), and the station could readily give tickets to nonwinners.

The second of the two classics is the "Stolen Call Letter." This game begins suddenly in a newspaper ad or a sign outside the station that reads for example, KFC instead of KFRC. The idea is that someone has stolen the R from the station's call letters. In this example from 1970, listeners had to discover that the R had been secreted in the R of Presidio (near San Francisco where KFRC is located).[6]

Once program and promotion directors began to strain for variations on these contests, radio found a whole new area for invention: television. Until about 1960, radio did not acknowledge that television existed. After all, it had been the executioner of network entertainment radio.[7] But by the 1960s the wounds had healed and radio *needed* television as a source of material.

A new genre of on-air promotions evolved using contests based on hit television shows such as *Laugh-In*, *Star Trek*, *Bonanza*, and *Columbo*. Because popular radio recognized that their audiences also watched the top-rated television shows, this cross-fertilization was immensely successful through the 1960s and early 1970s. But it was this interrelationship that eventually led to the darkest days of on-air promotion—typified by the "Rip-Off" game.

Rip-Off Games

The rip-off-the-station strategy is often credited to Buzz Bennett, erratic but brilliant programmer of the cosmic school.[8] Bennett decided that his listeners did not want to listen for clues, and his station did not have to maintain continuous listenership to be a ratings winner. He

---

[6]This promotion was also used in Boston by WRKO in 1973.
[7]It was in 1951 that television's terrible swift sword cut off the head of network radio.
[8]Bennett and the "cosmic" sound prevailed on KUPD, Phoenix, in 1971.

therefore devised the instant winner game—without clues, without an-swers, without fun—based solely on greed. He advocated *buying* lis-teners with big cash prizes won instantly just by calling in and winning.[9] The DJ rap now changed to "If you are the seventh caller on 599-9999, you win $100."

No longer was there a need to invent new games. Gone was the clever association with local communities, specific audiences, and local interests. Stations throughout the 1970s vied to see which could give away the most money the fastest. And the ratings on the stations run-ning these promotions were surprisingly high.

Since these promotions are primarily teen-oriented, stations using them acquire the "teeny-bopper" label, irrespective of the type of rock music they play. Moreover, this type of giveaway has a lasting effect on a station's image. Most stations that have been labeled "rip-offs" have trouble changing that image. Nevertheless, this type of on-air activity can be accomplished very rapidly; there is no contestant to deal with, no sound to play, no time to wait for a guess. The DJ just gives out the invitation to call and the prize. Many promotion managers consider this practice fast, clean, and tight, but many listeners consider it unsa-vory. They object to the "rip off the station" implications and often reject stations that engage in this promotion.

Ratings Hype Strategy

Another discovery came at about the time the rip-off syndrome peaked: The era of continuous promotion was over. In the 1960s, on-air pro-motions ran fifty-two weeks a year. Stations became so adept at man-aging secret sound contests that they could predict a contest's end to the day with astonishing accuracy. But by the early 1970s, rests between promotions sometimes permitted a gap of two or three weeks. Man-agement was startled to find no decline in listenership reflected in the ratings. After six years of constant on-air promotion on top forty radio (1965 to 1971), the time for a rest had arrived.

The 1970s signaled the frantic diary stage of commercial radio devel-opment. On-air promotion shifted toward elevating ratings. Since most markets are rated two or four times a year (six times in the major mar-kets) for a maximum of sixteen weeks, top forty stations began concen-trating their promotion during those rating weeks in the early 1970s. This concentration caused a dramatic increase in the size of prizes, since dividing the same total number of dollars among fewer giveaways results in larger amounts per game.

[9]KUPD, Phoenix, 1971.

Audience Flow Strategy

As a result of increased audience research in the 1970s, audience flow strategy surfaced in radio also. Programmers began looking for ways to recycle their audiences. They wanted 6 to 10 pm listeners to tune in at 7 am in order to build morning drive audiences for advertisers. Several means to this end are especially suited to top forty radio.

One is to give away expensive tickets to sold-out concerts—for example, to the Rolling Stones or Wings. It is common practice for DJs to read a seat and row number on the air at 8:06 pm and tell listeners that the morning personality will take a call at 7:06 am. The first caller to correctly name the row and seat number given out the night before wins. The strategy carries the night listener into the following morning's audience.

One objective of flow strategy is to get listeners to cross two quarter hours while staying tuned to one station. This flow increases average quarter-hour ratings and makes the station a more attractive commodity in the marketplace.

THE FUTURE OF TOP FORTY PROMOTION

In the 1980s, the most innovative promotional device for radio is direct mail. This strategy was inspired by the Publishers' Clearinghouse idea. This company has been highly successful using sweepstakes mailings to the general public. The possibility of winning a prize with little effort causes many people to open and read their junk mail.

Direct-Mail Contests

As used by commercial radio, the direct-mail contest involves a print brochure outlining a set of prizes appealing to the dominant demographic group in the industry (in 1980, the 25 to 44 group). Typical prizes are groceries for a year, rent or mortgage payments for a year, the car most coveted by the audience, food, cash, and stereo equipment.[10]

Each brochure contains several potentially winning tickets, numbered for identification. The brochures are mailed to the zip codes in which listenership is strongest and to zip codes that the originating station shares with key competitors. These brochures are intended to saturate the homes of real and potential listeners in the appropriate geographical areas.

---

[10]Stations often ask listeners to send in postcards indicating their most favored prizes, and these items turn up repeatedly, especially during "Christmas Wish" promotions. Studies by The Research Group in San Luis Obispo substantiate the items listed here as "most desired prizes."

Listeners are then asked on-air to watch for their winning ticket brochure. Listeners who do not receive a brochure in the mail are encouraged to call the station and have it mailed to their home. (The requested brochures have the advantage of going to self-identified listeners and create strong response during the on-air solicitation phase of the contest.) When the winning numbers are read on the air, listeners have 60 minutes to call and identify themselves and claim their prize.

Other media are especially useful for exciting interest in this type of contest. Billboards, newspaper ads, and television can be used singly or in combination, depending on the station's budget. Although direct mail is very expensive and has a low rate of return, for top forty radio it is highly effective compared to other on-air promotions.

Toward the 1990s

The future of radio promotion is tied to the extended measurement techniques of the rating services. Radio is being measured in the top 100 markets on a 48-week-a-year basis (starting in 1980) instead of 16 weeks as in the preceding twenty years. The 48-week ratings are designed to remedy the industry practice of hypoing in order to elevate station ratings during Arbitron diary periods. Extended measurement means that top forty, all-news, talk, beautiful music, and classical stations will now have to depend on program/format marketing.

Although extended rating measurement is still in its infancy, promotion and programming experts in the industry are already seeking ways to exploit the situation. Several strategies are certain: Giant on-air activities such as "Cash Call" will remain popular because they demand slow movement and can be sustained for a long time.[11] (Small amounts of prize money can be added, and the program director retains complete control over the jackpot total.) Entertaining games with clues will return along with low-reward, high-energy promotion recycling the audience. Audience flow strategies will be resurrected.

PRIZE STRUCTURES AND SCHEDULES

All on-air promotions should have consolation prizes. Listeners want to *feel* like winners, even if they are not. The consolation prize can be of nominal value and should relate to the contest itself. Record albums, concert tickets, film screenings, T-shirts, six packs of a soft drink—all have proved successful.

---

[11]In the Cash Call game, listeners are required to know a growing jackpot amount in order to win when they are telephoned by the station.

Prizes

There is a risk-versus-reward ratio involved in "mystery" promotions. Since they are rather trivial and more fun to play than win, the prize need not be large. Usually a station starts with $50 or $100 and adds $10 each time an incorrect guess is made. This mounting jackpot gives DJs something to talk about: "Next hour there's $155 in the KHJ Secret Sound Jackpot; listen for your chance to win!"[12]

There is a definite relationship between the difficulty of a contest and the size of the reward in the minds of audience members. A contest requiring listeners to stay up all weekend and list every Beatles record played over a 48-hour period, for example, should have no less of a prize than a $5,000 stereo or its equivalent. On the other hand, listeners have stated that as the prize escalates in worth, they lose faith in their ability to win. In certain cases there is a perceptual problem with prize structure. A New York study discovered that the audience of a certain station could not really differentiate between $1,000 and $10,000.[13]

This problem leads to an anomaly: A station may be overpricing its market in its contest reward structure. In 1971, WXLO offered a Mercedes-Benz automobile as a prize but received only a mediocre level of response. The station had neglected to uncover the fact that the most wanted car in its market was the Corvette. Right idea, wrong prize!

Schedules

On-air contests always run on weekdays and typically last ten to fourteen days. Weekends are devoted to music specials like "all Beatles" records. The classic on-air contest has four steps: (1) tease on-air for three days (Friday, Saturday, Sunday) while the music promotion is in effect; (2) start the contest on-air Monday at 6 am and run it until midnight; (3) have a winner the following Wednesday; (4) play congratulational promos with the winner until Friday, and then start the process all over again.

THE MECHANICS OF PROMOTION

There are four basic techniques of on-air promotion: the listener calls the station; the station calls the listener; the listener mails to the station;

---

[12]Used by KHJ in 1971.

[13]WXLO study in conjunction with The Research Group, San Luis Obispo, California. As a side note, it should be pointed out that the IRS requires all prizes of $600 or more to be reported by the broadcaster on Form 1099 Misc., "Statement for Recipients of Miscellaneous Income."

or the station mails to the listener. Variations on these themes have been legislated away. The "Treasure Hunt" concept, for example, current in the 1960s, had both amusing and malevolent sides. A station claimed to have hidden a prize of great value (the keys to a new car) in a secret but public place. Clues were announced on-air, and the first person to discover the keys won the car.

The potential for misuse soon became clear, however. One station directed its audience to City Hall because the local mayor had been an outspoken critic of top forty radio.[14] When hordes of angry listeners tried to dismantle his desk to find the keys, there was a riot. Although the station claimed the audience was really misinterpreting the clues, its case was never proved.

Another pitfall of this type of promotion is that unscrupulous operators may not bury the prize until the final days of the promotion— reasoning that an early winner would waste a rating period hype. Disruptive contest activities have been strongly discouraged by the Federal Communications Commission since 1966.[15]

Telephone Traps and Techniques

A telephone promotion can overload local circuits and cause a phone blackout that puts whole exchanges out of commission. In certain major cities this problem has been resolved by the installation of high-volume exchanges such as 520 in Los Angeles. Small-market stations with innovation in mind would be well advised to consult locally.

Some stations tried installing automatic answering services in their switchboards to notify callers that they were not winners.[16] Station management thought they were providing a service to callers, but in fact these installations cause callers to be charged for a completed call on every dialing. Imagine the shock to a parent in Massachusetts on receiving a $75 telephone bill for phone calls to WRKO in Boston for contest calls that only reached a recording.

The advantages of telephone call-in promotions are numerous. Since the respondent is there "live" and is always a potential winner, the DJ gets material for on-air promotional announcements, and the station gets the voices of actual listeners on the air. If, for example, a station is aiming for a slightly older audience to appeal to advertisers, it should strive for on-air contestants in the highly prized 25 to 34 demographic

---

[14]WITH, Baltimore, 1962.
[15]Contests and Promotions Which Adversely Affect the Public Interest, 2 F.C.C. 2d 464 (1966).
[16]Stations such as WXLD, New York, began using automatic answering equipment in 1977.

group. For listeners and advertisers, the on-air contestant provides an image of the station's audience, whatever the rating books may say.[17]

Call-out contests pose other problems. The telephone numbers for call-outs are picked at random from telephone directories. If the top-rated station in a market has a 6 percent share of the market, a not unusual number due to segmentation, it means that only 6 percent of radio listeners in that time period (not of the total population) are listening to that station.[18] Placing a random call that reaches a listener belonging to the small universe of listeners to a particular station is difficult. Compounding the difficulty by expecting the recipient of the call to know the jackpot amount or a secret phrase makes the contest almost impossible to win. From the station's perspective, this practice translates into having very few winners over a very long period of time.

To overcome the disadvantages of using a telephone directory, many stations request listeners with unlisted numbers to send them in so that they can be included in the mix of eligible contestants. When there is a lull in the audience's response rate, the station can then call numbers from the unlisted category—resulting in a much greater chance of winner response since the station knows they listen. This practice, however, alters the randomness of the winner selection process.

Station Mail-Ins

Contests requiring listeners to mail postcards to a station have been known to incur the wrath of the postal authorities: Stations often neglected to give their zip codes during the 1960s, causing great sorting and delivery problems. After 1970, moreover, stations had to react to the fact that cancellations on postcards, the most common form of evaluating mail response, no longer included the time of cancellation, only the date—which meant that on-air contests could no longer contain the immortal line, "The card with the earliest postmark will be declared the winner." This announcement has since been modified to read, "The card with the earliest postmark will be the winner, *and* in case of du-

---

[17]The telephone had an interesting ramification during the 1950s when rating services used telephone interviewing as their prime information source. The "Don't say hello" technique of on-air promotion required listeners to answer their phones with the call letters or slogan of a particular radio station. For example, listeners were encouraged to respond to the ringing of the phone with "99X is my radio station" instead of "hello." If listeners responded in that manner to the station's call, they won $5,000. If the caller was not the radio station but instead a rating service asking what radio station the respondent listened to, listeners had little option but to respond with the call letters of the station they had answered the call with. This practice was prohibited in the periods before and during ratings on the grounds that it influenced ratings.

[18]If 50 percent of all the radios in town are being listened to, only 3 percent are listening to that station.

plicate entries, the winner will be chosen at random from all cards received with identical postmarks."

Another complication arose in the mid-1970s involving a fast-food chain promotion in a midwestern community. The sponsor offered a prize and stated that the winner would be chosen at random from among all entries received. A group of enterprising college students in the community used the school computer to print out some absurd number of entries (about 650,000) on IBM burst sheets and submitted them. Naturally they won, since 90 percent of the entries bore the group's name. Stations then reacted with new rules stating that entries had to be handwritten in order to win.

The method of delivery can also make a difference. It is more or less standard that entries must be "delivered by U.S. mail" in order to be eligible. This stipulation prevents local residents from hand-delivering entries to the station in order to beat the postal service.

Station Mail-Outs

Mail from a station to listeners operates like direct-mail advertising. It is costly but can be narrowly targeted to the desired audience. Although the typical rate of return is only 3 to 5 percent, direct-mail pieces can serve more than one purpose. They can introduce new personalities, for example, or include posters, stickers, bumper strips, or a contest brochure with winning tickets. New sorting and bulk mailing regulations have reduced the postage rates, but the cost-versus-return rate is unlikely to become equitable in the immediate future since the variables (paper, printing, design, folding, stuffing, posting, and handling) are subject to 10 to 12 percent inflation.

ON-AIR PROMOTION FOR OTHER MUSIC FORMATS

Promotional tactics should be tailored. One can design the prize structure, the entry technique, the method of on-air presentation, and the payoff to fit the psychographics of the intended audience.

KHJ in Los Angeles shifted to a country format after fifteen years as a top forty station. To reinforce its new cowboy image, it asked listeners to call in and tell, on the air, "what makes a cowboy a cowboy." To complement this promotion, the station ran television spots and posted billboards containing the positioning statement, "We all grew up to be cowboys." Since KHJ's format appeals to a broad spectrum of the middle class with a traditional accent on blue-collar workers,[19] the prize

---

[19]One of the big fads of 1981 involved the cowboy image as a result of movies and songs like *Urban Cowboy.*

structure included such items as free groceries for a month, mortgage or rent payments up to $1,000, and $25 in gift certificates at a fast-food chain.

WGMS AM/FM in Washington is a classical music station that has an annual celebration surrounding Beethoven's birthday in December. In years gone by, in cooperation with a host of sponsors, the station printed a crossword puzzle and invited listeners to fill it in. Then they picked at random, from all the correct entries, a winner who was sent on a trip to the Bayreuth Ring Festival. They have also had trivia quizzes based on the same celebration. Classical music stations rarely exhibit consistency in on-air promotion of this type, however, and therefore have not established distinct promotional philosophies.

ON-AIR PROMOTION FOR INFORMATION RADIO

Talk and all-news stations have occasionally tried on-air promotion with games or contests as a programming tool but with limited success. Information radio capitalizes on the "promo event" (generally a public service activity) and encourages community participation. KABC and WOR provide several illustrations.

KABC, a major talk station in Los Angeles, has over the years exemplified the participation type of promotion. In fact, the station has even married people in its parking lot after soliciting couples on air as part of its early morning team's "5 O'clock Club" activities. KABC has sent a couple on a yacht race to Ensenada, Mexico, and on a trip for two to Hawaii for a second honeymoon. These promotions are based on random selection of postcards or selection of letters that best explain why couples want a second honeymoon. Such promotional activities encourage participation and strengthen the station's image but they do little to enhance the quarter-hour ratings.

Information radio and certain music stations tend to associate on-air promotion with top forty formats and shy away from it. Some program directors are quick to point out that their stations "don't believe in on-air promotion and contests." They claim that these activities are "rock and rollish" and appeal only to juvenile audiences. They are not entirely correct. The desire for something for nothing tends to be universally distributed.[20]

WOR in New York, for example, has played a birthday game in which listeners are invited to send in postcards giving their date of birth. The station then selects a card corresponding to the numbers

---

[20]Organizations such as Exxon, *Reader's Digest,* and McDonald's rely heavily on on-air promotional contests using radio as a prime medium for exposure.

generated by randomly rotating a wheel. The card contains the telephone number of the listener who submitted it. The winner is announced on the air and awarded a specified amount of money ($100 to $500). If the person announced, or a member of his or her immediate family, calls in quickly (generally within 30 or 60 minutes), the prize escalates to $1,000. The number of entries at WOR has been incredible (Figure 10-2). The problem with this promotion, however, is that it does not require listening to win. Moreover, the named person need not respond; a family member may do so and win the larger prize. If the object of on-air promotion is to enhance quarter-hour listenership, this promotion fails to meet the challenge.

COOPERATIVE PROMOTION

Promotion need not be a high-budget item. Station managers frequently complain that they cannot sustain an expensive contest budget. One problem is that radio promotion budgets cannot be formulated mathematically. There is no set procedure for basing the promotion budget on a percentage of profits, billings, or the company's market

Figure 10-2 WOR Birthday Entries (*Used with permission.*)

position.[21] The promotion budget is one of the few expenditures in a radio station that management can freeze in case of a bottom-line crisis. Promotion's flexibility may contribute to management's complaints about costs.

These complaints are compounded by a common lack of understanding of (1) contest prize structure, (2) the most effective means for transmitting contest rules to audiences, and (3) the escalating costs of cross-media buys. In mid-size and major markets, however, the beneficial effects of successful on-air promotion on station ratings have been all too evident.

Cooperative promoting is an effective budget-saver. Record companies are especially eager to promote locally appearing groups and artists on the air. Stations can arrange associations with the record companies based on the words of a song or the theme of an artist that can work for the benefit of both at minimal cost. A record like "Escape" by Rupert Holmes lends itself to an on-air promotion in which a pair of listeners win an escape to a glamorous vacation spot. In cooperative arrangements, the record company usually provides the prize and any additional costs (such as for direct-mail brochures). Listeners do not care who actually pays for this kind of promotion.

Detailed coordination between station and supplier ensures that all the fine points of the arrangement are carefully spelled out in advance so that neither party gets shortchanged. It is wise to start small in order to test the ability of the cooperating company to fulfill its commitment before initiating big events that could embarrass the station. Although winners may not remember that the prizes they won really came from a shoe store, they do know which radio station they won them on. And they will lay any blame at the station's door.

Sale orders for spots often accompany cooperative promotions, but advertising sales should not be the sole criterion for the promotion. Above all, the promotion should fit the station's desired audience profile and enliven its programming.

COMMUNITY SERVICE BENEFITS

Another aspect of on-air promotion on radio is its role in public service. The March of Dimes has reaped millions of dollars with its walking campaigns. For these walks, jogs, or runs around a city on a prescribed course, local sponsors of individuals and groups donate so many cents

[21]Chapter 4 presents a systematic approach to television station budgets that can be applied to radio.

per mile to the charity. There are two obvious benefits of this type of on-air activity: It associates a station with a well-known public service agency, and it draws attention to a display of listener strength. If 25,000 people come out on a drizzly, cold morning in April to march 10 miles around New York for WXLO's Superwalk, raising $300,000 for March of Dimes research, WXLO gets valuable publicity in addition to having a dramatic story to tell on-air and to potential sales clients.[22]

The cost to the station is minimal because most large public agencies have staffs and volunteers eager to participate. Although it is not unusual for stations to take their expenses off the top of the proceeds and donate the remaining sum to the charity in question, superior benefits accrue to the station from being able to say, for example, "Every cent gathered by WXLO listeners in Saturday's Superwalk will go to the March of Dimes research efforts to conquer birth defects." Suspicion surrounds telethons and other fundraising events; stations that cover some expenses will gain a brighter image with the public, advertisers, and local government. If budgetary considerations make this impossible, it should be possible to find a cooperative sponsor who will pick up the station's expenses. Another alternative is to state on-air that "X percent of every dollar raised goes to . . . ," reminding the audience that any money raised is money that the charity did not get before the promotion.

Recent interest in jogging and running has stimulated a flood of events. Hardly a day went by between 1975 and 1980 without a 10-kilometer run somewhere for something sponsored by a broadcasting station and a host of shoe manufacturers or food products to benefit some group. For the station, community service promotions can do good, result in sales, and not cost much.

THE RADIO PROMOTION MANAGER

The role of promotion managers is changing in contemporary radio. Many who have taken on the job in recent years have research and marketing backgrounds. Although their professional training has increased the quality and sophistication of promotion at mid-size and small-market stations, the mix of promotion managers needs to be leavened with graduates of artistic and communications disciplines if radio is to respond adequately to the creative challenges ahead.

The new improved promotion manager will examine newspapers and television news to convert current events into happenings for sta-

---

[22]According to general manager Erica Farber, the figures for WXLO's Superwalk went up annually from 1975 to 1978. KFRC, San Francisco, raised over $1,500,000 in their Superwalk for the March of Dimes in 1980.

tions that will excite and invite listeners. Promotion successes in the 1980s will go to descendants of the old Hollywood press agent and the check-suited snake-oil salesmen. Those who cringe at these labels are unlikely to be successful at promotion.

Research is vital, too, but it functions best to confirm strategy, not create it. A well-known research company sends its client stations their raw information in booklets that include the company's recommendations suggested by the data. Station managers, sales, promotion, and program managers typically go directly to the recommendations to see if a viable solution has been suggested to the problem that instigated the research in the first place. This practice forestalls creative solutions, eliminates skeptical examination of the raw data, and undermines the relationship among members of a management team. It would be better if the research company sent only the raw data for the station's analysis and then later, under separate cover, forwarded its recommendations. In the meantime, the station management could formulate its own solutions and then compare the two sets of conclusions. The results might be identical, but bright solutions would gain a chance to be articulated. In the current system it seems as if layers and layers of consultants extract the vital choices from client stations, resulting in parasitic relationships that may ultimately be fatal to many stations and staff members.

Promotion managers can play a role in expanding thinking at stations—not only about promotion activities, but about the station's image, its market position, and its relationship to competitors. On the everyday level, though, the role of promotion is to astonish, confound, and amaze.

THE TREND IN RADIO PROMOTION

On-air contests and promotion seem to be taking a back seat to the magic of the word *marketing*. Stations are embracing marketing strategies and veering away from contest techniques. The love affair between radio and television advertising is beginning to devour promotional budgets. In fact, some industry experts suggest that as much as 50 percent of the radio promotion budget should go to television spots.[23] The attraction of television is based on the desire to see advertising and promotional efforts in less ephemeral form than radio sounds. Radio station managers want to see their stations on the television screen as if there were a certain magic to video advertising. This can be an ex-

---

[23]Suggested by Jene Norris of WCOZ (FM) in Boston on a Broadcasters Promotion Association panel in 1980 (*Broadcasting*, 1 September 1980, p. 30).

traordinarily expensive trap—and sometimes, due to specific spot schedules and air times, it is less than effective. Radio is one of the most creative and effective media and is, as Joe Singer once said, the only medium where "not seeing is believing."

SUMMARY

This chapter traces commercial on-air radio promotion from its beginnings in the 1950s, through the era of continuous games and contests in the 1960s, through the period of sporadic promotions to hype the ratings characterizing the 1970s, to radio's cyclical return in the 1980s to ongoing games that invite the audience's participation. The strategy of the 1980s will see small contest prizes and amusing games along with application of sophisticated audience flow research. These practices will affect, in varying measures, top forty, album-oriented rock, talk, all-news, beautiful music, and classical stations. The costs of on-air television spots loom as an immediate threat to radio promotion budgets, but consistent, year-round on-air radio contest promotion remains the most effective promotional strategy for popular music radio.

Public Station Promotion

by
David L. Crippens

David L. Crippens became station manager for KCET-TV in Los Angeles in 1980, also retaining his position as vice-president of educational services for the station. Before coming to KCET in 1973, he was a producer for WQED-TV in Pittsburgh (1971–1973) and KPBS-TV in San Diego (1969–1971). He holds a B.A. from Antioch College in Ohio (1964) and an M.S.W. from San Diego State University. He received a Corporation for Public Broadcasting Fellowship in 1969. In addition to numerous on-air and producing credits, he has published articles in Variety, Education Broadcasting Review, *and other periodicals. He currently serves on the PBS Transponder Allocation Committee, the California State Instructional Television Advisory Committee, and the California Council for the Humanities. Among his media honors are the 1978 Minority Telecommunications Award from the National Association of Broadcasters and a 1975 Recognition Award for Service from the San Diego Chapter of the NAACP. Rae Amey of KCET-TV provided editorial assistance on this chapter.*

Promotion and marketing are becoming increasingly important for the survival of public television. Hit with declining federal financial support and the growth of alternative media such as cable and subscription television, public stations who want to stay in business in the 1980s are scrambling to meet a multitude of challenges. Public stations, more and more, are looking to their audiences to provide the support base that will enable survival.

Competition from alternative media and a growing challenge from commercial stations have forced public stations to reexamine their established modes of building an audience for programs and to expand their methods of fundraising from the public. A circular dictum operates in public television: Without an audience there can be no support or money; and without support or money, there can be no audience. Consequently, promotion becomes an integral part of public television's overall strategy. However, the details of strategies vary for large-market stations and small-market stations and vary also between public radio and public television.

PROGRAMMING AND PROMOTION

Before 1979, promotion at public stations was a catch-as-catch-can prop-osition. It tended to be sporadic rather than consistent, program ori-ented rather than image promoting, low budget rather than high priority, even at the major market stations. In 1979, however, after pres-sure from the president of the Public Broadcasting Service, Lawrence Grossman, among others, major public stations began devising active strategies to counterprogram competing commercial television stations in order to maintain and even build public television audiences.[1]

The pivotal event was an agreement by public stations in the major markets to carry PBS's **"common carriage schedule"** (**core schedule**) during primetime from Sundays to Wednesdays. This practice began in the fall of 1979 and has since raised public television audience levels by 30 percent.[2] To support this consistent programming in the evenings, extensive advertising and promotional campaigns have been built around the core programs at major market stations.

In 1980, major stations began acquiring programming outside of PBS in large quantities for the first time. The amount and quality of pro-gramming available through PBS did not satisfy audience demands for high-quality primetime entertainment in sufficient numbers, and the stations sought visibility to attract new audiences by programming more general entertainment programs. For example, the kinescope of *Requiem for a Heavyweight* and other programs such as *All Creatures Great and Small* came from the Interregional Programming Service (IPS). Al-though these programs did not garner ratings numbers adequate for commercial stations in most markets, they usually did very well for public television. In the Los Angeles market, *Requiem for a Heavyweight* gained a rating of 2.8 and a share of 5.4 in a one-evening showing.[3] The role of promotion for such programs was simply to let the public know about them and to state that PBS presents programs that are clearly alternatives to commercial station programming.

The image promotion of individual public stations has often been limited to the locally produced pledge and auction campaigns. Unfor-tunately, this image of the stations always "begging for donations" is a negative one. During regular programming periods, moreover, the

---

[1]Lawrence Grossman entered public television from commercial broadcasting and advertising: "My whole theory when I left NBC was to use the skills and experience and techniques that I had learned in the commercial marketplace—advertising, promotion and marketing—and make them available to the public sector." (David Crook, "Public TV: Ivory Tower or Bunker?", *Los Angeles Times*, 10 February 1981.)

[2]Dale M. Rhodes and Kenneth R. Wirt, *An Evaluation of the Common Carriage Experience* (Washington, D.C.: Public Broadcasting Service, 1980).

[3]Nielsen ratings, Thursday, 21 August 1980 (9 pm to 10:45 pm).

station breaks between programs have in the past often consisted merely of a logo slide with background music. New emphasis on promotion and marketing has spurred stations to reevaluate their images. KCET-TV in Los Angeles is a telling case study.

In early 1980, KCET-TV took a survey among its staff members seeking collective thoughts on the station's on-air image. Staff members were assigned different nights for viewing the station between 7 pm and midnight and were asked to comment on the following points:

- What image or look does KCET project?
- What is the "feel" of the station?
- What are your comments on the logo and station breaks?
- Is the programming flow effective?
- What audiences do you think KCET is reaching?

The responses were amazingly similar: Like many public stations, KCET was projecting a sluggish, passive image during the station breaks, despite excellent PBS programming. Furthermore, the flow of programming seemed to lack considered planning. Staff complaints included the following:

- Station breaks, consisting of merely the predictable logo slide with a classical music background, were wasted time. Why were there no spots promoting and previewing upcoming programs?
- The logo slide itself was considered uninspiring.
- The locally produced news program, *28 Tonight*, was considered a major disappointment. Its set was uninteresting, and its interviewers were not hard hitting, even when most issues demanded punch.
- KCET did not have enough local productions on the air, which promoted the feeling that the station was a mere distributor of programming, not a producer.

Since this study, changes subtle and not so subtle have resulted in an improved image for KCET. Specifically, local production has increased and is drawing on Los Angeles' most noteworthy resource, the entertainment industry. Moreover, the logo was redesigned. A variety of slides are now used during station breaks (Figure 11-1), and promotional spots for upcoming programs are aired regularly (Figure 11-2). The news program, *28 Tonight*, was revamped and reinstated as *Newsbeat* (Figure 11-3). More attention is now directed to sets for local productions, whether they are public affairs interviews or entertainment specials aired during pledge weeks.

Figure 11-1 KCET's Logos (*Used with permission.*)

PROMOTIONAL BUDGETS

Public television budgets for promotion usually have three elements: print advertising, on-air promotion, and radio promotion. In the allocation of promotion budgets, public stations are virtually identical to commercial stations.

Print Advertising

Major public broadcasters expend approximately 5 percent of their budgets for promoting and publicizing scheduled programming. The average major public station has ten to twenty employees working on program promotion and advertising. In addition, PBS and the national underwriters promote individual shows. Recent increases indicate that public stations have come to understand that in an increasingly fractionalized and competitive market, viewers have to be told when a given program will air and what to expect by way of content.

An example of changes in management's attitude toward promotion is exhibited by alterations in budget divisions at major public television stations. Until 1978, KCET in Los Angeles spent 80 percent of its pro-

Figure 11-2 KCET's Program Promotion On-Air (*Used with permission.*)

motion dollars advertising in daily newspapers. Although newspaper advertising continues, a larger percentage of promotional dollars has been targeted for specific media possessing the specific demographics of the intended audience for a given program. This strategy has proved effective for KCET since many of its programs are designed especially for children, minorities, cultural devotees, or public affairs enthusiasts.

Figure 11-3 KCET's News Slides: Old and New (*Used with permission.*)

Old

New

In addition to acquiring paid advertisements, community newspapers and weeklies are usually eager for background information on public television programs. Therefore, major stations use them as free media for promoting program schedules. Since public television fare tends to be targeted for specific rather than for general audiences (unlike commercial network entertainment), local periodicals can take station press releases and fit them to their readerships.

Smaller public stations are similarly targeting their print advertising. In many instances, they are better able than major stations to take advantage of free advertising because of the smaller size of their markets.

On-Air Program Promotion

Many in the business have traditionally viewed on-air promotion as too commercial. Stations skimped and showed slides, as did KCET in the case study, played music, or aired a ticking clock. This attitude is changing for both small and large public stations because of pressure to remind the "faithful" of upcoming programs and demonstrate the quality of offerings to the "daily switchers." Figure 11-4 shows an outstanding example of on-air promotion by KQED-TV in San Francisco.

On-air promotion is the one mode that quickly and concretely demonstrates to viewers the wide diversity of programs—from children's programs to high culture—that can be seen in a day on a public channel. The public television audience does not turn to a public channel and keep the dial there; they are quite selective and tune in and out.

Figure 11-4 KQED-TV's On-Air Illustration for *Crossroads* (© *KQEDesign, 1981. Used with permission.*)

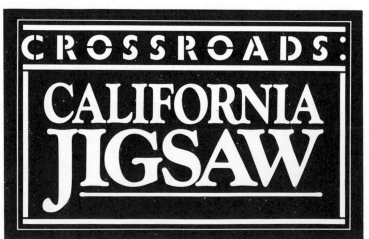

PBS audience figures suggest that the typical viewer watches a public station an average of 1 to 2 hours a week.[4]

On-air promotion at many stations is becoming slicker, more informative, and targeted to demonstrating the difference between the public station and its competition. Most station effort is now directed toward the 6 to 11 pm hours. Promotional budgets at large and small stations have increased by 25 percent in the last two years, and more money is likely to be spent in the next few years.

Radio Promotion for Public Television

The name of the game is targeting. Radio is beginning to take a more prominent role in public television's pursuit of specialized audiences. In Los Angeles, there are eighty-three radio stations ranging in format from all-news to jazz. Each station has carefully defined its listeners and actively seeks drivetime audiences. These attributes are especially useful to public television stations. Since the late 1970s, in fact, commercial radio has been considered an essential element in public television's major advertising campaigns.

KCET, for example, has deliberately set out to promote programming on radio stations with demographics similar to those of specific KCET television programs. News programs are promoted on all-news radio stations, and big band jazz on a "big band and blues" radio station. Since smaller public television stations usually have fewer radio stations in their markets, the same demographic advantage from utilizing radio does not necessarily accrue.

COMMUNITY SUPPORT

Major public television stations raise more than 30 percent of their budgets from their viewing publics. KCET in Los Angeles raised $4.5 million from audience subscriptions in 1980. An average of $40 was paid by 150,000 people to support basic operations in response to major station fundraising activities. At KCET, this fundraising consisted of two on-air pledge drives during 1980, one special emergency appeal, and an on-air auction that raised $500,000 from bids on items ranging from paintings to cars.[5]

---

[4]*National Audience Estimates for the Period September 29 Through October 5, 1980.* PBS Research Department, 1 December 1980.
[5]In the fall, after the August pledge, KCET conducted an emergency appeal campaign to cope with an increasing deficit. The appeal consisted of on-air spots asking for support by various members of management in conjunction with a mass mail campaign to subscribers. The response was overwhelming; in consequence, management canceled the December pledge and for a month ran special thank you spots featuring talents such as Rod Steiger, Hal Linden, and John Houseman.

Fundraising Strategies

Raising money from the public is a hard job under the best conditions, and it is becoming harder under conditions less than optimal. Until 1976, there was little competition from major-market commercial stations in on-air fundraising. Only four fundraisers a year for needy causes were conducted by commercial television stations in the Los Angeles market. In 1980, there were twelve. In New York and Chicago, the numbers are similar. Moreover, subscription and cable television are capable of siphoning off fundraising viewers. All of this translates into lost revenues for public television.

In California, Proposition 13 effectively cut back money to both governmental and nonprofit institutions in 1978. More organizations in the state are competing for less public money. In other states new competition affects public television because stations have to fight for a fixed quantity of dollars with a greater number of groups and organizations. Creating the identity of an alternative community institution (whether the station is community, public school, university, or state licensed) becomes increasingly important to staying in business.

Pledge Drives

Despite these depressing facts, on-air contributions have increased dramatically over the past two years for most major public television stations. A good part of the credit at most stations must go to effective promotion. The typical large station holds three pledge drives a year. The average pledge period lasts ten days and includes two weekends. Ideally, pitches begin after 6 pm and occur before and after every program until approximately 11 pm. During this time, the public phones volunteer telephone operators on a "hot" stage (before live television cameras), and each caller pledges a minimum of $20 or $30.[6]

The programs aired during a pledge must be selected carefully to meet two criteria: (1) to demonstrate why the audience should watch *public* television and (2) to show that this station's programming, which is not available on commercial outlets, deserves financial support. Many stations use charts and tape clips to show the importance of the local station and why it deserves financial support. Audiences are constantly reminded that a program such as *MacNeil/Lehrer* is not available on any commercial station and appears on public television daily. The station's message goes something like this: "Yet *MacNeil/Lehrer* costs

---

[6]Smaller amounts are accepted but usually do not entitle contributors to premiums or membership. Pledge amounts commonly range as high as $100 or $200 when special premiums are offered, but the role of premiums in fundraising is not clear and currently being studied by PBS.

money, some $118,000 for KCET in 1980. Very little on public television is free. You, the viewer, are our major source of financial support."

Pledge commitments made for specific programs indicate what the local public will support financially. Generally, the best-supported programs are music, drama, and general interest, in that order. There are wide differences according to geographical location, however. Rural audiences do not necessarily support the same programs as urban viewers. Although *MacNeil/Lehrer* and *National Geographic* have garnered sizable pledge dollars nationally, these are broad-appeal programs. The majority of programs on public television appeal to more specialized audiences; in consequence, targeting specific audience segments is a central part of planning a pledge to enlarge all audiences. Women outnumber men in viewing programs such as *Dick Cavett*, *Great Performances*, and *Julia Child*; the ratio of men viewers is higher for *Nova*, *Star Soccer*, and *The Advocates*. Other programs are targeted at specific age groups. For example, adults over 50 years view *Wall Street Week* and *Washington Week in Review* more than younger adults, and the opposite is true for *Yoga for Health* and *Visions*.[7]

Effective pledge strategy also requires an overall theme for each ten-day drive in order to focus the promotional campaign. A theme is usually chosen for its relationship to the individual programs the station intends to carry and its promotional value.

Programming and fundraising staffs must work closely in choosing the programs for the pledge period as well as in writing the pledge copy. A unified effort is essential for a pledge drive to work. (A style sheet covering copy for pledge-drive breaks appears later in this chapter.) Stations can also integrate their monthly television guide covers into the pledge theme, gaining additional promotional value.

KCET's August 1980 pledge was planned around the theme "Heat Wave." The viewers' guide cover picked up the theme, slogans such as "Don't Let Us Cool Off Now" were used in advertising, and the on-air pledge copy played on the same theme. Even balloons were printed with the message. They were brilliant yellow and gold, and the stage for the live performances was lit with dramatic red, yellow, gold, and blue lighting. The live music performances were "hot" (jazz and cabaret). Unfortunately, a week after the first production meeting, after the viewers' guide had been printed, and after correspondence had been sent out under the new logo, the theme was changed. A very real heat wave had hit the country resulting in deaths throughout the South and Midwest. Under the circumstances, management decided to rename the pledge "KCET Belongs to Southern California." Last-minute changes

[7]KCET Subscriber Survey, October 1979.

were made to the copy, and balloons were turned away from the cameras. All in all, the change was made rather gracefully. The set fit either theme.

Between-show air times are instrumental in pledge promotion strategy. These breaks should be written and produced to feature professionals and celebrities extolling the virtues of the public television concept, the programming, and the station.

The concept of community-supported television ("our" television) is essential to the future of public stations and is a prime motivator of viewers in appeals for support. Therefore, the alternatives that PBS offers, as well as local station programs, are essential selling points for potential subscribers. Local professionals and celebrities serve as role models when they become involved and encourage support for "our" community station, "our" alternative to commercial television.

In the availability of locally residing celebrities, large-market stations used to have distinct advantages over small-market stations. The top talent in small communities may be the local newscasters for commercial stations, whereas the top talent in Los Angeles (who are also community members) are national and international figures such as Jack Klugman, Brock Peters, and Steve Allen. This advantage faded in the 1980s, however, as PBS began distributing to all member stations prerecorded spots of celebrities appealing for public television.

Specific break pitches should be written to support the particular program aired in conjunction with the break. Call-in pledges received during a break can be regarded as direct support for the preceding program. For this reason, programming aired during pledges must be chosen very carefully, and on-air appeals can tell viewers about the high cost of the specific programs.

An appeal made by KCET to viewers of *Star Soccer* during its August 1980 pledge illustrates this strategy. This program was in danger of being dropped from the schedule due to increased costs. The situation was explained to soccer fans during a break within *Star Soccer,* and their response was immediate and favorable. As a result, station management decided to make a special effort to retain the program.

Other new approaches to the pledge drive were tried out at KCET in March 1981. Breaks were cut from 15 minutes to between 5 and 6 minutes (shorter than commercial station breaks). Production values were given increased thrust. Pitches were delivered directly from a set without the usual carnival atmosphere. Demographic analysis indicated that this sophisticated approach was especially effective with new subscribers.[8]

---

[8]KCET overshot its goal of $750,000 during this pledge drive by $250,000—a record for the station.

Once a theme has been chosen, the programming, publicity/promotion, and development departments of a station need to support a distinct advertising campaign. Approximately 80 percent of budgeted promotion funds should go to print media advertising; the remaining 20 percent should go to radio. This breakdown is in direct proportion to the sources of information on programming used by viewers. Whatever the market, most viewers check their newspapers and *TV Guide* for television listings, as well as for related feature stories. Although commercial television spots are too expensive to include in a pledge campaign, some commercial stations donate time or review certain pledge week offerings as a public service.

Tradeoffs

Public television stations can also stretch their promotional dollars by trading air time with radio stations. Offering an underwriting credit for a specific show to a local radio station is the usual means of trade. In exchange for a spot commercial—such as "Watch *Superstar* tonight on KCET/28 at 8 pm" or "The best in jazz on KCET"—the radio station gets a mention before and after the show. During its 1980 summer pledge, KCET had underwriting for four programs with three different commercial radio stations. The equivalent value of those spots in dollars was $40,000.

Auctions

Auctions have been a major source of fundraising for big and small public stations for more than a decade. They have, like pledge drives, also been a source of promotion for the tie-in between funding and public television programs. Auctions are much more targeted activities than pledge drives, however. Whereas pledge programs get ratings, auctions usually do not. Only serious "auctionites" watch for 6 hours a night in primetime for seven days. Increasingly, auctions (traditionally held in April, May, or June) are becoming too expensive in terms of personnel and production costs. Moreover, there is a dramatic drop in viewership for at least two months after an auction.

Thus big and small stations are beginning to gear their auctions toward "big ticket" items such as artworks, major appliances, cars, and vacations. The station's return is greater. Promotion in station magazines, print media, and radio should be directed toward the audience members who are willing to pay for these items. Events such as "Art Previews" in New York, San Francisco, Los Angeles, and Chicago are held in those cities' public television stations so that prospective bidders can preview the artwork to be auctioned. Since these events bring out the people who are normally shown on society pages, other media coverage is assured.

WRITING BREAK COPY

This section presents a guide to structuring and writing **break copy**.[9] Some of the principles apply to auction continuity, but most deal with program promotion. These principles can be most useful in suggesting directions; strict adherence to a formula is not intended. The contents fall into three categories: structure, content, and approach.

Structure: The Skeleton

The *program* is the major source of content inserts. Breaks should illustrate and evoke the program without breaking the mood. The viewer's motivation is deeply connected with emotions elicited by the program.

- *Break starts* must vary, but they must be related to program and theme.
- The *appeal to call* the number on the screen should be made immediately after a succinct break start. The appeal should be related to the program just seen and carefully tied to a pitch.
- A *program-related bonus* should be offered or teased near the top of the break.
- During the break, *bonuses* should be offered in ascending order— lower-priced bonuses first. Bonuses do not all require equal time and presentation.
- There should be *no more than 1 minute of talking head* on camera. A variety of visuals, static and moving, related to pitch and program, should continue to flow throughout.
- **Roll-ins** (inserts) should be related to membership ties. Important content of any montage that is not identified by type font or voice-over should be identified during the setup. The type, look, appeal, and content of roll-ins within a given break should vary.
- There should be no extremes in a break. The *pacing* should reflect a tension between substance and pitch. A lively pace (approximately 1 minute per element maximum) is preferred. No droning.
- Vary the *elements and format* to avoid predictability.
- *Break lengths* listed on the schedule include air time from the end

---

[9]This fundraising style sheet was written by Harry Chancey, Jr., senior producer at WNET, New York, in 1979–1980 for the station's writer/producers and is reproduced here with permission.

of closing credits through ID. Announce copy at head and tail is included in the time alloted. This copy should be short, crisp, and informational, especially at the top of the break.

- *Specials* are not long breaks. They are shows with their own content, theme, and tone, usually tied specifically to a prior show. There should be no generic pitching or use of standard cliches—especially at the top. The opening must be exciting with billboards, teases, previous program reactions, visuals, and the like. The body of the break should continue to tie the pitch to the program/series and special material. The pacing of a special should also be lively and evenly distributed, never missing a pitch opportunity. The no-more-than-1-minute-talking-head rule holds, but the 1-minute-pacing-of-elements guideline can be stretched to longer periods—generally 2 to 2½ minutes. A few elements (interviews, montages) may exceed 3 minutes when warranted.

Content: The Flesh

A break is not the traditional promotional appeal, but rather a sale. It asks for immediate *action*. All information, visuals, and thoughts should be framed in relation to telling the viewer how the phone call relates to whatever content is being presented by talent or tape.

- During the *closing credits*, thank members with a specific reason related to the program; tease the next program (and introduce the talent if there is no PBS logo). Do *not* ask for money or pitch in any direct way. Keep this copy very short—three sentences maximum—and informative with thanks.
- *Each break is a case study* of how the viewers' dollars bring them what they want and how their call specifically translates into the programs they want to watch—such as the one just seen (or to come).
- Everything ties to station *membership*, even introductions to talent.
- Each *pledge night week or event* has a special need, reason, theme, and appeal to be described.
- Every *break* has a special need, reason, and appeal to be expressed to the viewer.
- No appeal to call should be registered without answering at least one of the pertinent questions. *What* is the call? *Why* make a call? *How* does the call pertain to the program? No generic appeals!
- Relate the call to the program just seen or being seen. *Thematic* pitching, developing one theme for the break, is more effective than a series of disconnected reminders.

- *Specific details*—quotes, facts, figures, dates, information, visuals—should be incorporated as often as possible throughout the break in order to explain clearly and substantively how the call relates to the programming. Generic pitches must be avoided.
- All *promos* should be tied to pitches.
- *Bonuses* should be attractively described and illustrated.
- *Informational points* should be tied to a pitch.
- The *goal* should be clearly defined and explained.
- Members should be *thanked* as often and in as many ways as possible.
- Each break should reinforce the idea that all amounts are welcome. Every contribution helps the push toward the goal.

Some points relate specifically to calling:

- "Each program is special and unique—and your call supports it."
- "Our programming is special and unique—and your call supports it."
- "When you call, you applaud what we've done in the past and help us prepare for tomorrow."
- "Public television is different. There is no imitation. Instead there is imagination and risk."
- "Your support assures diversification of programs."
- "Consider the cost of a membership compared to the cost of ___ (tickets, subscriptions, and the like)."
- "A very special thanks and welcome to our new members and supporters. During the last intermission of ___ , nearly three hundred of you responded with a call."
- "Your membership means more fine programs of the caliber you are seeing tonight."
- "In the past, we have taken some calculated risks to bring you the kind of programs you're seeing tonight. We took these risks based on your response to our efforts in the past. Your phone call tells us your preference."
- "People make us possible. That's how we set our goals. During this membership drive we need ___ new members and time is running out. We need your phone call now."
- "When you call, we *know* you're standing behind the risks we take because, quite simply, they are the risks you ask us to take."
- "If you are already a member and you're enjoying tonight's programs, don't hesitate to let us know. Your additional contribution will be especially welcome, and you'll be making a loud and clear statement of support for our unique programs."

- "Right now only one person in ten supports public television. Imagine what would be possible if every one of our viewers were to make a call."
- "Our goals are based on our need to replenish the coffers that are drained each and every day in order to bring you the very best."
- "If you are already a member and want to be in on tonight's excitement by expressing your vote of confidence in the programs we're offering, then give us a call to boot."
- "We're here to please you and only you, our supporters. We have no commercial restraints. When you call, you register your pleasure with our efforts."
- "We need your guidance. Let us know how you feel with your phone call now."

There are many points related to budgets and funding, as well. The following points must be updated continually, but they add the specificity necessary to color the cliches and generic statements:

- "Our budget for '79–80 will go down from $43 million to $40 million from the previous year due to a falloff in major underwriting. Your support is that much more essential to maintain the quality of programming."
- "In that $40 million budget, $15 million is discretionary. The rest is tied to specific programs."
- "The Carnegie Commission Report states that if public television is to reach maturity over the next decade, the budget must increase from $540 million to $1.6 billion by 1985. This increase depends on the continued and expanded participation of the viewing audience. Whether public television maintains its stance as an indispensable tool for the future depends on . . . you."
- "Your support has added impact because of matching funds from the federal government."

Approach: The Heart of the Matter

You can say "Stop smoking" or you can say "Children love to imitate their parents. Do you smoke?" It is obvious which one is more effective. Form and content are important, but the right approach makes the difference. Here are a few tips on approaching the audience:

- Continue the mood of the program right into the break, and, at the proper point, bring in the next show. The audience will be calling for a variety of reasons—the strongest, for more shows like the ones they have tuned in. The program is the strongest emotional roll-in of the break. The break should be conceived in the context of the setting. And all roll-ins need tight, specific set-ups and reactions.

- The break should be conceived not only as it lies between two programs or program segments but in relation to the whole fund-raising period. It should be clear from the script that the break is part of a larger event so that momentum can work as a motivator. ("We're nearing the end" or "This is the final night.")

- Motivation is the answer. The task is to motivate the viewer to perform a specific act: picking up the phone and making a call. Thus the question to ask is this: "What can I say to the viewer that will motivate him or her to call?" The best response to this question is not so much intellectual or argumentative as it is emotional. That is why each break must continue the mood of the program while making the appeal to call in order to ensure more programs like the one just seen.

- In the emotional context, the appeal to call must be clearly stated so that viewers realize it is in their best interest to call. There are no sure-fire methods for motivating, no easy formulas. It takes vision and assessment.

- Appeal to the viewer's personal self-interest: "Do it for the kids." "Do it for yourself. You owe it to yourself." "You're looking for something different, unique, and you've found it right here. Support it."

- Take the "institutional" out of public television. Mention the viewers whenever possible. Instead of "these shows are funded by membership dollars," personalize the message with a direct reference to "you" or "your dollars." Institutional words should be avoided in the copy as much as generic pitching.

- Indirect approaches sometimes work better than direct approaches. To say "It's chic to become a member of Thirteen," is not very convincing. But *associating* the station with chic can be very effective. There should be no direct snob appeal. It bores even the snobs. We communicate our distinction best by association with what is chic, not by patting ourselves on the back.

- Another controversial motivation is guilt. It can be employed with sensitive scripts and high production values, but warrants extreme caution.

- Subtle references to sensual appeals can also be carefully injected into the approach. Once again, this motive must be suggested, not clubbed over the viewer's head.

- Interrogatives can turn a dull declarative statement into an engaging prospect that involves the viewer. They are particularly good at the top of a break. Go for the viewer's undivided attention:

"Do you know what just happened? You just watched a show
  that was aired."
"You may wonder what⸺has to do with you and your mem-
  bership dollars."
"Maybe you're asking yourself 'why should I give?' "
"I can tell you're not the average viewer. How do I know that?
  You're watching Channel Thirteen, aren't you?"

- Tone is very important. At no time should a viewer feel that he
  or she is being talked at. We are talking *to* the viewer. Never use
  the third person. Personalization comes from use of the first and
  second person: "the dollars we give," "our support," "my
  feelings."
- Urgency must be projected into every break. A year is a long
  time, and fundraising appeals do not come often. Therefore it is
  important to stress the urgency of the appeal, the break, and the
  event in the context of the rest of the year, which is programmed
  without interruption.
- Talent is a valuable resource. Each talent is a role model, an example. Some may have stronger demographic appeal than others, but all of them are devoted viewers who are volunteering
  their time to support the station's efforts. These points should be
  reflected in their scripts. On lucky occasions the talent may be
  directly linked with the previous program, thus making it easier
  to carry the mood of the program right into the break.
- The talent can engage the viewer personally by such approaches
  as "if you feel as I do. . . . "
- Sincerity, energy, enthusiasm, immediacy, and personalization
  should all be part of not only the scripts but also the delivery.
  The talent must be prepared so that the delivery is neither too
  casual nor mechanical. This means informing the talent of the
  real reasons for your need to raise funds for the station.
- The approach to premiums must also be fresh and appealing.
  Colorful adjectives do make a difference. Premium presentations
  should not sound or look alike.

DECISION MAKING FOR PROMOTION

Increasingly, decision making for promotion is becoming integrative.
The thrust of programming, whether one-time-only programs or series,
determines the promotion. The programming director works closely
with the head of publicity and promotion to determine promotional
emphasis. Even though the publicity/promotional staffs plan a campaign, the program director has the final say about it.

The key element is the number of dollars available for promotion.
As with most things in public television, dollars are in quite short sup-

ply. Thus how to stretch the station's dollars becomes a major factor in decisions. Big stations have more money and promotion staff than smaller stations. Besides size, the other factor is underwriting. Most underwriting grants for programs also include dollars for publicity and promotion—Gulf Oil, which underwrites *National Geographic Specials*, spent as much money for publicity and promotion as it did for producing the series.[10] Small stations typically depend more on their internal budgets to cover promotion costs than do the big stations. In many cases, consequently, small stations spend very little on promotion.

THE NEW COMPETITION

Approximately $5.5 million of KCET's $14 million budget was raised from the Los Angeles metropolitan area in 1979–1980. There are over 10 million people in this area covering Los Angeles, Orange, Ventura, San Bernardino, and Kern counties.[11] However, the demographics of those who support KCET are virtually identical to those of the supporters of pay cable and subscription television.[12] The basic question arises: Will people continue to support public television or will they substitute monthly pay-television fees for their "alternative" programming dollars? Although the big stations will feel the full brunt of competition from pay-cable systems before the smaller ones, the smaller stations will eventually have to grapple with the same challenges. Hartford Gunn, first president of the Public Broadcasting System and well-known communication futurist, points out:

> It could be argued that if the 1980s were to see the 30 percent penetration [of pay-cable] increase to 50 percent, with an accompanying growth in pay-cable programming, the networks would be affected as well. At the very least, the cost of creative and performing talent and sporting event coverage could rise substantially. At the worst, the audience for network programming could drop enough to cause a substantial reduction in network advertising rates. Rate reduction could lead to a reduction in programming—leading, in turn, to diminished audiences, and so on. It is the opposite of what seems to be happening in pay-cable.
>   The great "unknown" in this kind of speculation is the role of the federal government. The government could, as it has in the past, act to

---

[10]According to Thomas Skinner, WQED-TV, Pittsburgh.

[11]Los Angeles has seventeen VHF and UHF stations, more than eighty cable franchises, three subscription television channels, and eighty-three AM and FM radio stations.

[12]The demographics of the KCET viewer (typical of public stations in general) are male, 40+ years old, 5+ years of higher education, and a yearly income of $35,000. Source: "KCET Subscriber Survey," October 1979.

dampen these movements or adopt a neutral position of "letting the marketplace decide." Or it could make it federal policy to accelerate these changes. My own belief is that there is a significant body of people in government who are committed to the latter course.

If my assessment of the government's position is correct, the view that the next decade will lead to substantial and inevitable changes in American broadcasting also would seem correct. Broadcasting as we have known it for more than 50 years—dynamic, ever growing, and the most powerful of all media—could begin to change, and change dramatically.[13]

PUBLIC RADIO PROMOTION

Public radio, like its video counterpart, is becoming increasingly dependent on promotion to garner public support as federal funding slows. Even more than public television, radio suffers from insufficient funds for promotion. Thus efficient targeting is essential.

The Corporation for Public Broadcasting (CPB) contributes between $250,000 and $300,000 to an average station's yearly operational budget. Very little of that amount is allotted to promotion. KUSC-FM in Los Angeles is exceptional. Approximately 10 percent of its yearly operational budget of $1.2 million ($100,000) goes to promotion.[14] This is a monumental figure in comparison to the norm for public radio. According to CPB's *1978 Annual Survey*, stations affiliated with National Public Radio (NPR) invested a total of $2,418,896 for promotion while reporting $65.5 million income for that year—a 4 percent average investment. This figure means that there had been no growth in promotion activities since the *1975 Annual Survey*. To promote promotion, CPB is considering matching grants to local station promotion dollars.

Moreover, 60 to 70 percent of the public radio stations in the country have a combination development/promotion/advertising staff consisting of one person full-time or, in many cases, part-time. This one person generally begins as a development director whose duties expand to promotion as the two activities become pertinent to success in the eyes of station management. Usually this person functions without a professional staff, although there may be volunteers. This staffing naturally limits what can be achieved on a local level.

---

[13]Hartford Gunn, "Window on the Future: Planning for Public Television in the Telecommunications Era," *Public Telecommunications Review* 6, July/August 1978, p. 11.

[14]Selma Halpern, director of public relations, KUSC-FM, Los Angeles.

The Role of NPR

Much of the promotion for public radio originates with National Public Radio in Washington, often in conjunction with the Corporation for Public Broadcasting. Some of this promotion is in the form of packaged programming/promotion related to such national productions as *All Things Considered* and *Morning Edition*. These promotional efforts are widely successful due to the strength of the specific programs and the enthusiastic audience response. Approximately 20 percent of the average public radio station's programming and promotion is in the form of packages from NPR.

As a parent organization, NPR acts as a conduit for information exchanges between the stations, encouraging alliances and the pooling of resources for cost-effective campaigns. Member stations are encouraged to share their local promotion relating to programming offered nationally, thus eliminating waste and duplication of effort and cost.

Many of the alliances are quite successful. One example is the Washington Public Radio Campaign of 1980–1981 begun by WAMU-FM, WETA-FM, and WPFW-FM of Washington, D.C. (see Figure 11-5). These stations commissioned an advertising campaign and then arranged a "group buy" for other NPR stations for a cost of $25 per station—an amazing buy for camera-ready ads that could be targeted to each station's local audiences with minor changes to the copy.[15] The Washington campaign resulted, as of February 1981, in $18,975 in free advertising in major magazines such as *Business Week, Newsweek, New York,* and *Time* for the Washington stations.[16] Moreover, CPB and NPR also serve as sources of information on promotion by offering workshops and circulating such material as the *CPB Radio Development Handbook.*

An example of an outstanding national campaign to promote public awareness (it began originally as a membership campaign) was the "Discover Public Radio" campaign in the fall of 1980. To implement the project, CPB provided $900,000 to NPR, which then gave matching grants to the individual stations. Most stations solicited matching funds from local corporations and listeners, some matching by as much as two to one. Local stations also negotiated to include promotion of their local shows within the campaign.

At the conclusion of the project, an 8.1 percent increase in awareness was noted.[17] This growth was attributable both to the "Discover Public Radio" promotion and the *Morning Edition* package that had been cir-

---

[15]*i.e. development*, November 1980, pp. 3–11, published by CPB/Radio Development.
[16]*i.e. development*, February 1981, p. 4, published by CPB/Radio Development.
[17]Nel Jackson, assistant radio development manager, CPB, March 1981.

Figure 11-5 Public Radio Promotion (*WAMA-FM, Washington, 1980. Used with permission.*)

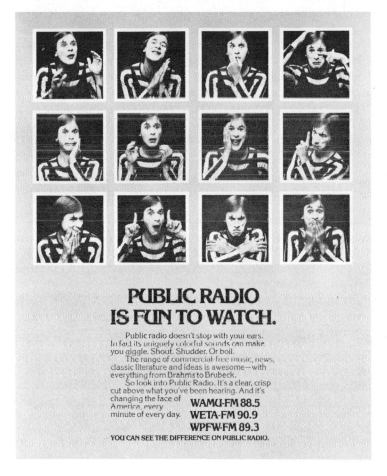

culated to member stations. Perhaps the real success is that most of the stations rallied and matched the NPR funds. The ability to raise money locally will be a crucial factor in the survival of individual public radio stations.

Tradeouts

As in public television, tradeouts for public radio promotion help to make up for lack of funds. WABE-FM, Atlanta, acquired $15,000 in free advertising in *The Atlanta Constitution* and *The Atlanta Journal* for Christmas programs in 1980 underwritten by those newspapers. In exchange, the newspapers promoted their image via their underwriting credits. This arrangement led to another tradeout with a neighboring community's daily paper that provided $5,000 in advertising space to underwrite local transmission costs for *All Things Considered* in return for promotion.[18]

Public radio stations in Los Angeles have received free spots on public television in an exchange of promotional "in-kind" services with KCET. Spots sold public radio for a month, promoting all seven of the Los Angeles public radio stations at once—"88.1 to 91.9 on your FM band." Like public television, public radio will be making more and more of these exchanges in order to realize its goals. Certainly cash to pay for such promotional activities is likely to be scarce in the 1980s.

THE FUTURE

Public stations are having to become more sophisticated to stay in business. And they are having to become more creative to grow. One of the likely trends of the 1980s for television may be an increase in the number of public stations working closely with their competition–subscription television and cable operators.

The advantage of joining forces is quite simple: It may keep many public television stations in business. Hartford Gunn, in *Window on the Future*, bluntly says that public stations have no other option:

> The alternatives facing public television on the issue of cable importation, simply put, are to "fight 'em, forget 'em, or join 'em." We cannot "fight 'em" because our resources are too limited, the forces in the government too strong, and our own concern for expanding public service too great. Nor can we "forget 'em," at least in most areas, and certainly not for any length of time. Only some major producing stations in places where the cost and complexity of installing cable is prohibitive can afford to ignore cable developments for any length of time. However, even in these instances, there would be an indirect effect. There is only one alternative left, and that is to work with cable.[19]

SUMMARY

Public television and radio have been late in realizing the importance of sophisticated, targeted on-air and print promotion by comparison

---

[18]*i.e. development*, March 1981, p. 10, published by CPB/Radio Development.
[19]*"Window on the Future,"* p. 14.

with commercial stations. Nevertheless, major-market public stations began demonstrating on-air promotion quality comparable to that of commercial stations by the early 1980s and refined their procedures for pledging and auctions. The success of these efforts is made plain by the increased size of community support in the form of dollar donations and pledges. Competition from new media such as cable and pay-television is likely to alter even further the promotional practices of public broadcasting on the local and national levels. The 1980s will also demand that each public station know its demographics and its targets. Without these adjustments, public stations may not survive the 1980s. Promotional strategy will directly reflect the drive of public stations to inculcate their image as a "quality alternative."

Pay-Television and Cable Promotion

by
Robbin Ahrold

Robbin Ahrold has headed Home Box Office's public relations and publicity department since 1978. He joined Home Box Office in 1974 as coordinator of special programming and moved to manager of affiliate communication and associate director of public relations. He came from Time Inc.'s corporate pay-television research team, where he served as a member of the corporate study group on satellite programming and networking (SPAN). From 1966 to 1972, he moved from researcher for Time/Life Books to editing and reporting for Time's *Washington Bureau, becoming manager of educational projects for Time/Life Cable in 1972. Robbin Ahrold holds a B.S. degree from Georgetown University (1965) and was awarded an Adenauer Fellowship in 1966. He is presently working toward a Ph.D. degree at Georgetown University. In addition to more than fifty articles for* Time *magazine and contributions to Time/ Life International Books, he edited* Pay-TV Guide: An Editor's Reference to Pay-Television, *published by Home Box Office in 1981. He also teaches classes in pay-television at the New School for Social Research in New York.*

This chapter does not recount the graveyard of broken promises, the foundering of hopes, and the multimillion-dollar investments that characterize the early experiments in cable and pay-television programming. It is sufficient to note that cable and pay-television programming, as of the early 1980s, is only beginning to drive a forceful wedge into the structure of the business of home entertainment, a structure that will undergo dramatic changes during the 1980s.[1]

---

[1]Cable will continue to face a difficult and often contentious regulatory environment at the local and state level along with substantial vested-interest opposition. Recent FCC deregulation of cable television rates and programming has opened the opportunity for more vigorous regulation of subscriber fees, programming, and marketing strategies by city councils and state cable commissions. The Manhattan cable television franchise contract, for instance, requires that cable operators offer each pay-television channel at an individual price to the consumer. This requirement prohibits the **bundling** of pay services in a single package price, a technique now very popular in cable and pay-television marketing. National policy favors letting marketplace forces set the rates for pay-television services. In 1980, the FCC lifted restrictions on distant signal importation and syndicated program exclusivity. These deregulation efforts were promptly challenged in the courts, and by 1982 the FCC's ruling had been upheld. Although the FCC's authority in rate regulation has prevailed in every case that has come before the courts, cable operators have become extremely cautious in asking for increases in the monthly subscription fees for both cable and pay-television services— largely due to the high cost of litigation. However, these issues have limited effect on promotion; they bear directly on business and operations strategy.

Already many channels of specialized television programming are included in basic cable services for which consumers receive no separate billing; charges for these services are borne by the cable system operator out of basic monthly cable subscriber fees. These channels provide news, sports, cultural, children's, religious, black, and Spanish-language services—with more being introduced all the time. Many of these services accept advertising. The term *pay-cable* specifically refers to channels of programming available on wired cable systems for a monthly fee (in addition to the fee for the basic cable service), while the broader term *pay-television* includes both **pay-cable** and over-the-air **subscription television.**

PAY-CABLE'S ROLE

To a much greater degree than elsewhere in the book, this chapter represents a "snapshot in time" of the promotion strategies practiced by dynamic new entrants in the field of home entertainment via cable and subscription television. The major pay-cable services as of December 1981,[2] each providing a single channel of pay programming, are Home Box Office (8.5 million subscribers), Showtime (2.8 million subscribers), The Movie Channel (1.7 million subscribers), and Cinemax (1 million subscribers).[3]

The advertising support system of broadcast television, as well as the relative scarcity of over-the-air transmission frequencies, demand that every program, network, or channel attempt to reach the broadest possible audience. Cable television couples the potential of a virtually unbounded number of channels with a financial mechanism that permits *direct* consumer payment for program services, allowing for the provision of highly valued special-audience programming.[4] Broadcast television seeks pennies from tens of millions of viewers day after day (via cost-per-thousand charges to advertisers); cable and pay television seek dollars from hundreds of thousands, or a few million, through monthly subscription charges.

MARKETING CONSIDERATIONS

The typical cable television system's balance sheet reveals why the bulk of promotion, advertising, and publicity activity for this industry has

---

[2]Defined as those with a million or more subscribers.

[3]According to Nielsen figures for 1981, the total number of pay-television subscribers exceeds 13 million households (and they tend to be younger, larger, and more affluent than broadcast television households).

[4]With both pay and non-pay national services active in marketing and promotion, the major advertising-supported channels are becoming a larger and larger force in the marketplace.

been devoted to pay-cable program services. From homes that subscribe to pay-cable, many cable operators realize twice the revenue they
receive from homes without pay-cable. The attraction of pay-cable programming has become the *primary* reason for subscribing by households.[5]

Pay-television is a monthly subscription medium. The viewer/sub-
scriber is asked to pay an established rate for one or more pay-television services once a month.[6] Every one of the millions of pay-television
subscribers must write a check every month to renew these services for
the month to come.[7] A pay-television service's monthly renewal (or
retention) figures are often more significant than figures representing
the acquisition of new subscriber homes. Subscribers are being asked
to assess the value of pay-television service only once a month when
they sit down to pay the bill. This places a special burden on both
programming and promotion to find ways to draw the subscriber's attention to the value of the *total* monthly package rather than individual
programs or program series—in other words, it obliges them to devise
a packaging strategy.

Package Strategy

One of the implications of persuading consumers of the "package
value" of a pay-cable channel is that it creates the need to promote the
network or program service's name, logo, and identity. Distinct identity
is particularly important because many cable subscribers already pay
for (and view on a regular basis) more than one pay-cable service.

Initial marketing studies have shown that many multiple pay-cable
service subscribers are not certain whether they have seen a particular
film on Home Box Office, Showtime, or The Movie Channel.[8] Their
confusion is understandable in view of the fact that all three frequently
schedule the same Hollywood feature films during the same period of

---

[5]This phenomenon, known as *cable lift*, is experienced primarily in major markets where broadcast
television signals are easily received with rooftop antennas. Although present measurement
techniques make it impossible to establish this cable lift percentage with precision, HBO experience
has shown lift to vary from *5 percent* to *30 percent* or more. Moreover, Nielsen surveys of pay-
cable households show dramatically heavier usage of pay-cable channels than of other cable
programming channels (such as superstations, Cable News Network, and ESPN). While many pay-
cable programs receive ratings and shares on a par with the most popular broadcast offerings,
viewing of all other cable program services combined averages about a 2 rating, 3 share.

[6]Approximately $8 to $12 per channel for Showtime, Home Box Office, and The Movie Channel as
of 1981.

[7]In addition to a basic cable subscription fee ranging from $7 to $10 per month.

[8]This phenomenon was noticed consistently in a series of focus group interviews with pay-cable
subscribers conducted by Home Box Office during 1980 as part of market research in planning
HBO's second pay-cable channel, Cinemax, which was launched in August 1980.

time; in fact, they often feature the same movie on the cover of their program guides.

All three major program services have now adopted promotion techniques aimed at differentiating their program services from those of competitors, a differentiation that must be accomplished by reinforcing the attributes of the total program package rather than the individual program. Because of the duplication of major film titles, HBO and Showtime differentiate themselves by focusing the viewer's attention on original programming.

Showtime's promotion and publicity, for example, carry the tag line "America's most original pay-TV." Its program guide builds the viewer's interest under specific product umbrellas—*Carousel* for children's features, *Broadway on Showtime* for dramatic presentations, *Hot Ticket* for live music and variety programs, *Critic's Choice* for classic and foreign films.

Home Box Office's promotion also uses original programming umbrellas (*Standing Room Only, On Location*) and often points out that HBO is the only pay-television network to offer "the best in films, specials, and sports." Both HBO and Showtime make heavy use of the logo graphics of their services in program guides, on-air promotion, and advertising.

The Movie Channel promotes its program package with a simpler, more direct approach: *24 Hour Movies*. The key to all pay-television promotion, whether on-the-air or pay-cable, is selling subscribers on the entire program package; topical movie and program promotion supports this total effort.

Audience Availability Strategy

After package value, the second important marketing factor for cable services is that, unlike broadcast television, cable subscribers must be *hard-wired* to the cable network. Television households only a stone's throw from the end of a municipally granted cable franchise will not have access to the cable service. Similarly, the construction of new cable systems often requires years—years during which television viewers, although they are within the boundaries of the cable franchise, do not have access to the system because the cable has not been laid in their neighborhood.

Promotional efforts that do not take the availability of cable into account result in low media efficiencies (advertisers paying too much for the size of the audience) and wasted promotion dollars. Moreover, they can produce a backlash of ill will from those who want to subscribe to cable service but are presently denied it and are therefore denied the opportunity of pay-cable subscription.

Broadcast network and national magazine advertising, for instance, are the smallest parts of Home Box Office's marketing campaign and do not figure at all into those of Showtime and The Movie Channel. All the pay-television networks as well as local cable operators rely much more heavily on more targeted media, such as local newspaper advertising, direct mail, and door-to-door sales.

On the other side of the question, it is extremely helpful to pay-cable marketers to have an exact record of the names and addresses of every cable subscriber in a franchise. This precise register of prime prospects facilitates direct-marketing techniques. Mailers and fliers left at doors play a significant role in pay-television and all cable marketing. Billing lists also permit accurate measurement of the effectiveness of marketing and promotional campaigns since the number of new subscribers attributable to these campaigns can be known with precision.

BUDGETS AND MARKETING

Pay-cable marketing and promotion budgets are usually represented in marketing and promotion planning as the number of cents or dollars spent per present or potential pay-television subscriber home ("cents-per-home-passed" in industry jargon). Nationally distributed pay-cable networks allocate a few cents per month of every subscriber's monthly payment for promotion and marketing; a local cable operator's expenditures for promotion and marketing fall in the same range.[9] Over-the-air pay-television systems (STV), such as SELECTV or ON TV, charge much higher monthly subscription fees than cable and pay-cable services.[10] Typically, they devote more than a dollar a month per subscriber to promotion and marketing activities.

Since most cable television systems offer a package of basic channels including one pay-cable service for approximately the same fee as the one-channel service of an STV station, STV is at a competitive disadvantage when competing against cable television for the same subscriber homes. STV's main target audiences are homes in major markets not yet served by cable. In the future, STV stations will have the option of offering their services to cable subscribers as one of the pay-cable channels available through cable systems. They might well reduce their wholesale charges to cable operators to make their retail rates comparable to those for national pay-cable networks. Since this option is not

---

[9]These figures do not include expenditures for launch marketing in new cable systems and major remarketing efforts in established systems, which may be substantially higher.
[10]Fees for SELECTV in Los Angeles were $21.95 monthly in January 1982.

yet exercised, however, it is impossible to predict its impact on the promotional activities of STV stations.

These high levels of expenditure have characterized only the last half of the 1970s and early 1980s. Until the mid-1970s, cable operators offering a television reception service in isolated communities where cable was a prerequisite for any television viewing often satisfied themselves with a Yellow Pages listing and occasional newspaper advertising. With rare exceptions, there were no attempts at year-round promotion and marketing campaigns before 1975.

Four factors have led to rapid growth in both promotion expenditures and the professionalism of cable promotional campaigns: (1) the advent of pay-cable services (the first truly discretionary offering for many cable operators); (2) the rapid advance of cable franchising and construction in major markets well served by broadcast television (where cable services were not needed merely to receive a clear picture); (3) the entry of several major marketing-oriented companies into cable ownership and pay-television network programming; and (4) the availability of increasing numbers of satellite **transponders** for national program services.

An explosive growth of interest in cable and pay-television marketing has created rapid expansion in the specialized marketing and promotion departments of the nation's top twenty-five cable multiple-system operators (Teleprompter, American Television & Communications, Warner-Amex, Times-Mirror, and others), as well as by all the nationally distributed pay-television networks.

As in many growth industries, this explosion in pay-television marketing and promotion has created a sharp discontinuity within the industry. Side by side with the large, sophisticated, and well-funded marketing and promotion departments of the big companies are the small-budget, sporadic marketing approaches of the locally owned rural cable television operators. Not surprisingly, the entire management "team" in thousands of small cable systems consists of one general manager whose primary expertise is in the technology of cable transmission. Small rural cable systems owned by large cable **multiple-system operators** (MSOs) or affiliated with national pay-cable networks have benefited from the campaigns, materials, and on-site assistance of the national company's marketing and promotion departments.

Prepromotion of Movies

When releasing a major film to pay-television networks, some film distributors limit prepromotion of the film's appearance on pay-television while the film is still in theatrical distribution. The primary impact of this policy has been to restrict a key promotional strategy: prepromotion of films. A ban on the prepromotion of major film titles often prevents the national pay services from announcing their strongest upcoming selections to consumers until shortly before the title appears on the screen. Effective promotion, however, would include on-air promotion, print publicity, paid advertising in newspapers, and prepromotion in monthly program guides for major films.

Because subscriber retention month after month is of primary importance, the inability to let subscribers know that their continued subscription payments will provide a film such as *Jaws* or *Close Encounters of the Third Kind* is obviously a major problem. Yet it is often precisely these "powerhouse" titles that fall under the film distributors' prepromotion ban. Imagine the frustration of a broadcast network's promotion staff unable to mention in any context—even to the trade press—that a major attraction such as *Roots* or *Shogun* is appearing until just a few days before it appears on the screen!

Pay-television promotion staffs, extremely conscious of the pulling power of major film titles in retaining current subscribers, are even more frustrated than their colleagues in broadcasting. Loss of viewers for a program or mini-series on broadcast television has no predictable effect on viewership for another program the following month. In pay-television, the inability to prepromote major film titles can mean substantially reduced pay-television sales and higher than necessary disconnects among present subscribers. Pay-television promotion staffs are able to point out to subscribers only that most major films eventually do appear on the pay-television networks.

Cross-Media Advertising

Opposition by local television broadcasters and national networks to the growth of cable television has resulted in the denial of the most natural and powerful promotion tool for cable and pay-television services—the on-air television commercial. In 1981, ABC and NBC and many local broadcast television outlets were still refusing to accept cable and pay-television advertising. But that opposition is lessening as the broadcasters also become more active in cable.

Cross-Media Effects of Pay Television

A test using saturation pay-television screening of *Blazing Saddles* in Long Island cable systems, just prior to a rerelease of the film to local theaters, resulted in higher theatrical revenues for rerelease of the film than were garnered in the film's initial theatrical rerelease (before pay-cable screening).[11] In other words, airing on pay-cable helped theater ticket sales in this study. On a broader scale, national box office receipts have been continually increasing over the past five years (according to *Variety Annual*, 1980) while national pay-television subscriptions have almost quintupled from 2 to almost 10 million.

PAY NETWORK SALES PROMOTION

Network activities aimed at the cable television industry resemble sales promotion activities undertaken by broadcast networks and magazine publishers aimed at advertisers and agencies. Direct mail, heavy schedules of trade advertising in leading cable trade magazines, in-person presentations to major cable operators—all focus on the additional revenues to be gained by cable operators from offering the pay service of a particular network.

Until 1979, the three major pay networks competed among themselves to be the single pay service offered by cable operators to their consumers. Home Box Office, able to demonstrate through independent surveys[12] that it achieved, on an average, significantly higher market penetration (and thus revenues), won most of the battles for the prized spot as the first or "foundation" pay-television service.

Beginning in mid-1979, however, Showtime—and later The Movie Channel—were able to demonstrate that consumers would purchase more than one pay-cable service. They redesigned their trade promotion activities to persuade cable operators to *add* their services on top of HBO. The change of tactics proved highly successful, permitting both of HBO's competitors to increase their roster of affiliated cable systems dramatically.[13] The battleground shifted to persuading cable operators to make a network pay service the primary offering to consumers in the multipay marketing environment.

Cable has thus become a supermarket for television channels as the pay networks compete for space, visibility, and position on the shelves. And the cable television operator has become the manager of this video supermarket, controlling the retail price of the product, billing, installation, and service.

Subscriber acquisition campaigns by both Home Box Office and Showtime have two aspects. They involve (1) a national marketing um-

[11]United Artists, 1978.

[12]Paul Kagan Associates, *Annual Census of Cable and Pay-Television Subscribers, 1976 Through 1980* (Carmel Rancho, California: Paul Kagan Associates, 1981).

[13]Showtime grew from approximately 600 to 900 cable affiliates in 1980—as many affiliates as were added to the network in the entire preceding four-year period (excluding new affiliates associated with the sale of 50 percent of Showtime to Teleprompter in 1979).

brella developed, paid for, and executed by the pay network (2) in support of local consumer marketing using a similar copy and graphic approach managed and paid for by the local cable affiliate.

NATIONAL MEDIA CAMPAIGNS

Home Box Office's $10 million media plan for 1981 called for broadcast network television commercials, print advertising in *TV Guide* and *People* magazine, local spot television, and newspaper advertising in major market dailies. The HBO-sponsored campaign in the first three weeks of each month is designed to build consumer awareness and demand for the service; the fourth week is reserved for local advertising. Both the HBO and the local cable advertising list telephone numbers for ordering cable and pay-television service.

The creative approach, using the tag line "HBO People Don't Miss Out," focused the viewer's attention on blockbuster movies to be aired by the service in the next month and drove home the value of the service through the use of such copy lines as "HBO people are getting *Alien* and much more. With no cuts or commercial interruptions. What are you getting?" Additional copy promotes "big hits like *Starting Over* and *Dressed to Kill*, plus smashing specials like *Paul Simon in Concert*, exciting sports, and a new family series featuring exclusive Disney classics." Figures 12-1 and 12-2 show some examples of this approach. A monthly advertising kit is sent to all HBO cable affiliates containing camera-ready **ad slicks** using the current theme with space provided for details of the local offer and telephone numbers to assure that ads placed by cable operators build on the theme and graphic approach of the national campaign.

Showtime, with a distribution base about one-quarter of HBO's, operated a more modest advertising campaign in 1981 using the creative theme "America's Most Original Pay TV." Like HBO, the campaign focused on blockbuster movies and the value of pay-cable subscription. Local television and newspaper spots were used instead of national television and national magazine advertising. The advertising campaigns of both networks seek strong national brand name recognition to boost cable operators' local marketing activities.

Sellathons

Both Showtime and HBO operate regular national or regional **sellathons** supported by newspaper advertising and direct mail in close collaboration with their cable affiliates. During the sellathon, the cable operator makes the pay service available for a one-or-two-day period to

Figure 12-1 HBO "Don't Miss Out" Strategy *(HBO, 1980. Used with permission.)*

all cable subscribers as a "free sample" of the pay-television program service.

Like broadcasters during the rating sweeps, the pay networks assemble their best product for the sellathon program schedule. Intermissions between programs are devoted to sales pitches by network television hosts and personalities, sweepstakes, and promotion of upcoming programming reminiscent of charity or public television telethons.

At HBO, participating cable affiliates precede the sellathon weekend with a direct-mail package containing details of the local offer (monthly subscription fee, installation charges, and so forth) mailed directly by the pay network to cable subscribers who have not yet become subscribers to the HBO service. During the sellathon, operators in a national telephone center take orders for HBO using toll-free numbers; they then pass the orders along to individual cable operators for installation. Cable operators pay only for the cost of the direct-mail packages and any local newspaper or radio advertising they choose to run in support of the sellathon. Because the sellathon is highly targeted to the primary sales prospects—present cable television subscribers—sales volume and cost per sale results are impressive, averaging 5 to 7 percent increases of pay-television penetration in a single weekend at less than $10 per sale.

Figure 12-2 HBO Movie Strategies *(HBO, 1980. Used with permission.)*

Showtime, using the same general plan, has taken a different approach to collaboration with the cable operator. Showtime affiliates pay nothing for direct-mail materials but are billed $2 per subscriber by the pay network for each order transmitted to the affiliate.

Launch Marketing Techniques

Although national sellathons are used as a primary **remarketing** device, the same concept has produced excellent results in the *initial* introduction of a pay-cable service to an operating cable system with good penetration of its franchise. Typically, the local cable operator introduces the pay service with a two-to-seven-day "free preview" of the new pay service for all cable subscribers. This campaign is supported by newspaper and radio advertising and direct mail. Often (as they do during the national sellathons), cable operators offer for a limited time a reduced installation fee for "charter subscribers." Cable operators with facilities for television origination can fill the time between programs during the free preview with sales pitches and local sweepstakes. The cable system manager often acts as on-camera host for the proceedings. All three pay networks offer local publicity support to cable operators—

including press releases customized with details of the local offer and news conferences and open houses for local VIPs and influentials—as a way of softening the market and creating consumer awareness for the upcoming free preview.

The resurgence of cable franchising by hundreds of communities in 1979 and 1980, including many of the nation's major markets, has led to the development of new tools to introduce both cable and pay-cable services to new markets. Here the sellathon or free-preview technique is not effective since there are, by definition, very few cable subscribers (if any) on the system as it begins construction.

In these new cable communities, direct mail, telephone sales, and door-to-door sales are the most cost-effective techniques. Many cable operators divide a franchise into several geographical areas for construction and marketing purposes. As the main or "trunk" cable is energized in each section, direct-mail brochures are sent to each home passed by the cable. These brochures explain the various levels or "tiers" of cable and pay-television service and the rates for each. After a short waiting period, door-to-door salespeople armed with glossy pitch books describing the programming services make a sales call on each house in the energized section, taking orders and collecting an initial installation charge and the first month's subscription fee. Other cable operators may use telephone sales personnel to call each home in the energized section. Pay networks offer direct-mail material and door-to-door pitch books for these launch campaigns; they often describe not only their own service but the entire lineup of cable channels, including competitors' pay services.

Some of the larger multiple-system operators have developed their own direct-mail and door-to-door materials designed to promote the complete range of cable and pay services instead of asking subscribers to pick and choose among several service options. Cable operators often promote a local brand name ("Metrovision," "Cablevision," and the like)—a technique that obscures the identity of the individual pay services (called "smudging") and facilitates the sale of a higher priced multichannel package. If the viewer is unwilling to accept the maximum-priced package, the door-to-door or telephone salesperson may discuss the individual cable and pay-cable services and invite the consumer to select among them.[14]

---

[14]Since all new cable television systems have the channel capacity to offer multiple pay-cable services, most systems constructed after 1980 will offer two (or even three) national pay networks. It is in the cable operator's financial interest to sell as many subscribers as possible on the complete package of cable and pay services. Some have experimented with marketing strategies containing substantial financial penalties for consumers who order less than the top-price package. However, communities are now more frequently requiring in their franchise agreement that cable operators permit the consumer to choose freely among the various options in the cable package.

SUBSCRIBER RETENTION STRATEGIES

Retention is the other major component of pay-television consumer marketing strategies (in addition to acquisition). It is aimed at decreasing pay-cable **disconnects.** Most cable television systems experience an average of 3 percent nonrenewals or disconnects per month due to moves, deaths, delinquent payments, and dissatisfaction with the transmission or quality of service. An additional 1 percent or more per month of pay-cable subscribers disconnect only their pay services—a combined turnover of almost 50 percent, or half the entire population of pay-cable subscribers, each year. Although the pay networks generally regard the 3 percent monthly cable disconnects as "uncontrollable," the additional 12 percent yearly turnover among pay-cable subscribers has become a major focus of marketing programs. The chief tactics used by the pay networks to increase subscriber retention are the program guide, on-air promotion, program publicity, tune-in advertising, and program listings in local newspapers and *TV Guide.*

Program Guides

The monthly program guides produced by the pay networks are perhaps the single most important tool in the promotional arsenal. The 16- to 24-page four-color guides combine daily program listings with copy and graphics promoting each new program for the current month as well as prepromotion of coming months' attractions (where distributors prepromotion contracts permit). Figure 12-3 shows a page from one of HBO's monthly program guides.

Typically, the covers of the guides display blockbuster movies in the networks' monthly schedules. Guides are mailed to pay-television subscribers monthly in the same envelope as the cable operator's bill for cable and pay-television service. This arrangement offers the pay networks the chance to promote the coming month's programs at *exactly* the time that the subscriber is being asked to write out a check to sustain the network subscription. (Using the same envelope means that the total weight of the program guide must be kept under one-half ounce so that first-class postage for the guide, bill, and return envelope does not exceed the one-ounce charge.)

The program guide also, almost without exception, forms the core of direct-mail packages soliciting new subscribers in sellathons, previews, and other remarketing campaigns. (Pay networks therefore have print runs for the guides that sometimes exceed the number of subscribers by as much as 100 percent.)

Figure 12-3 Monthly Program Guide (*HBO, 1980. Used with permission.*)

Multipay and Cable Program Guides

Newly constructed cable television systems ("new builds") offering multiple channels of pay-television as well as other satellite-distributed cable program services and locally originated cable programs are faced with a painful choice. They must either mail two or more individual program guides published by the pay networks to their multipay subscribers or publish (or commission the publication of) a local program guide that combines the listings and promotion of all the pay services—often including listings for non-pay-cable networks and locally originated programs. Publishing houses began to spring up in 1980 to cater to this specific need.

The large print runs of the pay-television network guides create significant economies of scale that permit them to be offered to cable operators at ten cents or less per copy. The cable operator's costs for self-published or commissioned program guides average twenty-five cents or more per copy, even after defraying some publishing costs by carrying local and national advertising. However, the self-published guides have the distinct advantage of permitting the cable operator to list every program available on a cable service—thus enhancing the consumer's perception of the value of the total cable package. Both

HBO and Showtime make special kits of text and graphic materials available to cable operators and guide publishers to facilitate the production process while assuring that each program is carefully promoted to the correct audience with the best possible graphic enhancement.[15]

On-Air Promotion

Another subscriber retention tool used by the cable networks is on-air promotion. Although the casual viewer would find pay television's on-air promotion similar to that used by broadcasters, there are striking differences in creative and scheduling strategies. Unlike broadcast television, which seeks the largest possible audience for every program, pay-television programs are often targeted at specific segments of the viewing audience (male vs. female, older vs. younger viewers, fans of classic films, and so forth). In pay-television promotion, it is more important to attract the *right* audience (who will be most inclined to appreciate the program) rather than the largest audience.

On-air promotion for pay-television does not have the tight time constraints of broadcast television. In fact, a promo may run a minute or longer if the time is needed to explain a program concept to viewers. Because the pay networks want not only to promote individual programs but the entire lineup of programs offered in the monthly schedule, HBO, Showtime, The Movie Channel, and the over-the-air services all produce stacked promos promoting their packages or substantial portions of them. HBO's on-air promotion department, in addition to producing promos of various lengths for each program to be aired, produces 1-minute promos promoting all the major programs to be aired on the coming weekend (*HBO Weekend*) as well as a 6-minute promo highlighting key programs for the entire month ahead (*Calendar of Events*). There are also separate promos on films, sports, and original pay-television specials.

HBO's programming department also produces a monthly half-hour program promotion entitled *Sneak Preview* that airs several times during the month in primetime. Surprisingly, the program—which combines clips of movies, sports, and specials with humorous vignettes—has achieved Nielsen ratings comparable to those for some original pay-television sports and entertainment special presentations.

Moreover, HBO's on-air promotion department produces "service spots." These promote the network's brand name and logo and key

[15]With 8.5 million subscribers, the monthly print run on the HBO program guide is enormous, equaling the *combined* distribution of these publications from its parent company, Time Incorporated: *Time, Life, People, Sports Illustrated, Money, Fortune.*

service attributes (such as the fact that major feature films and specials are aired six to seven times over a four-week period) to help subscribers make better use of the program schedule. In a sense, the service spots are part of an effort to educate the viewing public to the differences between broadcast and pay-television programming and scheduling—thus maximizing subscriber satisfaction with the pay-television program service.

Showtime and The Movie Channel are also regularly producing their own on-air promos. Showtime uses much the same approach as Home Box Office, creating original promotional spots targeted specifically at pay-television audiences, while The Movie Channel leans more heavily on edited broadcast television and theatrical movie trailers.

Program Publicity

Program publicity for all pay networks is patterned closely on the techniques developed for broadcast television—not surprising since the pay networks are competing with the broadcast networks for space on the entertainment pages of the newspapers. While broadcast networks have mailing lists of a few hundred newspapers in affiliated station markets, however, pay networks deliver materials to thousands of daily and weekly newspapers in rural and suburban America where their affiliates are located.

Tune-In Advertising

Tune-in advertising or topical advertising, a major component of broadcast television promotion, is probably the least important technique for subscriber retention at the pay networks. With rare exceptions, pay networks do not place national or local tune-in advertising themselves. Rather, they prepare camera-ready **ad mats** for placement in local newspapers by their cable affiliates. Even these ads, however, do not solely invite consumers to tune in; instead they use the appearance of a particular program as an opportunity to ask consumers to become subscribers to the pay network.

This striking difference in promotional techniques between broadcast and pay-television is another reflection of differences in programming philosophy. In pay-television, where most programs are aired six or more times over a period of a month, the number of viewers tuned in for a single program is irrelevant. It is much more important that the *right* audience be attracted to the *right* program and that they be satisfied with the viewing experience.[16]

Program Listings

Daily program listings in newspapers and other mass circulation print media are one of the most effective awareness-builders available for the television medium. Although broadcasters may take program listings in daily newspapers and *TV Guide* for granted, they have become a major focus of attention for pay networks. Editors of newspaper listings and magazines such as *TV Guide* have not readily accepted the addition of pay-network listings in their pages. Home Box Office and superstation WTBS have borne the major burden of convincing these media that the regular listing of programs is a valuable reader service. In the pay-television field, the battle has been arduous since many editors have responded to requests for pay-television listings, program reviews, and feature stories on programming by claiming that their editorial coverage of pay-television would constitute an endorsement and "free advertising" for pay-network programming. Public relations executives for HBO, Showtime, and The Movie Channel appeal in these cases to publishing executives, often with dramatic results. As pay-television programmers demonstrate substantial penetration of available television households within local readership areas, pay-television and other cable network listings are added.

In early 1980, *TV Guide* executives agreed to a long-term plan to phase in program listings for national cable networks and services for *TV Guide*'s more than one hundred editions. At approximately the same time, nationally syndicated listing services such as TV Compulog made listings for the major pay networks available to all their newspaper clients on the same basis as their broadcast television listings. Syndicated feature services (such as United Features Syndicate) have begun regular cable columns and feature stories. Syndicated television columnists now report on programs of exceptional interest produced and aired by pay networks.

---

[16]Members of the broadcast trade press often ask whether or not the pay networks counterprogram broadcast television. The question is naive. Pay programmers have no incentive to counterprogram broadcast offerings—in fact, quite the opposite. From the pay programmer's point of view, if viewers enjoy watching a regular broadcast television series, it makes more sense to urge them to watch their favorite broadcast program *and* view the competing pay-television program on one of its alternative play dates. Nielsen pay-television statistics confirm that this is exactly what happens. On the average, viewers in pay-television homes watch about the same number of hours of broadcast programming as the national Nielsen sample, but they add to it several hours a week of pay-television viewing. Pay-television thus seems to be not so much a replacement as an addition to regular broadcast viewing habits. However, network primetime audience shares are gradually shifting to cable programming and to independents.

By early 1981, consumers in most cable marketplaces were regularly exposed to these daily program listings, columns, and feature stories and were readily able to compare the quality of pay-network programs with those from the conventional networks. Significantly, an HBO research survey in mid-1980 showed that consumers in several major markets attributed awareness of pay-cable programs to newspaper listings and reviews of these programs.

STRATEGIES FOR CABLE OPERATORS

The diversity of strategic approaches, campaigns, and tactics used in marketing cable systems to the public is far greater than the diversity of approaches in pay-network promotion. This difference reflects the varying stages of development in channel capacity, delivery, **denial technology,** and the many types of entertainment, informational, and security services offered. At one end of the spectrum, a substantial group of cable operators offers broadcast retransmission services with a maximum capacity of twelve channels, only one of which is a national pay network. Many of these systems promote themselves as local utilities with occasional newspaper and Yellow Pages advertising the mainstays of their media plans, along with a small amount of direct mail and door-to-door sales.

At the other end of the spectrum are cable systems offering sixty or more channels, two-way or "interactive" services, up to a half-dozen nationally distributed, advertising-supported cable networks, superstations (WTBS, WGN, WOR), Cable News Network (CNN), The Entertainment and Sports Programming Network (ESPN), USA Network, Nickelodeon, Music TV, CBS Cable, ABC Arts, Bravo, Playboy and others, several national pay-television services, and locally originated pay-per-view options permitting consumers to select and pay for individual films, sporting events, and other programs. Pay per view is seen as a major cable marketing concept of the future. Here marketing and promotion will match the sophistication of the technology and the programming and utilize many or all of the techniques successfully pioneered by the national pay networks.

Tiered Marketing Techniques

The large and technically sophisticated cable systems being built in major markets such as Houston, Dallas, Cincinnati, Pittsburgh, Chicago, and Los Angeles during the early 1980s are the testing grounds for a new wave of marketing and promotion campaigns by cable operators. One marketing strategy that is growing rapidly in acceptance is the packaging or **tiering** of groups of television channels. Under this plan, cable reception of local broadcast stations and a handful of public-access municipal channels is offered at a relatively low monthly price ($1 to $7) as the first tier or "basic cable television service." A second tier of service called "extended" or "expanded basic" service typically includes four to six of the nationally distributed non-pay-cable networks (ESPN, CNN, WTBS, Christian Broadcast Network, for example) for a small additional fee ($3 or $4). The third tier consists of two or more channels of pay-television service sold separately or in combination.

Warner-Amex Cable Communications' pioneering effort in Columbus, Ohio (and later Cincinnati, Dallas, and Pittsburgh) offers its two-way interactive **Qube service** as an additional level between the basic package and the pay-television tiers. The Qube technology permits consumer polling, shop-at-home services, and several channels of pay-per-view entertainment programming—all accessible to viewers at the touch of a button on a special **key pad device** connected to their television set. After heavy direct mail and local newspaper advertising, the majority of basic cable subscribers opt to take the Qube service.

On the horizon, leading cable operators foresee the possibility of extending basic service to all homes in the cable franchise free of charge; certain basic channels (**barker channels**) are already used for promoting additional levels of service. This strategy assures that the video promotion (commonly **teletext**) is seen by all homes in the franchise area—thus obviating the need for broadcast television advertising and permitting the collection of a precise list of names and addresses of all potential pay-television subscribers for direct-mail, door-to-door, and telephone sales efforts.

Non-Pay-Cable Network Promotion

The leading advertiser-supported cable services, such as ESPN, WTBS, CNN, and USA Network, provide cable affiliates with a monthly package of camera-ready newspaper ads for tune-in and subscriber acquisition purposes—together with descriptions of program highlights to be used by door-to-door and telephone sales staffs. To date, these non-pay-cable networks have not invested in separate program guides, national direct-mail materials, but are engaged in national media campaigns or program publicity operations. The burden of attracting viewers for individual programs falls largely on their on-air promotion, which closely resembles the strategies and techniques used by broadcasters.

STV AND MDS PROMOTION

In the late 1970s, the FCC began considering dozens of applications for UHF frequencies to provide broadcast pay-television services in major markets. By the end of 1980, there were ten subscription television (STV) licensees operating in eleven markets. Each local STV station acquires schedules and broadcasts its programming independently, and although several STV stations under common ownership may jointly negotiate for film packages, there is no networking of pay-television programming.

Over-the-Air Pay-Television

One of the first subscription television operations, and by far the most successful, is ON TV, counting almost half a million subscribers in the Los Angeles metropolitan area at the end of 1980. Typical of most STV operations, ON TV offers a monthly subscription package of films and specials similar to those offered by the national pay-cable networks, augmented by live coverage of the Los Angeles Kings and Lakers and other local sporting events. The monthly subscription price was about $20 at the beginning of 1981. There is an installation fee to cover the costs of installing a high-gain UHF antenna to assure the best possible reception of the station's programming.

As with other forms of pay-television, the promotional objective is to acquire new subscribers and retain the current ones. Although ON TV makes occasional use of direct mail and door-to-door techniques for subscriber acquisition, the key marketing strategy has been the heavy use of broadcast television and newspaper display advertising. As with pay networks, advertising focuses on the schedule of films (often listing thirty or more titles) and the lack of commercial interruption, editing, or censoring—and prominently displays a telephone number for "immediate installation." At ON TV headquarters, banks of telephone sales personnel write up the orders and dispatch installers who collect the first month's subscription fee and installation charge.

The most remarkable difference between ON TV's marketing and that of the national pay networks, however, is the level of media spending. In 1980, when Home Box Office spent $6 million for media nationwide, ON TV is rumored to have spent $3 million in newspaper and broadcast advertising in the Los Angeles market alone. This heavy commitment to local media has rapidly produced almost complete awareness of ON TV's name, logo, and attributes as well as making it one of the fastest-growing pay-television operations in the nation. (On a per-subscriber basis, HBO spent $1 per subscriber per year whereas ON TV spent $6 per subscriber per year.)

To an even greater extent than with the national pay networks, ON TV's most significant means of retaining subscribers is its large, glossy, four-color program guide, estimated to cost $1 per-subscriber-per-month delivered (versus seven to fifteen cents per month delivered for the program guides produced by HBO, Showtime, and The Movie Channel and distributed by local cable operators). The larger size of ON TV's guide permits effective use of big four-color display graphics, longer articles describing key programs, and more detailed daily program listings.

Multipoint Distribution Service

Multipoint distribution service (MDS) uses microwave frequencies for transmission of pay-television programming. Like STV, MDS is a phenomenon of the late 1970s as an entertainment medium; by the end of 1980, there were some three-quarters of a million subscribers in major markets. Unlike STV, many of the MDS operations are local affiliates of Home Box Office and Showtime. Thus these national pay networks can deliver their services where cable television does not have substantial penetration of the market.

Until the 1980s, the sophisticated and expensive ($600 to $1,500) reception equipment for MDS services has made it financially practical only for large apartment complexes where individual subscribers are served through a master antenna system connected to the MDS receiver and converter located on the roof of the building. Recent advances in integrated chip technology have reduced the cost of some lines of reception equipment, however, permitting installation on individual homes and smaller garden apartments at a cost of approximately $200 to $300.

It is not surprising, then, that MDS marketing and promotion resemble a blend of techniques used by cable and pay-television services on the one hand and STV on the other. Because it is a broadcast signal capable of reaching all the homes in a market, use of newspaper display advertising linked to telephone orders is a typical strategy. Apartment complexes offering MDS transmitted through the CATV system are targets for direct mail and door-to-door marketing techniques. Some MDS marketers also use videotape players and television monitors in lobby demonstrations of the pay program package when the service first becomes available in an apartment complex.

THE FUTURE

Predicting the future of promotion techniques for an industry that sees dramatic structural changes every year verges on the foolhardy. Will some pay-television services begin accepting commercial advertising?[17] If so, the accumulation of large audiences for certain programs supported by advertising would refocus pay-television promotion away from techniques promoting the entire package to resemble more closely broadcast tune-in advertising and promotion.

Will advancing technology create a place for pay-per-view programming in which cable subscribers are charged individually for the viewing of each film or sports program? If so, there will be a major refocusing of marketing and promotion techniques toward accumulating the largest possible audience for specific programs.

Will cable television systems become major providers of such services as home security and shopping at home? Some industry observers predict that revenue from such nonentertainment services could far outstrip that from present pay-cable and basic cable services. If so, major national cable operators and national service providers can be expected to develop marketing and promotion staffs, campaigns, and budgets that would dwarf the present efforts of cable and pay-television programmers.

Will direct-broadcast satellites, interconnecting individual homes through inexpensive earth stations, become a major form of pay-television networking? Comsat Corporation proposed such a plan in 1979 and petitioned the FCC in late 1980 to begin a three-channel, direct-broadcast, pay service to consumers along the entire eastern seaboard. The initial marketing for such a service would undoubtedly require multimillion-dollar mass media campaigns comparable to that developed by RCA for the national introduction of its videodisc in 1981.

Will teletext services—allowing consumers to order specific news and information from computerized information banks managed and edited by national publishers—permit cable television to replace the functions of the daily newspaper, news magazines, libraries, and archieves? Certainly Time Incorporated, Knight-Ridder, Gannett, and CBS Inc. have all announced well-funded experiments to explore the viability of such video information banks, some supported by advertising, others supported by subscriber fees.[18] Moreover, AT&T is explor-

---

[17]To date, Home Box Office, Showtime, and The Movie Channel have strong corporate positions against accepting advertising. Nevertheless, leading national advertising agencies continue to predict that they will break the pay-television barrier some time in the 1980s. A new pay-television entrant, the ABC-Hearst Daytime service, carries advertising, and all the news and sports networks have carried advertising since their inceptions.

[18]One of the principal reasons for the formation of Warner-Amex Cable Communications (50 percent owned by American Express Company) is the establishment of a national shop at home network through cable television systems. Certainly, American Express is well positioned in terms of experience and sophistication in marketing and promotion for this line of business, an experience matched by adequate capital for the investment necessary to pioneer such an effort. One large multiple-system operator, the Times Mirror Corporation, has introduced a shop-at-home service available to cable subscribers in all of its franchises. Revenues are shared between manufacturers of goods sold, a national distribution and marketing company (Compucard), and the local cable operator.

ing the possibility of offering a classified advertising service ("Yellow Pages") by means of cable television.

What is the future of advertising-supported services? Their sales are already aided by an industry association, the Cable Television Advertising Bureau (CAB), which is working to increase the sophistication of multiple system and local cable operations in building local sales efforts and regional advertising interconnections. Most advertiser-supported services allow a certain number of minutes per hour for local sale. Cable sales promotion activities will expand significantly on the national, regional, and local levels.

These developments are not merely "blue sky" ideas for the remote future. Some, perhaps all, will come to pass in the early to mid-1980s. Each will bring with it a restructuring of the cable and pay-television industries' marketing and promotion priorities—a series of mini-revolutions that will dramatically change the face of the industry by 1990.

SUMMARY

The initial promotional goal for cable system operators is to attract the largest number of subscribers possible. The major strategy is to offer an attractive array of services ranging from basic cable to additional non-pay and pay-television networks (tiering). The networks' goal is to amass the largest possible number of cable affiliates. The shared objectives of both are the acquisition of new subscribers and the retention of present subscribers. Over-the-air pay-television (STV) has the special problem of offering only a single service in competition with multi-channel services. For promotion, as for the cable industry itself, only change is constant. Career opportunities will spring up much like campsites in the Gold Rush of the 1840s. The promotional strategies being developed in the early 1980s will be tempered within the coming decade.

Part II ■ Suggested Readings

Friedman, Mel. "PTV's Fund Raising Methods Proliferate and Draw More Fire." *Television/Radio Age* (22 September 1980): 41–43.
Examination of alternative methods of underwriting costs of public television programming.

"Is Public TV Going Commercial?" *Media Decisions* (October 1977):76.
Review of the effects of commercial funding on public television programming; includes a discussion of public television as an alternative medium for advertising and corporate public relations.

LeRoy, David J. "The PTV Conundrum." *Public Telecommunications Review* 6 (November/December 1979): 50–58.
Results of a 1976 national ascertainment survey performed by the Office of Communications Research of the Corporation for Public Broadcasting; includes suggestions for increasing numbers of viewers and viewing time through program placement and promotion.

Lindsay, Carl; LeRoy, David; and Novak, Theresa. "Public Television: Whose Alternative?" *Public Telecommunications Review* 7(March/April 1979): 18–23.
Audience analysis showing that public television viewers may not fit the intellectual stereotype, but may instead be regular commercial television viewers who simply spend more time in front of television sets and have more opportunity to view public stations.

"The Many Worlds of Radio." *Broadcasting* (27 September 1976):33–82, (25 July 1977):31–76, (24 July 1978):37–74, (10 September 1979):35–67, (25 August 1980):40–102, (17 August 1981):39–86.
Annual reports on radio covering many facets of the field including promotion, advertising, and public radio.

Meistrich, Ira J. "On-Air Graphics: The News, Now." *Print* (March/April 1980):45–47.
Review of the way computers have changed the style of network news by creating composite graphics and exciting visual effects.

"News: Badge of Honor for the Independent." *Broadcasting* (6 February 1979):40.
Discussion of the role of local news programs in promoting independent television stations.

O'Daniel, Michael. "Programming for Basic Cable." *Emmy Magazine* (Summer 1980):26.
Overview of recent changes in cable and pay-cable economics including the role of advertising and promotion.

"Radio Promoters Have Tough Task Getting Listeners to Twist Dials." *BPA Newsletter* (December 1976):5.
Results of a radio industry survey of large markets showing that most radio listeners tune in to an average of 2.5 stations per week and that few listeners routinely change stations while listening.

"Razzle, Dazzle, Flash, and Splash." *Cable Marketing* (January 1982):30–31ff.
A report on image promotion by cable systems.

Rosenthal, Edmond M. "Two Webs Start Early: More Local Tie-Ins Seen." *Television Radio Age* (16 July 1979):27.
Analysis of the fall 1979 promotional strategies adopted by the three commercial television networks.

"A *View* Special Report: The Channel Capacity Crunch." *View* (October 1981):43–54.
Three-part report on marketing cable covering the shortage of cable channels, from the perspectives of program distributors, operators, and suppliers of nonentertainment services.

Walker, Jean. "Spending More Money on Promotion Doesn't Necessarily Make Stations Happier." *Television/Radio Age* (25 August 1980):42.
Results of a nationwide study of the top 100 markets sampling the attitudes of radio stations that (1) create their own promotional material in-house, (2) use advertising agencies, and (3) use syndicated promotion.

Part

III

Sales Promotion

Whereas Part II dealt with marketing to the general public, Part III discusses marketing *within* the broadcasting industry. The term *sales promotion* covers informational and persuasive efforts to reach broadcast advertisers and their agents, the media buyers, and similar efforts by syndicators of series and feature films to reach stations and group management. Effective sales promotion is of increasing concern to all decision makers in tightly competitive markets. This trade perspective will be of use to students of advertising and sales as well as media management, programming, and promotion.

Chapter 13 outlines the needs of sales executives for both broad and customized promotion. It describes the tools of sales promotion and examines the problems of using tradeouts and merchandising. This chapter covers the basic strategies of radio and television station sales promotion.

Chapter 14 turns to marketing of programs to stations (and networks and pay-cable suppliers) by syndicators. Their clients are station management rather than station audiences, although syndicators often sell their programs by providing their clients with especially useful and reliable audience promotion materials without charge.

Although the concepts and vocabulary of sales promotion have traditionally been the province of commercial broadcasters and program syndicators, it is becoming increasingly evident that the techniques of sales promotion must be adopted by public broadcasters if they are to survive in the competitive race for corporate funding. Just as audience promotion increased greatly in value to both commercial and public stations during the 1970s, so will the methods of sales promotion become the tools of noncommercial broadcasting. The gradual relaxation

241

of restrictions on on-air credits for underwriters by the Federal Communications Commission (begun in 1981) is expected to result in longer, animated spots on public television resembling commercials. However, the strategies used to persuade corporations to underwrite programs must increasingly resemble the methods of promotion used by syndicators to sell films and series to stations. The major difference is that syndicators attempt to reach many stations simultaneously with their messages while strategies to acquire underwriters must be tailor-made for specific corporations.

Station sales strategies also have applications in pay-television where the pay networks must persuade cable systems to carry their services and market them effectively to audiences. This subject was discussed in Chapter 12, although it relates to sales promotion. Part III, then, describes the current concepts and practices of commercial sales promotion that may be translated into innovative practices for public broadcasters and pay-television.

Promotion to Advertisers

by
Dick Newton

Dick Newton, national creative services director of PM Magazine, *is responsible for all advertising, publicity, and sales promotion for the daily primetime access program syndicated to more than 100 markets by Group W. He developed the original advertising and publicity campaign for the 1976 introduction of* Evening Magazine— *the program's title on stations owned by Group W. At that time, he was West Coast creative services director for Group W's KPIX, the position he held before moving to* PM Magazine *in 1979. Prior to his transfer to San Francisco, he was headquarters station promotion manager for all Group W television and radio stations. Before joining Group W in 1960, he worked in various broadcast promotion capacities at television and radio stations in Chicago, Los Angeles, and Portland. He received an Emmy from the San Francisco Chapter of the National Academy of Television Arts and Sciences in 1975 and a Best in the West award from the Advertising Agencies of the West in a 1977 competition. Dick Newton is a past director of the Broadcasters Promotion Association and frequently lectures on broadcast promotion at San Francisco State University.*

The operation of a commercial radio or television station is made possible by the revenue generated from the sale of broadcast commercial time to advertisers. Sales promotion is the supportive effort that arms the station's sales account executives with tools and information enabling them to sell their station time effectively. Sales promotion also helps to position the station positively in clients' minds to provide a favorable reception for sales efforts.

THE ROLE OF SALES

A salesperson who is not backed up with strong sales promotion walks naked into clients' offices. Even before the wide use of computers by media buyers and sellers, broadcast media buying had become highly sophisticated. Buyers demanded detailed information about a station's market, ratings, demographics, image, and competitive situation. These data are considered essential to gain maximum productivity from advertisers' media dollars.

243

Sales promotion provides the means to communicate this information effectively with materials ranging from simple printed pages to multimedia presentations, from small trade magazine ads to four-color sales brochures. In the fight for media dollars, a carefully planned and executed sales promotion effort can make the difference between winning or losing the buying decision.

A television or radio promotion manager is responsible for two separate station marketing efforts. The first is to attract the target viewing or listening audience—the consumers of the station's programming. The second is to attract the advertisers (or their advertising agency representatives) who buy commercials (buyers)—the consumers of the station's advertising time. The two goals are equally important to the station's success. This chapter focuses on the marketing effort to sell advertising time.

Most stations receive the largest percentage of their sales from local accounts. The balance comes from national advertising bought through advertising agencies in major cities. To get this national business, a station uses a national sales representative firm. Representing other stations as well, these reps call on the ad agency media buyers in New York, Chicago, Los Angeles, and other large cities. Sales promotion strategy, therefore, must be planned to meet the needs of both the local and the national sales efforts.

While sales promotion and audience promotion are aimed at different groups, there is often some overlap. In a station's market, advertising agencies and direct client customers are also viewers and listeners, exposed to the station's on-air and print promotion. The two promotion images should be compatible, and the trend is for stations to use one marketing theme for all their audience promotion, music, and visual identity. By putting the sales promotion components under this one umbrella, sales efforts benefit from the campaign's total impact.

SELECTING A STRATEGY

A station's first objective in developing an effective campaign is to determine the sales promotion goals of the sales department. Promotion managers need a thorough knowledge of how the sales effort operates. In addition to establishing a close working relationship with the sales manager and sales staff, promotion managers should periodically attend sales meetings, accompany salespersons on calls, and be familiar with the department's sales objectives and performance.

Ideally, the sales manager and promotion manager should jointly formulate sales promotion objectives and strategies. The first step is identifying the basic sales targets. In medium and large-market stations, the primary prospects are local advertising agencies. Secondary prospects are large and small retailers and other direct accounts. At independent television stations and all stations in smaller markets, the emphasis is reversed. Therefore, stations whose most important customers are ad agency media buyers put more emphasis on producing sophisticated research data. Stations whose sales staff is calling principally on direct accounts need materials designed for people with less experience of media buying.

Another consideration in formulating small-market station strategy is determining the relative importance of selling the market as well as the station. For markets ranking below the top fifty, selling efforts are largely directed toward persuading media people to choose the market. Some markets have special advantages the buyers should know about before decisions are made.[1]

A station's competitive position in the market determines its sales promotion strategy. Independent television stations and radio stations ranking below the top five must develop strategies to counter the client's tendency to think first of the market's leading stations. Stations ranking low in ratings can place their emphasis on merchandising support for clients, for example. Another strategy is selling "on the come." A station can point to format or program changes or other activities as indications that the station is on the move in ways that will soon be reflected in improved ratings. Above all, a station's strengths and weaknesses must be viewed as clients will perceive them. A sales promotion effort can then be developed to promote the strengths and counter the weaknesses.

BASIC SALES TOOLS

Most stations supply certain standard materials to their sales account executives. Produced continually and updated when necessary, these tools provide clients with basic information about the station. They are left by salespeople on calls, mailed out to lists of potential and actual clients, and included in presentations made to clients.

Because printed materials contribute significantly to the client's perception of a station's image, everything must be well designed and produced. Whether designed by a station's own artists or an outside resource, the material is most effective when it has a unified look.

Many stations develop a format that can be carried out in all their current sales promotion materials. An attractive folder or cover is produced for their presentations; for single information sheets, a pre-

---

[1]Radio station WOWO in Fort Wayne, Indiana, is a 50,000-watt facility that reaches a large area situated between Chicago, Indianapolis, Detroit, and Cincinnati. Since its coverage area is much larger than the standard Fort Wayne market, clients are sold on that fact.

Figure 13-1 Preprinted Format Shell (*Used with permission.*)

printed format shell can be produced.[2] Some stations preprint a number of format sheets titled for specific categories such as research, success stories, and program information. This material is often redone to tie in with the launching of a new television season or to relate to a new station identity campaign. The shell in Figure 13-1 is preprinted in red and black and can be used for a variety of promotional information.

Among the basic sales tools are rate cards, coverage maps, program schedules, and format information. Personality and program sheets and success stories are also appealing, and client rosters and press reprints are often enclosed.

Rate Cards

A **rate card** is a current listing of the station's time prices. It includes information on sales policies, special packages, and a few key facts

[2]Since only small quantities of these sheets are needed, it becomes expensive to print in more than one color. By preprinting the outside of the shell in two or more colors, it can first be run off in large quantities, with subsequent small runs made as needed for individual sheets with the information printed in black. The outside information usually includes the station's logo, address, phone numbers, and national rep's name.

Figure 13-2 Coverage Map (*Used with permission.*)

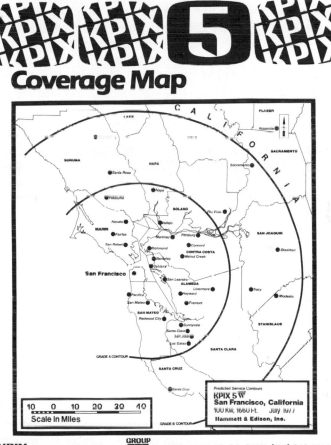

about the station such as the names of top management, coverage data, rep and network affiliations, and broadcast hours. When rates are changed, these cards must be reprinted. Because both television and radio rates are now commonly negotiated at the time of sales, rate cards are less important than in the past, particularly for television stations. As a result, rate cards are sometimes printed on a single page.

Coverage Maps

All stations print coverage maps showing their signal's reach. These maps, derived from the ones prepared by the engineering department for the Federal Communications Commission, are simplified for sales promotion purposes to show counties covered and areas reached by

primary and secondary signals. Coverage maps are especially important to radio stations that use their strong signal as a selling advantage.
Stations also make use of the coverage map sales sheet to list county
populations, buying power data, and other statistical market information (such as a listing of supermarket chains with numbers of stores,
freeway traffic data, automobile registrations). The coverage map in
Figure 13-2 uses a preprinted format shell. Two colors are preferred for
their attention-getting value.

Program Schedules/Format Information

In the summer, prior to a new fall season, television stations produce
schedules listing their programs.[3] These lists are often supplemented
with competitive schedules showing a side-by-side comparison of the
market's network affiliate stations. Generally, independent programming is ignored.

Personality/Program Sheets

The information encapsulated in program schedules or format sheets is
commonly expanded into numerous single program sheets. Television
stations produce sheets for important locally produced shows, news
operations, syndicated shows, and sometimes network shows. Radio
stations cover their personalities, news operations, sports, and other
programming features. The objective is to communicate basic facts and
selling points about the subject to inform and impress the client.

Success Stories

Success stories can be persuasive demonstrations of a station's selling
power—especially when the station is small. Larger stations find them
invaluable when concentrating on a specific sales category such as department stores or banks or automobile dealers. Success stories from a
client's own industry make an impressive selling point. Most stations
simply reproduce letters received from satisfied clients.[4] For better effect, the letters are slightly reduced to fit on a format sheet with a good
quote lifted out and reprinted boldly on top.

Client Rosters

Many stations print lists of their advertisers. Smaller stations find that
a printed roster of their advertisers makes an impressive tool for selling
other local advertisers on buying station time.

---

[3]These schedules are often updated at the year's end to reflect network program changes.
[4]The client is usually asked to write the letter.

Ad and Press Reprints

Important newspaper stories or trade ads are usually reprinted on a format sheet for client exposure. Newspaper stories have the appearance of unsolicited publicity, which can be especially effective in persuading new advertisers to take a chance.

SALES RESEARCH AMMUNITION

Broadcast clients buy advertising based on the size and makeup of audiences. The basic measurement of audiences derives from ratings, which are subject to much interpretation (commonly called "massaging" in the industry). Every station must carefully analyze its ratings to find its strengths, its competitors' weaknesses, and current audience trends. While this is a job for the sales staff (which generally includes a research specialist at larger stations), the promotion manager should be familiar with the analyses as they relate to the station's overall marketing effort.

Tangibles

The station's strengths can come from total audience size or an advantageous size in isolated demographic categories. Audience size, classified demographically, can also be measured against the price of spots and compared with competitors' rates to show cost-per-thousand (CPM) advantages. Specifically, individual dayparts and programs are also analyzed to find strengths. Much of a station's sales tool package (Figure 13-3) is produced from the analysis and interpretation of research data.

Television stations must do considerable advance selling of new programs and sports events when past ratings data are lacking. The sales department estimates future ratings by finding old figures or relevant figures from other markets that support projections.

All research data should provide clients with tangible evidence that they are making a wise buy. Advertising agency buyers demand accurate facts and figures to support their buying decisions. Ideally, these data should be based on the accepted Arbitron and Nielsen reports. Media-generated research carries less weight, though it is acceptable when commissioned through reputable, nationally known research firms. In addition to putting one's own best foot forward through positive research findings, exposing the competition's weaknesses is crucial. A station or program rated number two might be sold against a number one, for example, by showing that the latter's ratings or demographics are trending downward. Station A may have a 15 percent

Figure 13-3 Sales Tool for WBZ *(Used with permission.)*

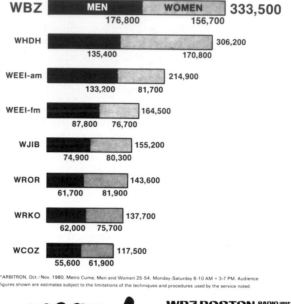

WBZ...The Station Adults 25-54 Turn to During Drivetimes*

Boston Metro Cume, Men and Women Listeners
for October/November 1980
Monday-Saturday 6-10 AM + 3-7 PM

Station	Men	Women	Total
WBZ	176,800	156,700	333,500
WHDH	135,400	170,800	306,200
WEEI-am	133,200	81,700	214,900
WEEI-fm	87,800	76,700	164,500
WJIB	74,900	80,300	155,200
WROR	61,700	81,900	143,600
WRKO	62,000	75,700	137,700
WCOZ	55,600	61,900	117,500

*ARBITRON, Oct./Nov. 1980, Metro Cume, Men and Women 25-54, Monday-Saturday 6-10 AM + 3-7 PM. Audience figures shown are estimates subject to the limitations of the techniques and procedures used by the service noted.

research

WBZ BOSTON RADIO 1030 W
Count on us.

Represented
Nationally by   **RAR** RADIO ADVERTISING REPRESENTATIVES, INC.

ratings lead over Station B, but the ratings for a year may clearly show that Station A's advantage was originally greater and has steadily declined. Station B might therefore assume it will soon surpass Station A in audience size.

Intangibles

While advertisers seek the biggest audiences made up of their potential customers at the best price, intangibles can influence buying decisions. Effective communication of strengths unrelated to ratings may be the deciding factor in a close selling contest. One example is the way a station is perceived by the community it serves. Banks, department stores, and other prestigious advertisers are concerned about the advertising climate surrounding their selling message. Thus a station's positive community image is a valuable selling factor that should be substantiated by brochures documenting its community involvement. Active support of local charities and civic activities, outstanding local sports coverage, documentary probing of community problems, awards won, and other evidence of a station's concern for its community should be conveyed to clients.

Higher advertising acceptance standards and less commercial clutter than the competition are other aspects of station policy that can be especially useful for sales promotion. On-air personalities who command remarkable audience loyalty are yet another strength. Extraordinary mail pull or personal appearance drawing power may be documented on sales sheets. Large community events staged by radio stations can also be promoted as part of the sales effort. Promotion managers must look at every aspect of station operations for activities and achievements that can be promoted to enhance the station's image and provide effective tools for sales staffs.

SALES PRESENTATION ASSISTANCE

Most broadcast sales efforts require written presentations. They typically contain one or two pages of sales pitch plus rate and spot availability data tailored to a prospective client. Presentations for major pieces of business become more elaborate. Along with a well-written explanation of how the client's needs can be served, reflecting the station's awareness of the client's own objectives and unique selling problems, major presentations occasionally include specially commissioned research findings.

When stations have an important message to communicate to clients, they often turn to audiovisual aids. A radio station's announcement of a format change, the introduction of the new fall television season, the findings of an expensive research study—all may warrant elaborate presentations produced by multiple-slide projection or on videotape or film, often by an outside production firm. These efforts vary greatly in scope, ranging from a short videotape announcement (shot and edited on videocassettes and shown on monitors) to a multimedia extravaganza on a giant screen. Videotape presentations are advantageous in that they can be shown by sales executives and national reps to clients in their offices by means of portable video equipment.

MERCHANDISING HELP

Merchandising is the bonus clients get for their money over and above contracted air time. How much merchandising should a station offer? The answer varies greatly among stations. For some, merchandising compensates for lower ratings or provides an edge in competitive selling situations. Four basic forms of merchandising specifically aid (1) package goods advertisers, (2) sports advertisers, (3) advertising staff morale, and (4) general retail advertisers.

Package goods advertisers can receive extra exposure in supermarkets for their products—such as end-aisle displays supplied through reciprocal trade agreements between a station and a supermarket chain; ads in grocery trade publications purchased by the station; or mailings by the station to supermarket managers informing them of a product's ad schedule. The announcement of a broadcast advertising schedule encourages stores to feature products in order to take advantage of the increased demand.

Stations with live sports coverage rights usually make commitments for large amounts of merchandising as part of their contracts with the teams. They agree to buy billboards and newspaper ads and in other ways promote their game broadcasts. This media advertising is then used as a merchandising opportunity for the sponsors of the broadcasts. Large sponsorship packages are made more attractive to prospective advertisers by offering them listings on billboards and in other promotional materials as team sponsors.

Other incentives include mentions in printed schedules of the season's games or counter card schedules made available to the sponsor to give away. The sponsor's dealers or sales staffs are usually invited to a dinner and a game with special treatment. These efforts have the attraction of involving the sponsor with a professional sports team.

In some cases, a station may promote a contest among a client's sales staff. These contests usually take the form of letters announcing the product's broadcast advertising schedule with an invitation to win a prize by guessing how many people will be exposed to the spots (ratings results). Prizes are supplied by the station. Such campaigns are typically announced to a client's regional sales staffs, dealers, or franchise holders at a luncheon or dinner hosted by the station.

The task of implementing a merchandising program generally falls to the promotion manager. An entirely different form of merchandising is offered to local retailers. As the broadcast share of retail advertising dollars has increased, broadcasters have provided more service to retailers. The station often offers them use of its production resources, some of which may be part of a merchandising package. The production portion of this program is sometimes part of the promotion manager's job.

Reciprocal Trades

Whether or not a station decides to trade unsold time for merchandise or services is always a policy decision. While there are arguments for and against trades, most stations trade for some of their needs.

Perhaps the simplest trades are reciprocal trades ("recips" or **trade-outs**) made with other media for space or time. The promotion manager usually makes these trades in negotiation with counterparts at other media companies. Some stations assign a sales executive to service trades instead of cash sales; others require the promotion manager to act in this capacity. While trade deals are one more burden in a crowd of job commitments, the process gives promotion managers an education in sales procedures.

Apart from media space or time trades, stations often trade for merchandise, restaurant meals, sports and theater tickets, and other desirable items with which to stock the prize closet. Stations with liberal trade policies use this means to pay for everything from automobiles to transmitters. Large-item trades usually involve dealing through a third party known as a barter house; promotion managers frequently participate in these transactions.

Gimmicks

One function of sales promotion is to smooth the way for sales executives by providing reminders in the form of leave-behinds and mailers. Certain gimmicks and advertising specialties work primarily as reminders of the station's advantages as an advertising medium rather than to provide specific ratings or other information.

Media buyers receive great quantities of sales promotion mail from broadcasters. If they buy other media such as newspapers and magazines as well, they become targets for constant media promotion. Local direct clients such as car dealers and store owners are also the recipients of heavy sales pressure from media salespeople.

To increase the salience of its messages, a broadcast station occasionally supplements its informational sales tools with gimmicks or advertising specialties. For executives confronting large stacks of mail every day, the arrival of a small package has special impact. Whether the package contains a mug with a station's logo or some other small object tieing in with a new program or personality, these small gifts always get opened (which is not always the case with direct-mail advertising).

If the item has real utility, it may remain on the desk or, in the case of a poster, be displayed on a wall. Sales account executives making direct calls on advertisers also use these items as leave-behinds. The promotion manager must therefore be aware of the latest specialty items and be on the lookout for unusual gimmicks.

Although the promotion manager is generally behind the scenes producing useful tools for the sales staff, there are times when the manager can play a more direct role in sales efforts. On occasion, a sales executive brings other station executives along on calls to provide authoritative information. The promotion manager's presence can be especially useful in describing an unusual merchandising program or a tie-in with a new public service campaign.

Parties, Prizes, and Payoffs

In the name of good client relations, most stations periodically throw parties for their clients. Whether to introduce the new fall television season, show a presentation, or celebrate an anniversary, the station's objective is to impress the clients and show them a memorable time.

Promotion managers traditionally plan the station's parties. These are excellent opportunities to demonstrate originality in creating a theme cleverly tied to invitation, choice of location, and menu selection. Most client parties include entertainment, contest prizes, and perhaps a small gift for each guest. Such gifts should enhance the station's image and be unusual enough to make conversation pieces for family, friends, and business acquaintances.

Contests for clients can be handled by direct mail. Provided clients are aware that they have been specially targeted, the station's messages often gain extra impact from getting the respondent involved.

As the station's valued customers, clients are the beneficiaries of many free gifts from sales account executives—tickets to sporting events, restaurant dinners, Christmas presents, travel accommodations, and other desirable items. Most, if not all, of this largesse comes from the station's prize closet. The items are supplied by trading with other companies.

SUPPORTING THE NATIONAL SALES EFFORT

Many local sales promotions also benefit national sales efforts. Since national reps (and their clients) are geographically separated from the station, however, and because the reps represent many stations, extra support is necessary. The national rep needs fundamental information about the market and station in explicit and handy form. To their clients, reps must appear experts on the specific stations and local markets they sell. The key to servicing reps effectively is keeping them regularly supplied with pinpointed station selling ammunition and updated market information.

Many stations keep reps up to date with video presentations or newsletters covering local market developments. The following items might be covered in such a newsletter: news of program or personality changes, success stories, news of local promotions or stunts, advance information on upcoming station developments, information on the competitive situation.

A station's relationship with its rep firm often entails visits by rep firm executives escorting key national clients. These visits challenge the promotion manager to offer activities the guests will long remember. Tightly organized schedules, introductions to well-known personalities, and visits to fine restaurants are basic to red-carpet visits.

TRADE PRESS ADVERTISING

Another valuable avenue of communication between stations and clients is through ads taken in advertising trade publications—such as *Ad Age, Ad Week, Variety, Broadcasting, Marketing and Media Decisions,* and *Television/Radio Age.*[5] Added to this list are various informational sources for time buyers such as *Standard Rate and Data Service.*

For maximum effectiveness, a trade advertising campaign, like any other, must meet planned objectives with appropriate media strategies. Because most station trade advertising has the goal of increasing sales, trade press ads should convey information about the station that will be of help and interest to buyers. Trade press ads are used to relate ratings success stories, announce the winning of important awards, provide market information, or enhance the station's image by revealing significant community service efforts (Figure 13-4). Some stations run trade press ads consistently to keep their call letters regularly before buyers. Station groups, such as Group W and Post-Newsweek, also advertise collectively for their stations.

Stations and groups can use their trade press advertising to reach other audiences as well as clients. Station image ads, intended to be seen by opinion leaders including the Federal Communications Commission and politicians, often report a station's successful public service efforts.

Trade press advertising is sometimes expanded by stations to include the trade publications of other industries such as the grocery,

[5]This subject is covered in detail in Chapter 15.

Figure 13-4 Trade Ad for WOWO (*Used with permission.*)

garment, or furniture businesses. The station's objective is to sell directly to advertisers (who may not see the media trade publications that ad agencies do). Another goal is to interest potential advertisers in the broadcast medium as well as in individual stations.

A final resource used to convey information to clients is publicity in trade publications and the advertising columns of metropolitan newspapers—stories of ratings shifts, programming changes, important media buys, and personnel changes are examples. Pictures taken of advertising agency and client figures at station parties are also accepted by some publications. The guidelines for getting program publicity outlined in Chapter 15 are applicable to sales promotion publicity as well.

COMPETITION IN THE 1980s

A new consideration affecting the priority of sales promotion came with the electronic communications revolution—the growth of new communication technologies that ushered in the 1980s. Cable television, two-way cable, subscription television, satellite broadcasting, and microwave networks will be competing for attention on the air and on screens that used to be the exclusive preserve of commercial and public radio and television stations. Advertisers are showing more and more interest in these new opportunities to reach viewers as the traditional broadcast audience is diluted. The relaxation of broadcast regulation in the 1980s with the resulting proliferation of new radio and television frequencies adds a further competitive factor.

All these changes clearly indicate that broadcasters will be fighting harder for advertising dollars. If a station's sales goals are to be achieved, there must be more and better sales promotion support. New approaches must be developed while existing techniques are improved.

Perhaps more important, the heightened competition for both audience ratings and sales dollars will elevate the stature of promotion managers. Their advertising and promotion skills will become even more valuable competitive resources in station operations of the future.

SUMMARY

The growth of broadcasting in the 1960s and 1970s has been accompanied by a corresponding increase in the competition for advertising sales. As broadcast sales staffs have developed more effective techniques for selling time, advertising media people have become more sophisticated in buying it. This trend has increased the importance of sales promotion's role in the station's total marketing mix. The basic sales tools of coverage maps, format sheets, and rate cards are effective only when combined with detailed analysis of the demographic composition of the station's audience. Research is the key to sales efforts, but gimmicks, merchandising, and parties can be the extras that hold the interest of satisfied clients. The trade press is a powerful aid to the national as well as local sales effort.

Syndicated Series and Feature Film Promotion

by
Jerry Greenberg

Jerry Greenberg has been vice-president for advertising, public relations, and promotion for Twentieth Century-Fox Television since 1978. He steers the company's efforts in advertising, sales promotion, graphic arts, and public relations. Before joining Twentieth Century-Fox, he was director of communications for CBS-owned WBBM-TV in Chicago and director of information services for CBS Radio Spot Sales and for CBS AM Stations Administration in New York. He has also held positions with WQXR Radio, the ABC Radio Network, and Young and Rubicam Advertising in New York. He holds a B.A. from Columbia University and has won a large number of awards, including two Clio Finalist Awards, the 1977 Broadcast Media Award from San Francisco State University, the 1976 Andy Award from the Advertising Club of New York, the U.S. Television Commercial Festival Award for outstanding creativity in 1976, and a 1977 award from the Broadcasters Promotion Association. He was honored twice by the American Research Bureau for radio sales promotion with first-place innovation awards.

The market for domestic syndication consists of more than seven hundred commercial television stations programming over 100,000 hours each week, the three commercial networks, public television, and pay-television. A special type of sales promotion reaches this market.

THE ROLE OF THE NETWORKS AND GROUPS

The Federal Communications Commission has ruled that no company can own more than five VHF television stations or seven stations if two or more are UHF.[1] This rule applies to the three commercial networks (CBS, ABC, and NBC) as well as other group owners. CBS's owned and operated (O&O) stations are located in New York, Los Angeles,

---

[1]Proposals for additional UHF stations ("drop-ins") and low-power television stations considered by the FCC since 1980 may radically change this picture, but it is unlikely that the market will feel major effects before 1990.

258

Chicago, Philadelphia, and St. Louis. ABC's owned and operated stations are in New York, Los Angeles, Chicago, Detroit, and San Francisco. NBC's owned and operated stations are in New York, Los Angeles, Chicago, Washington, and Cleveland. Obviously, with key stations located primarily in the nation's top ten markets, the influence of the three networks is enormous. Moreover, their influence does not end with their O&O stations, since network shows are also viewed by affiliated stations.[2]

Independent stations are, of course, not affiliated with a network. But some independent stations are owned by groups, and some of these groups have standardized their stations' time in such areas as news, weather, station identification, and promotion. In addition, independent and affiliated stations can form their own "networks" for showing specially prepared programs as was done recently and successfully with Operation Prime Time (OPT).[3]

The market for syndicated programming also includes cable systems, subscription television, and, to a lesser extent, public television stations. The needs of all these buyers differ by type, by market size, and by intensity of competition.

SUPPLY AND DEMAND

Most of the product in the field is supplied by the television subsidiaries of the major Hollywood studios (Paramount, Twentieth Century-Fox, Columbia, MGM, Warner, and others), independent producer/syndicators (Metromedia, Group W, Viacom, and others), and independent syndicators acting as sales representatives for various producers.

The programming most in demand for syndication falls into four primary categories: motion pictures, off-network reruns, talk-variety/magazine formats, and game shows. The major television studios as well as independent producers have discovered that syndication to television stations is more important than creating original series or specials for the networks. Certainly syndication is more profitable. With the exception of first-run series and films, syndicators sell programs whose major costs have long since been defrayed. Moreover, syndicated programs are typically more durable in syndicated runs than on

---

[2]Affiliation contracts specify that certain programs (generally news and primetime) will be carried at certain times and restrict the amount of delay that stations may give (especially to news). Affiliates control their own time, however, and by their own option carry all the shows they deem desirable. Affiliates may also carry programs from competing networks.

[3]Operation Prime Time is a group of independent and affiliated television stations that have joined together to create, fund, initiate, and broadcast programs as a mini-network. Most of the programs OPT has distributed have been dramatic mini-series.

network runs. Even the longest-running network hits have longer re-runs in syndication. And, finally, many syndicated programs can be sold over and over again.

Syndicators need to communicate their promotional messages to al-most three thousand executives around the United States—general managers, program directors, station managers. These decision makers are, in effect, the advertising audience. Any of them can participate in a final program purchase decision. And these executives at the more than seven hundred commercial television stations around the country continually receive one clear advertising message from the nation's pro-ducers: "Buy my syndicated show."

As of 1980, the cable market almost exclusively involves the licensing of feature films for pay-cable services and subscription television. The demand for films is so much greater than the supply that promotion is limited to the establishment of identity for the companies that supply films or act as distributors.

The quality of a program may be the major determinant of whether it can be sold, but the speed at which the program is sold and used and the terms of the sale are the primary determinants of whether a show will be profitable. To a syndicator, promotion is a key element in assuring the speed of sale.

THE MESSAGE

With more than seven hundred stations and nearly three thousand ex-ecutives spread across the country, there is no way that even a major studio with a nationwide sales force can effectively promote every show on a personal basis. Just as any corporation does, syndicators rely heavily on trade media, trade conventions, and collateral materials to get their messages across and augment the work of their sales staffs.

Personal relationships *can* make a difference, however. Once estab-lished, personal relationships can be extremely valuable to a sales staff. They are particularly crucial when selling against competition in situa-tions when no company has a clear advantage in program quality. In fact, in an oversupplied market they can provide the extra element that swings a sale. This factor encourages personal relationships between station executives and members of sales teams and is always consid-ered an important element of sales strategy.

In most cases, however, the established methods of marketing—through conventions, trade publications, and collateral materials—are the ones that play the strongest roles in promoting shows to the sta-tions. Although the strategy for promoting a feature film package is markedly different from promoting an off-network series, they both use the same vehicles to accomplish their goals. There are only so many important trade publications, so many conventions, and so many ways of preparing a brochure. While messages may differ, all syndicators use the same means to reach their goals.

Conventions

While several conventions throughout the year highlight syndicated products, the one major convention that all studios and independent producers gear up for is that of the National Association of Television Program Executives (NATPE)—a once-a-year gathering that usually takes place in February and brings together almost all the station executives for a week of entertainment, food, drink, and a grand survey of everything new in the market. No one can say how many shows are actually bought at NATPE, but it is quite clear that many of the programs that show up on television sets in the fall were introduced at this key convention.

To gear up for an event of this importance, ads are placed in special editions of the major trade publications, brochures are created, giveaways arrive by the carton, hotel suites are decorated, personal appearances are arranged, and studio personnel and producers arrive by the planeload. At NATPE, a television executive and spouse can stuff themselves on shrimp, watch all the new television shows, and have their pictures taken with anyone from Spider Man to Dinah Shore.

Trade Publications

Producers or syndicators who want to bring their product to the attention of the stations automatically buy space in the major trade publications and use a *major* unit of space in those publications. The leaders, *Broadcasting*, *Television/Radio Age*, *Variety*, and, to a lesser extent, *Hollywood Reporter*, are ideal promotional tools because they deal with daily industry problems, solutions, and news.[4] All these publications are important reference sources for television executives who wish to stay abreast of industry trends.[5]

Collateral Materials

Collateral materials come in many forms. Simple one-sheets (an 8½ x 11 inch page printed both sides) are often used to promote off-

---

[4]Minor publications are often used as well, such as *Emmy* (the publication of NATAS), *P.D. Cue* (NATPE's official journal), and *Facts & Figures*.

[5]The cable industry is developing a number of trade publications that provide suitable vehicles for promoting programming to that market. The *Kagan Reports*, *Multi-Channel News*, *View*, and *Cable Marketing* already carry a substantial amount of advertising for syndicated services, films, and equipment.

network shows as well as network series and specials. More elaborate four-color brochures are used for similar purposes, as well as to introduce first-run syndicated programs. Still more elaborate is the press kit. (Anything from a miniature suitcase to a beach chair can be considered a press kit if it will get the attention of station managers or program directors and encourage them to advertise and publicize that show.)

DAYPART STRATEGIES

Television is as rigidly formatted as a Swiss watch. Ask anyone in almost any part of the country what is playing at a certain hour, and, given time differences and the baseball and football season, the answer is probably the same. This uniformity is due as much to the federal government as to stations' assumptions about American tastes and habits. The FCC's creation of **access** time radically altered programming sales patterns.

PTAR

In the early 1970s, the Federal Communications Commission decreed that the first half hour of primetime had to be filled with locally originated programming—or, more specifically, could *not* be filled with network entertainment programs or off-network reruns on affiliates in the top fifty markets. The intent of the primetime access rule (PTAR) was to give local programs and talent greater access to television's largest audiences by forbidding network-originated fare and to encourage new program producers by reducing network dominance. The federal government envisioned a half-hour filled with locally produced public service shows.

The result has been far different, of course. Network affiliates acquired an extremely valuable half-hour to sell in the spot market. They quickly learned that audiences will sit through a half-hour of almost anything between the end of network news and the beginning of network entertainment programming. Rather than creating a venue for locally produced shows of local interest, PTAR created a need for cheap, first-run programs that could be syndicated at high prices. This part of the FCC's goal was technically fulfilled. It also created opportunities for independent stations to counterprogram affiliates with off-network syndicated programs that had proven appeal. Thus prime access time on affiliates has been filled with the likes of *The Gong Show, The Newlywed Game, Tic Tac Dough,* and *Face the Music;* on independents, it has been filled with reruns of primetime network series. A few original access programs of quality are syndicated (such as *The Muppets* and *PM Magazine*).

Of all the television dayparts, prime access time generates the most revenues for stations. At the same time, it is the most competitive time period for syndicators because it generates the most money for their half-hour programs. As a result, the greatest portion of syndicators' sales promotion and advertising focuses on access time.

Changes in Lifestyle

Other changes in American life during the 1970s have influenced the way syndicators market their programs. In 1970, some 28 percent of adult American females 18 years and older were employed outside the home. In 1980, the figure was 54 percent, and there is every indication that this extraordinary change in American life will persist. Families are being formed somewhat later, too, and the trend is toward smaller family units. These social conditions increased the numbers of homes watching television and, consequently, increased the market value of daytime on weekends and early and late fringe time and early morning time on weekdays.[6] At the same time, daytime HUTs on weekdays declined and primetime HUTs leveled off after a decline, for the first time in history, in the fall of 1976.[7]

There are four net results of these social trends for syndicators. First, on affiliated stations, daytime syndicated shows earn relatively less money; the networks compete more aggressively for late night and early morning clearances; and weekend daytime and early and late fringe time are enhanced in importance. Second, independent stations have become more important to the syndicators. Third, as with the affiliates, daytime is less lucrative to the independents. And fourth, the market for quality early morning, early and late fringe, and primetime is enhanced.

METHODS OF PROMOTION

The major syndicators advertise to attract superior program proposals from leading writers and producers. As in any industry, the hottest companies are the ones that attract the biggest talents.

"Image" advertising in trade publications—announcing new affiliations with producers as well as prestigious awards and nominations—is an obvious but necessary means of communicating a company's successes to the industry. Having attracted the talent and the ideas, the next step is to produce and promote the product.

---

[6]Time periods preceding and following primetime. On the East and West coasts, early fringe time is 4:00 to 7:30 pm; late fringe time is 11:00 pm to 1:00 am.

[7]The HUT level (homes using television) is a Nielsen term defined as the percentage or number of television homes using one or more sets during the average minute of a 15-minute time period or during the average minute of a specific program.

A program can be promoted in a number of ways; in fact, most major syndicators use all the methods to ensure that their message is effectively communicated in the marketplace. Syndicators support their products with extensive use of broadcast trade media, public relations, brochures, fliers, and promotional mailers. They bolster media promotion with personal sales calls that reinforce the media message. Personal sales calls are also used to close major market purchases. And the larger producers and syndicators provide postsales support to promote programs and hold them on the air.

Trade publications offer other advantages for sales and promotional messages. Since these magazines are written especially for the television industry, they reach a high concentration of senior television executives and decision makers. Exposure in these magazines ensures both the right readership and cost efficiency. Figure 14-1 shows a typical trade advertisement for a syndicated access series.

Advertising units range from black and white pages to four-color spreads. Using a major unit of space provides numerous benefits: Two-page spreads tend to dominate other advertising in a publication by their size and advantageous position, frequently taking the center spread. These attributes save the sales message from being overshadowed by competitors' messages. They provide visual impact as well as prestige.

Obviously, marketing syndicated programming is very different from marketing network programming. The procedures depend on the process of program development, the number of prospects, and the prospect needs. Working relationships between producers and syndicated prospects differ from relations with networks, and postsale service requirements are more complex. Seeing how feature films and first-run syndicated programs are handled shows how complex the marketing needs are and how elaborate the advertising can be.

FEATURE FILMS

More money is invested in the production of promotional materials for feature films than for any other type of syndication. The networks, pay-television, stations, producers of videocassettes and videodiscs—all vie for the limited supply of Hollywood-produced feature films. Because of the potential for great profit, extraordinary investments are made in promotional materials. They tend to be innovative, four-color, glossy, design-oriented, award-winning showcases of promotion. They are totally in print and largely for trade advertising publications and leave-behinds. The key characteristic of these promotional materials is the

Figure 14-1 Trade Ad for a Syndicated Series (*20th Century-Fox, 1980. Used with permission.*)

distributor's name (Paramount, MGM, Twentieth Century-Fox, MCA) because the promotional objective is *prestige*. These film promotions also act as showpieces for the distributor's line of syndicated programs.

FIRST-RUN SYNDICATION

First-run syndicated programs seldom reach pilot stage without agreement in principle from some network owned and operated stations or a major group to air the program. There is more risk in first-run syndication than in off-network syndication or movie packages. Breaking even is contingent on selling a program in enough major markets and keeping the show on long enough to recoup development costs.

Services

First-run syndication also requires a large number of postsale services. Syndication operations have aptly been described as mini-networks, and parallels exist between the postsale activities of a studio's sales force and the activities of a network's affiliate relations department.

A studio or syndicator's advertising/public relations department supplies materials and services comparable to those provided by networks for their affiliates, although the syndicator must use all available trade publications as well as brochures to encourage sale of the show to other markets. After a show has been introduced in trade publications, ads usually continue to appear, announcing how many and what markets the show has been sold in. To encourage a show's longevity, ads often appear after each major rating sweep to announce how well the show has done in a variety of different demographic situations.

In the case of both first-run and rerun products, syndicators supply stations with general press kits, specific press releases, and black and white glossies for the show and its stars. They produce and supply on-air television spots (encouraging audiences to tune in at a specific time), on-air slides, radio spots, ad mats, and ad art slides. And, as discussed previously, syndicators often undertake cooperative promotional advertising with stations or will pay for tune-in advertising themselves if the show and the situation merit it.

Merchandising other kinds of syndicated shows—movie packages, off-network shows, specials—requires similar, if more specialized, efforts from the syndicators' advertising and public relations departments. But whatever the program or marketing strategy, the use of the major trade publications, collateral materials, and the trade conventions is a constant.

Scheduling

A syndicated show, once it has been sold to a television station, is like a child given away for adoption. The station that purchases the show assigns it an on-air time period (which may not be to the producer's liking), assigns a dollar value to the advertising time in the program, and finally advertises and promotes the program on its own. Because this last function can greatly affect the success or failure of a program, syndicators and studios have recently abandoned the passive, hands-off, let-the-station-handle-everything role and are now developing marketing objectives and strategies for their important shows, just as any corporation would.

Support

Support for their programs comes in the form of direct media advertising in individual markets through the use of local newspapers, television newspaper supplements, *TV Guide, TV Log,* network and local radio spots (occasionally), and other key consumer media such as billboards.

Figure 14-2 shows three ad slicks supplied by the distributor of *A Perfect Couple* that stations can use for *TV Guide* ads. Several sizes are supplied so that stations can choose the size that fits their promotional needs and budgets.

Advertising support for a station can also be handled cooperatively by offering the station matching funds in its market. The timing for these activities falls into two primary sequences: during the introduction of a new program and during the key rating sweeps (usually in November and February).

Figure 14-2 Ad Slicks for a Feature Film (*20th Century-Fox, 1980. Used with permission.*)

ADVERTISING ART

While it is clear that producers can do a great deal to control a show's image at the viewer's level, and will probably become more involved in direct consumer advertising during the 1980s, they are still scrambling to create the kind of programming that will get them into the most lucrative time periods, an element over which they have much less control.

PARALLELS IN PUBLIC BROADCASTING

Public broadcasting must sell its programs. Just as commercial broadcasters promote their series to advertisers and distributors sell to stations, public broadcasters sell major national corporations on underwriting their costs. Public broadcasters employ many of the promotional and selling techniques associated with commercial broadcasters and syndicators. They need similar audience research and promotional brochures and materials.

Managerial support for demographic audience research and funds for sophisticated sales materials have been slighted in public broadcasting, however, partly because of inadequate station budgets. Individual stations have had to sell their programs with little promotional assistance from PBS. And the two central advantages of public broadcasting over its commercial competitors—its lower-cost programs and its upscale audiences—are rarely articulated as marketing strategies.[8] Although the language of selling is usually rejected by public broadcasters as too "commercial," the life-and-death competition for money is forcing a new awareness on many public station managers. They are beginning to adopt the marketing perspective of sales promotion and allocate funds for support materials. The "development director" of public broadcasting increasingly resembles the "vice-president for sales" at a syndication firm.

THE FUTURE

The future for syndication—that is, programs supplied to broadcasters independent of established networks—is especially bright. The marketplace is expanding, choices are proliferating, and producers and syndicators will have to broaden their product to meet the new demands. The major areas for growth will be motion pictures, original programming, and program services; each will demand greatly expanded pro-

---

[8]David J. LeRoy and Judith M. LeRoy, untitled manuscript prepared for the Corporation for Public Broadcasting, 1981.

motional activities. The key question is how great a financial stake the major producers acquire in programming for the newer media such as cable and videodiscs. If, as anticipated, the expansion of cable creates a parallel expansion in the demand for new feature film material, promotion and advertising will have to create audiences for new films faster than ever before—and faced with much greater competition—in order to maximize revenues from the "home box office." It is hard to tell whether videodiscs will consist largely of already marketed films and series—requiring special remarketing techniques directed toward consumers—or will require substantial amounts of original programming.

Moreover, the commercial stations will probably require a much greater variety of first-run programming to replace the previous supplies of off-network product. First-run programming will have to operate without the aid of network promotion to millions of homes at a single moment. Producers and syndicators may well involve themselves in the creation and distribution of programming and promotion for a variety of program formats. News and information features, dramatic and comedy programming, pop music formats, variety shows— these are just a few of the possibilities. However it evolves, the market will be considerably different from anything broadcasters have known. The opportunities, in turn, will be enormous.

SUMMARY

This chapter draws together the promotional practices used by syndicators of series and feature films to television stations, networks, and pay-television systems. The practices are virtually the same as those used in the sale of any product, but the supply and demand characteristics of the broadcasting market are unique. Film sales promotion requires only information on the identity of distributors because the demand for films is so great. Conventions, trade publications, and collateral print materials play especially important roles in promoting syndicated series sales. First-run programming requires expanded postsale services from distributors. The changing marketplace and the shifting lifestyles of television viewers have induced syndicators and studios to begin to play active roles in the scheduling and audience promotion of their series and films. The growth of cable and projected expansion in numbers of television stations suggests a broadening market for syndicated programs and increased demand for well-promoted first-run programming.

Part **III** ■ Suggested Readings

Aspley, John Cameron. *The Dartnell Sales Promotion Handbook.* **5th ed.** Chicago: Dartnell Corporation, 1966.
Basic industry guide covering sales promotion and including case studies.

Horowitz, Norman. "Syndication" in *Inside the TV Business,* Steve Morgenstern, ed. New York: Sterling Publishing Co., 1979.
Interview-style article covering economics of feature film and second-run series syndication.

Mayer, Michael F. *The Film Industries: Practical Business/Legal Problems in Production, Distribution and Exhibition.* New York: Hastings House, 1973.
Advice for film producers, agents, exhibitors, and distributors on financial and legal considerations in feature film marketing; covers talent rights, exhibition contracts, copyright, publicity, and promotion.

Mueller, William S. "What Does Your Film Contract Say?" *Broadcast Financial Journal* 3(June 1973):14.
Analysis of the technical languge of contracts for syndicated films aimed at broadcasters.

Wurtzel, Alan, and Surlin, Stuart. "Viewer Attitudes Toward Television Advisory Warnings." *Journal of Broadcasting* 22(Winter 1978):19–31.
Study concluding that viewer advisories may act as promotions for movies and shows although networks claim they are intended only as warnings about possibly objectionable material.

Part

IV

Public Relations

$\mathbf{P}$art IV contains two chapters crucial to understanding the most so-phisticated strategies of broadcast and cable marketing. One covers communicating to others by means of the trade press; the other discusses communication by means of a positive public service image.

Although public relations is the parent to promotion, the duties of dealing with the trade press are only an ancillary responsibility of station promotion departments. Networks, groups, the pay services, and the larger commercial and public stations maintain in-house public relations staff and generally place them in structural units separate from promotion. They may also employ outside specialists. But mid-sized and smaller television stations and most radio stations add the job of public relations on a day-to-day basis to the workload of the on-air and print promotion department. Cable systems rarely give prominence to public relations as an activity separate from subscriber marketing.

In these two chapters public relations is divided into its trade and community service aspects; publicity is included as a subsidiary concern since it is normally handled by station promotion departments. Chapter 15 looks at the basic techniques of trade relations that can be used by networks, groups, cable, pay services, and stations to realize their overall strategies. The chapter reviews the fundamental concepts behind "PR" and gives numerous examples of attention-getting ideas.

Chapter 16 deals with community involvement that affects a station's entire programming schedule, binding the station's public image to its public service activities. This highly visible brand of public service promotion uses a station's own on-air, its programs, its public service announcements, and its logos and image devices to promote community involvement in a major public service activity. Station identity de-

271

rives from community presence. This comprehensive view of the role of promotion is advocated by a limited number of public service promotion companies. The chapter opens with a classification of the types of public service that radio and television stations have traditionally attempted; it then details the phenomenal community service successes of WBZ in Boston. What gives this chapter special value is that it proposes the means for evaluating the accomplishments of public service promotion in concrete, objective terms.

This part of the book sums up perspectives on promotion using largely unpaid forms of marketing. The chapters examine techniques for reaching station and network goals within the larger framework of industry trends and community needs. They conclude the book's comprehensive examination of the current strategies of television, radio, and cable promotion at the beginning of the 1980s. Even though changes in the economic configuration of the industry by the mid-1980s are likely to refine the practice of these strategies, the importance of promotion will be increasingly recognized as a major element in the achievement of audience-related goals.

Trade Press Relations

by
Robert A. Bernstein

Robert A. Bernstein has been president of his own New York public relations firm, March Five Inc., since 1975. His clients include the National Association of Television Program Executives (NATPE), the International Radio and Television Society (IRTS), the Broadcasters Promotion Association (BPA), Time/Life, Viacom, Post-Newsweek Stations, Metromedia, Globo Network of Brazil, Scholastic, and Eastman-Kodak. Before starting his own firm, he held public relations positions at the Dumont Television Network, Westinghouse Broadcasting Company, Triangle Publications, and Viacom International. He has a B.A. from Columbia University and an M.F.A. from Yale University. Robert Bernstein won the Silver Anvil Award from the American Public Relations Association in 1961.

> They meet in a singles bar. If he says he owns a Picasso, makes a great fettuccine, and ran the Marathon in 2:59 . . . that is advertising.
>
> If he says Jackie O wants to buy his Picasso, he could have won the Marathon if Halston, Capote, and Liza hadn't kept him up till three over fettuccine, and she has the most incredible eyes . . . that is promotion.
>
> But if she has heard from her friends that his Picasso is the biggest and his fettuccine the best, and she immediately suggests they go up to his place . . . that is public relations.

It used to be called publicity. When P. T. Barnum practiced it, it was press agentry. When St. Paul did it, it was gospel. Hollywood made it tawdry; corporations made it suspect; the White House made it controversial. Yet today, everyone and everything has a need and usually a plan to reach certain publics and create certain images.

THE FUNCTION OF PUBLIC RELATIONS

Public relations is not a luxury. In America at least, it is a necessity, and it costs less than advertising or promotion. Public relations makes images and molds public opinion; it gives durable general impressions of companies by imaginatively translating their features.

273

In broadcasting, public relations must whet the appetites of the financial community, industry professionals, advertisers and their agencies, government, educators, opinion makers, and listening or viewing audiences. In addition to telling a company's overall story, public relations must position each ingredient in a substantive, invigorating manner. It is a business of creative ideas and professional skills masquerading as effortless and natural processes.

Broadcasting lives with scrutiny as a bedfellow. To imagine that a new White House will inaugurate a honeymoon with the press or a sabbatical from congressional investigations, FCC filings, or public interest group inquisitions is unrealistic. The explosive power of radio and television on daily living, the inadequate defense of the industry by its spokespersons, and some tangible failures by broadcasters have made it fashionable and comfortable to attack not only programming but all facets of broadcasting. The right to engage in a business that brings an inordinately high return on dollars invested requires constant care and thoughtful representation of that business if it is to flourish in a relatively unimpeded manner.

The public relations expert's role cuts across all station departmental lines and corporate organizational charts. That individual deserves to be fully informed on every subject because, just as ads and sales calls are expected to return money, knowledge, and goodwill, so public relations expenditures must produce a fair return.

Although there is no special time or place the role is played, the particular responsibility of public relations is to visualize, assess, and articulate both internal and public announcements, to conceive community projects, and to package specific office activities as attractively and effectively as possible. The public relations manager helps management restate its goals in periodic sequences of self-examination. After delineating corporate objectives, emphasis must always be placed on the current climate and the future in the same breath. Publicists have to be schizophrenic, devoting one mind to press coverage amid current pressures while devoting a second mind to anticipation of tomorrow's changes.

Station Groups

Station groups are groups of stations. The definition thus includes the networks and their owned stations, sets of stations scattered geographically but licensed to one parent corporation, and electronically joined broadcasts from syndicators. All groups have characteristics setting them apart from non-group-owned stations that affect the practice of public relations.

Groups tout programs and image concepts that touch many markets at once. The large number and variety of their concerns produce undercurrents that affect the freedom of individual stations in their public announcements. Higher management's eyes are frequently turned toward Washington and associated politics. Although group budgets for public relations may be higher than for an equivalent number of separately owned stations, group management's publicity expectations are concomitantly higher.

The larger the station group, the more complex its geography and its cast of executive characters. Ergo delays are more frequent, and a publicist's ability to get basic information is put to ruder tests. One practical strategy is to invent the needed information and offer it to management for correction. Using a mailgram is effective since busy executives rarely read long memos. They will respond, however, in order to correct mistakes.

The dragging of executive feet is endemic, epidemic, and pandemic. Hooray for Steve Labunski, executive director of the International Radio and Television Society, who is credited with inventing the time bomb memo. This device can save a publicist's life. Whenever upstairs management delays a project until it is in danger of collapse, the idea is to send the boss a note including the phrase: "Therefore, unless I hear from you to the contrary by noon tomorrow, I'll go ahead with . . ." The project will be able to proceed safely or the promotion department will rapidly hear why it should not.

Networks

For the twenty American syndication networks, the thirty leading station groups, and ad hoc programming networks such as **Operation Prime Time,** the central public relations problem is the intense competition they face from the most sophisticated professionals in the field: the three commercial networks. In all these situations—at syndicators, groups, and networks—there is greater tension in executive suites than at stations, and tougher internal politics. Moreover, there is great concern over broad social and regulatory issues—requiring homework from public relations staffs—and a rapid pace in day-to-day developments easily creating ulcers.

THE METHODS OF PUBLIC RELATIONS

Implementing a public relations campaign in the typical broadcast company requires efforts in the following areas:

- Sales publicity
- Programming
- Corporate publicity
- Community relations
- Governmental relations
- Special projects
- Executive education (education of management in public relations strategies and techniques)
- Glamour

Seven of these are acknowledged to be proper, normal concerns of public relations requiring continuing involvement. The eighth, glamour, is often dismissed as the province of the cosmetics industry or furriers.

The truth is, however, that broadcasting is the most glamorous medium yet invented. It brings into homes the excitement of an external universe. A Washington crime indictment or an antitrust suit never diminishes the size of an audience or lowers a sales price. A series that sounds boring surely will. Lack of glamour encourages tune-out and loses sales.

Corporations yawn or frown when public relations firms suggest they can and should be glamorous. Broadcasters especially should know better. If nations of television viewers can be stimulated into panting over who shot J. R., they certainly can be motivated more than once a season to stay home for a show "everybody is talking about," one that simply cannot be missed.

This goal may sound too grandiose for small-market stations on tiny budgets, but glamour can be adapted on a lower level. If local management refuses to understand the strategies of public relations, good staff should move as quickly as possible to larger markets.

Public relations methods are basically the same for broadcast stations, station groups, networks, producers, distributors, newspapers, schools, professional associations, star talent, and foundations. The ultimate goal of every one of them is the same: profit. The intensity of public relations efforts varies, however, depending on available dollars and emotional commitment from management. The method boils down to five concepts that encompass complex strategies appropriate to all public relations situations: friendship, optimism, credibility, knowledge, and momentum.

Friendship

It is *who* the public relations expert knows that counts. Every media person within reach should be made into a personal friend. This especially includes media people in New York and Los Angeles because these two cities have unique media concentration. No matter how geographically distant, other media people are easily reachable by telephone and mail from anywhere else. On the local level, it is important to disarm editors and turn their objectivity into conflicting loyalties by becoming a friend who shares common pastimes and ethnic restaurants. This may require getting tickets to hockey games though one hates hockey; it definitely requires elaborate lists of spouses' birthdays.

Optimism

The old axiom that says "smile" is best. If a public relations expert does not care, who will? Enthusiasm is contagious, and lack of conviction leads to unnecessary defeat. If first efforts do not succeed, send over the press release again, this time wrapped around a bottle of wine. The ploy of "I need this as a favor" works about once a year at most.

Credibility

There is astronomical value to having a publicist's words respected, especially because those of so many colleagues are not. Never lie, unless you are absolutely brilliant at permanent concealment of the truth. Broadcasting is truly a small world. Everyone knows everyone, and a best friend's secretary confides in a sister-in-law who plays bridge with an editor's aunt. Tell the truth up to the point at which management balks, and then decline to answer press questions.

Knowledge

Know the subject. Few reporters are content to accept only what is announced. It is appropriate for them to ask questions, and a public relations spokesperson should have adequate answers or sources for reference. When management claims the station is doing the first game show ever to have animals as contestants, call the Broadcast Information Bureau or the Broadcast Promotion Association library to check the facts out; the press may well know that the assertion is untrue.

Momentum

Continuous activity is vital. The cumulative impact of week-in/week-out contact with the press gives a station importance as a source of news and inspires the press to seek out the station as a resource. "Quickie press flights" are soon forgotten; a steady flow of information can produce increasing quantities of results and beneficial long-term press relations.

A Word to the Wise

These five concepts should be the basis of each day's public relations schedule. The need for credibility must surface, for example, when a sales manager wants to claim a sold-out spot schedule; it is likely, after all, that thirty-six Red Cross public service announcements will strike editors as excessive even for a station of pronounced civic responsibility.

And when the general manager asks for wedding announcement placement for a niece's nuptials, call up some optimism before expressing a realistic but negative response. When the sportscaster slips the public relations staff four seats for the big game, invite a choleric local reporter instead of a good old buddy.

Few stations employ full-time public relations directors. Promotion managers, usually overworked and underpaid, inherit this function, often almost as an afterthought. The promotion manager may have to fight for a seat at staff meetings, but a clipping service is a useful lever if the manager's name appears in a healthy percentage of clippings. When management executives assure public relations staffs that they do not need ego trips, do not listen.

THE ROLE OF THE NATIONAL TRADE PRESS

When a station has a major story worthy of the national *consumer* press, the nearest wire service correspondent will quickly be responsive. *Trade* press interest is harder to ascertain, but the average station has more stories of trade press interest than pessimistic promotion managers attempt to place. Nothing is more irritating to a trade press editor, though, than to receive inappropriate materials. One common example is a log listing that no national publication uses. *Variety* never uses photos; to send one is to imply that your staff does not read the publication. The two British-based trade publications in the following list prefer an angle of international interest but actually print local U.S. items without any international connection. In contrast, *Solomon Newsletter* is published in the United States but deals only with global perspectives of media events. The lesson for public relations staffs is that what goes out to a national mailing list cannot be identical to local press mailings.

The trade publications that may use local market stories vary in the quantities they use and whether they use only radio or only television or both. The following national trade publications should be approached with items of national interest:

Advertising Age (Crain Communications, Chicago)

Ad Week (Lee Kerry, publisher, New York; also Los Angeles)

Backstage (New York)

Billboard (Los Angeles)

BPA Newsletter (Broadcasters Promotion Association, Lancaster, Pennsylvania)

Broadcast (London)

Broadcasting (Broadcasting Publications, Washington, D.C.)

Broadcast Management/Engineering (BM/E) (Broadband Information Services, New York)

Business Week (New York)

Channels (Media Commentary Council, New York)

Daily Variety (Los Angeles)

Facts, Figures & Film (Broadcast Information Bureau, Syosset, New York)

Gallagher Report (New York)

Hollywood Reporter (Hollywood)

Marketing and Media Decisions (New York)

Media Industry Newsletter (Terry Poltrack, editor, New York)

Merchandising Week (New York)

Millimeter (Alice Wolf, New York)

Movie/TV Marketing (William Ireton, editor, Los Angeles; also Tokyo)

NAB publications (various) (National Association of Broadcasters, Washington, D.C.)

New York Times (New York)

P.D. Cue (National Association of Television Program Executives, New York)

RAB publications (various) (Radio Advertising Bureau, New York)

Radio & Records (Hollywood)

Scholastic Publications (various) (New York)

Screen International (London)

Solomon Newsletter (Kenneth Morris, publisher, Beverly Hills)

Telek (Eastman-Kodak, Rochester, New York)

Television Digest (Washington, D.C.)

Television International (Hollywood)

Television/Radio Age (New York)

TVB publications (various) (Television Bureau, New York)

TV Guide (Radnor, Pennsylvania)

TV World (London)

Variety (New York)

Wall Street Journal (New York)

A rapidly growing number of newspapers and magazines in related industries—advertising, cable, satellites, home video, education—allot limited space to traditional broadcasting news and should be cultivated when time permits or the subject matter is especially appropriate. A single telephone call can produce the basic details on deadlines and procedures. The following list covers the most established of these publications as of 1981:

Cablecast (Paul Kagan Assoc., Carmel, California)

Cable Source Book (Broadcasting Publications, Washington, D.C.)

Cablevision (Titsch Publishing, Denver)

Home Video Newsletter (Knowledge Industry Publications, White Plains, New York)

Multicast (Paul Kagan Assoc., Carmel, California)

Multi-channel (Fairchild Publications, Denver)

Pay Television (Television International Ltd., Hollywood)

Pay TV Newsletter (Paul Kagan Assoc., Carmel, California)

Satellite Communications (Cardiff Publishing, Denver)

Sat Guide (Satellite Program Guide, Hailey, Idaho)

TVC (Cardiff Publishing, Denver)

Video (Reese Publishing, New York)

Videocassette & CATV Newsletter (Martin Robers & Assoc., Beverly Hills)

Videography (United Business Publications, New York)

Videoplay (C. S. Tepfer Publishing, Danbury, Connecticut)

Video Week (Television Digest, Washington, D.C.)

View (Macro Communications, New York)

Watch (Titsch Publishing, Denver)

THE IMPORTANCE OF LOCAL PRESS CONTACTS

When suburban papers, weeklies, and monthlies are added to the diminishing number of daily newspapers, no American market lacks a press corps. Unlike the trade press, newspapers may occasionally be hostile to broadcast public relations, perceiving themselves as rival media. In rare instances, a ban on news of a particular station is rigid and fully supported by newspaper ownership. Generally, however, reporters and editors are fair but human, requiring the same tender loving care advocated in the five magic public relations concepts: friendship, optimism, credibility, knowledge, and momentum.

One error made by many station promotion or public relations managers is to clutch the local press to one exclusive bosom. This penalizes the station by restricting the number of individuals who can approach the press. Department heads can usually be trusted to speak with press representatives as long as the public relations staff knows what is happening. National sources such as the syndicators of programs the station airs often have personal ties with local editors and can take some of the promotion department's workload onto their competent shoulders.[1]

Wise minds throughout the industry are proclaiming more and more forcefully that localism is the key to station survival in an era of incredible technological innovation. Identification with the local community must reach beyond mere publicizing of new on-air personalities to the positioning of the station as an integral part of the market. The station's best weapon remains the local press; in most markets, the national press carries little weight.[2]

For all publications, local or national, the most widely used device is the press release. There are almost ten thousand radio and television stations in operation; consequently, five hundred releases in an editor's mail each day is a modest number. No wonder editors toss two-thirds in the wastebasket unread. But when they have met or talked periodically on the telephone with an individual, they are likely at least to open the envelope and give the story a glance.

The rules for effective press releases are logical and obvious, but many publicists forget them. To wit:

- Use a dateline, as other publications do, to indicate when the information was released.
- Double space.
- Use one side of a page only.

---

[1]The degree of support (and competence) demonstrated by syndicators may vary widely.
[2]The obvious exceptions are the major markets of New York and Los Angeles.

- Include a contact name—normally that of the public relations person who created the release—in case editors want more information.
- Adopt a straightforward news style in keeping with the publication's writing style. Eliminate all the adjectives that belong in promotional brochures and advertisements.

Sportswriters claim that teams not only beat their opponents—they crushed, jolted, buried, walloped, edged, trounced, set back, stymied, subdued, topped, blanked, upset, or overwhelmed them! Public relations writing can be as inventive; management need not always "announce" something: They can also reveal, point out, note, confirm, enunciate, declare, and explain it.

LET'S HEAR IT FOR GIMMICKS

An instinct for slogans, tricks, quotable quotes, themes, and funny titles is a talent worth perfecting. The enemy of public relations is dignity (frequently an overrated virtue anyway). *Variety* taught a jarring lesson some years ago when it failed to print a polite release about a corporate triumph but, in the same issue, gave several column inches to three lesser stories.[3]

One story pointed out that a small FM outlet in New Haven had to go off the air for three days while its new transmitter was being activated. The publicist suggested that the dead air time be sold to an advertiser using the simple sign-off line, "The following 72 hours of silence are brought to you by First City Bank."

In another item the same day, the mayor of Philadelphia announced his pride in his administration's encouragement of the still-new television medium with this statement to a Rotary lunch: "We fought a bloody battle to bring the coagulated cable in."

In the third story, a syndication company stuck with a dull documentary about the Paris Zoo, famed for its lions and tigers, found no one would write a line about it until a publicist headlined a release "French Cat House on TV."

These stories illustrate the power of the gimmick. Publicists must stoop to conquer. The U.S. Health Department once declared a sick bird "ill-eagle." The "NEWS" was described as standing for "North-East-West-South" and later for "News/Editorial/Weather/Sports" on station KDKA, Pittsburgh. New Jersey's Highway Department launched

[3]*Variety*, June 1961.

Route 9-W with this gem: "The answer is 9-W. What's the question? Does Wagner get spelled with a V?" Nein, it vos not genius, but the joke worked and started a year of similar jokes.

A pun is the lowest form of public relations wit. A bun is the lowest form of wheat. It may not be well-bread to roll on in the rye fashion, but it can bring in the dough. Opponents of alliteration might be reminded that the most famous headline in trade press history is "Sticks Nix Hick Pix."

To find empathy in individual press contacts, then, look for a gimmick and exploit it. And enlist the aid of station personnel. The salesman who wanted to be a singer and the secretary who tap dances can get involved in publicity stunts that please them, improve corporate morale, cost the station little, and generate column inches in the local press.

FIRST AID KITS

Every publicist needs a stockpile to draw from in real emergencies as well as day-to-day demonstrations of brilliance. The following are standard elements in a public relations CARE package:

- One executive in Sales, one in Programming, and one in Business/Finance who especially like you
- Two editors who like you enough to come through in a clutch with a decent story break
- One government contact, preferably in Washington, who will lend his or her name to open doors for you
- A private stock of devices to tap when the moment calls for "a fresh idea at today's meeting"
- A weekly bit of gossip about the competition
- An infallible, immaculate typist (neatness counts)
- A few terrific sourcebooks such as annual broadcasting encyclopedias
- A radio talk show that will agree to interview your corporate president
- Aspirin

These are the emergency supplies from which the tired, uncreative publicist draws. On creative days, replenish the stockpile.

A DOZEN IDEAS THAT WORK

Many publicity projects have perennial value. These are ideas whose time has come and come and come and, with a year's rest, can come again. Unless they have been noticeable in the local market lately, they can be tapped to a station's advantage at any time.

Information Brochures

Prepare an information booklet with data hard to come by in the market. Include such information as the names and addresses of all-night pharmacies; banks with late hours; where to rent costumes; all-night beauty salons; emergency plumbers/electricians/auto repairs; where to cash checks after bank hours; weekend medical/dental/optical/veterinarian services; key names for city and state departments of gas/water/sanitation/parks/highways; night food deliveries; locations and hours of public recreation facilities. Ideally, such a booklet leaves blank space for a sponsor's imprint so that a local advertiser can defray the cost. Such brochures are easy to update every year and accommodate a change in sponsors.

Films

Use film footage taken by school teams of recent games. When live interviews in the station's studio with coach and star are added, an inexpensive half-hour special has been created with advertiser and community appeal.

Audio Tapes

Announce that the station will make brief audio tapes for any viewer or listener who wishes to speak to a friend or relative overseas, especially military personnel, and mail the tapes with the station's compliments. This effort creates goodwill (at low cost) and can generate positive consumer news coverage.

Policy Statements

Publicize the station's official policy on political advertising, hiring practices, management training programs, contests, appeals and telethons, paid religious broadcasts, acceptability of advertising, libel and slander, ascertainment of community needs, the right of privacy, or current issues that are controversial. Clear statements on such subjects may be newsworthy at any time; they are especially likely to be drawn out of press files when a pertinent issue arises.

Children's Events

The station can hold regular children's events such as solicitations of drawings and paintings on given themes. Exhibit as many entries as possible in station lobbies, cooperating banks, or sponsors' store windows. Such activities have the ever-popular appeal of association with children for both station and sponsor.

Local Organizations

Connect each key station executive with a particular civic, fraternal, or philanthropic organization, local or national. Committee volunteers soon become chairpersons and officers and bring beneficial publicity to the station.

The Mobile Museum

The station can inexpensively rent a large display van to drive to shopping centers and schools throughout the station's coverage area. Generally, people enter public display vans, by means of removable steps and view an exhibit down one side and back the other. Voice commentary and music are prerecorded. Most exhibit materials can be gathered at no cost and can range from histories of the World Series to book displays for National Library Week, from Irish music celebrations to memorabilia on the birth of the nation or the city. As with the other public relations ideas, the station is both creating a newsworthy event (particularly for suburban weekly papers) and gaining a valuable community service image.

Station Participation

Another possibility is to invite a local reporter to sit in on the station's staff meetings for a week. This invitation should cement a personal friendship and probably will result in a feature newspaper story.

Parades

The station may want to stage a sports car rally or an antique auto parade with prizes. The station can also enter a float in the city's annual parades. One useful device is to invite the audience to appear at curbside carrying signs about the station for which the station distributes gifts and awards prizes. This type of activity has a high likelihood of receiving local television news coverage and newspaper photographs.

Polls

Instant polls provide quick reactions to local, regional, or national current events. For the price of a special telephone number, the station can pose both serious and frivolous questions and garner press coverage on the results. It is important to the station's credibility, though, never to misrepresent the nonrandomness of the poll's sample.

Station Awards

Create a station salute or award, monthly or annual, that honors a citizen, a local company, a cause, or a neighborhood. Plaques and framed scrolls awarded to recipients become permanent station call letter advertising as well as conversation pieces among potential advertisers and audience members.

Contests

A solid, old-fashioned event such as a treasure hunt, talent contest, golf competition, or charity costume party can involve the community. Some events lend themselves to annual repetition and become outstanding elements in the station's long-term community image.

A Baker's Dozen

Numerous other ideas can be borrowed by reading the trade press to see what has succeeded in other markets. The operation of a mini-bureau for speech platforms sometimes works—assuming that the station's top executives agree to be high on the list of available speakers. Celebrities are good ammunition under any and all circumstances. Always push for the biggest name available. At the same time, the dullest areas—accounting, engineering, furnishing—can yield publicity nuggets if mined. Sizable dollar contributions to local cultural institutions can generate tickets for entertaining press or advertising clients at performances. Another possibility is naming a board of experts as the station's "Think Bank" with the understanding that the station's news department will call on them as contributing editors when their fields of expertise are in the news.

Each of these ideas is reusable and lends itself to creative variation. All combine the two essential ingredients of public relations: community goodwill and newsworthiness. It is this last element—newsworthiness—that differentiates station promotion and station community service from the activities that genuinely reflect public relations genius.

SUMMARY

The public relations process is a pyramid. Reporters, industry committees, conventions, suppliers of materials, and useful contact names are all foundation stones. The lowest levels require more stones and a greater expenditure of time and care to position them properly. Higher in corporate strategy, fewer stones are needed, but it is always a mistake to skip a stone, leaving a gap that can weaken the superstructure.

The methods required of a publicist are friendship, optimism, credibility, knowledge, and momentum. They apply in dealing with both the local and national trade press and the consumer press. They apply whether the publicist works for a network, a group, or an individual station. The effective use of gimmicks can create news interest largely irrespective of an item's actual content; it is the gimmick that gets the envelope opened and the press release read. However, a large number of station activities reach beyond press releases to stimulate press coverage through community involvement. In addition to the concrete suggestions offered in this chapter, more elaborate campaigns are discussed in Chapter. 16.

This chapter has focused on the strategies and tactics for effective public relations that demand education of company management, community press leaders, and advertisers. A station's most important strategy is its articulated goals, and some employees have an instinct for communicating dramatically and effectively to the station's numerous publics. The public relations staff needs this ability most of all, but a roster of station spokespersons greatly eases the task. Flair, style, glamour, or class, a touch that becomes the station's calling card, are crucial to communicating a station's message reliably. And the successful publicist will have a unique signature over and above the station's message that communicates that individual's friendliness, optimism, credibility, knowledge, and momentum.

Perhaps the earliest explanation of publicity in the United States is dated 1789:

> He who whispers down the well
> About the goods he has to sell
> Will never reap the golden dollars
> Like him who stands up proud and hollers.

The author was, of course, Benjamin Franklin, but he neglected to point out that if everybody else is hollering, a whisper may do better. The successful publicist lets no day go by without some public relations activity, however pressing other commitments. If it is getting near 5:30 pm, start a rumor.

Promotion As Public Service

by
Jerry Wishnow

Jerry Wishnow formed his own public service promotion company in 1974, the Wishnow Group, to provide broadcasters, government, and businesses with a cohesive means for using public service as an advertising and promotional tool. His clients have included the U.S. Department of Justice, the U.S. Department of Energy, the General Federation of Women's Clubs, the CBS Television Network, RKO General Broadcasting, the Washington Star Broadcasting Company, Westinghouse Television, ABC Radio, and Montgomery Ward. Between 1973 and 1974, he coordinated public service promotions for the Westinghouse group of radio and television stations. Prior to that, he was creative services director and public services director for WBZ Radio in Boston. He holds a B.A. from Northeastern University and an M.S. from the Medill School of Journalism at Northwestern. He has won awards from Scripps-Howard, the Broadcasters Promotion Association, National Headliners, Esquire magazine, the Environmental Protection Agency, the American Medical Association, United Press International, Sigma Delta Chi, the Massachusetts Teachers Association, the National Tuberculosis Society, Billboard magazine, The Hatch Award for advertising, the National Conference of Christians and Jews, and the American Trial Lawyers Association.

The public service promotional approach to community involvement and station promotion is contradictory by nature. Broadcast public service is usually thought of as the ponderous explication of community problems while promotion has the crass image of drums beating. In actuality, public service promotion allows a station to position itself as the friend and ally of its audience and, at the same time, draw new audiences to its programs. While other stations in a market use their advertising, promotion, and public relations resources to tell their audiences how great they are, stations using public service promotion can actually perform invaluable services on behalf of their audiences. These services can enhance a station's image and improve its ratings by using public service announcement and public affairs programming air time rather than large quantities of commercial or promotional time.

THE BASIC TOOLS OF PUBLIC SERVICE

The two major elements of on-air public service are public service announcements and public affairs programming. Commitments to air a specified quantity of each are made periodically to the Federal Communications Commission when stations renew their licenses. The FCC has outlined a series of program categories and definitions to assist broadcasters. These guidelines distinguish between public service announcements and public affairs programming, but both are essential techniques of public service promotion that sometimes overlap.

Public Service Announcements

Public service announcements (PSAs) are announcements for which no charge is made to promote activities of federal, state, or local governments (such as military recruiting or sales of U.S. savings bonds), the activities of nonprofit organizations (such as the United Giving Fund or Red Cross blood donations), or any other announcement serving community interests (such as messages urging listeners or viewers to vote).[1] An example of a standard PSA is:

> *The Detroit area Red Cross Blood Drive is under way. You can take part by rolling up your sleeves at the WXYZ-TV Bloodmobile all this week from 5 to 9 pm. For further information on locations, call. . . .*

Information for PSAs is sometimes researched by the station, but more frequently it is sent or called in by representatives of nonprofit organizations. National service groups typically send well-packaged spots that provide space for the addition of local time and place or other specific information. Local nonprofit organizations are often poorly funded, and station personnel must package the information themselves.

Public service announcements take many different forms. On radio, they range from brief scripts read by announcers to elaborately produced 30-second and 60-second spots, complete with music and sound effects. On television, PSAs can take the form of simple slides with voice-overs or can be highly produced spots using station personalities at remote locations. Most radio and television stations also air a "community calendar" listing upcoming local activities.

At larger stations, the community affairs or public affairs director is responsible for writing and screening PSA materials. The director also

---

[1]This definition appears in FCC Section 73,1810, *Rules and Regulations*, but is intended as a general guideline only, not a rule.

makes sure that spots are noncommercial and customizes them to the station's time and format requirements. The PSAs are then scheduled by the station's traffic department. After airing, the time, date, and content of PSAs are logged so the station can demonstrate that it has met its license renewal commitments. At small-market radio and television stations, the promotion manager, traffic manager, or program director is often responsible for public service functions, or they may be a shared duty among the department heads.[2]

Most stations are inundated with local and national PSAs—often to the point where demand exceeds the supply of air time. Stations or local broadcast associations usually organize rotation plans that manage the flow of spots. These rotation plans generally work against the impact of any individual spot. Because public service announcements are a large part of a station's community outreach, they need to reflect current public issues and needs. Selection of appropriate spots also should give priority to community activities in a station's service area. Broadcast reform groups are quick to take note of stations that rely too heavily on nationally preproduced material. Quite often station policy allows PSAs to be aired at the least desirable times to avoid conflict with valuable commercial or promotional availabilities. Some stations, however, reserve air time for PSAs in all dayparts, including primetime, in advance.

Public Affairs Programming

Public affairs programs deal with local, state, regional, national, or international issues. They include, but are not limited to, talk programs, commentaries, discussions, speeches, editorials, political programs,

[2]A survey of the members of the National Broadcast Association for Community Affairs (NBACA) was conducted in 1980 to describe the backgrounds and current professional responsibilities of those specializing in public/community affairs. Eighty-seven television and thirty-eight radio members of NBACA participated in the mail survey. The respondents exhibited wide diversity in age, sex (56 percent female, 44 percent male), education, race/ethnic group, and previous broadcast experience. Reports of background experience emphasized production, news, talent/announcing, programming, and promotion.

The titles of those at stations most involved with public/community service demonstrate the separation of station/program promotion from public/community affairs. At the reporting television stations, 33 percent are called public affairs directors/managers and 32 percent community affairs director/manager; the remainder are divided among community relations/services/director/manager, vice-president, public service director/manager (28 percent), and other (7 percent). Approximately half or more take complete responsibility (as opposed to shared or none) for public affairs programming, PSA production, PSA scheduling, ascertainment, and community service involvement and projects. In fact, of those reporting, 57 percent said their major activity was public affairs programming, 23 percent said community service involvement and projects, and 13 percent said PSAs.

Demonstrative of the rising importance of public/community affairs is the fact that 58 percent of respondents report to the station or general manager, 11 percent to a corporate executive, and only 22 percent to the program manager (9 percent to other). Inadequate staff is the biggest single problem reported because over 60 percent of respondents have only one, two, or no other people in their departments, although 24 percent have five or more (three or four people, 13 percent). These results were reported in the *National Broadcast Association for Community Affairs Summer Newsletter* 1(6)(Summer 1980):1–12.

documentaries, mini-documentaries, panels, round tables, vignettes, and extended coverage (whether live or recorded) of public proceedings (such as local council meetings, congressional hearings, or political conventions). *Meet the Press* and *60 Minutes* are network programs that affiliates can log as public affairs. Local nonentertainment specials and documentaries on subjects such as schools, health, or politics equally satisfy public affairs commitments.

Production quality for local programs ranges from talking heads on a bare set to sophisticated, goal-directed series such as Westinghouse Broadcasting's *Impact*, a week-long station effort aimed at specific ascertained community problems, highlighted by a primetime special. *Impact* usually includes a five-part news series, PSAs, editorials, and segments in all locally produced programming (generally talk shows).

From the FCC's point of view, the *quality* of a program is not at issue; the commission's records ask for the number of minutes and hours logged under public affairs and the significance of the topics as measured by a station's ascertained community needs. Public affairs programming commitments are made yearly in each station's annual programming report to the FCC.[3]

As with public service announcements, many stations air their public affairs programming in the time periods with smallest audiences. Many programmers see public affairs as both non-revenue producing and of low audience appeal. Other stations, however, showcase their public affairs efforts. The best examples of public affairs programming are found in the larger markets that have greater resources to devote to local production and greater pressure from the community to emphasize these programs.

Public service announcements and public service programming can both contribute to a station's total promotional strategy. Instead of placing this material in time periods with small audiences, instead of allowing the spots and programs to lose their impact by covering a wide range of social issues, a station can harness some of this material under the umbrella of a specific goal-oriented campaign. The spots and programming will not only fulfill FCC requirements and serve the audience, but they can also be used to promote the station's own service campaign, adding to its community image.

STRATEGIES OF PUBLIC SERVICE PROMOTION

The strategies of public service can be divided into three broad categories: passive, active, and activist. Stations are often classified by com-

---

[3]See chap. 3 by Sydney W. Head in Susan Tyler Eastman, Sydney W. Head, and Lewis Klein (eds.), *Broadcast Programming: Strategies for Winning Television and Radio Audiences* (Belmont, Calif.: Wadsworth, 1981) for a description of ascertainment and the annual programming report.

munity groups and business organizations according to their public service policies and practices.

Passive Public Service

The passive stations present no more than the required share of public service announcements and rotate them in accordance with their license commitments. These stations run PSAs sent to them by national or local organizations. Infrequently they produce some of their own but see little need to showcase them in highly visible time periods, give them high production quality, gear them to the station's overall promotional needs, or carry out campaigns with flair or a sense of commitment.

It is difficult to estimate how many stations fall into the passive category. Many small-market stations with small staffs and minimal budgets are forced to take this approach. In larger markets, license challenges, community activist groups, FCC scrutiny, and market competition make it harder for stations to adopt a low-key strategy. The passive strategy includes (1) using preproduced materials; (2) not taking a great deal of time to screen preproduced PSAs to find those most relevant to the community; (3) doing little local production and independent research; and (4) airing PSAs during the least valuable time periods. Passive public affairs programming is exemplified by talking heads on bare sets in ghetto time periods.

A passive commitment lives up to the letter of the FCC guideline but not the spirit. Stations using a passive strategy, it should be noted, miss a great many promotional opportunities.

Active Public Service

Active stations involve their staffs and air time in advancing local causes. They typically associate themselves with established community projects and charities, furnishing enormous amounts of support to ongoing local institutions such as hospitals, rape crisis centers, and mental health facilities. They participate actively in services such as United Fund campaigns, Cerebral Palsy telethons, or Red Cross blood drives. These stations typically meet the minimal FCC guidelines for public service (PSAs and programming) in ways that take advantage of promotional opportunities.

Stations active in public service commonly take local fund drives and turn them into annual crusades. They use station personalities, tie in local sponsors, coordinate with dozens of community organizations, and powerfully persuade their audiences to participate. WKQX's "Christmas Is for Children" campaign in Chicago involved and benefited mentally retarded and handicapped children.[4] WKQX's on-air talents spent several days with the children at their treatment and rehabilitation center in Palatine, Illinois. The children were asked about their current projects, handicrafts, and thoughts on Christmas. Their responses were aired and listeners given the chance to pledge a particular Christmas gift for the children. The gifts were distributed along with some presents supplied by the station.[5]

Such active efforts involve station personalities, station staffs, and station budgets, and they tie in local sponsors and networks (if the stations are affiliates) with dozens of local community organizations.[6] Yet even an active strategy fails to realize fully the promotional value of the station's efforts.

Activist Public Service

One does not have to be a fireman to see that a number of social fires rage out of control on the far side of every broadcaster's door. They range from problems of energy and the economy to the environment and education. The average broadcaster's involvement with these fires is minimal after reporting their existence to audiences. Broadcasters are, to paraphrase reporter/commentator Rod MacLeish, "guilty bystanders" giving witness to the problems of their communities but reluctant to intervene directly. What follows are some of the most commonly given challenges to involvement in activist efforts. And the responses provide the rationale for activist public service promotion:

Challenge: Broadcasters are not responsible for solving social problems. Their responsibility ends with treating issues with fairness and balance.

Response: Under the FCC's Fairness Doctrine, broadcasters are clearly responsible for balanced treatment of controversial issues.[7] A greater responsibility, however, is to serve "the public interest, convenience, and necessity."[8] No more effective way exists for doing this than to intervene in the real problems faced by audiences.

[4]*BPA Newsletter*, December 1979.

[5]Another example comes from KMOX radio in St. Louis. The Illinois and Missouri Farm Bureaus started a 1980 "Holiday Harvest" campaign to help thousands of needy families in the bistate area to have a better Christmas. The outdoor event included a country-style barbeque luncheon at nominal cost and various activities typifying farm life. Music, square dancing, a decorated Christmas tree, carolers, a display of an alcohol still and farm machinery, and a cow-milking contest drew attention to the "Holiday Harvest" campaign and raised thousands of dollars. *BPA Newsletter*, November 1980.

[6]CKTM-TV's (Trois-Rivières, Quebec) twenty-first telethon, the "Noel du Pauvre," involved more than a thousand volunteers in a fundraising project. The station was successful in gaining pledges of $104,000 to be distributed to poor families. *BPA Newsletter*, March 1980.

[7]See discussion of the Fairness Doctrine in John M. Kittross and Kenneth Harwood, *Free and Fair: Courtroom Access and the Fairness Doctrine* (Washington, D.C.: Association for Professional Broadcast Education, 1970).

[8]This phrase is the cornerstone of the Communication Act of 1934 under which broadcasting is regulated.

Challenge: Broadcasters are entrusted with a force that is too powerful to be used to intervene in specific issues.

Response: Broadcasters have enormous power and responsibility—twin resources to be used on behalf of their audiences. Like the political process, broadcasting is one of the most effective vehicles our society has for social betterment and *should* be used to that end.

Challenge: The audience wants radio and television to provide entertainment and information only. And, in reality, that is all most broadcasters are equipped to provide.

Response: Broadcasting is rightly viewed as an entertainment and information medium. Nevertheless, broadcasters do have the tools at hand to participate in community issues in an activist way. Ongoing television community ascertainments mandated by the FCC spotlight issues of local concern. News, editorials, public service, advertising, and promotion staffs are active in community outreach as well as packaging and presentation. Most broadcasters have the knowledgeable staff and the time on air to influence community problems. Above all, each station's transmitter puts its signal directly into the lives of those who are most endangered by social fires as well as those who (along with broadcasters) propose and carry out solutions. The public needs all the help it can get. A resource as central as broadcasting should be more than just a conveyor of entertainment and information.

Challenge: How can solving community problems produce the three Rs of broadcasting: ratings, revenues, and recognition?

Response: Public service promotion can also be *self-serving* in the best sense. The public service promotional approach is designed to help ratings and revenues and to enhance the station's recognition. Public service is a friend-making function of broadcasting that can become the tail that wags the rest of the broadcast dog. It can become the platform from which many of the other functional needs of broadcasters are met. Properly done, public service promotion gives stations something important to advertise and promote, provides them with local and national publicity and awards, and allows them to position themselves as allies of the public. The station becomes more than another local news outlet or an extension of the network. Activist public service serves not only audiences but broadcasters.

Activist public service promotion is not just fundraising or appealing for assistance on behalf of local charities. The strategy requires that the broadcaster identify specific social problems and, in alliance with such partners as business, government, and organized volunteers, intervene in those problems on behalf of the audience while meeting a number of the station's public service, ascertainment, and promotional needs.

Most of the weapons in the firefighting arsenal of television have been adapted from radio, although the immediacy and pervasiveness of television make much of this weaponry as outmoded as the cavalry charge. None of the standard public service techniques are calculated to affect social problems directly.

Newscasts, documentaries, talk shows, and investigative reports *inform* audiences on the nature of specific social fires. They give the box score: "fire, 4; victims, 0." Education is appropriate to Jeffersonian democracies; electorates must be given unbiased information, and they can be expected to act on it through the political system. But this approach contributes very little to extinguishing social fires.

Public service announcements, editorials, and commentaries direct audiences to problems and suggest solutions. They are useful as far as they go, but editorial and commentary practices tend to be exhortative. They become the color story of the flames: "The fire is dreadful, and you should really get up and do something about it."

Both approaches have their place and are important, but neither education nor exhortation results directly in immediate social improvement. Activist public service promotions not only educate and exhort the public about social problems. They *intervene* on the public's behalf, using broadcasting as the medium for that intervention, and the broadcaster receives credit for any improved situation.

If it is properly tied in with a station's general advertising approach, public service promotion leaves the public with a strong image of the station as a substantial force in the community. Take, for example, the campaign of a Washington, D.C., radio station. Knowing that it was going to be seriously involved in service, this solidly entrenched, middle-of-the-road music and sports station created an overall campaign line (Figure 16-1). This campaign worked together with follow-up public service promotional projects to prevent other stations in the market from co-opting the "strong friend" image.

Activist public service promotion brings stations a wide variety of benefits. Although no single campaign should be expected to achieve all the benefits summarized below, different campaigns can aim at clusters of goals. Some can be targeted to enhance the station's image and garner accolades; others can serve as rating boosters and a means for creating teamwork at the station. Among the benefits of activist public service promotion are:

- Performance of meaningful, measurable service on behalf of the station's audience
- Intense, highly dramatic, relevant programming
- Short-term programming and promotions that increase ratings
- Long-term positioning of the station as a community leader and "friend" having a positive influence on all the station's on-air and off-air efforts

Figure 16-1 Activist Promotion at WMAL (*WMAL, 1974. Used with permission.*)

- Positive local and national public relations
- Tools for merchandising that the sales department offers clients
- Opportunities to advertise the station's identity legitimately as community friend and ally
- Provision of a management tool to encourage teamwork and morale at the station
- Attractions for local and national service awards
- Contributions to FCC public service commitments, thereby helping to ensure renewal of the station's license

The strategies for achieving these benefits are identifying and intervening in social problems while coordinating public service, promotional, and advertising efforts.

A CASE STUDY OF ACTIVIST PROMOTION

In 1968, WBZ-AM/FM and WBZ-TV, Boston's Westinghouse Broadcasting stations, undertook an unusual example of activist public service promotion.[9] This activity was followed by annual campaigns on WBZ that illustrate the strategies and benefits of activist promotion as well as the most frequently adopted types of campaigns.

What If?

In the late 1960s, one of the nation's major social fires was busing. In Boston, the conflagration was manifested in riots, broken bones, arrests, and, ultimately, in the closing of two black schools in Boston's ghetto. In turn, the school closings led to an unspoken commitment on both sides of the issue—black and white—to agree to disagree. Those monitoring local broadcasting (indeed, all media) during this period heard the play-by-play and color story of the crisis through newscasts and editorials, but the social fire, and the fires in the street, still burned.

WBZ radio and television asked the question "What if?" What if community leaders, both black and white, were all put in a tiny room with mattresses on the floor, some food, and a black and a white social psychologist? What if they were told they could not leave the room until the schools were opened? What if the door was locked while WBZ microphones and cameras were turned on?

That question "What if" turned into something called T-Group Fifteen—a 21½-hour black versus white marathon beginning with bitterness, acrimony, debate, and swearing.[10] After 18 hours came the realization that the political issues could not be solved by those present in the room. But they also realized that among them they had the power to open the schools and allow the children to return to classes. Two days later, the schools were opened as a direct result of WBZ's broadcast initiative.

The question "What if?" had turned into a powerful social and emotional tool. The local and national press showered WBZ with coverage, including full-page stories in *Newsweek* and the *Saturday Review*.[11] Six major awards were received by the station. This experience also gained WBZ something important to advertise and promote.

---

[9]The bulk of the promotions in this case study appeared primarily on WBZ-AM. Many of the programs were simulcast on WBZ-FM and cross-promoted on WBZ-TV. Occasionally, programs or projects were also aired on WBZ-TV.

[10]The content of the program was emotionally intense. At one point, 18 hours into the broadcast, a black housewife turned to Louise Day Hicks, head of the conservative Boston School Committee, and asked, "Louise, what about the children? Don't you have a boy? Isn't he in school? Don't you want my little boys to go to school too?" Hicks, a six-foot woman, judge's daughter, ex-mayoral candidate, and national symbol of antibusing, glowered down at the woman and then softened, saying, "You're right. I, too, want the best for my boy." And then she and the black woman began to cry. Call it emotional and physical exhaustion or change of heart—either way, these two human beings had communicated with one another. And the deadlock between them was broken.

[11]*Newsweek*, 13 January 1969, p. 60; Robert Louis Shayon, "Airing the Hang-Ups," *Saturday Review*, 15 February 1969, p. 36.

Since intense programming leads to ratings, ratings lead to advertisers, and, the way the equation goes, advertisers lead to dollars, important lessons were learned in T-Group 15. WBZ learned that activist public service promotion could not only have an impact on major community problems but could improve the station's position in its market generally.

Drug Campaign

In 1972, the social fire was drugs. WBZ mounted an all-out offensive, calling the campaign "The Flesh Is Weak and the Spirit Is Willing." By this time, the station was placing its unique service approach under an overall advertising umbrella line: "WBZ, The Spirit of 103."

Over a million kits, which included a drug slide rule, referral information, and a station listening guide, were printed and distributed free of charge to junior and senior high schools and major businesses throughout the state. Local civic and business groups paid for the printing costs in exchange for on-air mentions. Their responsiveness demonstrated that community service designed by a station can elicit the community's help to defray expenses.

A station can produce its public service promotional campaigns for little or no out-of-pocket expense if it is creative and resourceful. A community group or business that wishes to sponsor costs, provide staffing, or supply services (such as distribution) can usually receive on-air credit—a form of institutional advertising that may well bring them business. Spots crediting local service groups and businesses with support can often be counted by the station as part of its PSA commitment. Since each case is different, it is prudent to check station (and group) policy. If these obstacles are surmounted, a campaign has a powerful way to fuel itself with money and manpower.

Another approach is to sell a campaign to one or more clients, thereby increasing the station's revenue during slow sales periods. In this case, the on-air material must be logged in as commercial matter. A third approach—**split logging**—allows the station to log a campaign spot as "other" except for the sponsor's tag, generally logged as "commercial matter."[12]

Another segment of WBZ Radio's long-term antidrug campaign was "Home Sweet Hell." A family of eight with serious drug and alcohol problems was given live, on-air therapy throughout the two-month-long campaign. This project was an attempt to help the individuals

---

[12]If PSA or commercial logging is not appropriate, consider logging the spots entirely in the "other" category. In all cases, check with the station's attorneys. Shifting FCC interpretations and ambiguous rulings can trip up the unwary.

while showing audiences that there were ways for them to deal with their own drug-related problems. After each on-air session, the audience was invited to call in and ask the participating psychiatrists for specific referral information.[13] The station also set up drug referral clinics staffed by experts at remote locations throughout the state and aired 5 hours of specially produced programming on drugs that were heard by junior and senior high school students in assemblies all over the state. Their parents were asked by the schools to listen at home. The station provided free discussion guides and station program schedules (paid for by participating clients) to go with the on-air sessions for use by both parents and students.

The most substantial aspect of this campaign was its effect on drug legislation. Certainly the drug laws in Massachusetts up to 1973 were anachronistic,[14] so the changing of outdated laws became one of the goals of WBZ's campaign. In order to achieve their goal, the station invited two leading attorneys to discuss their differing points of view on the drug issue. Through PSAs, ads, editorials, and talk programs, the attorneys educated the audience about the peculiarities of Massachusetts' drug laws. Eventually, the attorneys brought in nationally and internationally known experts to explain how those laws could be changed and improved. Once the attorneys thought the audience was sufficiently educated about the situation and potential solutions, they essentially told the audience that:

> These are your children being victimized by these laws. We were all taught in seventh grade civics that as members of a democracy, we have the right and ability to change the laws that govern us. We have the tools here to do just that with your help. What laws would you like to see? Call or write, and let us know.

During the next six weeks, WBZ was overwhelmed with thousands of responses. This outpouring of suggestions was then categorized by a committee of experts and audience members organized by the station for discussion and debate. Three key issues emerged. They were organized into a cohesive legislative package emphasizing public service work for drug users as an alternative to jail and the expunging of the records of first-time offenders.

The audience was then told how to lobby their legislators for or against the bill.[15] All the station's departments worked together to ed-

---

[13]The on-air session became a serialization of one anonymous family's growth and change.

[14]The laws included such contradictions as a three-year prison sentence for using marijuana, but up to five years in prison for merely being in the presence of someone using marijuana.

[15]Although the station wanted change, it did not *direct* the audience to accept a specific point of view. It used the media as a road along which the station's vehicle (the drug campaign) could travel; the audience then drove the vehicle down that road to whatever legislative destination they wished.

ucate the public about the pending legislation—through editorials, talk shows, public relations, print ads, and special programs. Finally, the bill was brought into public hearings before the Massachusetts State Legislature. The hearings were held before an overflow audience at the State House and were aired live by WBZ-AM. From all over the country the station brought in guest experts for and against the bill, including the former head of the National Institute of Mental Health. On 12 November 1973, a drug bill was signed into law by the governor of Massachusetts. It is commonly referred to as "The WBZ Drug Bill."

This campaign gave WBZ-AM something important to advertise, something important to promote, several local and national awards, a quantity of good programming—and the opportunity to participate with its audience in changing laws that harmed their children.

Operation Shape-Up

In 1974, WBZ-AM decided to "Shape Up Boston." This campaign, centered on diet, exercise, and nutrition, attempted to break new ground for the station. In the past, WBZ's campaigns had been utterly serious. In this case, although the topic was serious, the station wanted to make its presentation light and entertaining as well as helpful. It wanted to present serious medicine with the traditional promotional sugar-coating of contests, songs, and parties.

To prepare for the campaign, the station organized a committee of leading community health organizations. They were responsible for the content of the campaign. The committee then explained to the station's personalities what they should and should not say on the air. Since the station was dealing with people's health, it did not want to risk misleading the audience while trying to help them.[16]

To launch the campaign, the station held a giant on-air eating bonanza, sort of a Mardi Gras before the fast.[17] Invitations to advertising agencies, civic leaders, and the public health agencies went out in a set of wind-up, plastic chattering teeth.[18] Once the campaign was under way, several features were aired during each typical broadcast hour.

---

[16]All station participants were given thorough physical checkups by the participating health agencies. By taking part in the campaign responsibly, they set good examples for the audience and did not risk harming themselves.

[17]Before one could even get out of the car at the party, chubby clowns offered enormous Swedish meatballs through the vent windows of the guests' cars. Once in the hall, there were four bands, three bars, Alka-Seltzer in the water coolers, and waiters burdened down with stuffed pig flambé and rounds of beef.

[18]In Los Angeles, where the campaign was replicated for KABC Radio in 1979 under the title of "Go to Health," the invitations came in the form of tape-measure belts with the station's dial position in place of a measurement. The attached copy read "Have a belt on us."

They included 40-second exercises; consumer and investigative reports on nutrition-related topics; editorials called "Dietribes"; and The WBZ Waistline, a phone-in service staffed by the state's Dietitian Association that gave the audience customized dietary information for 40 hours per week. In addition, the station's omsbudsman service, Call For Action, directed listeners regarding specific consumer problems. On-air clinics were also held each evening to challenge spurious health approaches.

The campaign also used a contest, outside promotion, and client merchandising. The station selected 103 overweight listeners and turned them into "The Shaplies"—a costumed band trained to do 20-minute exercise demonstrations in shopping centers throughout the

Figure 16-2 Shape-Up Strip Art (*WBZ, 1973. Used with permission.*)

You have nothing to lose but the worthless pounds...
useless foods and assorted ills that go with careless eating habits.
WBZ Radio is going all out for good health. May 23-June 16.
It's a 24-hour-a-day wall-to-wall tip-to-toe diet. Hourly exercises with Maggie Lettvin.
Consumer Reports from Ellie Green. How-to-Diet Tips. Evening Clinics with Jerry Williams.
Dr. Jean Mayer and other Harvard nutritional experts.
Editorials ("Dietribes"). All aimed at getting Boston in condition.
So tune in. And tone up. That's the spirit!

WBZ RADIO 103 W̄

station's coverage area. Other ingredients in this campaign included agency contests, the printing and distribution of 2 million health pamphlets for schools, and on-air clinics. Figure 16-2 shows an example of the artwork used in the campaign.

One of the long-term results of the campaign was the design and setup of a series of Shape-Up Strips—mile-and-a-quarter jogging and exercise strips organized by the station in cooperation with state government. The most conspicuous strip was located on the Boston Common and, for over four years, it was used by hundreds and seen by thousands daily. Again, the campaign gave WBZ-AM something important to advertise and promote, local and national awards, invaluable publicity, and fun.

Some Lessons Learned

After seven major public service campaigns, WBZ-AM began using an umbrella advertising line: "WBZ, Where Entertainment Is Concerned." The station's strategy was to identify their station not only in terms of entertainment but also involvement.

Public service promotion does not, and for the most part should not, change a station's programming format. Activist promotion should be designed to fit into program "islands." It should harness the bits and pieces of programming that occur on almost all stations (editorials, PSAs, commentaries, mini-documentaries, consumer reports) to promote and explain a project. On-air reinforcement by radio personalities or television newscasters may be appropriate. Some highly successful campaigns, like Shape Up Boston, were carried out entirely in program islands. Some topics lend themselves to large blocks of programming, however; T-Group 15 is a good example of how a station took large chunks of its air time for intense, highly dramatic programming. Such examples are exceptional, however, and occur only when the importance of the content demands it.

Effects on WBZ

WBZ was chosen for the case study in this chapter because of its long and consistent history of activist public service promotion. During the six-year period (1968 to 1974) when public service was most intense, the station went from sixth in overall ratings (men and women 18+, Monday through Friday) to first in overall ratings.

Obviously, it is difficult to pinpoint why a station's ratings climb. During this period, new station personalities were added, sports and other features were expanded, advertising budgets were increased. Nevertheless, it is fair to say that WBZ's public service promotional strategy was an enormous part of the station's overall presentation to its public. It played a large, if not easily measurable, part in the station's improved ratings. During this period, the station received twenty local and national awards for service, and its campaigns were the subject of eight major articles in the general and trade press.[19]

WBZ was also credited by its listeners for performing services ranging from reducing racial tension and passing major drug legislation to saving lives. Continued audience feedback, much of it unsolicited, during that period (and even years later when its promotional emphasis had changed) demonstrated that the station was consistently regarded by its audience as being "service oriented," "helpful," and "concerned."

ACTIVIST PROMOTION FOR NATIONAL TELEVISION

Other stations besides WBZ have adopted activist public service strategies. Some have developed their own campaigns tied to local issues or events; others have incorporated nationally distributed campaigns in their programming and promotion. Two of the most widely known national campaigns were Hands Up and H.O.T. Car.

Hands Up

Hands Up was a national effort to halt crime that was launched in 1975 for the Justice Department in cooperation with 600,000 members of the General Federation of Women's Clubs. In this campaign, the money, organization, and staffing came in great measure from outside broadcasting stations. All participating stations had to do was air the materials, thereby becoming the promotional arm for a nationwide process. Figure 16-3 shows the Hands Up logo.[20]

The General Federation of Women's Clubs sent representatives from all fifty states to meet in Washington, D.C., with national community leaders, ex-criminals, law enforcement personnel, and victims. The group, numbering some four hundred, spent a full day in small meetings to set priorities for local anticrime programs. They then returned to their communities and, where possible, formed alliances with local broadcasters. Once a broadcaster agreed to participate, the station received the materials necessary to carry out the campaign (public service announcements, a half-hour documentary, print ads, national and local

---

[19]In *The Wall Street Journal, Variety, Saturday Review, Newsweek, Time, New York Times, Broadcasting, Television/Radio Age.*

[20]Klein & designed and produced all materials related to the campaign as well as many of the advertising materials used in the preceding examples.

Figure 16-3 Hands Up Logo (*Used with permission.*)

A NATIONAL
VOLUNTEER EFFORT
TO HALT CRIME

public relations, decals, stationery, T-shirts). In addition, the local members of the General Federation of Women's Clubs, along with other organizations and individuals who agreed to ally with them in this anticrime effort, worked with stations on specific local anticrime projects. The campaign was mounted in a total of twenty-six states and lasted for over three years with a number of measurable local successes.

H.O.T. Car

Another national campaign was H.O.T. Car (an acronym standing for Hands Off This Car). This anti–auto theft campaign was a complete approach to auto theft protection for viewers' vehicles. Participating stations received all necessary ingredients from the campaign's sponsor, the Montgomery Ward Auto Club. Stations then distributed and aired the campaign pamphlets, PSAs, editorials, mini-documentaries, and specials about auto theft, explaining how one could join a club designed to protect cars.[21]

[21]People who signed up received, without charge, a membership card, decal, antitheft door lock buttons, and a computerized record of information pertinent to the automobile. If a participant's car was stolen, an on-air description was given by the local broadcaster and a $1,000 cash reward was offered. The free package was tested in both Boston and Los Angeles and had resounding success. The campaign recruited over 200,000 members in a little over one year in Boston—which meant more than one out of every twenty-two cars in Massachusetts carried a H.O.T. Car sticker proclaiming its owner's participation in the campaign.

Equally impressive was the fact that the H.O.T. Car campaign, according to the Boston police, was in a large measure responsible for reducing auto theft 26 percent in Boston and over 11 percent statewide during the first year of operation. Ultimately, the state of Massachusetts reduced the cost of comprehensive auto insurance 5 percent for those who used H.O.T. Car devices. After being tested, the campaign was distributed to stations nationally as a free public service by the Montgomery Ward Auto Club.

Other Campaigns

A number of stations throughout the country have done public service promotion campaigns. Free health screenings were offered to Pittsburgh area adults over 18 years of age during Health Spirit '80—a weeklong health fair sponsored by WIIC-TV, Pittsburgh, Aluminum Company of America, the United Way Health Foundation, and the Pittsburgh–Allegheny County Chapter of the American Red Cross. Health Spirit '80 was based on a model originated by the National Health Screening Council for Volunteer Organizations. More than 140,000 abnormalities worthy of follow-up were detected within one week.[22]

Each community in the four-county area offered free medical screenings for height and weight, blood pressure, anemia, sickle-cell anemia, and vision. Other services available at Health Spirit '80 sites included counseling, referral, health exhibits, and demonstrations. Depending on the needs of the community, some sites offered oral screening and podiatry tests.

WJZ-TV, Baltimore, sponsored a weekend of classes in cardiopulmonary resuscitation (CPR) in 1980 in conjunction with the American Heart Association and the American Red Cross. The channel's "Save-A-Life Saturday" CPR courses covered early signs of heart attack, risk factors of heart disease, and instruction in the steps to be taken in an actual emergency. Taught by Red Cross and Heart Association volunteers, the courses were open to anyone aged 12 and older.[23]

Each of these national campaigns resulted in something important to advertise, something important to promote, local and national prestige awards, station esprit, higher ratings, public recognition, and increased revenue for the stations that participated. These are the potential benefits of activist public service.

ORGANIZING A CAMPAIGN

Ascertainment and community outreach are the best ways of identifying local issues. One should look for an issue that:

- Is important to a large segment of the station's audience
- Can be dealt with in a fresh and exciting way
- Can actually show measurable change

[22]*BPA Newsletter*, May 1980.
[23]*BPA Newsletter*, April 1980.

- Has natural allies in the community who can be of help
- Takes advantage of the station's strengths

The judicious selection of a problem is crucial to whether or not a campaign will work. Obviously, a local television station is not going to solve the issues of world peace and nuclear disarmament. But it might help mediate a school board problem or provide a mechanism that trains volunteers to help fill a service need created by a tax cut.

A station should be wary of taking on a campaign topic that its audience might regard as dull or depressing. Unless handled properly or carried on-air for just short periods of time, some topics may cause the audience to tune out. This does not mean that a station should ignore these topics, only that it should be aware of the pitfalls. Moreover, those designing public service campaigns should be sure that their efforts are truly constructive. A health campaign that gives people faulty medical information can only tarnish the station's image.

Intervention is at the very heart of public service promotion. Unless a campaign finds an imaginative way to deal with a problem, it does not meet the criteria for activist public service. What one has to do is:

- Isolate a community problem.
- Talk to those in the community who are trying to deal with the issue. Ask them what they would do if they had a broadcast facility at their disposal.
- Make a list of those who can actually work on the campaign and resources they might be able to commit.
- Determine what the station can hope to achieve.

The Basic Steps

There can be no set formula for designing, launching, and administering an effective public service project. Each approach will vary according to the station and the community. There are, however, certain guidelines that can be used to steer a station campaign, especially for the first time. The initial steps include:

1. Explain the approach to the general manager and other department heads in order to gain their support for an activist public service campaign.
2. Study community ascertainment and local newspapers, and consult various community interests and others at the station about social problems suitable for a campaign.
3. Isolate a primary topic and a backup topic.

- Research the content of each.
- Research national and local market resources.
- Develop the concept and determine the goals of the project.
- Enlist community participation.
- Develop a budget.
- Approach outside sources for funding if necessary—business, government, private agencies.
- Package the presentation.
- Present it to station personnel.
- Gain the staff's commitment to the overall project and their individual participation.

The campaign packaging phase covers the physical materials of the campaign, the involvement of key people, and the campaign itself:

1. Prepare the campaign materials and gain approval from all departments.
   - Advertising/public relations/promotion
   - Programming
   - Public service (PSAs)
   - Sales/merchandising
   - News
   - Editorials
2. Solidify the station's commitment.
   - Present the formal concept to station personnel.
   - Select key station personnel responsible for supervision.
   - Work with department heads to customize the concept to the station and market.
   - Specify: timing, personnel, budget.
3. Gain community involvement.
   - Present the concept and enlist the involvement of interested community groups to provide: credibility and endorsement, expertise, staffing, administration, and distribution.
4. Finalize all aspects of the campaign.
5. Launch the campaign. Schedule the major elements.
   - Advertising and public relations
   - Tease and promotion
   - Major launching event
   - Campaign underway with aid of all participants: advertising,

programming, promotion, public relations, public service, community process

6. Maintain the campaign.
    - Follow through on original campaign commitments.
    - Remain open to new campaign directions as they develop.
    - Monitor, gather, and promote measurable results of the campaign.
    - Consider making the campaign a long-term community institution.
7. Follow up on the campaign.
    - Promote campaign achievements to the staff and audience.
    - Preserve relevant materials for award presentations.

Obviously, the preceding steps are meant to be general guidelines only. Each station and project will take its own path.

Small-Market Involvement

The major difference between large-market and small-market participation in activist public service is a matter of scale. Social problems are as easy to find in small cities as in large ones. But the key challenge faced in conceiving and mounting the public service/promotional approach in small markets is securing staffing and dollars. One is advised to select only projects that can be realistically implemented and to take advantage of the close community ties usually found in smaller cities by leaning heavily on local resources.

Organizing the Station's Personnel

An organizational form can be used to demonstrate how a station's departments and personnel will participate in a public service campaign. The topic headings across the top of the chart should reflect the different departments involved in the campaign. The left-hand column should delineate the different stages of the campaign. Each department head can determine what he or she could contribute to the campaign, who will be responsible for that activity, and what the budget will be. Once the form is completed, department heads and the campaign coordinator should be able to explain the timing, budget, and tasks to the station's general manager. If all the points are accepted, they can carry out the campaign. If not, they can refine the timing, budget, and tasks until agreement is reached. The outline then becomes the working plan for the campaign.

The station coordinator is the pivotal person in a public service project. This person should be someone within a station who has not only the time to devote to a major effort but the respect of those above and below, since these projects usually cut across all station departments. Experience with programming, advertising, and promotion is also helpful. The coordinator must have the confidence of the station manager, since he or she will not only be directing station personnel but will usually be working with representatives of outside civic and governmental organizations, and perhaps with advertising clients as well.

COUNTERPROMOTION

A very effective way for a station to counterpromote the public service approach of a competing station is to emulate it. A more common approach, unfortunately, is to blunt the impact of a competitor's campaign by advertising a similar approach without delivering real service. The H.O.T. Car campaign provides an example. When the campaign was first launched in Miami, a rival station countered by promoting "Hot Iron," a mini-documentary series on stolen cars, a week before the H.O.T. Car campaign began. Obviously, the competing station hoped to blur the identity of the station actually carrying the H.O.T. Car campaign. The competing station's one-shot approach had little success, however, since the original campaign was designed to air for a full year. In fact, if anything, the competitor *aided* the promotion of the H.O.T. Car campaign by raising the community's awareness of its serious auto-theft problem.

EVALUATING A CAMPAIGN

Campaigns must be evaluated from three separate points of view: the public's, the organized community's, and the station's. The public obviously refers to the general mass of viewers or listeners. Their reaction can come from formal polls, from call-in programs, or from question naires added to ascertainment or other surveys of the general public. The organized community—government agencies, volunteer organizations, nonprofit charity groups—can be reached through ascertainment or by surveying them directly about the project. The station's response is most accessible. Generally, a station's reactions are obtained from informal feedback, but they are most valuable when obtained systematically. (A side benefit is that station personnel continue to feel involved in the project.)

The simplest and most organized way to gather campaign evaluations from the perspectives of all involved is to use a form like the one shown in Figure 16-4. Items on the questionnaire can be scored from a

Figure 16-4 Public Affairs Campaign Evaluaton Form* (*Used with permission.*)
(Score: Low = 1, High = 10)

I. **Campaign**—From public's point of view

A. *Presentation*   Was it creative, arresting, interesting, involving? Was it designed to get the public into the tent?

B. *Education*   Did it educate audience? Provide new insights? Comprehensive overview? Did it avoid rehashing the same tired information?

C. *Exhortation*   Did it rev up audience to take some action or have some point of view?

D. *Intervention*   Did it provide any measurable outcome (e.g., legislation, clinics, reduction in crime statistics, etc.)?

E. *Follow-up*   Was it designed not to be a "one shot," but rather with follow-up of the problem built in?

F. *Promotion*   Was it an outstanding promotion for the station, garnering good public relations and possible awards and generating the station's image as a friend and ally of the audience?

II. **Campaign**—From organized community's point of view

A. *Alliances*   Were a number of appropriate community organizations involved (e.g., government, volunteer, business)?

How active was their involvement? (Talking heads? Use in clinics? Help in distribution? Funding? Labor? Material contributions)?

III. **Campaign**—From station's point of view

(Add 5 points for each participating department)

A. How many of the following departments participated? How?

1. News, public affairs, community services
   —Investigative reports
   —Consumer reports
   —Mini docs
   —PSA spots
   —Community outreach
   —
   —

2. Programming
   —Specials
   —Access programming
   —Minority programming
   —Talk shows
   —Remotes
   —

3. Editorial
   —Series
   —Rebuttals
   —
   —

4. Advertising, Promotion, PR
   —Ads
   —Promo spots
   —Pamphlets
   —Signs
   —Displays
   —Press conferences
   —Releases
   —

5. Sales
   —Business involvement
   —Distribution of campaign materials
   —
   —

*Copyright by the Wishnow Group, Inc., 1978

high of 10 points to a low of 1 point. The maximum score that can be obtained is 105 points. This evaluation form is designed to measure the success of a project from all points of view. A truly successful campaign is one that helps the audience, community organizations, and the station achieve their respective goals. It is very difficult not to have at least limited success with a public service promotional project. If a campaign helped to intervene in a social issue, it must be considered a success whether or not it garnered great acclaim or did much for staff morale.

SUMMARY

Public service promotion can be passive, active, or activist. Activist public service is an innovative way to garner advertising, promotion, public relations, ratings, awards, and revenue for a station. At the same time, campaigns can involve station staffs in significant activities for their communities. Public service promotion is not something that should be done once and then put aside. The activist approach works most effectively only if it becomes part of the station's philosophy. Ideally, stations should plan on one major service-oriented project a year, as well as smaller service projects during that period. In this way, broadcasters can be identified with community services in the eyes of their audience. Not many broadcast companies stress activist public service promotion, but the number is growing. Westinghouse Broadcasting, Post-Newsweek Stations, and King Broadcasting are among the leaders. Stations owned by NBC and CBS are also now involved in this approach. Moreover, a number of individually owned stations throughout the country actively pursue public affairs promotional projects. Activist public service takes broadcast facilities beyond the information and entertainment business and makes them *service stations* functioning as friends of their audience. Public service promotion can separate a station from its competition by creating an ally for audience members in a common struggle. This strategy builds loyalty and enhances many other station goals at the same time.

Part **IV** ■ Suggested Readings

Anthony, Elle. "Doing Creative Public Service Announcements." *Educational and Industrial Television* (October 1980):37–39.
Step-by-step outline for producing creative public service announcements.

Cutlip, Scott M., and Center, Allen H. *Effective Public Relations.* 5th ed. Englewood Cliffs, N.J.: Prentice-Hall, 1978.
Widely used text in public relations, first published in 1952; covers major topics of management techniques, press relations, planning processes, publicity, and research.

Golden, Hal, and Hanson, Kitty. *How to Plan, Produce, and Publicize Special Events.* Dobbs Ferry, N.Y.: Oceana Publications, n.d.
Handbook on advance preparation and implementation of special promotions.

Halstead, W. "Is Corporate Underwriting Effective PR?" *Public Telecommunications Review* 7(January/February 1979):48.
Discussion of the use of underwriting public television programs for publicity and public relations by large corporations.

Lesly, Philip, ed. *Public Relations Handbook.* 2nd ed. Englewood Cliffs, N.J.: Prentice-Hall, 1978.
Comprehensive reference guide to the fundamentals of modern public relations.

Mechling, Thomas. "Is Public Service Public Relations Practical—And Desirable?" *Public Relations Quarterly* 20(Summer 1975):10.
A five-year survey of what public relations professionals think about promoting public interest information.

Weiner, Richard. *Professional's Guide to Publicity.* 2nd ed. New York: Richard Weiner, 1978.
Manual for the publicist working with the press.

Glossary

access programming: Programs produced or purchased that have not been previously aired on the commercial networks and are scheduled during prime access time (7:30 to 8 pm in the top 50 markets). See also *PTAR*.

action news: Television news reporting style emphasizing news film, rapid pace, and visuals; frequently includes informal dialogue among anchors.

actuality: On-the-spot news report or voice of a newsmaker (frequently taped over the telephone) used to create a sense of reality or to enliven news stories, generally broadcast at a later time.

ad mat: Papier-mâché mold into which molten metal is poured to form a duplicate for printing artwork for an advertisement.

ad slick: Glossy print of an advertisement.

ADI: Area of dominant influence. There are 211 geographical designations defining each television market exclusive of all others. ADI is Arbitron's term; Nielsen's term is DMA (designated market area), indicating the area in which a single station can effectively deliver an advertiser's message to the majority of homes.

adjacency: Commercial spot next to a specific program, especially local spots next to network programs.

affiliate: Commercial radio or television station receiving more than 10 hours per week of network programming. This term is occasionally applied to individual cable operators contracting for a *pay-television* or *superstation* service and to *PBS* and *NPR* stations that air national noncommercial programming.

AFTRA: American Federation of Television and Radio Artists; labor union representing performers whose voice or image is used on radio or television.

air time: The actual broadcast time a station is in transmission; also, the starting time of a program.

alphanumeric news service: Television news created on a *character generator* and distributed as lines of text to be displayed on television receiver screens.

313

amortization: The allocation of syndicated program series' costs during the period of use to spread total tax or inventory and to determine how much each episode costs the purchaser per airing.

animation: Images recorded on traditional film animation stands as well as any type of frame-by-frame recording of calculated stop/start sequences.

AOR: Album-oriented rock; a contemporary music format playing a broader range of songs than the top forty.

ASCAP: American Society of Composers, Authors, and Publishers; organization licensing musical performance rights; see also *BMI*.

ascertainment: Two-part examination of local audience needs required by the FCC to retain broadcast licenses.

audience flow: The movement from one program or time period to another, either on the same station or from one station to another; includes turning sets on and off; positive flow is encouraged by similarity between contiguous programs.

availability: (avail) Spot advertising positions offered for sale by a station or network.

barker channel: Cable channel reserved for promotion of programs appearing on the other channels.

barter: Exchange for the use of a television program by a station in return for commercial announcements (usually aired within the program being bartered but sometimes elsewhere in a station's schedule); barter eliminates the exchange of cash and thus reduces a station's financial commitment; *Hee Haw, Lawrence Welk, Mickey Mouse Club, Mike Douglas,* and *Phil Donahue* are bartered or partially bartered programs.

basic cable: Standardized package of cable channels priced as lowest-cost unit.

beautiful music: Radio format emphasizing low-key, mellow popular music, generally with extensive orchestration and many classic popular songs (not rock or jazz).

bicycling: Transfer of syndicated or group program tapes or films by means of wheeled delivery services or mail (in contrast to wired or microwave transmission).

billboard: Highway display sign.

block programming: Several hours of similar programs placed together in the same daypart to create audience flow. See *stacking*.

BMI: Broadcast Music, Inc.; music licensing organization created by the broadcasting industry to collect and pay fees for musical performance rights; competes with *ASCAP.*

BPA: Broadcasters Promotion Association; major trade organization representing the promotion executives of the broadcasting industry.

break: Time between or during programs for insertion of commercials, IDs, or other announcements.

break copy: Continuity that fills the spaces between spots at the hourly (and half-hourly) interruptions.

bumper: On-air tease preceding a series of commercial spots that encourages viewers to stay tuned (uses copy such as "Stay tuned for . . . right after these messages").

bundling: Offering groups of programs at a single price; common practice of cable and pay-television. See *tiering.*

cable lift: The percentage of homes subscribing to cable solely to acquire a pay-cable channel (such as Home Box Office).

camera card: Channel number or station logo design (or other illustration) generally dry-mounted on 11 x 14 inch card.

camera ready: Completed graphics suitable for placing on-air.

cel· Individual frame of movie film; the fundamental unit of animation.

character generator: Equipment capable of generating lines of text or effects to appear on the TV screen.

churn: Rate of turnover in homes subscribing to cable or a pay-television system.

clip: See *film clip.*

clutter: Material that is nonprogram and noncommercial; term often applied to public service announcements and promotional announcements.

combo spot: Spot with content and cost shared between a network and its affiliate.

common carriage schedule: The set of primetime programs that most public television stations have agreed to carry at the same times in order to take advantage of national promotion. Also called core schedule.

contemporary: FCC radio term covering popular music formats, generally referring to rock.

co-op: Cooperative arrangement whereby producer or syndicator makes partial payment for promotional announcements; also, print ad with costs shared by network and station.

copy: Script for the audio portion of an announcement or written portion of an advertisement.

core schedule: See *common carriage schedule.*

counterprogramming: Scheduling programs against the competition in order to appeal to a segment of the audience not being served (usually contrasting programs such as off-network reruns versus local news).

courtesy: Announcement of last-minute cancellation of a program.

credits: Listing of the personnel responsible for the production of a program, usually run at its conclusion.

crossover: Use of a character from one program in another.

cross-plug: Specific reference to a following program inserted within the preceding show; used of on-air promos intended to stimulate viewing of subsequent programs.

cumulative audience: The net audience tuning into a station over the period of one week; "cumes" count each listener or viewer only once irrespective of how often they tune in.

cut-in tag: Live voice-over instruction to viewers to tune in upcoming episodes or programs.

daypart: Period of 2 or more hours considered as a strategic unit in program schedules—such as morning drive-time in radio (6 to 10 am) and primetime in television (8 to 11 pm).

dedicated channel: Cable channel restricted to a single type of program or aimed at a single audience—such as sports or children's or barker channels.

demo: Demonstration; a tape intended to reflect the content, style, and quality of a musical composition, program, or on-air personality.

demographics: Descriptive information on an audience, usually the vital statistics of age and sex.

denial technology: The means for preventing nonsubscribing homes from receiving pay-cable channels being distributed to nearby subscribers.

disconnect (DC): Subscriber who cancels cable service.

distant signal importation: Acquiring television signals from distant stations by satellite or microwave for inclusion as cable channels over and above local broadcast signals.

distributor: Syndicator or marketer of programs to stations and groups of stations.

donut: Promotional form consisting of a fixed opening (introduction) and a fixed ending (tag). The middle is open and modular, designed to be filled with topical promotional materials. Also referred to as sandwich or wraparound.

double truck spread: Print ad that occupies space on both left-hand and right-hand pages of an editorial layout. Artwork runs across the fold, connecting the two pages.

drivetime: In radio, 6 to 10 am and 4 to 7 pm.

edit point (music): Spot at which an electronic edit is made by erasing old sounds and adding new ones.

episodic promo: Topical on-air promo; this term is particularly used by ABC and NBC. See *topical promo*.

exclusivity: The sole right to air a program within a given period of time in a given market; imported signals may undermine exclusivity agreements.

feature: News program material other than hard news, daily sports /weather /stock market reports, or music.

filler: Audio copy read or ad-libbed by DJs.

film clip: Selected scene, generally from a feature movie.

first run: The first airing of a program (not counting theatrical exhibits of feature films); especially used of programs not aired on the three commercial television networks.

fixed-position promotion: System in which promotion department contracts with sales department to reserve certain spots during the day for on-air promos that cannot be sold to commercial advertisers.

focus group: Group of approximately a dozen people assembled to elicit their reactions to a program or personality (or product or spot advertisement).

format: Overall programming design of a station.

franchise:	Local agreement between municipal government and cable system operator permitting exclusive service in a geographic area. Less often, two cable operators are granted franchises to compete in the same area.
fringe time:	The television time periods adjacent to primetime— (EST) from 5 to 7 pm and 11 to midnight or later; early fringe time includes the hour from 4 to 5 pm.
generic promo:	Promotional spot highlighting intrinsic qualities and appeal of a program format or service rather than describing specific episode plots.
graphics:	Illustrations for television or film; generally consist of drawings, logos, charts, or mounted photographs on camera cards or slides, and animation.
gross ratings point:	The sum of the average quarter-hour ratings for all the commercial positions in a program (or series of availabilities); used to estimate the number of ratings points delivered by an advertising buy.
group-owned station:	Radio or television station licensed to a corporation owning two or more stations.
gutter:	The fold connecting two facing pages in a magazine.
hard news:	Daily factual reporting of national, international, or local events.
hot clock:	Wheel divided into segments showing program, promotion, and commercial elements by the hour.
HUTs:	Households using television; rating industry term for the total number of sets turned on during an average quarter hour—that is, the actual viewing audience divided among all stations in the market.
hypoing:	Unethical promotion of a program or airing of special programs in order to increase audience size during a rating period.
ID:	Identification; in broadcasting, an ID must state call letters and community of license (with FCC waiver, city of origin, or area of dominant influence) and may include channel number or frequency; in television, an ID may be audio or video.
independent:	Commercial television broadcast station that is not affiliated with a national network (or, by one FCC definition, carries less than 10 hours of network programming per week).
interactive:	Cable television system having twelve or more channels for video signals to the subscriber and one or

more channels for electronic responses by the sub-scriber (such as Warner Communications' Qube).

inventory: The amount of on-air promotional material on hand.

key pad device: Hand-held electronic unit used by subscriber to respond to cable operator's receiving equipment.

kinesthesis: The moving of cutout images along plotted paths as they are recorded on film. This technique looks like stop motion filming.

lead-in: Immediately preceding program (usually intended to encourage audience flow to subsequent program).

lead-out: Immediately following program.

lead sheet: Initial paragraph of a story.

leave-behind: Printed material, usually brochures or rate cards, used by sales personnel to promote the station or a feature film.

library: Storage area for printed, taped, or filmed materials.

live action: Not prerecorded on tape or film.

local: Program or commercial generated 50 percent or more within a station's broadcast coverage area; contrasts with network originated and syndicated programs.

log: The official record of a broadcast day, kept by hand or automatic means such as tape, noting opening and closing times of all programs, commercials, and nonprogram material and other facts mandated by the FCC.

logo: Concise and striking image representing a network, station, or programming service.

long form: Longer than the usual 30 minutes for entertainment series or 60 minutes for specials (for example, a 60- or 90-minute fall season premiere for a new series) or playing the entire 2 or 3 hours of a film in one showing.

make-good: Spot announcement run at no charge by a station to replace a commercial announcement that was run at the wrong time, did not run at all, or had technical problems in transmission.

MDS: Multipoint distribution service; a television relay system radiating programs over a small area to private rooftop antennas. Commonly used by hotels, office buildings, and large apartment complexes not served by cable systems.

merchandising: Selling by offering products; in sales promotion, encouraging clients to purchase advertising by creating goodwill with gifts; also, offering giveaways such as T-shirts to the general public.

mix session: Production session where all the components of a promotional announcement are assembled; usually involves editing the video component and combining it with the audio portion; may also be a sound mix only, in which case it means assembling voices, music, and special effects.

MSO: Multiple-system operator; a corporation that owns two or more cable systems.

multiple spot: On-air promo containing mentions of several programs used especially to promote a series of prime-time programs; see also *stack ad* and *piggybacking*.

music bed: Music track edited under voice-over copy or the sound track of a promotional spot.

music package: Specially produced music (usually a *music signature* combined with a *music bed*) to be used in a promotional campaign.

music signature: Musical version of identification (or logo); may be combined with a video element; see *signature*.

NAB: National Association of Broadcasters; the major trade association of the broadcasting industry.

narrowcasting: Designing programs for specific ("narrow") audiences.

NATAS: National Academy of Television Arts and Sciences; the organization that makes annual Emmy awards for excellence in television production and performance in conjunction with ATAS (Academy of Television Arts and Sciences), its Hollywood counterpart.

NATPE: National Association of Television Program Executives; the major organization representing the program executives of the television industry and the distributors of programming.

NCTA: National Cable Television Association; the major trade organization representing cable system operators and cable networks.

needle drop: Short selection of music or sound effects purchased from a sound library.

network: Interconnected chain of broadcast stations or national cable program suppliers; refers to the administrative and technical unit that distributes or originates schedules of programs.

network-owned station: Radio or television station licensed to one of the three commercial networks (ABC, NBC, CBS); limited to no more than seven television stations (five VHF and two UHF) and seven AM and seven FM radio stations.

new connect: Home recently wired for cable television service.

NPR: National Public Radio; an organization supplying radio programming to public radio stations that are members.

O&O: Broadcasting station owned and operated by one of the three commercial networks.

off-line preediting: Editing procedure wherein *rough footage* is coded and transferred to cassette for previewing, planning, and sometimes rough assembly.

off-network rerun: Television series that originally ran on one of the three major commercial networks, later offered by a syndicator to local stations.

off-network syndication: Selling programs (usually series) that have appeared at least once on the national networks directly to stations or pay-television.

on-air: Taped or live video or radio spots as distinguished from printed promotional material (ads, billboards).

on-the-spot coverage: Term used to denote the new "reality" of on-air television promotions utilizing tape rather than film; usually associated with promoting programming that has been shot on tape.

one inch tape: Configuration of magnetic videotape; though one of the current broadcast standard configurations, one-inch tape has less resolution capability because of its small surface area.

open-entry policy: FCC policy permitting common carriers unrestricted access to commercial satellite channels.

Operation Prime Time: Association of stations and producers contributing funds on a prorated basis for the production of high-quality, first-run drama intended for primetime airing.

outdoor: Billboards, signs, and display cards used for advertising.

pay-cable: Cable-television programming service for which the subscriber pays an extra fee beyond the monthly cable fee; see *pay-television, basic cable, tiering*.

payola: Illegal payment for advertising a song or recording (or other product or service) on the air.

pay-television: Any programming for which a fee is paid by viewers; includes *pay-cable* and *subscription television*.

PBS: Public Broadcasting Service; the noncommercial federally supported service that distributes programming nationally to member stations and serves as a representative of the public television industry.

per inquiries: Commercials that are paid according to the number of viewers responding (customer inquiries).

personality research: Information on the audience appeal of anchors, DJs, and other on-air personalities.

personality spot: Promotional announcement focusing on a particular on-air personality.

piggybacking: Carrying promotional information for one program along with information on another program in the same spot or ad; also refers to commercial spots advertising more than one product. See also *multiple spot* and *stack ad*.

pitch book: Printed and graphic materials assembled to aid sales executives in selling commercial time.

plugola: Material or copy included in a program for the purpose of covert advertising without disclosing that payment of some kind was made.

positioning: Persuading the audience that one station is really different from its competitors.

preemption: Cancellation of a program by an *affiliate* subsequent to agreement to carry the program; cancellation of an episode by a network in order to air a news or entertainment special; or cancellation of a commercial sold at a special price to accommodate another commercial sold at full rate.

primetime: The period of peak television set use, commonly 7 to 11 pm in the East and West, 6 to 10 pm in the Midwest, three hours of which are programmed by the networks. See also *PTAR*.

print crawl: Device to move printed copy vertically in front of a television camera.

program clip: Short scene excerpted from a program.

promo: Broadcast advertising spot announcing a new program or episode or encouraging viewing of a station or network's entire schedule.

promo cutting: Creating and editing promotional spots from prerecorded video and audio materials.

promotion: Informational advertising of programs, stations, or networks; commonly subdivided into audience promotion and sales promotion.

psychographics: Information on the attitudes, interests, and opinions of audience members (as opposed to demographics that include only the age and sex of audiences). Also called lifestyle data.

PTAR: FCC's primetime access rule; limits evening network programming to 3 hours of entertainment material between the hours of 7 and 11 pm (EST) in the top 50 markets.

public station: Noncommercial station (prior to 1967 called educational station); licensed by the FCC to offer noncommercial/educational service.

quarter-inch tape: Configuration of magnetic videotape designated by its width, 1-inch, 2-inch, and ¾ inch tape are currently the broadcast standard configurations for video.

Qube: Warner Communications' two-way cable system; first installed in Columbus, Ohio.

rate card: Current listing of a station's commercial time prices.

rating: Audience measurement unit representing the percentage of the total audience (whether sets on or not) tuned to a specific program (by average quarter-hour periods); also, average percentage of audience viewing a station or network.

record library: Stored recordings and tapes suitable for airing on radio music programs.

remarketing: Campaign to reach potential subscribers in a geographic area who did not sign up when cable service was initially introduced.

remote: Live production from locations other than a studio (football games, live news events).

rerun: Repeat showing of episodes in a series first aired earlier in the season or some previous season (usually on a network).

rights use contract:	Legal agreement covering the number of airings of a program and restrictions on the use of segments to advertise scheduled showings.
roll-in:	Videotape insert used within another program or within pledge breaks for content changes.
rough footage:	Unedited, raw film or videotape footage from which the final edited version of an on-air promotional announcement is taken.
royalty:	Compensation paid to copyright holder for the right to use copyrighted material.
runs:	Number of times a spot or film is aired.
sampling:	Trying out programs by tuning in; especially important for new programs.
sandwich:	See *donut*.
sellathon:	On-air sale or auction of merchandise to raise money for the station.
share:	Measurement unit for comparing audiences; represents the percentage of total listening or viewing audience (with sets on) tuned to a given station; total shares in a designated area in a given time period equal 100 percent.
shared ID:	Identification that combines station and program identification—that is, title, day, and time. Varies in length from 2 to 10 seconds and usually constructed for television so that part of the information is visual and part aural.
shelf life:	The length of time a spot can run before it suffers from overexposure.
shell:	See *donut*.
shortflighting:	Trying out.
sign-on/sign-off:	The period during which a station is on the air (as from 6 am to 2 am).
signature:	Identification, with same function as a logo; signatures may be audio or video identifications, but logos are always visual.
sound bite:	Short clip of both audio and video recorded from a program or news story; designed to give the viewer a quick taste of the actual program or story.
specific promo:	Promotional spot showcasing a specific program and giving time, day, and station or network.

split logging: Procedure in which a spot is recorded in more than one FCC content category (usually "commercial" and "other").

sponsor: The advertiser featured in commercial announcements.

spread: Two facing pages sold for a single advertisement, typically in magazines. See *double truck spread*.

stack ad: Several promotional segments placed in one 30-second on-air spot or print advertisement. See also *multiple spot* and *piggybacking*.

stacking: Sequential airing of several hours of the same kind of programs; similar to *block programming*.

station: Facility operated by a licensee in order to broadcast radio or television signals on an assigned frequency; may be affiliated by contract with a *network* or may be *independent* (unaffiliated); may be commercial or noncommercial (*public*).

station program cooperative: Arrangement permitting public station participation in choosing the national program schedule carried by *PBS*.

station representative: Firm acting as sales agent for a client station's advertising time in the national market

still: Most basic graphic in promotion; includes various camera cards, slides, mounted photographs, drawings.

stripping: Putting successive episodes of a program into the same time period five days a week—for example, placing *Star Trek* every evening at 7 pm.

stunting: Frequent shifting of programs in a schedule; also using *long form* for a program's introduction and using character crossovers from one program to another in order to attract viewers; frequently used in the week preceding the launch of a new fall season combined with heavy *promotion*.

STV: Subscription television; a form of *pay-television* typically using an *independent* station's channel during *primetime* hours for broadcast of scrambled television signals to subscribers with decoding devices.

subscription television: Over-the-air *pay-television*; see *STV*.

superstation: *Independent* television station that has its signal distributed by satellite to distant cable companies for retransmission to subscribers.

sweeps: The four periods during each year when Arbitron and Nielsen gather audience data for the entire country: November (fall season ratings become base for rest of the year); February (fall season programs again plus replacements); May (end-of-year ratings); July (summer replacements). The ratings on the sweeps determine network and station rates for advertising time until the next sweep.

syndication: The marketing of programs on a station-by-station basis rather than through a *network* to *affiliates, independents,* and *pay-television* for a specified number of plays.

syndicator: Company that holds the rights to distribute programs nationally or internationally.

tag: Short summary statement, usually a command, often at the end of a *promo;* tells the viewer or listener the program's title, day, and time and the station's channel number or call letters.

tease: Brief news item or program spot intended to lure an audience into watching or listening to the succeeding program or news story by provoking interest; usually incomplete in order to intrigue viewers or listeners. Also called a teaser or *bumper.*

telecine film chain: Unit made up of one or more 16-mm projectors and often a 35-mm slide projector focused into a prism or multiplexor for video transmission by a television camera.

telops: Device for optically projecting photographs or other opaque artwork into television film cameras.

three-quarter-inch tape: Configuration of magnetic videotape; though one of the current broadcast standard configurations, ¾-inch tape has less resolution capability than 1-inch and 2-inch tape because of its small surface area.

tiering: Different pay schedules offered by cable systems to subscribers for added channels of programming.

topical advertising: Information on the same or next day's program content, especially on content of newscasts.

topical promo: Promotional spot showcasing a specific episode or program by using edited highlights from the show.

tradeout: Exchange of spot air time for merchandise useful for gifts to clients or as contest prizes or for advertising time or space in another medium. Also called "recips" (reciprocal trades).

trailer: Short segment of film used to announce program contents.

tune-in advertising:	Information on date, time, and channel of a program.
TvQs:	Ratings for television personalities and programs reflecting both their popularity and familiarity to audiences.
two-inch tape:	Configuration of magnetic videotape; one of the three current broadcast standard configurations; has the highest quality due to fine resolution of image.
type font:	Set of printer's type with one size and face.
typography:	The style of printed matter in an ad or spot.
underwriting:	Grants from foundations or private corporations to cover costs of producing or airing a program or series on public television or radio.
video switcher:	Electronic unit controlling which of a series of video sources (cameras, videotape recorders) is transmitted to a broadcast antenna or videotape recorder.
visual signature:	Animated version of a signature (or logo); usually combined with an audio element that complements video action. See *signature*.
voice-over:	The narrative portion of a commercial; usually recorded by an announcer and containing vital information for the spot
voice-over copy:	Announcer's copy to be read as narrative over video.
web:	Another term for *network*.
wheel:	Visualization of the contents of an hour as a pie divided into wedges representing different content elements; used in radio to visualize a program format by showing designated sequences and lengths of all program elements—musical numbers, news, sports, weather, features, promos, PSAs, commercials, IDs, time checks.
wild footage:	Unedited, raw film or videotape footage from which the final edited version of a program or on-air *promo* is taken.
wraparound:	See *donut*.

Guide to Suppliers and Consultants

This is a briefly annotated reference guide to promotion resources for television and radio station and cable promotion staffs. It contains representative samples of nationally known companies. A complete list would necessarily be inaccurate because of the changing demands of the marketplace. These companies were selected for their prominence and their familiarity with the broadcast field. Inclusion does not imply endorsement by the editors. The guide is divided into three sections covering suppliers of music, suppliers of animation, and firms specializing in media campaigns. An additional resource is the Broadcasters Promotion Association Library of videotapes and audiotapes, promotional campaigns, print and newspaper ads, and notebooks of sales materials, community involvement activities, and campaigns. It is located at San Diego State University.

Music Suppliers

This section lists companies that write, produce, or syndicate original or prepackaged themes, jingles, and background sounds that can be used in on-air program and identity promotion. These firms provide a variety of kinds of music. The list includes radio promotion consultants.*

Chuck Blore & Don Richman, Inc.
1606 N. Argyle
Hollywood, California 90028
(213) 462-0944   M,R

Otis Conner Productions
2829 W. North-West Highway
Dallas, Texas 75220
(214) 358-5500   M

Eye
3518 Cahuenga Blvd.
Los Angeles, California 90029
(213) 851-6377   M,R

Klein &
1111 S. Robertson Blvd.
Los Angeles, California 90035
(213) 278-5600   M,R

Terry Murphy Ltd.
4 Ascot Ridge
Great Neck, New York 11021
(516) 829-9229/(212) 895-7708   M

No Soap Radio/Bryan Wells Music
161 W. 54th St.
New York, New York 10011
(212) 581-5572   R,M

Peters Productions
9590 Chesapeake Drive
San Diego, California 92123
(714) 565-8511   M,R

TM Productions
1349 Reagle Row
Dallas, Texas 75247
(214) 634-8511   M,R

Tuesday Productions, Inc.
4429 Morena Blvd.
San Diego, California 92117
(714) 272-7660   M,R

*M: music; R: radio promotion.

Animation Suppliers

This section lists companies that supply film and video animation services for television. It indicates whether the firm specializes in graphic animation, cel

329

animation (cartoon), video animation, computer animation, or live action animation.*

Robert Abel & Assoc.
935 N. Highland Ave.
Los Angeles, California 90035
(213) 462-8100   GA

Bajus-Jones Film Corp
5250 W. 74th St.
Edina, Minnesota 55435
(612) 835-4490   GA,CA

Calico Creations
8811 Shirley Ave.
Northridge, California 91324
(213) 855-6663   GA,CA

Campbell/Gericke
2322 Lyric Ave.
Los Angeles, California 90027
(213) 665-0048   GA

Computer Image Animation Corp.
2475 West 2nd Ave.
Denver, Colorado 80223
(303) 934-5801   VA, CO/A

Digital Effects
321 West 44th St.
New York, New York 10036
(212) 581-7760   CO/A

Digital Image
1440 San Pablo Ave.
Berkeley, California 94702
(415) 526-7161   CO/A

Dolphin Productions
140 E. 80th St.
New York, New York 10021
(212) 628-5930   VA

Duck Soup Productions
1026 Montana
Santa Monica, California 90403
(213) 392-4984   GA,CA

Edstan Studio
240 Madison Ave.
New York, New York 10016
(212) 686-3666   GA

Roger Flint Productions
1075 N. Orlando Ave.
Los Angeles, California 90069
(213) 650-6546   GA,LA

Harold Friedman Consortium
420 Lexington Ave.
New York, New York 10017
(212) 697-0858   GA,CA

Bo Gehring Aviation
13431 Beach Ave.
Venice, California 90291
(213) 823-8577   CO/A

R/Greenberg Associates
240 Madison Ave.
New York, New York 10016
(212) 689-7886   GA,CO/A

IF Studios
328 East 44th St.
New York, New York 10017
(212) 683-4747   GA

Image Factory
18 East 53rd St.
New York, New York 10022
(212) 759-9363   GA,VA,CO/A

Image West
845 N. Highland Ave.
Los Angeles, California 90038
(213) 466-4181   VA,CO/A

Information International
5933 Slauson Ave.
Culver City, California 90230
(213) 390-8611   CO/A

Klein &
1111 S. Robertson Blvd.
Los Angeles, California 90035
(213) 278-5600   GA,CA

Kurtz & Friends Films
1728 N. Whitley Ave.
Los Angeles, California 90028
(213) 461-8188   CA

Lumeni Productions
1727 N. Ivar
Los Angeles, California 90028
(213) 462-2110   GA

Magi-SynthaVision
3 Westchester Plaza
Elmsford, New York 10523
(212) 462-7272   GA

Moore Graphics & Film, Inc.
729 N. La Brea Ave.
Los Angeles, California 90038
(213) 462-8363   GA,CA,CO/A

Motion Graphics
801 N. La Brea, #103
Los Angeles, California 90038
(213) 934-5263   GA

*GA: graphic animation
 CA: cel animation
 VA: video animation
 CO/A: computer animation
 LA: live action

Rebecca Singer Studio, Inc.
111 W. 57th St.
New York, New York 10019
(212) 541-4552   GA

Robert Story Co.
1620 Vista Del Mar
Hollywood, California 90028
(213) 467-6700   GA,CA

Triplane Films & Graphics
1545 N. Wilcox, #201
Los Angeles, California 90028
(213) 463-8131   GA

Zeplin Productions
850 Seventh Ave.
New York, New York 10019
(212) 582-6633   GA

Media Consultants

This section lists advertising agencies, creative and production services, and news promotion consultants.*

Bozell & Jacobs/Pacific
10850 Wilshire Blvd.
Los Angeles, California 90024
(213) 879-1800   A

Charisma Productions Ltd.
32 E. 57th St.
New York, New York 10022
(212) 832-3020   P

Consolidated Visual Center
2529 Keniworth Ave.
Tuxedo, Maryland 20781
(301) 772-7300   P

D.J.M.C.
3435 Wilshire Blvd., #18
Los Angeles, California 90010
(213) 383-3332   A

W. B. Doner & Co.
26711 Northwestern Highway
Southfield, Michigan 48034
(313) 354-9700   A

Frank Magid Assoc., Inc.
1 Research Center
Marion, Iowa 92302
(319) 377-7345   N

Future Media Corp.
6526 Sunset Blvd.
Los Angeles, California 90028
(213) 460-6301   P

Goldberg/Marchesano & Assoc., Inc.
1910 Sunderland Pl., N.W.
Washington, D.C. 20036
(202) 785-0600   A

Harold Friedman Consortium
420 Lexington Ave.
New York, New York 10017
(212) 697-0850   C,P

International Communications/
Media Consultants, Inc.
8111 Beverly Blvd.
Los Angeles, California 90048
(213) 657-4410   P

Jacobs & Gerber
731 N. Fairfax
Los Angeles, California 90036
(213) 655-4082   A,C,N

Klein &
1111 S. Robertson Blvd.
Los Angeles, California 90035
(213) 278-5600   C,P,N

Kramer/Rocklen
1312 N. La Brea
Hollywood, California 90028
(213) 462-2680   P

New York Communications
207 S. Stater Rd.
Upper Darby, Pennsylvania 19082
(215) 352-7472   N,P

PFT Advertising
10200 Riverside Dr., #203
Taluca Lake, California 91602
(213) 760-3885   A

Promotion Plus
2007 Wilshire Blvd.
Los Angeles, California 90057
(213) 413-0567   A

Reymer-Gersin
4000 Towncenter
Suite #655
South Hill, Michigan 48075
(313) 354-4960   N

Sieracki & Gree
Peddler's Village 425
Lahaska, Pennsylvania 18931
(215) 794-5107/348-8169   P

Jerry Smith Studio, Inc.
205 W. Highland
Milwaukee, Wisconsin 53203
(414) 765-0080   C,P

*A: agency
 C: creative services
 N: news
 P: production

Robert Story Moving Pictures
6922 Hollywood Blvd.
Los Angeles, California 90028
(213) 467-6700   P

Telesound, Inc.
P.O. Box 1900
San Francisco, California 94101
(415) 863-4880   P,C

Visual Resources, Inc.
1556 N. Fairfax
Los Angeles, California 90048
(213) 851-6688   P,C

Bibliography

This is an annotated listing of books, guides, reports, theses, dissertations, journal articles, and trade press articles relating to broadcast and cable promotion. An item is included (1) it it contributes substantively to understanding the strategies or techniques of broadcast television, radio, cable, or pay-television promotion, publicity, and public relations or (2) if the article illuminates current promotional issues. This bibliography emphasizes publications since 1970 and includes all books and articles cited in the Suggested Readings but omits minor footnoted material.

Anthony, Elle. "Doing Creative Public Service Announcements." *Educational and Industrial Television* (October 1980):37–39.
Step-by-step outline for producing creative public service announcements.

Appel, Valentine; Weinstein, Sidney; and Weinstein, Curt. "Brain Activity and Recall of TV Advertising." *Journal of Advertising Research* 19(August 1979):7–15.
A physiological study of the impact of attention-attracting advertisements on viewer recall.

Archer, Eva. "Producing and Using Radio Promotions." *BPA Newsletter* (February 1980):14–15.
General guidelines for producing radio promotion spots to fit specific audiences and individual stations.

"ARMS II: Will It Lift Radio in the Media Mix?" *Media Decisions* (June 1976): 60–61, 92–94.
Report on the All Radio Marketing Surveys (ARMS) performed by the Radio Advertising Bureau to measure the relative audience positions of radio, television, and newspapers in both New York and Los Angeles.

Arnold, Dave. "Television." *Media Decisions* (April 1976):72–74.
Analysis of the negative effects of too many nonprogram/promotion breaks concluding that they clutter television viewing and reduce the value of advertisements.

Aspley, John Cameron. *The Dartnell Sales Promotion Handbook.* 5th ed. Chicago: Dartnell Corporation, 1966.
A basic industry guide covering sales promotion, including case studies.

Avery, Robert, and Pepper, Robert. "Politics in Space: The Struggle over PTV Satellite Governance." *Public Telecommunications Review* 7(January/February 1979):19–28.
An in-depth report on the state of satellite broadcasting for PTV; a historical perspective on the problems of using satellites for television.

333

Backstage (13 June, 1980):69 ff.
Includes a special section on the Broadcasters Promotion Association and the role of promotion in broadcasting economics.

Barban, Arnold M., and Krugman, Dean M. "Cable TV and Advertising: An Assessment." *Journal of Advertising* 8(Fall 1979):4–8.
An analysis of cable television's growth and its relationship to advertising.

Bergendorff, Fred; Smith, Charles Harrison; and Webster, Lance. *Broadcast Advertising and Promotion: A Handbook for Radio, Television and Cable.* New York: Hastings House, 1982.
BPA-sponsored handbook emphasizing the techniques of promotion.

"The Booming Sound of Network Radio." *Marketing and Media Decisions* (December 1980):62 ff.
Details the growth of network radio between 1966 and 1980 emphasizing the role of advertising.

Borg, Dan. "Television." *Media Decisions* (February 1976):82.
Critique of current station promotions, identifications, and other "clutter" items arguing that they detract from the value of advertisements and make television less enjoyable to watch.

"BPA Big Ideas." *BPA Newsletter* special reports.
Each "Big Ideas" report covers a single subject of special interest to broadcast promoters with examples of supporting promotions from stations all over the country.

"The Broadcast Promoter: No Longer the Last to Know, the First to Go." *Broadcasting* (5 June 1978):32–33.
Special report on promoters and marketing in the broadcast industry; covers the future of promoters and the importance of modern marketing techniques.

Broadcast Promotion Survey—United States and Canada. Lancaster, Pennsylvania: Broadcasters Promotion Association, n.d.
A 1976 survey of broadcast promotion managers conducted jointly by the Broadcasters Promotion Association and the Department of Journalism at Bradley University, covering demographics and individual responsibilities.

Broadcasting and Government: A Review of 1979 and a Preview of 1980. Washington, D.C.: National Association of Broadcasters, 1980.
Review of government regulations and new technological advances in broadcasting; covers a variety of issues, including advertising, cable and pay-cable, ownership, and engineering issues.

"Cable Advertising Growth." *Broadcasting* (30 October 1978):45.
Analysis of increases in local and national advertising on cable television resulting from low spot prices and tight targeting of cable audiences.

Commercial Radio Programming: Recommendations for Expanding Diversity and Excellence. New York: Center for Public Resources, 1980.
Report based on the 1979 Center for Public Resources analysis of commercial radio; chapters cover public affairs, new technologies, and other aspects of contemporary radio.

"The Competition Gets Keener as the Pie Gets Larger." *Broadcasting* (4 June 1979):37–61.

Special report on television advertising agencies and station representatives; covers their competitive positions, their roles in the industry, and predictions for the future.

Coons, Joseph. "Using Promotions to Build Audience and Sales." *Broadcast Management/Engineering* (August 1965):20–23.
An evaluation of radio and television audience promotions focusing on the general rationales behind them and their usefulness for building audiences and sales.

Crawford, Tad. *The Visual Artist's Guide to the New Copyright Law.* New York: Graphic Artists Guild, 1978.
Guidelines for artists for obtaining copyright protection, transferring and terminating transfer of copyrights, including special rules for magazines.

Cunningham, Marianna. "RISE: A Promotional Challenge." *BPA Newsletter* (December 1979):13–14.
Describes the special problems of promoting RISE (radio information service for the blind and physically disabled).

Cutlip, Scott M., and Center, Allen H. *Effective Public Relations.* 5th ed. Englewood Cliffs, New Jersey: Prentice-Hall, 1978.
Widely used public relations text, first published in 1952; covers major topics of management techniques, press relations, planning procedures, and research.

Davis, Donald M.; Sebring, Penny A.; and Ziegler, Michael J. "Audience Duplication: A Powerful Promotional Tool." *Public Telecommunications Review* 8(September/October 1980):61–66.
Results of an audience duplication study for two markets showing how duplications help in the scheduling of on-air promotions.

Dusek, Alex S. "Promotion Managers Improve Status; Need to Review Promo Content." *BPA Newsletter* (March 1979):15–16.
Review of recent trends in broadcast promotion, with guidelines for responsibly promoting radio and television.

Engle, James F.; Wales, Hugh G.; and Warshaw, Martin (eds.). *Promotional Strategy.* Homewood, Illinois: Richard D. Irwin, 1975.
Textbook using a managerial approach to promotional strategy; includes sections on "processing and the promotional message," demographics and psychographics, and legislation on promotion.

Fierro, Robert D. "You PR Men Are All Alike—A Survey of PR People Under the Age of 30." *Public Relations Quarterly* 18(Fall 1973):11.
Survey of sixty men and women in the public relations field (under age 30); includes their ideas, attitudes, and opinions about their own positions and the role of public relations in business.

Fitch, Dennis. *BPA Big Ideas: Creatively Servicing the Budget.* Lancaster, Pennsylvania: Broadcasters Promotion Association, 1981.
A booklet based on a 1981 BPA seminar workshop on promotion budgets; contains a budgeting system and sample forms.

French, Warren A., and McBrayer, J. Timothy. "Managing Television Commercial Time." *Journal of Advertising* 7(Fall 1978):17–23.

Description of the process television stations use to divide commercial time to obtain the most profitable rates with a minimum risk of losing business.

Friedman, Mel. "New Dimensions Seen in Battle for Listeners." *Television/Radio Age* (10 December 1979):51 ff.
Recommendations for using radio promotions to increase a station's listening audiences and using publicity to improve station image.

Friedman, Mel. "PTV's Fund Raising Methods Proliferate and Draw More Fire." *Television/Radio Age* (22 September 1980):41 ff.
An examination of methods of underwriting public television programming costs.

Gantz, Walter. *Uses and Gratifications Associated with Exposure to Public Television.* Washington, D.C.: Corporation for Public Broadcasting, 1980.
A 1980 study for CPB analyzing motivations of public television viewers.

Gell, Frank. "When TV Seems Too Good to Be True." *TV Guide* (26 April 1979):72
Discussion of the problem with sweeps weeks and how the networks, affiliates, and advertisers feel about them; some alternatives are suggested.

Giovannoni, David. "The Musical Trademark of Public Broadcasting." *Public Telecommunications Review* 6(March/April 1978):14–17.
Report on the use of Voegleli's electronic music at 96 percent of public radio stations, 97 percent of public television stations, and the PBS.

Golden, Hal, and Hanson, Kitty. *How to Plan, Produce, and Publicize Special Events.* Dobbs Ferry, N.Y.: Oceana Publications, n.d.
A handbook on advance preparation and implementation of special promotions.

Gompertz, Rolf. *Promotion and Publicity Handbook for Broadcasters.* Blue Ridge Summit, Pennsylvania: TAB Books, 1977.
Examples and case histories of promotional campaigns with emphasis on publicity; includes the use of other media, such as newspaper and magazines, to promote stations, personalities, and programs.

Guidelines for Radio: Promotion. Washington, D.C.: National Association of Broadcasters, 1981.
The first in a series to be produced by the NAB, this booklet combines promotions and articles relating to promotion that have appeared in *RadioActive,* the NAB's monthly radio magazine.

Gunn, Hartford N., Jr. "Window On the Future." *Public Telecommunications Review* 6(July–August 1978):5–55.
Overview of the factors influencing the direction and quality of public television funded by the Public Broadcasting Service.

Halstead, W. "Is Corporate Underwriting Effective PR?" *Public Telecommunications Review* 7(January/February 1979):48–52.
Discussion of the value of underwriting public television programs by large corporations for publicity and public relations.

Harlow, Rex F. "The Successful Public Relations Practitioner—A Composite Profile." *Public Relations Quarterly* 22(Fall 1977):8–12.
A survey of the success factors in current public relations personnel based on demographics, activities, and interests.

Henderson, David E. "Radio–Print Ad Mix Could Be Ideal for Retailers." *Advertising Age* (21 May 1979):5.
Prescription for the advertising mix for local retailers.

Hershberger, John. "A Place in the Sun: Reaching Out to the Elderly." *Public Telecommunications Review* 5(July/August 1977):34–37.
Details a successful effort by local volunteers to help produce and promote a public service program for the elderly.

Hesbacher, Peter, and others. "Radio Format Strategies." *Journal of Communications* 26(Winter 1976):110–119.
Case study testing the theory of relationships between music programming and audience size and composition.

Hodgson, Richard S. *Direct Mail and Mailorder Handbook*. 3rd ed. Chicago: Dartnell Corporation, 1980.
A guide to copy preparation and the mechanics of production; includes case studies.

Huriburt, John. "BPA—There's Cable in Your Picture." *BPA Newsletter* (September 1979):3.
Recommendations for the role of the Broadcasters Promotion Association in cable promotion.

If You Want Air Time. Washington, D.C.: National Association of Broadcasters, 1979.
Booklet designed to help organizations get air time on commercial radio and television for their public service announcements.

"Is Public TV Going Commercial?" *Media Decisions* (October 1977):76 ff.
Review of the effects of commercial funding on public television programming; discusses public television as an alternative medium for advertising and corporate public relations.

Kernan, Jerome S.; Dommermuth, William K.; and Summers, Montrose S. *Promotion: An Introductory Analysis*. New York: McGraw-Hill, 1970.
Theoretical marketing text, not specific to media promotion, but with brief sections on adoption, diffusion, and broadcast promotion.

Klayman, Ron. "It Seemed Like a Good Idea at the Time." *BPA Big Ideas: Special Events*. Lancaster, Pennsylvania: Broadcasters Promotion Association, 1980.
Humorous review of some promotions that seemed good in the planning but turned into disasters during completion.

Kleppner, Otto. *Advertising Procedure*. 6th ed. Englewood Cliffs, New Jersey: Prentice-Hall, 1973.
Comprehensive text covering basic advertising methods and techniques.

Krasnow, Erwin G., Lawrence D. Longley, and Herbert A. Terry. *The Politics of Broadcast Regulation*. 3rd ed. New York: St. Martin's Press, 1982.
The latest edition of a respected analysis of the forces and institution-shaping regulation of electronic media; includes five case studies.

Legal Guide to FCC Broadcast Rules, Regulations and Policies. Washington, D.C.: National Association of Broadcasters, 1977.
Explanation of FCC rules and regulations as they apply to broadcasters.

Lem, Dean P. *Graphics Master 2.* Los Angeles: Dean Lem Associates, 1977.
Text covering printing processes, screens, halftone values, duotones, process color, proofing methods, typography, copyfitting, proportional scale, binding and finishing, paper size and weights, envelope sizes and weights.

LeRoy, David J. "The PTV Conundrum." *Public Telecommunications Review* 7(November/December 1979):50–58.
Results of a 1976 national ascertainment survey performed by the Office of Communications Research of the Corporation for Public Broadcasting; includes suggestions for increasing number of viewers and viewing time through program placement and promotion.

Lesly, Philip (ed.). *Public Relations Handbook.* Englewood Cliffs, New Jersey: Prentice-Hall, 1978.
Comprehensive reference guide to public relations, including public affairs, communication techniques, analysis and research, writing for readership, and emerging trends.

Levitan, Eli L. *Electronic Imaging Techniques.* New York: Van Nostrand Reinhold Company, 1977.
Handbook on the workings of conventional and computer-controlled animation, optical, and editing processes.

Lindsay, Carl; LeRoy, David; and Novak, Theresa. "Public Television: Whose Alternative?" *Public Telecommunications Review* 7(March/April 1979):18–23.
Public television audience analysis showing that public television viewers may be regular commercial television viewers who spend large amounts of time viewing and have more opportunity to view public stations.

Lipton, Mike. "Poetry in Promotion." *TV Guide* (16 August 1980):39–40.
Informal report on the use of on-air promotional themes by the three commercial networks.

Longman, Kenneth A. *Advertising.* New York: Harcourt, Brace Jovanovich, 1971.
Basic advertising text with chapters on writing ads, choosing media, typical promotions, and ad campaigns; includes chapters dealing with mass communications and audience perceptions of ads.

MacDonald, Jack. *The Handbook of Radio Publicity and Promotion.* Blue Ridge Summit, Pennsylvania: TAB Books, 1970.
Sourcebook of radio promotions with instructions for using them.

"The Many Worlds of Radio." *Broadcasting* (27 September 1976):33–82, (25 July 1977):31–76, (24 July 1978):37–74, (10 September 1979):35–67, (25 August 1980):40–102, (17 August 1981):39–86.
Annual reports on radio, covering many aspects of the field including promotion, advertising, and public radio.

Marx, Gary. *Radio: Get the Message.* Washington, D.C.: National Association of Broadcasters, n.d.
Booklet designed to show local school board officials how to use radio public service announcements.

Mayer, Michael F. *The Film Industries: Practical Business/Legal Problems in Production, Distribution and Exhibition.* New York: Hastings House, 1973.
Advice for film producers, agents, exhibitors, and distributors on financial

and legal considerations in feature film marketing; covers talent rights, exhibition contracts, copyright, publicity, and promotion.

Mechling, Thomas. "Is Public Service Public Relations Practical—And Desirable?" *Public Relations Quarterly* 20(Summer 1975):10–22.
Result of a five-year survey on what public relations professionals think about promoting public interest information.

Meistrich, Ira J. "On-Air Graphics: High Tech in Motion." *Print* (March/April 1980):33–44.
Review of the increased use of special effects visuals and computers in television during the late 1970s and the ensuing revolution in television graphics.

Meistrich, Ira J. "On-Air Graphics: The News, Now." *Print* (March/April 1980):45 ff.
Discussion of the role of computers in changing the style of network news by allowing for composite graphics and specialized visual effects.

Morrell, Gail. "Programming and Promotion Managers: Talk to Each Other If You Expect Top Ratings." *Broadcaster* (April 1980):6–7.
Excerpts from a speech in Canada by the president-elect of the Broadcasters Promotion Association.

Mueller, William S. "What Does Your Film Contract Say?" *Broadcast Financial Journal* 3(June 1973):14.
Analysis for broadcast managers of the technical language of contracts for syndicated films.

Mullally, Donald P. "Public Radio: Options in Programming." *Public Telecommunications Review* 6(March/April 1978):8–13.
Block programming and format programming in public radio; prescriptions for using programming and promotion to build audiences and improve station image.

"News: Badge of Honor for the Independent." *Broadcasting* (6 February 1978):40.
Discussion of the role of local news programs in promoting independent television stations.

Nickels, William C. *Marketing Communications and Promotion.* Columbus, Ohio: Grid, 1976.
Textbook using a systems approach to marketing communications; includes useful chapters on public relations and publicity, sales promotion, and the promotion of nonprofit organizations.

NRBA Resource Service. Washington, D.C.: National Radio Broadcasters Association, n.d.
Resource book containing weekly letters informing NRBA members of various radio station activities; one letter each month deals with new promotions used by stations from all areas of the country.

O'Brien, Dan. "Measuring the Effectiveness of Advertising." *BPA Newsletter* (June 1980):24.
Three-part series reviewing the uses and effects of promotion and advertising for the broadcasting industry.

O'Daniel, Michael. "Programming for Basic Cable." *Emmy Magazine* (Summer 1980):26 ff.
Overview of recent changes in the economics of cable and pay-cable systems including the role of advertising and promotion.

"On Air Graphics." *Print* (March/April 1980):33–79.
Special issue devoted to the use of graphics on television.

On-Air Promotion Handbook. Lancaster, Pennsylvania: Broadcasters Promotion Association, 1980.
Handbook of broadcast promotional ideas including using your own air, viewers motivation, tools, styles, and scheduling.

Pavitt, William H., Jr. "Legal Protection for Broadcast Promotion Campaigns." *BPA Newsletter* (May 1980):21–22.
Review of the legal protection of original ideas and original artwork in promotional films.

Peck, William. *Radio Promotion Handbook.* Blue Ridge Summit, Pennsylvania: TAB Books, 1968.
Practical guide to radio promotional techniques written for students of promotion; emphasis is on advertising ideas and creative promotion ploys.

Pocket Pal: A Graphic Arts Production Handbook. New York: International Paper Company, 1976.
First published in 1934 and now in its eleventh edition in paperback, this handbook presents material in accessible form for beginners; includes a guide to printing processes, type and typesetting, copy preparation, photography, stripping and imposition, platemaking, printing, binding, paper and inks; a glossary; a section on copyfitting; and many tables and charts.

Pokorny, Wilma J. "A Case Study of Effectiveness of WBGU-TV Program Promotion Methods." Masters thesis, Bowling Green State University, 1970.
Study reporting the relative efficiency of nine promotional methods employed by WBGU-TV in 1970.

Potts, Joseph. "Accounting for Trade-Outs: Solving an Industry Headache," Parts I and II. *Broadcast Financial Journal* 3(November 1973):8–10; 4(January 1974):6–7.
Budgetary procedures for evaluating traded promotional air time.

"PR Operations Merged into Ad Agencies See Enhancement of Broadcast Services." *Television/Radio Age* (24 March 1980):53 ff.
Discussion of the benefits to stations of combining public relations agencies with advertising agencies.

"Programming and Promotion." *P. D. Cue* (April 1979):31–33.
Synopsis of promotional recommendations made by a panel of promoters at the sixteenth national conference of the National Association of Television Program Executives in March 1979; includes suggestions for increasing creativity in promos and for increasing audience awareness of promotions.

The Public Broadcasting Report. Washington, D.C.: Television Digest, Inc., 1979 to date.
Biweekly bulletin on news, programs, and promotion in public broadcasting.

Public Service Advertising Bulletin. New York: The Advertising Council.

Bimonthly report reviewing all the public service announcements supported by The Advertising Council; includes text, visuals, and addresses for further information.

"QUBE—A Marketing Tool That Puzzles Its Owners." *Marketing and Media Decisions* (May 1979):72 ff.
Article covering the problems and potentials of the Qube system.

Rabin, K., and Lehrer, B. "Cable vs. Broadcast TV Public Relations: What Selected Target Audiences Think." *Public Relations Quarterly* 23(Fall 1978):13–17.
Study of the perceptions of senators, educators, and FCC staff members on the public relations information value of cable television distributed by the National Association of Broadcasters and the National Cable Television Association.

The Radio Code. 22nd ed. Washington, D.C.: National Association of Broadcasters, 1980.
The code developed by the National Association of Broadcasters for radio.

Radio Program Department Handbook. Washington, D.C.: National Association of Broadcasters, n.d.
Basic guide for program directors of small stations; includes material for on-air and off-air promotions, publicity, and public service announcements.

"Radio Programming and Production for Profit." *Broadcast Management/Engineering*, monthly series, January 1977 to date.
Discussions of program formats along with reports on syndicated programs and features.

"Radio Promoters Have Tough Task Getting Listeners to Twist Dials." *BPA Newsletter* (December 1976):5.
Results of radio industry survey of large markets showing that most radio listeners tune in to an average of two and a half stations per week and that few listeners routinely change stations while listening.

"The Radio Reps: Down in Number But Up in Ambition." *Broadcasting* (2 July 1979):39–63.
Special report on the role of station representatives in radio, dealing with their influence on the radio industry and their importance to advertisers.

"Radio Stations Pouring More Money into TV as They Compete to Make Their Sounds Visible." *Television/Radio Age* (24 March 1980):52 ff.
Analysis of the cost vs. return ratio in audience size of television spots for radio.

"Radio, TV Promotion Execs Happy with Work, Average over $22,000, Survey Indicates." *Television/Radio Age* (2 June 1980):41 ff.
Findings from a 1980 survey of Broadcasters Promotion Association members covering salaries, professional experience, and job satisfaction; includes members' evaluations of suppliers' promotional materials.

"Razzle Dazzle Flash and Splash." *Cable Marketing* (January 1982):30–31 ff.
A report on image promotion by cable systems and networks.

Reidy, John S. *Evolution of the Media in the 1980's.* New York: Drexel, Burnham, Lambert, Inc., 1979.
Report on future economic prospects for the advertising media based on

studies performed by the investment firm of Drexel, Burnham, Lambert; covers satellites, regulatory trends, pay-television, video recorders.

"Retailers Research Broadcast Effectiveness." *Television/Radio Age* (28 February 1977):36 ff.
Analysis of advertising effectiveness as a promotional technique broadcasters can use to increase station advertising.

Rockford, John. *On-the-Air Promotion Techniques.* New York: MCA-TV Publication, n.d.
Handbook covering the methods, techniques, and production of broadcast promotion for radio and television.

Rosenthal, Edmond. "Emerging Local TV Sales Change Market's Shape." *Television/Radio Age* (4 June 1979):37 ff.
Describes the growth in local advertising on television cutting into the national advertising market.

Rosenthal, Edmond. "Fall Network Promotion: Two Webs Start Early; More Local Tie-ins Seen." *Television/Radio Age* (16 July 1979):27 ff.
Overview of the timing techniques used in 1979 network television promotion by CBS, NBC, and later ABC.

Routt, Edd; McGrath, James B.; and Weiss, Fredric A. *The Radio Format Conundrum.* New York: Hastings House, 1978.
Includes numerous references to promotional strategies and gives useful details on radio contest practices.

"Roving Reporter." *P. D. Cue* (February 1979):44–45.
Collection of opinions from broadcasting executives on the role of promotion managers and their positions in the industry.

Rubens, Williams S. "A Guide to TV Ratings." *Journal of Advertising Research* 18(February 1978):11–18.
Review of the ratings process and the effects of the ratings on the advertising and broadcasting industries.

Schultz, Don E.; Block, Martin P.; and Custer, Stephen J. "A Comparative Study of Radio Audience Measurement Methodology." *Journal of Advertising* 7(Spring 1978):14–22.
Analysis of the methods used in measuring and analyzing radio audiences, covering ARMS, RADAR, and the techniques of the ratings companies; a comparison of diaries, day-after interviews, and coincidental telephone surveys.

Slakoff, Morton A. *Program Promotional Materials Supplied by Distributors.* Lancaster, Pennsylvania: Broadcasters Promotion Association, June 1977.
List of promotional materials available from syndicators of series, features, specials, and mini-series.

Slakoff, Morton A. "Promotion—The Job Is Bigger Than You Think." *Broadcasters Promotion Association Newsletter* (July 1980):23 ff.
Detailed listing of the duties of a promotion manager; covers audience and sales promotion, publicity, and public relations.

"Small Station Promotions Said to Be Discouraged." *Television/Radio Age* (24 March 1980):29.

Analysis of trend toward decreased television spot spending by small radio stations combined with record use by larger stations.

Smith, Donald R., and Rabin, Kenneth H. "What Broadcasters Want in Public Service Spots." *Public Relations Review* 4(Spring 1978):29–36.
Summary of what radio broadcasters say they want in public service announcements based on a 1977 mail survey of radio station managers.

"Special Supplement on Self Promotion." *RadioActive* (November–December 1980):20–29.
Collection of examples of visual print material from radio stations in the form of logos, T-shirts, bumper stickers, rate cards, and sales folders.

Stanley, Richard E. *Promotion: Advertising, Publicity, Personal Selling, Sales Promotion.* Englewood Cliffs, New Jersey: Prentice-Hall, 1977.
Concise text on marketing strategies with rules and prescriptions for what will and will not work; chapters on sales promotion and public relations; does not cover broadcast or cable promotion.

"Study for CPB Says Much of Commercial TV's Success Stems From Promotion, Viewer Lethargy." *Broadcasting* (23 October 1978):57 ff.
Overview of the role of on-air promotion and intellectual content of commercial and public television as they affect audience size.

Sullivan, Tobie. "Promos Gobble Up Attention." *Advertising Age* (21 May 1979):5 ff.
Discussion of the increased role of radio promotions in recent years covering changes in the size and expense of campaigns.

Sunoo, Don, and Lin, Lynn W. S. "Sales Effects of Promotion and Advertising." *Journal of Advertising Research* 18(October 1978):37–40.
Comparison of two marketing variables (promotions and advertisements) on sales of consumer products using a dual-system cable to collect the data.

The Television Code. 21st ed. Washington, D.C.: National Association of Broadcasters, 1980.
The code developed by the National Association of Broadcasters for television.

"Tooting the Horn for 'The Bastard'." *Broadcasting* (22 May 1978):60–62.
Analysis of independent station promotional efforts accompanying MCA-TV/Universal's mini-series.

Toran, William B. "Radio: Fertile Ground for Non-profit Public Service Spots." *Public Relations Journal* 33(August 1977):24–25.
Discussion of the problems and potential of using radio for public service announcements; includes tips for improving spots.

Trade and Barter Guidelines. Chicago: Broadcast Management Institute, 1979.
Twelve-page publication on trade and barter transactions including suggested accounting and reporting procedures, recommended agreement proposals, and trade agreement forms.

"TVB Feels Its Promotional Edge Is Pretty Sharp." *Television/Radio Age* (22 May 1978):31 ff.
Reviews of some Television Bureau of Advertising campaigns with comments on their effectiveness.

"TV's Hot Potato: How to Use CATV?" *Marketing and Media Decisions* (January 1980):60 ff.
Discussion of the functional differences between cable and commercial television from the viewpoint of advertisers.

"Update on Cable TV—Big Impact, Weak Numbers." *Marketing and Media Decisions* (January 1979):60 ff.
Analysis of the cable television audience compiled from recent research.

Vella, JoAnn. "Production Houses: A Survey of Rates." *Video Systems* (October 1979):24–26.
Results of a cross-country survey of video production houses reviewing rates and cost averages for remote productions, studio productions, and post production editing.

"A *View* Special Report: The Channel Capacity Crunch." *View* (October 1981):43–54.
Trade cable magazine analysis of the shortage of programming channels during the 1980s.

Vorce, Betsy. "The Care and Feeding of ITV." *Public Telecommunications Review* 8(January/February 1980):21–30.
Overview of instructional television and its usefulness in the classroom; stresses the value of recent promotion of ITV, including awareness campaigning, to increase ITV's use and improve its image.

Wald, Richard. "Possible Courses for News and Public Affairs." *Public Telecommunications Review* 6(May/June 1978):50–57.
Goals for news and public affairs programming for public television by a former network head of news.

Walker, Jean. "Spending More Money on Promotion Doesn't Necessarily Make Stations Happier." *Television/Radio Age* (25 August 1980):42 ff.
Results of a nationwide study of the top 100 markets sampling the attitudes of radio stations that (1) create their own promotional material in-house, (2) use advertising agencies, and (3) use syndicated promotion.

Weiner, Richard. *Professional's Guide to Publicity.* 2nd ed. New York: Richard Weiner, 1978.
Manual for the publicist dealing with the press.

"What Everyone Should Know About Radio Listening." *Television/Radio Age* (4 July 1977):23 ff.
A review of the findings from the first two RADAR (Radio's All Dimension Audience Research) studies conducted by Statistical Research, Inc., for CBS, NBC, ABC, and MBS in 1976 and 1977.

"Who Gets the Minute?" *Marketing and Media Decisions* (April 1978):68 ff.
Reactions from networks, affiliates, and advertisers on adding an extra minute of commercial time to primetime viewing hours.

Wurtzel, Alan, and Surlin, Stuart. "Viewer Attitudes Toward Television Advisory Warnings." *Journal of Broadcasting* 22(Winter 1978):19–31.
Study concluding that viewer advisories may act as promotions for movies and shows although networks claim they are intended only as warnings about possibly objectionable material.

Index